THE *SENATUS CONSULTUM DE CN. PISONE PATRE*

The *Senatus Consultum de Cn. Pisone Patre* is a senatorial decree issued in AD 20 following the trial of Gnaeus Calpurnius Piso, the governor of Syria, who was accused of rebellion against Tiberius following the death of his heir, Germanicus. It survives on several inscriptions and is among the most important documents from the early Principate. This new edition, with translation and commentary, sets the text within its contemporary context, considering it alongside other texts (including Tacitus' *Annales*), coins, and monuments, and focuses on their complementary roles in developing Tiberian political discourse. It explores how contemporary observers (including Valerius Maximus and Velleius Paterculus) understood and contributed to the shaping of dynastic rule at Rome after the death of Augustus in AD 14. It analyses how the Principate continued to evolve under his successor Tiberius, and explores the role of different individuals and groups in negotiating these political changes.

ALISON E. COOLEY is Professor in Classics and Ancient History at the University of Warwick. She has published extensively on topics relating to Roman epigraphy and the politics of early imperial Rome. Her books include an edition of and commentary on the *Res Gestae divi Augusti* (Cambridge, 2009) and *The Cambridge Manual of Latin Epigraphy* (Cambridge, 2012).

THE *SENATUS CONSULTUM DE CN. PISONE PATRE*

Text, Translation, and Commentary

ALISON E. COOLEY
University of Warwick

Shaftesbury Road, Cambridge CB2 8EA, United Kingdom

One Liberty Plaza, 20th Floor, New York, NY 10006, USA

477 Williamstown Road, Port Melbourne, VIC 3207, Australia

314–321, 3rd Floor, Plot 3, Splendor Forum, Jasola District Centre, New Delhi – 110025, India

103 Penang Road, #05–06/07, Visioncrest Commercial, Singapore 238467

Cambridge University Press is part of Cambridge University Press & Assessment, a department of the University of Cambridge.

We share the University's mission to contribute to society through the pursuit of education, learning, and research at the highest international levels of excellence.

www.cambridge.org
Information on this title: www.cambridge.org/9781108494458
DOI: 10.1017/9781108638050

© Cambridge University Press & Assessment 2023

This publication is in copyright. Subject to statutory exception and to the provisions of relevant collective licensing agreements, no reproduction of any part may take place without the written permission of Cambridge University Press & Assessment.

First published 2023

A catalogue record for this publication is available from the British Library.

ISBN 978-1-108-49445-8 Hardback
ISBN 978-1-108-71456-3 Paperback

Cambridge University Press & Assessment has no responsibility for the persistence or accuracy of URLs for external or third-party internet websites referred to in this publication and does not guarantee that any content on such websites is, or will remain, accurate or appropriate.

In memory of Miriam Griffin and Fergus Millar

Contents

List of Figures	*page* ix
Acknowledgements	xi
List of Abbreviations	xii

Introduction 1
1 The Importance of the *Senatus Consultum de Cn. Pisone Patre (SCPP)*   1
2 Historical Context   2
3 The *SCPP* and Tacitus   20
4 The Inscriptions of the *SCPP*   34
5 The Senate and its Relationship with the Imperial Family   44
6 The *SCPP* and the Creation of Tiberian Political Discourse   62
7 The Punishments of Piso   82
8 Later Pisones   95
9 'Some Justice': Piso in Robert Graves' *I, Claudius* and Jack Pulman's BBC Production   100

The *Senatus Consultum de Cn. Pisone Patre*: Text and Translation 111
Explanatory Note   113
Heading   114
Lines 1–4 Preamble (*praescriptio*)   114
Lines 4–11 Four Items for Discussion in the Senate, Introduced by Tiberius (*relatio*)   114
Lines 12–22 Thanks to the Gods for Thwarting Piso, and to Tiberius for Facilitating his Trial   114
Lines 23–70 Description of the Circumstances that Led to Piso's Prosecution   116
Lines 71–123 Senate's Recommendations on the Four Items under Discussion   120
Lines 123–51 Praise for Members of the Imperial Family   124
Lines 151–54 Praise for the Equestrian Order   126
Lines 155–58 Praise for the Plebs of Rome   126

Lines 159–65 Praise for the Army ... 128
Lines 165–72 Instructions for Publication of the Decree ... 128
Lines 172–73 Senatorial Procedure ... 128
Lines 174–76 Addendum (*subscriptio*) by Tiberius ... 128
Notes on Variations between Copies of the Text ... 130

Commentary ... 141

Bibliography ... 242
Index Locorum ... 262
Thematic Index ... 265

Figures

1 Family tree of the *domus Augusta* in December AD 20 (courtesy of M.G.L. Cooley) *page* 3
2 Bronze coin minted at Italica. Obverse (A): a bare-headed Tiberius, with the legend IMP TI CAESAR AVGVSTVS PON MAX ('Imperator Tiberius Caesar Augustus, pontifex maximus'). Reverse (B): an image of an altar, inscribed PROVIDENTIAE AVGVSTI ('To the Foresight of Augustus') and the legend [M]VNIC ITALIC PER DI[VI] AVG ('Municipium of Italica by permission of deified Augustus'). *RPC* I 64; source: gallica.bnf.fr / Bibliothèque nationale de France) 42
3 Heading of *SCPP* on Copy A (photograph: A.E. Cooley) (by kind permission of the Museo Arqueológico de Sevilla, Colección Museística de Andalucía, Junta de Andalucía: MAS inv. D09579) 48
4 Prescript of Copy B (photograph: A.E. Cooley) (by kind permission of the Museo Arqueológico de Sevilla, Colección Museística de Andalucía, Junta de Andalucía: MAS inv. D09479) 49
5 Paragraphing on Copy B at line 84 (photograph: A.E. Cooley) (by kind permission of the Museo Arqueológico de Sevilla, Colección Museística de Andalucía, Junta de Andalucía: MAS inv. D09479) 49
6 *Dupondius*. Obverse (A): Laureate head of Tiberius, facing left, with the legend TI CAESAR DIVI AVG F AVGVST IMP VIII ('Tiberius Caesar Augustus, son of the deified Augustus, imperator for the eighth time'). Reverse (B): male portrait framed within a shield with the legend CLEMENTIAE S C ('To Clemency, by decree of the Senate'). *RIC* I² Tiberius no.38. Münzkabinett, Staatliche Museen zu Berlin, 18211825. Photograph by Dirk Sonnenwald. Courtesy of Dr Karsten Dahmen (Münzkabinett, Staatliche Museen zu Berlin) 67

7 *Dupondius*. Reverse: male portrait framed within a shield with the legend MODERATIONI S C ('To Moderation, by decree of the Senate'). *RIC* I² Tiberius no. 39. American Numismatic Society: 1944.100.39284, available at numismatics.org/collection/1944.100.39284 — 68
8 Silver didrachm, mint of Caesarea in Cappadocia, depicting the coronation of Artaxias by Germanicus. Obverse (A): head of Germanicus, with the legend GERMANICVS CAESAR TI(BERI) AVG(VSTI) F(ILIVS) CO(N)S(VL) II ('Germanicus Caesar, son of Tiberius Augustus, consul for the second time'). Reverse (B): Germanicus, standing on the right, crowning Artaxias with a diadem, with the legend ARTAXIAS GERMANICVS. *RPC* I 3629,2 (Münzkabinett, Staatliche Museen zu Berlin, 18200231). Photograph by Lutz-Jürgen Lübke (Lübke und Wiedemann). Courtesy of Dr Karsten Dahmen (Münzkabinett, Staatliche Museen zu Berlin) — 175
9 Map of Rome (adapted from Bodel, 1999) — 197
10 Modern view of area of Piso's house on the Capitoline Hill, overlooking the Roman Forum, with the *curia Iulia* to the left (photograph: A.E. Cooley) — 207

Acknowledgements

It is a pleasure to be able to thank Concha San Martín and her colleagues at the Museo Arqueológico de Sevilla for granting me access to the *SCPP* bronzes, large and small, in their museum. I am grateful to the University of Warwick for granting me a year's research leave in 2018/19 and to the Leverhulme Trust for a Major Research Fellowship in 2020/22, which enabled me to devote my time to researching and writing this monograph. I would especially like to thank the librarians of the Institute of Classical Studies, London, for their prompt help in supplying books by post in times of CoVid, as well as to staff at the Bodleian Libraries, Oxford, for speedy assistance in scanning print materials. I am grateful to Suzanne Frey-Kupper and Susan Treggiari for their expert guidance on numismatic and legal matters. For help in acquiring images for the book I am indebted to Clare Rowan and Dr Karsten Dahmen (Münzkabinett, Staatliche Museen zu Berlin). I am grateful to William Graves and The Robert Graves Copyright Trust for permission to reproduce Robert Graves' poem, 'Bringing the Dead to Life', reproduced from TO BRING THE DEAD TO LIFE by Robert Graves (Copyright © Robert Graves Trust 1936) by permission of United Agents LLP (www.unitedagents.co.uk) on behalf of Accuro Trustees (Jersey) Ltd as trustees of the Robert Graves Copyright Trust. I also benefited from feedback received from audiences attending seminars at the Universities of Birmingham, Macquarie, Oxford, and Warwick, and from the comments of Cambridge University Press readers. As always, I have enjoyed unwavering support from my family, and particularly thank my parents, Melvin, Emma, and Paul for all their help at various stages of writing and for their tolerance in living with the Piso decree for some years.

Abbreviations

AE	*L'Année épigraphique* (1888–)
CFA	J. Scheid, Commentarii fratrum Arvalium qui supersunt. *Les copies épigraphiques des protocoles annuels de la confrérie arvale (21 av.–304 ap. J.-C.).* (Rome: École française de Rome / Soprintendenza archeologica di Roma, 1998)
CIL	*Corpus Inscriptionum Latinarum* (ed. T. Mommsen et al., 1863–)
Dig.	*The Digest of Justinian*, Latin text edited by T. Mommsen with the aid of P. Krueger; English translation edited by A. Watson, vol. 4, rev. edn (Philadelphia, PA: University of Pennsylvania Press, 2009)
EDCS	Epigraphik-Datenbank Clauss / Slaby: http://db.edcs.eu/epigr/epi_ergebnis.php
ILN-Vienne	*Inscriptions Latines de Narbonnaise*, vol. 5.3, XLIVe supplément à *Gallia*, ed. B. Rémy (Paris: CNRS Editions, 2005)
ILS	*Inscriptiones Latinae Selectae*, ed. H. Dessau, 3 vols (Berlin: Weidmann, 1892–1916)
Inscr.It. XIII.1	*Inscriptiones Italiae. XIII – Fasti et elogia. Fasc. 1 – Fasti consulares et triumphales*, ed. A. Degrassi (Rome: Libreria dello stato, 1947)
Inscr.It. XIII.2	*Inscriptiones Italiae. XIII – Fasti et elogia. Fasc. 2 – Fasti anni Numani et Iuliani*, ed. A. Degrassi (Rome: Istituto poligrafico dello stato / Libreria dello stato, 1963)
IRT2009	*Inscriptions of Roman Tripolitania*, ed. J.M. Reynolds and J.B. Ward-Perkins, enhanced electronic reissue by Gabriel Bodard and Charlotte Roueché (2009), http://inslib.kcl.ac.uk/irt2009/
LACTOR 17	*The Age of Augustus*, ed. M.G.L. Cooley, LACTOR 17 (London: London Association of Classical Teachers, 2008)
LACTOR 19	*Tiberius to Nero*, ed. M.G.L. Cooley, LACTOR 19 (London: London Association of Classical Teachers, 2011)

LACTOR 20	*The Flavians*, ed. M.G.L. Cooley, LACTOR 20 (London: London Association of Classical Teachers, 2015)
LTUR	*Lexicon Topographicum Urbis Romae*, ed. E.M. Steinby, 6 vols (Rome: Quasar, 1993–2000)
MAS	Museo Arqueológico de Sevilla
OCD[4]	*Oxford Classical Dictionary* (4th edition), ed. S. Hornblower, A.J. Spawforth, E. Eidinow (Oxford: Oxford University Press, 2012)
OLD	*Oxford Latin Dictionary*, ed. P.G.W. Glare (Oxford: Clarendon Press, 1982)
PIR[2]	*Prosopographia Imperii Romani Saec. I. II. III*, 2nd edn, 9 vols (Berlin: De Gruyter, 1933–2015)
P.Oxy.	*Oxyrhynchus Papyri*
RGDA	*Res Gestae divi Augusti* (edition used: Cooley 2009)
RIC I[2]	*The Roman Imperial Coinage*, vol. I (rev. edn) *31 BC–AD 69*, ed. C.H.V. Sutherland (London: Spink)
RPC I	*Roman Provincial Coinage*, vol. I: *From the Death of Caesar to the Death of Vitellius (44 BC–AD 69). Part I: Introduction and Catalogue*, ed. A. Burnett, M. Amandry, P.P. Ripollès (London: British Museum Press / Paris: Bibliothèque nationale de France, 1992)
RRC	*Roman Republican Coinage*, ed. M.H. Crawford (Cambridge: Cambridge University Press, 1974)
SCPP	*Senatus consultum de Cn. Pisone patre*
SEG	*Supplementum Epigraphicum Graecum*
TLL	*Thesaurus Linguae Latinae*

Abbreviated references to classical authors follow the conventions in the *Oxford Classical Dictionary* (4th edition).

Introduction

1 THE IMPORTANCE OF THE *SENATUS CONSULTUM DE CN. PISONE PATRE* (*SCPP*)

If Augustus' account of his achievements in the *Res Gestae* deserves the accolade of being known as the 'queen of inscriptions',[1] then it is only fair to follow Yakobson in hailing the senatorial decree concerning Gnaeus Piso senior (*Senatus consultum de Cn. Pisone patre* = *SCPP*) as the 'princess of inscriptions'.[2] Not only does the inscription give fresh insights into one of the crisis points in Roman history, which witnessed the sudden death of Tiberius' heir Germanicus and the threat of instability in the eastern Mediterranean on the fringes of the Roman empire (see §2), but it also illustrates the development of political discourse under Tiberius, as the Senate sought to define its relationship with the imperial family. In this way, it complements other Tiberian voices – notably Valerius Maximus and Velleius Paterculus – in illuminating the ways in which the leadership of Roman society by members of the imperial family became justified (see §5–6). This decree is particularly valuable in offering a contemporary, alternative interpretation of events to what has been until recently dominated by the colourful narrative of Tacitus, who deals with these same events in books two and three of his *Annales*, describing them with the benefit of having experienced the Principate as a political system for over a century (see §3). Unlike Tacitus, the Senate of AD 20 could not know how the Principate was to develop in successive years: its perspective reveals instead the shifting relationship between Senate and imperial family, and the Senate's role in creating a new imperial political discourse. The fact that Tacitus devotes so much space to Germanicus' activities in the East and the subsequent trial of Piso demonstrates that he regarded this episode as pivotal for the shaping of the Principate. What this inscription now confirms is that the importance of these events was equally recognised by contemporary observers. As will also become clear, analysis of this inscription shows that readers need to be just as conscious about authorship, bias, and rhetoric in interpreting this inscribed decree as any literary text.

---

[1] Mommsen ([1887] 1906) 247; discussed by Cooley (2009) 1–3. [2] Yakobson (1998).

As well as providing new insights into politics at Rome, the proliferation of copies of the decree also offers a fresh opportunity to assess the relationship between the provinces – particularly Baetica in southern Spain, where almost all of the known copies of the text have been found so far – and the centre of power at Rome. By considering the multiple copies of the inscription within the wider context of the coins minted in the province, we can trace how the local elite of Baetica reacted to the train of events unfolding at Rome (see §4).

In short, whereas the establishment of the Principate at Rome has generally been considered to have been the achievement of Augustus, close reading of the *SCPP* in the context of other contemporary texts, coins, and inscriptions reveals the importance of the Tiberian era in further shaping the evolution of dynastic rule at Rome. It also allows us to analyse the contribution made by different individuals and groups in negotiating the political changes that were taking place in the aftermath of Augustus' death in AD 14, and how the Principate was not simply inherited from Augustus as a fixed entity but was further transformed under his successor Tiberius.

2 HISTORICAL CONTEXT

On 10 October AD 19, Germanicus Caesar died aged thirty-three at Antioch on the Orontes following a period of illness whilst on a mission in Syria.[3] He was a key link in the dynastic chain of the Caesars, as not only was he married to Augustus' granddaughter, Agrippina, but he had also been adopted by Tiberius as his son in AD 4, having up until then been his nephew (son of Tiberius' brother, the elder Drusus, and Antonia) (Fig. 1).[4] After Augustus' death, Germanicus was in effect second in command to Tiberius,[5] something which – along with Ovid's conceit that he was simply a fellow-poet – helps to explain why Ovid turned to him for help from exile.[6] Both Germanicus and the younger Drusus, Tiberius' son who was a few years younger than Germanicus, were regarded as helping Tiberius to govern Rome in the view of the contemporary observer, Strabo:

At any rate, never has it been permitted to the Romans and their allies to enjoy so much peace and abundance of good things as both Caesar Augustus supplied from the moment he took on absolute power and as now too his successor, his son

---

[3] For a narrative of the period from AD 15–20, see Seager (2005) 81–100, largely a summary of Tacitus. Germanicus' death: Degrassi (1963) 209 – *Fasti Antiates Ministrorum*, 10 Oct. = LACTOR 19, J7g. Birthday on 24 May: Scheid (1998) 30 – *CFA* 12c, 31 = LACTOR 19, A38j; age at death: Suet., *Calig.* 1.2 – *annum agens aetatis quartum et tricensimum diuturno morbo Antiochiae obiit* – with Wardle (1994) 105. Contrast Levick (1966) 238–39, who argues that Germanicus was aged thirty-four.
[4] *PIR*² I 221, Germanicus Iulius Caesar.
[5] Tiberius' son Drusus was younger than Germanicus, and so his career at this time was slightly behind that of his adoptive brother: Sumner (1967).
[6] Herbert-Brown (1994) chapter 5; Ov., *Pont.* 4.8.27–88, with Myers (2014).

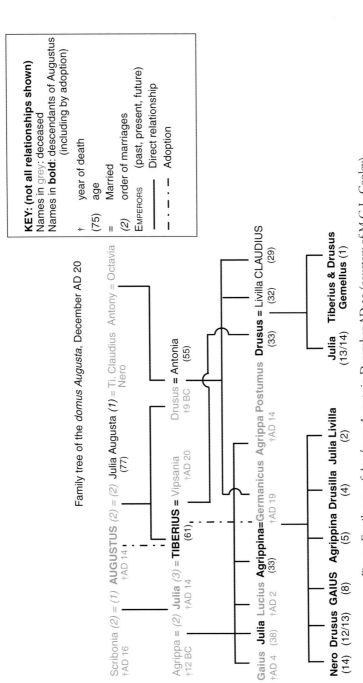

Fig. 1. Family tree of the *domus Augusta* in December AD 20 (courtesy of M.G.L. Cooley).

Tiberius supplies, who is making Augustus the model for his administration and edicts, whilst Tiberius' sons Germanicus and Drusus in turn assist their father.[7]

Their role in Augustus' hopes to hand down his *statio* ('position') to the next generation and beyond[8] is reflected in their inclusion in dynastic statuary groups from at least AD 7/11.[9] During Augustus' lifetime, Germanicus had gained experience first as quaestor and then as consul in AD 12. Commanding troops in Germania from AD 13, he resisted pressure from those mutinying to seize power from Tiberius, recovered the standards lost in the Varus disaster of AD 9, and led his men on an expedition as far as Ocean, albeit with rather mixed results, before returning to Rome to celebrate a triumph in AD 17.[10] He must have been viewed as an ideal Roman in many respects, being of noble family, a military victor, and happily married with nine children.

Tacitus draws a vivid picture of Germanicus that presents him as an emotional, popular figure, known for his *comitas* ('approachability'); but the multivalent nature of his depiction also challenges the reader to make sense of its complexities.[11] Rather than representing Germanicus as an undiluted heroic figure,[12] Tacitus' characterisation of Germanicus is full of complexities and ambiguities, whereby he emerges potentially both as a 'naive and innocent youth' and a 'clever and dangerous image-maker'.[13] Tacitus implicitly challenges his readers to make sense of Germanicus as a character in whose actions past and present interact,[14] and whose open behaviour may be taken as illustrating an alternative to the secretive world of the Principate.[15] To some extent, it is true that Tacitus creates the character of an emotionally demonstrative Germanicus as a foil to the secretive Tiberius, commenting in the passage that formally introduces his character in the *Annales*: *nam iuueni ciuile ingenium, mira comitas et diuersa*

---

[7] Strabo 6.4.2: οὐδέποτε γοῦν εὐπορῆσαι τοσαύτης εἰρήνης καὶ ἀφθονίας ἀγαθῶν ὑπῆρξε Ῥωμαίοις καὶ τοῖς συμμάχοις αὐτῶν, ὅσην Καῖσάρ τε ὁ Σεβαστὸς παρέσχεν ἀφ' οὗ παρέλαβε τὴν ἐξουσίαν αὐτοτελῆ, καὶ νῦν ὁ διαδεξάμενος υἱὸς ἐκεῖνον παρέχει Τιβέριος, κανόνα τῆς διοικήσεως καὶ τῶν προσταγμάτων ποιούμενος ἐκεῖνον, καὶ αὐτὸν οἱ παῖδες αὐτοῦ Γερμανικός τε καὶ Δροῦσος ὑπουργοῦντες τῷ πατρί.

[8] On the distinction between passing on a *paterna statio* rather than the *principatus*, see Cooley (2019).

[9] Examples before AD 14: Rose (1997) 96, cat.24, portraits of Germanicus and Drusus from Nomentum (Latium); 132, cat.59, portaits of Livia, Drusus and Germanicus from Asido (Baetica); 134, cat.62, inscriptions of Germanicus and Drusus from Segobriga (Tarraconensis); 138, cat.68, inscribed base for (in order) Drusus, Tiberius, Augustus, Germanicus from Athens (Achaea); 174, cat.114, inscribed base for Germanicus, Drusus, Tiberius from Ephesus (Asia).

[10] Tac., *Ann.* 1.31–52 (mutiny); 1.55–71 (response to Varus disaster and campaigns of AD 15); 2.5–26 (campaigns of AD 16); 2.41 (triumph).

[11] Brief overview of scholarship on Tacitus' presentation of Germanicus in Goodyear (1972) 239–41; further analysis in Pelling (2012, a revised version of a chapter first published in 1993); O'Gorman (2000) chapter 3; Williams (2009); B. Kelly (2010) on Germanicus in Egypt, which is complemented by Low (2016) on his activities in the Black Sea region; Poulsen (2020).

[12] View of Daitz (1960) 37, 48, challenged by Shotter (1968).

[13] Rutland (1987), 164.   [14] O'Gorman (2000) 46–69.   [15] Pelling (2012).

2 Historical Context

ab Tiberii sermone uultu, adrogantibus et obscuris ('for the young man had an unassuming character, and an approachability that was remarkable and the opposite of Tiberius' conversation and demeanour, which were arrogant and secretive').[16] Nevertheless, documentary sources support the view that Tacitus did not entirely invent this character for him. Fragments of a speech and edict delivered by Germanicus in Alexandria, which are preserved on contemporary (or near-contemporary) papyri, fit the rather histrionic tone of his character as depicted by Tacitus.[17] In addressing an enthusiastic crowd in Alexandria, Germanicus dwells upon the personal hardships he is facing in being wrenched away from his family and close friends in order to be sent on his mission to the East, but flatters his audience in stating that being able to see Alexandria and receiving such a warm reception has made it all worthwhile.[18] In the edict, he turns down divine honours, threatening (humorously?)[19] to 'appear before you seldom' (μὴ πολλάκις ὑμεῖν ἐνφανίζεσθαι) if disobeyed, and stating that the acclamations 'are hateful to me and fitting for the gods' (τὰς δὲ ἐπιφθόνου[ς] ἐμοὶ καὶ ἰσοθέους).[20] These papyri texts therefore support Tacitus' depiction of Germanicus as someone who speaks effusively and informally, expressing his personal feelings, and in return receiving enthusiastic responses from his audiences. At the same time, Tacitus' Germanicus is not without his faults, particularly in his lacklustre handling of the mutiny on the Rhine in AD 14, which contrasts so starkly with the competence of Drusus' handling of the parallel mutiny in Pannonia.[21]

News of Germanicus' death did not reach Rome until 8 December, whereupon the Senate decreed a *iustitium*, a period of public mourning when the temples closed and all business ceased.[22] This official period continued throughout the rest of December, even interrupting the usual celebration of the Saturnalia, and lasted until the end of March, when Germanicus' ashes were interred in the Mausoleum.[23] The outpouring of public grief that ensued, however, was unprecedented in its scale and intensity: it had already begun even before the official announcement of his death was made, and it continued for some weeks, causing Tiberius to

---

[16] Tac., *Ann.* 1.33.2, with Goodyear (1972) 252. Ross (1973) 220, however, argues that Germanicus is closer to a counterpart than a foil to Tiberius.
[17] Shotter (1968) 206–07.
[18] *P.Oxy.* no.2435 recto, with commentary ad loc. = LACTOR 19, J7e. [19] Post (1944) 82.
[20] Hunt and Edgar (1956) no.211 = LACTOR 19, J7d, with analysis of dating from handwriting by Zucker in von Wilamowitz-Moellendorff and Zucker (1911) 795–96.
[21] Tac., *Ann.* 1.16–52. Ross (1973) 211–20; Fulkerson (2006); Pelling (2012) 285–97.
[22] Bargagli and Grosso (1997) 23 – *Fasti Ostienses* frag.Cd left 33–34 = LACTOR 19, J7h. Goodyear (1981) 432–33 wonders whether the inscription is an accurate record, on the grounds that it seems surprising for such news to take almost two months to reach Rome, but arguably the Senate delayed making this announcement (cf. Wardle 1994: 121): such a delay would help to explain why mourning first broke out unofficially among the people.
[23] Suet., *Calig.* 6. On the duration of the official *iustitium*, compare Fraschetti (1988: it ceased at the end of December) and Crawford (1996, 539–41: it continued until Germanicus' ashes were interred, as had happened for Gaius Caesar).

issue an edict towards the end of March in an attempt to restore normality to the city.[24] The grief at Rome is described by Tacitus as exacerbated by the fact that rumours of Germanicus' death had earlier reached Rome, but had subsequently been contradicted by false reports of his recovery, leaving the populace ill-prepared for the eventual news of his death. Suetonius adds dramatically to this picture by describing the extreme response to Germanicus' death by the people of Antioch, in whose city he had died, as they stoned temples, destroyed altars, cast out their household gods, and even exposed newborn infants.[25] Another echo of extravagant responses to Germanicus' death can be found in a Greek epigram by Bassus, who has Hades declare that the entrances to the Underworld should be blocked since Germanicus is destined for the stars.[26] The equestrian Clutorius Priscus too is known to have composed a poem lamenting the death of Germanicus, for which he was rewarded by Tiberius.[27] Such responses to Germanicus' death may have reflected the shifting of people's affection away from the abstract idea of the state onto the state as represented in the person of their leader, along with a shift towards associating the welfare of the state with the welfare of that leader.[28] The degree to which public distress at his death led towards social disintegration will be relevant when we later consider the way in which the Senate responded to this crisis through the passing and publication of their decree in AD 20.

By the end of December, the Senate had held two meetings in order to decide what honours would be fitting in Germanicus' memory, and the incoming consuls for AD 20 were instructed to present the Senate's proposals to the people for formal ratification. In addition to Tacitus' selective account of these honours, we also have much more detailed epigraphic evidence in the form of the *Tabula Siarensis* and *Tabula Hebana*, inscribed on bronze, of which the *Tabula Hebana* (found in Etruria) overlaps with and continues the text of the *Tabula Siarensis* (found in Baetica).[29] Three bronze fragments of a tablet from Rome also overlap with thirty lines of the *Tabula Siarensis*.[30] In addition, a new fragment of a bronze inscription from Umbria has now been published which also partially overlaps with the *Tabula Siarensis*, but includes just over nine new lines of text, which record part of the motion (*relatio*) introducing the subject of Germanicus' honours for discussion in the Senate.[31] The epigraphic and literary accounts are not identical, since Tacitus chooses to focus upon the new

---

[24] Tac., *Ann.* 3.6. [25] Suet., *Calig.* 5. [26] *Palatine Anthology* 7.391 = LACTOR 19, J7j.
[27] Tac., *Ann.* 3.49; Cass. Dio 57.20.3. [28] Versnel (1980).
[29] Tac., *Ann.* 2.83; *Tabula Siarensis*: *AE* (1984) 508; *Tabula Hebana*: *AE* (1949) 215, overlapped by another fragment from Baetica, from Carissa Aurelia: *AE* (2000) 725; Crawford (1996) no.37 = LACTOR 19, J8; Lott (2012) sections 2.3–2.4, 3.3–3.4. On the Todi fragment, compare Crawford (1996) 507, 542–43 and Lott (2012) 49–50. Cipollone (2012) 83–86 reviews all the epigraphic fragments.
[30] *CIL* VI 31199; Crawford (1996) no.37; Lott (2012) sections 2.5, 3.5.
[31] Cipollone (2012) = *AE* (2012) 467.

honours being devised for the occasion.³² These include three arches: in the Circus Flaminius at Rome; on Mount Amanus in Syria; and next to the burial mound of Germanicus' father Drusus beside the river Rhine in Germania.³³ These arches commemorated the different spheres of Germanicus' activities, centrally in Rome, and on the western and eastern borders of the empire.³⁴ In addition, other honours were modelled upon those previously granted by the *lex Valeria Cornelia* to Lucius and Gaius Caesar on their deaths in AD 2 and AD 4,³⁵ and Tacitus simply omits some of these, notably the decision to establish five new *centuriae praerogativae* named after Germanicus to supplement the ten *centuriae praerogativae* already created in honour of Lucius and Gaius in AD 5: these were privileged groups who were permitted to be the first to cast their votes at elections for consuls and praetors, giving a strong steer as to which candidates should be preferred. The *Tabula Hebana* contains extensive instructions about exactly how this should be done, on the model of the previous electoral centuries named in honour of Lucius and Gaius.³⁶ Overall, Tacitus' selection of some honours but not others seems designed to convey that Germanicus' death was being treated as an exceptional crisis, and to avoid giving the impression that his honours simply followed the pattern set under Augustus in the cases of Lucius and Gaius Caesar.

Germanicus' death was not just regarded as an unfortunate tragedy: rumours soon spread that he had been poisoned. The senator Cn. Calpurnius Piso and his wife Plancina were suspected of having had a hand in his death, with the arrest in Syria of Martina, who was both a notorious poisoner and friend of Plancina;³⁷ this created a crisis for Tiberius and his mother Iulia Augusta, since if this were true, they might likewise be implicated in this murder.³⁸ A charge of poisoning was brought against Piso at his trial, as Pliny the Elder records the existence of a speech for the prosecution made by Publius Vitellius, in which the failure of Germanicus' heart to burn during cremation at Antioch is cited as evidence that he had been poisoned.³⁹ It is likewise a prominent theme in Tacitus' account of the trial: he chooses to conclude the episode by alluding to it as 'the end of avenging the death of Germanicus' (*is finis fuit ulciscenda Germanici morte*),⁴⁰ despite the fact that it was the one charge that had been dismissed.⁴¹ The accusation seems in part to stem from Germanicus himself, given that he is described as accusing Piso as being the cause of his death in the *SCPP* (see line 28). In addition, Tacitus creates a still more sinister atmosphere by describing in vivid detail the discovery of

---

³² González (1999).
³³ Remains of this arch have been identified at Mainz-Kastel: Frenz (1989). ³⁴ Potter (1987).
³⁵ *CIL* XI 1420–21; Lott (2012) sections 2.1–2.2, 3.1–3.2.
³⁶ *Tabula Hebana* lines 6–16 = Crawford (1996) no.37 = LACTOR 19, J8m–n.
³⁷ Tac., *Ann.* 2.74.2.   ³⁸ Tac., *Ann.* 2.69.3, 3.12.2.
³⁹ Plin., *HN* 11.187 = LACTOR 19, P2c.   ⁴⁰ Tac., *Ann.* 3.19.2.   ⁴¹ Tac., *Ann.* 3.13–14.

incantations, curses, and lead tablets inscribed with Germanicus' name, as well as sinister human and organic remains, which all pointed to the deployment against Germanicus of magical practices.[42] If such details were in circulation at the time of the trial, these may point to the common tendency to associate charges of poisoning with witchcraft, and reflect the atmosphere of paranoia and anxiety that surrounded Germanicus' death at Rome.[43] They also feature in Suetonius and Cassius Dio,[44] although they are completely absent from the *SCPP*. The silence of the *SCPP* need not, however, indicate that Tacitus invented these details as dramatic enhancements of his narrative,[45] given that the Senate does not choose to dwell on the charge of murder in its official account of events.

The death of Germanicus occurred at a time of ever worsening relations between Germanicus and Piso, for which several reasons can be put forward. Firstly, the circumstances of Germanicus' appointment for a special mission in the East in AD 17 were not conducive to creating a good working relationship between the two men.[46] The types of problems which had arisen in the East were considered to require the authority of Tiberius himself or of one of his sons,[47] especially since they involved delicate negotiations with kingdoms on the fringes of the Roman empire, and notably with the powerful Parthian empire. For some years the royal succession in Armenia (a crucial 'buffer-state' client kingdom between the Roman and Parthian empires) had been disputed, and tensions between pro-Roman and pro-Parthian factions had come to a head in AD 16 with the detention (albeit with the retention of his dignity and luxuries, according to Tacitus) in Syria of the former Parthian king Vonones by the Roman governor, Q. Caecilius Metellus Creticus Silanus,[48] after strong protests against his position in Armenia had been made by the Parthian king Artabanus III.[49] Eldest son of the Parthian king Phraates IV (who ruled 38–2 BC), Vonones had been sent by his father along with his three brothers to be brought up in Rome before eventually being nominated as king of Parthia at the Parthians' own request by Augustus in AD *c.*11/12.[50] Deposed a few years later by the Parthians, who considered him too Roman in outlook, Vonones had then become king of Armenia, but repeated military pressure from the Parthian king, Artabanus III, forced him by AD 15 to flee to Syria, where he was subsequently detained by Silanus, in an attempt to prevent a further outbreak of fighting in this tense region.

Nor was this delicate situation the only challenge: in addition, the newly annexed kingdom of Cappadocia needed to be set up as a province, whilst the deaths of the kings of Commagene and Cilicia – both

---

[42] Tac., *Ann.* 2.69; Tupet (1980); Damon (1999b) 158–60 on Tacitus' decision to focus on the alleged murder, in contrast to the *SCPP*.
[43] Versnel (1980) 614–15. [44] Suet., *Calig.* 3.3; Cass. Dio 57.18.9.
[45] Contra, Gordon and Simón (2010) 9 n.36. [46] Tac., *Ann.* 2.43. [47] *SCPP* lines 29–32.
[48] *PIR*² C64. [49] Tac., *Ann.* 2.1–4. [50] *RGDA* 33, with Cooley (2009) 255; *PIR*² V994.

2 Historical Context

westerly neighbours of Armenia – prompted uncertainty over the futures of those territories.[51] Consequently, according to the *SCPP* (lines 33–36), a *lex* was passed formally giving Germanicus *imperium* greater than that of other Roman proconsuls, but lesser than that of Tiberius. Our other contemporary documentation, the *Tabula Siarensis*, recalls how Germanicus 'was sent as proconsul to the overseas provinces and in setting them and the kingdoms of that region in order according to the instructions of Tiberius Caesar Augustus …' (*pro co(n)s(ule) missus in transmarinas pro[uincias atque] / in conformandis iis regnisque eiusdem tractus ex mandatis Ti(beri) C<a>esaris Au[g](usti)*).[52] On the face of it, Germanicus' powers were in this way explicitly defined as greater than those held by the proconsuls currently governing the eastern provinces of Asia, Pontus-Bithynia, Cyprus and Crete/Cyrene, Achaea, and Macedonia.[53] It is not to be assumed, though, that Germanicus was not also supposed to have greater authority than the legates governing provinces (including Syria) who were Tiberius' nominees, and therefore did not themselves hold *imperium*.[54] Tacitus makes this explicit by specifying that Germanicus' *imperium* was to be greater than that of 'those who held office by lot or by being sent by the *princeps*' (*quam iis qui sorte aut missu principis obtinerent*),[55] thus avoiding any ambiguity about Germanicus' authority in relation not only to proconsuls (chosen by lot) but also to imperial legates (appointed by the *princeps*). Tiberius had replaced the current legate of Syria, Creticus Silanus, whose daughter was betrothed to Germanicus' eldest son Nero,[56] with Piso as his new appointee.[57] This was in itself unexceptional, given that Silanus had been governor since AD 11, but Tiberius perhaps also did not want Germanicus' actions in the East to go unscrutinised, especially since four legions were at the time stationed in Syria, and so he appointed Piso to replace Silanus.[58] Piso was instructed to act as Germanicus' 'aide' (*adiutor*), a term which denoted that he had a formal duty to work with

---

[51] Tac., *Ann.* 2.42. On the intertwined problems of Armenia, Commagene, Cilicia, and Parthia, see Olbrycht (2016); Germanicus' mission is summarised in Sawiński (2021) 88–90.
[52] *Tabula Siarensis* = Crawford (1996) no.37, frag. a, lines 15–16 = LACTOR 19, J8b.
[53] Eck, Caballos, Fernández (1996) 159 n.420.
[54] Eck, Caballos, Fernández (1996) 158–61; cf. Zecchini (1999) 316–19 and Hurlet (1997) 181–97 for a summary of the problem.
[55] Tac., *Ann.* 2.43.
[56] Her epitaph, *CIL* VI 914, commemorates her as *Iunia Silani [f(ilia)] / [spo]nsa Neronis Caes[aris] / [hic sita est]*, showing both the value given to this betrothal and her death before marriage, some time before AD 20, when Nero married Tiberius' granddaughter Iulia instead.
[57] Tac., *Ann.* 2.43.2, with pluperfect tenses *demouerat* and *praefecerat*.
[58] Shotter (2000) 345–48 accepts Tacitus' depiction of tensions between Germanicus and Tiberius. Drogula (2015) argues against accepting the logical implication of Tacitus' narrative, that Piso was appointed to keep Germanicus in check, suggesting (128) that the two appointments (of Germanicus and Piso) 'would barely seem connected'. This, however, ignores the fact that the Senate calls Piso the *adiutor* of Germanicus in *SCPP* lines 29–31, confirming Tacitus' use of this description at *Ann.* 3.12.1.

Germanicus, beyond his role as imperial legate.[59] In Piso's case, it appears that he interpreted his role as *adiutor* as being to challenge Germanicus if he felt that he was acting inappropriately; furthermore, Piso appears to have regarded himself as answerable only to Tiberius.[60] Given that Germanicus proceeded to enter Egypt illegally in AD 19,[61] interfering with the grain supply,[62] addressing crowds at Alexandria, and touring the country (ostensibly as a sightseer), it seems that there was a need for scrutiny of Germanicus' actions, especially since they may have resulted in a grain shortage in Rome shortly afterwards.[63] Admittedly, by the beginning of AD 19 Germanicus had successfully completed the specific tasks for which he had been despatched eastwards, having settled a new king in Armenia, and organised the administration of Cappadocia and Cilicia, but it is perhaps doubtful whether Tiberius had also mandated him specifically to intervene in Egypt.[64] Furthermore, the speech delivered by Germanicus to crowds in Alexandria illustrates how Germanicus embraced a distinctive conception of Roman imperial power. In the speech, he alludes to his having been sent 'by my father to settle the overseas provinces' (ἐγω πεμφθεὶς … ὑπὸ τοῦ πατρὸς [ἐ]πὶ τὸ καταστησάσθαι τα{ῖ}ς πέραν θαλάσ<σ>ης ἐπαρχίας):[65] this both echoes the official description of his mission found in the *SCPP* lines 30–31, when the Senate states that Germanicus 'had been dispatched by our *Princeps* in accordance with the authority of this body to put overseas affairs in order', and yet at the same time omits any mention of the role of the Senate in authorising his mission and granting him *imperium*. Another papyrus shows that Germanicus welcomed divine honours for Tiberius and Iulia Augusta, something which is at odds with Tiberius' own attitude to emperor-worship.[66] The fact that Germanicus was Antony's grandson was perhaps also difficult to forget.

From these contemporary documents, we can see how Germanicus' public statements were not always in tune with what Tiberius might have preferred him to say, suggesting that he was prepared to strike out on an independent pathway in representing the Roman rulers to the people of Alexandria. This may partly be explained by the geographical context, given

---

[59] Damon (1999b) 150 n.15.   [60] Shotter (1974) 234–37; Zecchini (1999) 312–16.
[61] Tac., *Ann.* 2.59.
[62] Joseph., *Ap.* 2.63; Suet., *Tib.* 52.
[63] On Germanicus in Egypt, see B. Kelly (2010), and Woodman (2015) 256–62 for echoes of Livy's Aemilus Paullus which underline Germanicus' naivety; cf. the way in which Tacitus' narrative implicitly justifies some of Tiberius' concerns about Germanicus' behaviour: Pelling (2012) 302–03; Rutland (1987) 158 points out that Tiberius was forced to compensate for the shortage of grain in Rome at Tac., *Ann.* 2.87, with Goodyear (1981), 376–77, although Wilcken (1928) observes that the timing of Germanicus' visit would have meant that the grain for Rome had already been shipped from Alexandria. Sawiński (2021) 31–32 briefly explores an alternative perspective.
[64] Hurlet (1997) 202–06 suggests that there may have been scope for Germanicus to believe that he was in fact entitled to enter Egypt, given the broad remit of his *imperium*.
[65] *P.Oxy.* no.2435 recto = LACTOR 19, J7e.
[66] Hunt and Edgar (1956) no.211 = LACTOR 19, J7d. Pani (1987), (1993) 236–49; cf. Levick (1999) 139–40.

that Alexandria was a city familiar with the traditions of Hellenistic monarchy, whilst Germanicus' desire to win popularity among the Alexandrian crowd is also apparent from his praise of Alexander as 'hero and founder, to whom there is a kind of common debt on the part of those who have the same ideals' (διὰ τ[ον] [ἥ]ρωα καὶ κτ[ισ]την προς τον κ῾οι῾νη<ι> τι ἐστιν ὁ[φ]ει[λημα] [το]ις των αὐτ[ων] ἀντεχ῾ο῾μενοις).[67] Nevertheless, Germanicus' words also demonstrate his willingness to embrace a monarchical, autocratic model of imperial power, and his independence – conscious or not – from Tiberius' own approach to the role of *princeps*. He may consequently have been regarded by Tiberius as potentially troublesome, something which may explain the appointment of Piso as his 'aide', even if we cannot be certain that Piso was given 'secret instructions' by Tiberius, according to rumours repeated by Tacitus.[68] The precedent of Marcus Lollius (consul, 21 BC), however, might have forewarned of potential tensions. Sent out to the Greek East in 1 BC to act as aide to Gaius Caesar, Lollius ended up in conflict with Gaius, accused of conspiracy and accepting bribes from eastern kings. Following Gaius' formal renunciation of friendship, Lollius poisoned himself.[69] This outcome could have shown only too clearly what pitfalls might befall a senior senator sent to advise a younger member of the imperial family far from Rome, and the scenario offers striking parallels to Piso's later fate.[70]

Another reason for the worsening relationship between Piso and Germanicus seems to have been a personality clash between Germanicus and Piso on the one hand and between their wives Agrippina and Plancina on the other.[71] Tacitus constructs a dramatic picture of antagonism between the two couples, setting up narrative episodes in which the actions of Piso and Plancina mirror actions taken by Germanicus and Agrippina.[72] Both wives, for example, intervened in person with the soldiers under their husbands' command, Agrippina by maintaining her cool at a time of confusion and preventing the demolition of a bridge over the Rhine, and Plancina by attending military training exercises.[73] Antagonism between Piso and Germanicus resulted in Piso refusing to send to Germanicus the troops he had

---

[67] *P.Oxy.* no.2435 recto = LACTOR 19, J7e.   [68] Tac., *Ann.* 2.43.4.
[69] Vell. Pat. 2.102.1, a description of Lollius which is perhaps influenced by the case of Piso: Potter (1998) 444; Plin., *HN* 9.118.
[70] Drogula (2015) argues for an alternative view, that Tiberius sent Piso to Syria so that Germanicus could keep watch over him, rather than vice versa, commenting that Tiberius had no reason to doubt Germanicus' loyalty. But Germanicus' visit to Egypt, on the contrary, may have offered plenty of grounds for Tiberius to suspect Germanicus of adhering to his own personal agenda.
[71] Köstermann (1958) 337–38; Suspène (2010) 849–52 goes further, to suggest a fundamental clash between Piso and Germanicus based upon conflicting conceptions of imperial power. For the Pisones as potential rivals to the Caesares, see §8.
[72] Pelling (2012) 296, 300–01, 311–12.
[73] Agrippina – Tac., *Ann.* 1.69. This episode is given particular emphasis by the fact that Tacitus unusually cites his source for this story, none other than Pliny the Elder's *German Wars*. Plancina – Tac., *Ann.* 2.55.6, cf. 3.33.3.

called for, and countermanding Germanicus' arrangements in Syria whilst he was travelling in Egypt.[74] Piso, perhaps, did not regard Germanicus' authority as retaining its validity when he was absent in another part of the empire. This antagonism ended up in open hostility, with Germanicus formally repudiating his friendship with Piso.[75] The *SCPP* (lines 55–56) describes how Piso challenged Germanicus' authority in the military sphere, encouraging partisanship among his troops, resulting in some soldiers calling themselves *Pisoniani* and others *Caesariani*. Such antagonism may have been the inevitable result of Piso's appointment as Germanicus' *adiutor*, or 'aide', as discussed above, but Tacitus outlines how the noble backgrounds of both Piso and Plancina made them reluctant to regard Germanicus as inherently superior to them as a consequence of his family ties.[76]

Piso's family background and his high status as a leading consular at Rome, along with the noble descent of his wife Plancina, made it unlikely that he was ever going to be a yes-man in his dealings with Germanicus.[77] Cn. Calpurnius Piso was the elder son of the Cn. Calpurnius Piso who had taken over from Augustus as consul during the crisis of 23 BC.[78] In turn, our Piso had served jointly as consul with Tiberius in 7 BC. His family pride is evident early in his career when as *tresvir monetalis* he issued coins bearing an image of Numa.[79] This was an allusion to his family's claim to be descended from the second king of Rome, via Numa's son, Calpus. This was one of the last series of coins to be minted honouring the family background of the moneyer rather than the imperial family.[80] The image of Numa had also appeared on coins alongside the name of Piso's father as proquaestor, issued in Spain in 49 BC.[81] Piso then served as proconsul of Africa at some point between 5 BC and AD 2 and legate of Hispania Tarraconensis in AD 9/10.[82]

Piso and his immediate relations (notably, his grandfather, father, and brother) could all be characterised by their fierce independence from Rome's establishment. His grandfather, suspected of involvement in Catiline's early attempts to create trouble for the state, was sent as propraetorian quaestor to Hispania Citerior, where he was assassinated by 'barbarians' in 64 BC: Sallust writes that some explained this as the consequence of Piso's

---

[74] Tac., *Ann.* 2.57.1, with Goodyear (1981) ad loc.; Tac., *Ann.* 2.69.1.
[75] *SCPP* line 29; Tac., *Ann.* 2.70. [76] Tac., *Ann.* 2.43.2–4. [77] Shotter (1974).
[78] Cn. Calpurnius Piso, consul 23 BC: *PIR*² C286, with Hofmann-Löbl (1996) 234–68; Cn. Calpurnius Piso, consul 7 BC: *PIR*² C287, with Eck, Caballos, Fernández (1996) 71–77.
[79] *RIC* I² 71–72, nos 390–96: *asses*, before 16 BC, perhaps minted in 23 or 22 BC: Burnett (1977) 49–52.
[80] Compare the *aurei* minted by L. Aquillius Florus depicting a flower: *RIC* I² 63 no.308, *c.*18 BC; Fullerton (1985) on the dominance of imperial themes thereafter.
[81] *RRC* I 463, no. 446/1.
[82] Di Vita-Évrard (1990); Fernández Ochoa, Morillo Cerdán, Villa Valdés (2005).

unjust, arrogant, and cruel commands.[83] In his youth, in 66 BC, Piso's father gave early indications of his determination to be independent of the dominant political forces in Rome, by prosecuting Manilius Crispus, a supporter of Pompeius Magnus.[84] Valerius Maximus records Piso's confrontation with Pompeius as a striking example (*exemplum*) of freedom of speech (*libertas*). He represents Piso as not being intimidated by the great man's support for the defendant, continuing his prosecution despite signs that Manilius Crispus was likely to be acquitted as a result of Pompeius' influence. We might wonder to what extent Valerius Maximus' account of this *exemplum* was influenced by the fact that he had also lived to see *libertas* as characteristic of our Piso and his brother in their dealings with Tiberius.[85] This same Piso went on to become a supporter of Brutus and Cassius, and later it was he whom Augustus persuaded to be suffect consul in 23 BC, precisely because he was easily recognisable as a former opponent of the Caesars.[86] The *libertas* of Piso himself is likewise emphasised by Tacitus on occasions when he was prepared to be outspoken in pointing to inconsistencies in the *princeps*' place within the Senate. Tacitus' use of the word *libertas* here should be understood as referring to an individual's independent way of thinking and speaking rather than to his adherence to a constitutional principle.[87] Tacitus recounts how Piso did not hesitate to challenge Tiberius' behaviour in the Senate in the *maiestas* case brought against Granius Marcellus in AD 15, describing his actions as displaying 'even then traces of a dying freedom' (*etiam tum uestigia morientis libertatis*).[88] The following year, too, Tacitus focuses upon Piso's willingness to challenge authority when he asserted that it was fitting for the Senate and equestrians to perform their duties even in the *princeps*' absence.[89] This is also a characteristic of Piso in Cassius Dio, who records an occasion on which Piso was prepared to dispute openly with members of the imperial family, opposing a motion about astrologers which had been introduced to the Senate by Tiberius and Drusus.[90] Furthermore, Tacitus narrates how Piso's brother, L. Calpurnius Piso Augur, behaved in a similar way towards the imperial family: not only did he summon to court one of Iulia Augusta's intimate friends, Urgulania, but he even went to Tiberius' home to extract her when she refused to appear. Besides this, he even threatened to

---

[83] Sall., *Cat.* 18.4–5: *sunt qui ita dicant, imperia eius iniusta, superba, crudelia barbaros nequiuisse pati.*
[84] Val. Max. 6.2.4.
[85] For more on the role of Valerius Maximus in reflecting and shaping political discourse under Tiberius, see §6.
[86] Tac., *Ann.* 2.43. On Piso's consulship of 23 BC, see Syme (1939) 334–35; Hofmann-Löbl (1996) 201–05 suggests that Augustus wanted to demonstrate to the Senate his willingness to compromise, and that Piso may even have bargained with Augustus in order to promote the careers of two members of his family, L. Calpurnius Piso Pontifex and his son Cn. Calpurnius Piso, in return for accepting the suffect consulship.
[87] Wirszubski (1950) 165   [88] Tac., *Ann.* 1.74.5.   [89] Tac., *Ann.* 2.35.
[90] Cass. Dio 57.15.9.

withdraw from public life as a protest at the corrupt way in which business was being handled.[91] In this way, Piso was an integral member of a family prepared to risk offending powerful agents at Rome in pursuit of *libertas*.

These same individuals were also characterised as sharing the family trait of *ferocia*. In Tacitus' narrative, *ferocia* is a dominant characteristic of Piso, his father, and his brother. At the point in his narrative where Tacitus pauses to comment upon Piso's character, just before he sets out for the East, he stresses Piso's natural insubordination and the *ferocia* which he has inherited from his father: 'He was violent by nature and insubordinate, and had inherited fierceness from his father Piso' (*ingenio uiolentum et obsequii ignarum, insita ferocia a patre Pisone*).[92] Later, Tacitus signals the turning-point in his narrative, when Piso decides to return to Syria after the death of Germanicus and sends a letter to Tiberius criticising his heir, with the words: 'It was with no great difficulty that Piso, ready for insubordination, was persuaded to adopt this opinion' (*haud magna mole Piso promptus ferocibus in sententiam trahitur*).[93] Similarly, Tacitus describes the brother of Piso, L. Calpurnius Piso Augur, as a 'noble and fierce man' (*nobili ac feroci uiro*).[94] The idea that members of the same family might share similar moral qualities (or vices) was typical of Roman aristocratic values: as Syme pointed out, the Popillii were regarded as intolerable, the Domitii stubborn, and the Cassii as upright and opposed to individuals exercising domination: 'from precedents or by mimesis, families transmitted characteristic features through the generations'.[95]

Munatia Plancina, in turn, was granddaughter (or less likely daughter) of Lucius Munatius Plancus, consul of 42 BC, erstwhile supporter of Antony who had defected to support Augustus only shortly before Actium but went on to be one of his most vociferous supporters, proposing for him the title Augustus in the Senate in January of 27 BC.[96] Tacitus suggests that Iulia Augusta encouraged Plancina in her enmity towards Agrippina,[97] and the way in which Iulia Augusta intervened in Piso's trial to secure her pardon clearly demonstrates that the two women were close allies.[98] But even without assuming that Plancina was working to undermine Agrippina at the behest of Iulia Augusta, there is another reason why Plancina may have been hostile towards the imperial couple on her own account: her brother, L. Munatius Plancus (consul AD 13), had almost been killed during the Rhine mutiny in AD 14 as a result of Germanicus' errors.[99]

---

[91] Tac., *Ann.* 2.34, 4.21. [92] Tac., *Ann.* 2.43. [93] Tac., *Ann.* 2.78.1. [94] Tac., *Ann.* 4.21.
[95] Syme (1986) 367. For the significance of this theme in the context of the trial of Piso, see further Cooley (1998).
[96] Munatia Plancina: *PIR*² M737; L. Munatius Plancus: *PIR*² M728; for a reassessment of Plancus' career, see H. Mitchell (2019).
[97] Tac., *Ann.* 2.43.4. [98] Tac., *Ann.* 3.15.1, 3.17.2–3, 3.18.1, 6.26; *SCPP* lines 109–20.
[99] Tac., *Ann.* 1.39.3–6; L. Munatius Plancus: *PIR*² M729.

2 Historical Context

Both the *SCPP* and Tacitus, then, set out a picture of ever-worsening hostility between Piso and Germanicus, which continued even after the latter's death. For Tacitus, it is central to his narrative to depict Piso as a friend of Tiberius, inviting his readers to believe that Piso and Plancina were acting in cahoots with Tiberius and Iulia Augusta in order to check the actions of Germanicus and Agrippina, even to the extent of poisoning Germanicus. Although it might seem illogical for Tiberius to be suspected of desiring to kill his adopted son, Tacitus paints a consistent picture of suspicion and dislike on Tiberius' part towards Germanicus, dating right back from AD 4 when he was forced by Augustus to adopt his nephew, even though he already had a son of his own.[100] Nor was his relationship with Agrippina any better, since Tacitus relates how she took pains to remind Tiberius that she was the one with direct blood ties to Augustus.[101] In his final letter, as given in Tacitus' account, Piso alludes to his positive relationship with both Augustus and Tiberius: 'once approved of by your father the god Augustus and your own friend' (*quondam diuo Augusto parenti suo probatus et tibi amicus*).[102] But is this just an invention of Tacitus designed to create a less than favourable picture of the *princeps* and his mother? On the contrary, do Piso's *ferocia* and pursuit of *libertas* make it unlikely that he was in reality a political ally or friend of Tiberius?[103] Plancina's friendship with Iulia Augusta is now evident from the *SCPP*, but it is true that the fact that Piso had served as joint consul with Tiberius in 7 BC is not in itself sufficient to demonstrate friendship between the two men. In order to tackle this question, we need to explore first evidence for a positive attitude towards Piso from Augustus, and then the separate question of whether we also have any independent evidence pointing towards friendship with Tiberius.

First of all, the *SCPP* (lines 85–86) reveals that Piso had been given a gift of land in Illyria by Augustus. The fact that he had served as proconsul of Africa also suggests that at this time he enjoyed a good relationship with Augustus.[104] As far as collaboration with Tiberius is concerned, it is possible that Piso first served as a legionary legate under Tiberius in 16/15 BC.[105] More significantly, however, the *SCPP* (lines 83–84) reveals that Piso had been a member of the *sodales Augustales*.[106] This is a clear sign of a favourable standing after the death of Augustus, given that this position was intimately associated with the imperial family, not just in terms

---

[100] Tac., *Ann.* 1.3.5. Cf. 1.62.2, 2.59.2; Seager (2005) 53–54, 60–61, 92–94 considers that Tiberius and Germanicus were simply 'incompatible'.
[101] Tac., *Ann.* 4.52.   [102] Tac., *Ann.* 3.16.4.
[103] Compare Shotter (1968) 205–06 and (1974) 231, who accepts the traditional view that Tiberius and Piso were friends, questioned by Rapke (1982), whose interpretation of passages in the *Annales* is in turn challenged by Bird (1987) and Eck, Caballos, Fernández (1996) 71 n.61. Drogula (2015) reprises this revisionist view that Piso was not an ally of Tiberius.
[104] Hofmann-Löbl (1996) 237.   [105] Hofmann-Löbl (1996) 237; Oros. 6.21.22.
[106] Rüpke (2008) 593 no.1052.

of its cult functions but also in terms of membership, since the *sodales* were high-ranking individuals and included all the main adult male members of the imperial family. Founding members in AD 14 included Tiberius himself, Drusus, Claudius, and Germanicus, as four out of the twenty-one *sodales*.[107] Finally, Piso was possibly the individual elected to replace the deceased Augustus in AD 14 as one of the Arval brethren, whose name was subsequently erased from the inscribed records kept by the Arvals. The (now lost) inscription records: 'in place of Imperator [Caesar] Augustus, the Arval brethren [co-opted and] called to its rites [[[Gnaeus Calpurnius Piso]]]' (*in locum Imp(eratoris) / [Caesaris] Augusti [[[Cn(aeum) Calpurnium Pisonem]]] fratres Aruales / [cooptauit et] ad sacra uocauit*).[108] Although it is also possible that the erased name could equally well have been that of Libo Drusus, who was condemned for plotting against the state in AD 16,[109] it is impossible to be certain which name was erased in this particular case, given the lack of consistency in erasing or retaining Piso's name on inscriptions in Rome (see §7). Nevertheless, Libo Drusus is not known otherwise to have been subjected to such a penalty, although he did suffer some memory sanctions after his suicide.[110] In addition, the fact that Piso's grandson was in his turn an Arval supports the idea that Piso himself may also have been a member of the priesthood.[111] Even without this, however, Piso's membership of the *sodales Augustales* is enough to suggest that he was in Tiberius' favour in AD 14.[112] For these reasons it seems more likely that the traditional view is correct, namely that Piso and Plancina were tasked by Tiberius and Iulia Augusta with keeping a watch over the activities of Germancius and Agrippina rather than vice versa.

We are largely dependent upon Tacitus for a narrative of events in the aftermath of Germanicus' death, including Piso's return to Rome and his trial. As a result, several important questions remain unresolved, notably the date at which the trial took place (see §3), but also whether shortly before his death Germanicus had explicitly ordered Piso to leave the province of Syria, or whether Piso did so on his own initiative, following Germanicus' renunciation of friendship with him.[113] At any rate, when

---

[107] On the foundation of the *sodales Augustales* and on their social status, see Tac., *Ann.* 1.54; Rüpke (2008) 9; Di Vita-Évrard (1993).

[108] *ILS* 5026, *CIL* VI 2023a, *CFA* 2 col. 1, 20–22, with notes at Scheid (1998), 6. The inscription is no longer extant, making it impossible to try to check the reading. Scholarly opinion remains cautiously split between Piso – Shotter (1974) 232 n.25; Syme (1986) 60, 369; Eck, Caballos, Fernández (1996) 75–76 – and Libo Drusus – Flower (2006) 228; Rüpke (2008) 881.

[109] Rüpke (2008) 881 no.2999.   [110] Tac., *Ann.* 2.32; Cass. Dio 57.15.4.

[111] Rüpke (2008) 593 no.1054; Flower (1998) 173 suggests that Piso's elder son Lucius (formerly Gnaeus) was also an Arval, but the evidence may relate instead to his uncle L. Calpurnius Piso Augur – Rüpke (2008) 593 no.1053.

[112] Eck, Caballos, Fernández (1996) 76.

[113] Tacitus' narrative hedges on this: contrast 2.69.1 'then Piso decided to leave Syria' (*dein Piso abire Suria statuit*), 2.70.2, 'many added that he had been ordered to leave the province' (*addunt plerique iussum prouincia decedere*), and 2.78, Piso's claim in a letter to Tiberius 'that he had been expelled' (*seque pulsum*).

2 Historical Context

Germanicus died in Syria, Piso was no longer in the province, but on the island of Cos: consequently it seems that his *imperium* over the province had also lapsed.[114] In the *SCPP* (lines 57–70), the Senate supplements Tacitus' description of the allegation that Piso did not conceal his joy on hearing the news of Germanicus' death, giving examples of what it regards as his behaviour constituting an affront to humanity.[115] Tacitus then relates how centurions from the Syrian legions came to Piso in order to ask him to resume command over them.[116] We are given the impression that Piso then decided to return to the province, despite advice to the contrary from his younger son Marcus.[117] This led in effect to a civil war, with Roman troops opposing each other under the command of Piso on the one hand and Cn. Sentius Saturninus on the other,[118] whom Germanicus' friends had appointed as governor of Syria following his death.[119] Although in principle this seems a somewhat irregular appointment, it was later confirmed by Tiberius.[120] Having been defeated, Piso was then, however, in no haste to return to Rome, making leisurely progress,[121] meeting Drusus en route in Illyricum,[122] and perhaps also visiting his estate in that region.[123] Piso then pointedly staged his arrival in Rome, disembarking from the Tiber next to the Mausoleum of Augustus, where Germanicus' ashes had recently been laid to rest. He is reputed to have held a lively party in his house on the slopes of the Capitol overlooking the Roman Forum.[124] In the meantime, Agrippina had arrived some time previously in Rome, bearing the ashes of Germanicus: exactly when this was is unclear, but Tacitus emphasises that she made the journey in winter.[125] This must have been an immensely tough journey. First, she sailed from Antioch on the Orontes along the coast of Lycia and Pamphylia to Corcyra – a journey of some 1,833 km, taking thirty days or more – where she recovered for a few days before continuing her much shorter voyage to Brundisium, of 282 km, which would have required more than four days. She then travelled by road to Tarracina – a distance of 455 km requiring at least fifteen days – and lastly from Tarracina to Rome, some 93 km over at least three days.[126] Given that the journey from Brundisium was in effect a funeral cortege, we might suppose that this part of the journey took considerably longer than this.[127] The whole journey, therefore, may well have taken more than two months to accomplish.

---

[114] Barnes (1998) 130.   [115] Cf. Tac., *Ann.* 2.75.2.   [116] Tac., *Ann.* 2.76.1.
[117] Tac., *Ann.* 2.76.2–3.   [118] Tac., *Ann.* 2.78–81.
[119] Cn. Sentius Saturninus: *PIR*² S395; Tac., *Ann.* 2.74.1.
[120] As confirmed by *CIL* III 6703, where he is named alongside Tiberius as *legatus Caesaris Augusti*.
[121] The chronological crux of the trial would mean that Piso either took weeks or months over this journey (see §3).
[122] Tac., *Ann.* 3.8; possibly during April/May.   [123] Cf. *SCPP* line 85.   [124] Tac., *Ann.* 3.9.
[125] Tac., *Ann.* 3.1.   [126] Tac., *Ann.* 2.79.1; 3.1.1–2.
[127] Journey distances and times calculated using The Stanford Orbis Project (http://orbis.stanford.edu/, accessed 23/03/21).

Piso's journey back to Rome was prolonged over many weeks (or even months), but as soon as he had arrived in Rome steps were taken to bring him to trial, charged under the Iulian law of *maiestas*.[128] Introduced either by Iulius Caesar in *c.*46 BC or Augustus in *c.*19 BC, this law was still evolving under Tiberius.[129] His prosecutors were L. Fulcinius Trio, who had earlier also successfully brought the case for *maiestas* against Libo Drusus in AD 16, and three of Germanicus' associates, Q. Servaeus, P. Vitellius, and Q. Veranius.[130] In AD 18, Veranius had been put in charge of Cappadocia by Germanicus, and Servaeus in charge of Commagene, whilst Vitellius had taken part in Germanicus' Rhine campaign in AD 15.[131] In Tacitus' summary of the speeches for the prosecution, he recounts how Fulcinius Trio launched the case for the prosecution with historic charges relating to Piso's time as governor of Hispania, before Germanicus' associates proceeded to raise charges relating to Piso's hatred for Germanicus and his desire for civil unrest. Specifically, he was accused of undermining military discipline, hostility towards Germanicus' friends, murder of Germanicus through curses and poison (along with Plancina), and waging war upon the state.[132] The *SCPP* (lines 23–70), however, differs from Tacitus' account, making no mention of the charge of poisoning Germanicus. Instead, it adds the following further charges: that Piso failed to obey Germanicus' commands, stirred up war with Armenia and Parthia having been bribed by Vonones, and violated the divine spirit of deified Augustus. In addition, the Senate gives vivid illustrations of actions whereby Piso showed his hatred for Germanicus and sought to stir up civil war. Piso was thus exposed to liability under the *maiestas* law for murdering a proconsul and taking up arms against the state. This is consistent with Ulpian's description in the *Digest* of those liable to the *maiestas* law 'by whose agency a plan is formed with malicious intent to kill any magistrate of the Roman people, or anyone holding *imperium* or power; or that anyone should bear arms against the state'.[133] He was also liable under the law for promoting war between Armenia and Parthia, according to Scaevola – 'or who so acts that allies of the Roman people become their enemies; or by whose malicious intent it is brought about that the king of a foreign

---

[128] Piso's return to Rome and trial summarised by Eck (1995b). See further §3 for the question of the chronology of the trial. See Paladini (1996) for an account analysing Tacitus' narrative.
[129] See further, commentary on *SCPP* lines 32–33. Castro-Camero (2000) in general, and esp. 39–44 for overview of *maiestas*; Williamson (2016) 337–40.
[130] L. Fulcinius Trio: *PIR*² F517 with Rutledge (2001) 234–35, later consul in 31 but committed suicide in 35 on account of his friendship with Sejanus; Q. Servaeus: *PIR*² S557; P. Vitellius: *PIR*² V743, also committed suicide in the aftermath of Sejanus' downfall; Q. Veranius: *PIR*² V388; Tac., *Ann.* 3.10.
[131] Tac., *Ann.* 2.56; 1.70.   [132] Tac., *Ann.* 3.13.
[133] *Dig.* 48.4.1.1 (trans. Watson 2009): *cuiusue opera consilio malo consilium initum erit, quo quis magistratus populi Romani quiue imperium potestatemue habet occidatur: quoque quis contra rem publicam arma ferat.*

nation fails to make submission to the Roman people'[134] – and refusing to hand over his province to a successor, as also mentioned by Ulpian ('who has failed to relinquish his province although his successor has arrived').[135] The discrepancy between the *SCPP* and Tacitus reflects the fact that the *SCPP* post dates the end of the trial, allowing the Senate to take account of the fact that the murder charge had been dismissed, and instead to make much more of the serious crimes of which Piso was found guilty, notably of waging war illegally and corrupting army discipline.

Piso's defence was undertaken by his brother L. Calpurnius Piso, M. Aemilius Lepidus (consul AD 6), and Livineius Regulus (consul AD 18).[136] The trial was held in the Senate with Tiberius presiding and making an opening speech, echoes of which appear to occur both in Tacitus and in the *SCPP*, and which the Senate ordered to be engraved on bronze for display in the city of Rome (*SCPP* line 168).[137] The decision to hold this trial (like other *maiestas* cases from AD 15 onwards) in the Senate was an important political decision.[138] Previously, standard procedure would have been to hear a case of *maiestas* in the court specifically designated for hearing such cases, the *quaestio maiestatis*, presided over by a praetor. The role of the Senate as a judicial court for Roman citizens was an innovation of the times. As Tacitus points out, it prejudiced the accused's chances of being acquitted. This was because of the difficulty which senators encountered in exercising independent judgement about individuals accused of offences against the *princeps* in a court where the *princeps* was present, especially in cases brought under a law that remained ill-defined and shifting in scope.[139] In effect, the Senate was arrogating for itself the role of judging cases of *maiestas*, even though it formally could not yet do so.[140]

Two days were allocated to the prosecution, followed by a six-day interval and then three days for the defence.[141] As the trial proceeded it became clear that Piso's conviction was close at hand. Even though the poisoning charge was dismissed, the other grave accusation of having waged war illegally in Syria was enough to convict Piso of *maiestas*.[142] Tacitus complicates matters by suggesting that the Senate wanted even so to convict Piso of having poisoned Germanicus, whilst it was Tiberius who was most exercised by Piso's military interventions, and further pressure for a con-

---

[134] *Dig.* 48.4.4 (trans. Watson 2009): *utue ex amicis hostes populi Romani fiant: cuiusue dolo malo factum erit, quo rex exterae nationis populo Romano minus obtemperet.*
[135] *Dig.* 48.4.2 (trans. Watson 2009): *quiue de prouincia, cum ei successum esset, non discessit.* Cf. Castro-Camero (2000) 44–50.
[136] Tac., *Ann.* 3.11.2. M. Aemilius Lepidus: *PIR*² A369; Livineius Regulus: *PIR*² L290.
[137] Damon (1999a).   [138] Castro-Camero (2000) 171–210.
[139] Tac., *Ann.* 1.74; Yakobson (2003).
[140] Richardson (1997) 515–17; see further the commentary on lines 120–23.
[141] Tac., *Ann.* 3.13.1; Flower (1999) 111 observes, however, that this merely outlines the planned structure of the trial, rather than what actually took place.
[142] Tac., *Ann.* 3.14.

viction was exerted by the people threatening to riot. It is no surprise to find that Tiberius was unrelenting in his attitude to Piso's interference in military matters. His sharp response in AD 32 to the misguided proposals by Iunius Gallio relating to ex-praetorians illustrates his resentment of the threat of interference in any military matter.[143] Possibly at the end of the second day allocated to the defence case, Piso committed suicide, a move calculated to salvage the inheritance of property for his heirs.[144] He would have expected that by doing so before he had been condemned, he would ensure a decent burial for himself and the continued validity of his will.[145] By contrast, conviction would have resulted in the confiscation of his property, with a proportion of it being given to those who had successfully prosecuted him (see §7).[146] Piso may also have calculated that his suicide was most likely to persuade Tiberius to intervene on behalf of his heirs and his co-defendants.[147] Despite the death of the accused, the trial continued with two further days, at the end of which his wife Plancina and son Marcus were granted pardon.[148] Penalties were then proposed in the Senate but subsequently extensively modified by Tiberius.[149] The *SCPP* (lines 71–90) gives a much more detailed picture of the penalties that were imposed, showing how completely the Senate attempted to erase all memory of Piso from both his family and from the state (see §7). Of the protagonists, therefore, Gnaeus Calpurnius Piso had taken his own life and his memory was condemned; Plancina was pardoned and continued to live under Iulia Augusta's protection until committing suicide in AD 33; their elder son Gnaeus Calpurnius Piso – whose loyalty had not been in doubt – changed his name to Lucius and went on to lead a successful political career, becoming consul in AD 27.[150] Finally, their younger son, Marcus, who had been in Syria, disappears from the historical record.

3 THE *SCPP* AND TACITUS

One of the most fascinating features of the *SCPP* is the way in which it overlaps with an account of the same events in Tacitus' *Annales*. Previously, the other major example of this kind of overlap was represented by the speech made in AD 48 by Claudius in the Senate recommending the admission of Roman citizens from Gallia Comata as members of

---

[143] Tac., *Ann.* 6.3.
[144] Flower (1999) 111 contends that the chronology of the trial's proceedings and of Piso's suicide is far from clear.
[145] This principle is described by Tac., *Ann.* 6.29; Griffin (1997) 261–62.
[146] G.P. Kelly (2006) 19 on *interdictio* involving property confiscation; Chilton (1955) 79 on a quarter of the confiscated property of a condemned person usually being assigned to the successful prosecutors.
[147] Tac., *Ann.* 3.15. On the impact of suicide, see Castro-Camero (2000) 37, with *Dig.* 48.21.3.8.
[148] Tac., *Ann.* 3.17.   [149] Tac., *Ann.* 3.17.4–18.4.
[150] Cn. / L. Calpurnius Piso: *PIR*² C293; M. Calpurnius Piso: *PIR*² C296.

3 The SCPP and Tacitus

that body: one version of this speech is to be found in Tacitus' *Annales*, and another is inscribed on bronze – the so-called Lugdunum Tablet.[151] In the case of a speech, it is no surprise to find that Tacitus did not choose to copy out a real speech verbatim, but preferred to rework the speech to suit his own thematic purposes and stylistic priorities.[152] He may also have included material in his version of the speech which was designed to respond to opponents of Claudius' proposal.[153] At any rate, he altered its historical perspective and enhanced its rhetorical effectiveness so as to make it a coherent analysis of the question of Rome's incorporation of newcomers within its citizen and governing bodies.[154] We might suppose a priori that Tacitus would have had more latitude for interpretation in incorporating Claudius' speech into his *Annales* than in giving an account of a trial held in the Senate. For these reasons, Claudius' speech on the Lugdunum Tablet and the Tiberian Senate's decree concerning Piso, even though both are inscribed upon bronze, offer quite different types of perspective upon Tacitus' historical methods.

The publication of the dossier of inscriptions relating to the death of Germanicus and the trial of Piso reveals clearly that the importance of Germanicus' death and Piso's trial was no invention on Tacitus' part, but that Roman society in Rome, Italy, and the provinces was encouraged to mourn Germanicus and condemn Piso's behaviour.[155] Together, the *SCPP* and Tacitus offer insights into contemporary political discourse (see §6), but they also raise questions about Tacitus' approach to writing imperial history.[156]

For many decades a recurring question in Tacitean studies has been the extent to which Tacitus used documentary sources in composing his histories.[157] For the Tiberian period, it is likely that Tacitus read accounts of the period by earlier writers such as Aufidius Bassus and Servilius Nonianus (consul, AD 35), who had likewise consulted letters which had been read in the Senate, as Tacitus himself noted (*Ann*. 2.88.1).[158] He very occasionally mentions the sources of his information explicitly, such as the *German Wars* of Pliny the Elder and Agrippina the Younger's *Memoirs*.[159] In Book 4, Tacitus gives the impression of having read widely among the historical texts available to him,[160] but he is also likely to have talked to

---

[151] Tac., *Ann*. 11.23–25.1; Lugdunum Tablet, *CIL* XIII 1668 = LACTOR 19, M11–M12; Malloch (2020).
[152] Miller (1956); Riess (2003) 214–222.   [153] Schillinger-Häfele (1965) 449–54.
[154] Griffin (1982).   [155] Griffin (1997) 260–61.
[156] Summary in Lott (2012) 39–41; Damon (1999b) analyses Tacitus' use of 'mirror stories' in order to offer multiple versions of a single narrative.
[157] Devillers (2003) offers a detailed study of Tacitus' historical methods and use of sources in the *Annales*, Potter (2012) a briefer overview.
[158] Syme (1958) vol. 1, 274–76; Devillers (2003) 12–17.
[159] Tac., *Ann*. 1.69.2, 4.53.2; with analysis of Devillers (2003) 160–61, 169 on the effect of Tacitus' unusual citation of his sources at these points.
[160] Tac., *Ann*. 4.11.2, 4.53.2; cf. 1.81.1, 3.3.2.

older contemporaries about what they remembered of the past. Tacitus alludes to hearing old men talk about the trial of Piso,[161] whilst Pliny the Younger's letters on the eruption of Vesuvius were written in response to a request from Tacitus for eye-witness information about the catastrophe.[162] Syme was firmly of the opinion that Tacitus extensively consulted records of senatorial business (*acta senatus*), which included accounts of speeches, motions, and decisions made in the Senate: 'Convincing and conclusive are the strings of personal names, the odd authentic details, the debates that led to no sort of action or legislation.'[163] Although Tacitus refers explicitly to the senatorial records only once,[164] there are many places in his works which appear to have used them directly.[165] His accounts of senatorial meetings are often very detailed, naming individuals who spoke in the Senate, recording proposals that were rejected, and maintaining the way in which matters for discussion arose over several meetings rather than pulling these together into a single passage.[166] In particular, there is a concentration of material which appears to have been derived from senatorial records in *Annales* Book 3, with twelve instances of such material catalogued by Syme.[167] Furthermore, Tacitus twice mentions the principles upon which he acted in choosing which opinions to record, and which to pass over: 'I have made it my custom not to set out senatorial opinions unless they are remarkable for their probity or because they are of notable disgrace – something which I consider to be the chief task of annals – so that virtues are not kept silent and so that wicked words and deeds should produce fear of infamy among future generations' (*exsequi sententias haud institui nisi insignes per honestum aut notabili dedecore, quod praecipuum munus annalium reor, ne uirtutes sileantur utque prauis dictis factisque ex posteritate et infamia metus sit*).[168] This implies that he was making his own selection of material directly from the archival records, and was not simply deriving it from a synopsis already created by an earlier writer.[169]

Even so, there is a risk that the image of Tacitus poring over documentary sources may be an anachronistic reflection of modern historical methods. Momigliano was one of the most determined and influential proponents of this view, stating that 'we must resist any attempt at presenting Tacitus as a researcher on original evidence' and avoid an 'anachronistic image of

---

[161] Tac., *Ann.* 3.16.1; as Woodman and Martin (1996) point out, ad loc., it should be noted that Tacitus does not claim that the old men were eyewitnesses of the trial themselves, but that they were passing on reports about the trial that circulated at the time.
[162] Plin., *Ep.* 6.16 and 6.20.
[163] Syme (1958) vol. 1, 278–86, quotation from 278; Syme (1982) 73–81; cf. Goodyear (1981) 136 on *Ann.* 1.72–81, substantial parts of which he judges to be based on senatorial records; Barnes (1998) 135–40 summarises the divergent approaches to the question by Syme and Momigliano.
[164] Tac., *Ann.* 15.74.3.   [165] Devillers (2003) 55–64.   [166] Talbert (1984) 326–34.
[167] Syme (1977) 247–51.
[168] Tac., *Ann.* 3.65.1, with Woodman and Martin (1996) ad loc.; cf. 14.64.3.
[169] Syme (1958) vol. 1, 281.

3 The SCPP and Tacitus

a Tacitus passing his mornings in the archives of the Roman Senate'.[170] He maintained that Tacitus was likely to have carried out original research only for recent events of which he was the first to produce a narrative historical account, but would have relied on earlier texts and separate publication of imperial speeches for the period we are concerned with here. In the case of the Lugdunum Tablet, for example, it is possible that Tacitus read Claudius' speech in a published collection of that emperor's speeches rather than as recorded in the senatorial archive,[171] but in either case Tacitus' account of the episode does demonstrate his desire to engage with what we would regard as a piece of primary historical source material. We should also be aware of Tacitus' use of what has been termed 'substantive self-imitation',[172] whereby the historian elaborated freely upon an episode in the *Annales* by imitating a passage already composed for the *Historiae*. Woodman has traced how the account at *Annales* 1.62.2 of Germanicus' visit to the battlefield site of Varus' defeat was inspired in its details by the account Tacitus had earlier composed of Vitellius' visit in AD 69 to the battlefield at Cremona at *Historiae* 2.70. This is not to claim, however, that Tacitus simply invented the whole episode: Woodman suggests that both Suetonius and Tacitus 'are independently indebted to the official records on this matter', and probably derived information about Tiberius' criticism of Germanicus burying the remains of Varus' army from the senatorial records.[173] The visit made by Germanicus to the battlefield, then, can be regarded as an actual historical event, but the details with which Tacitus described it should be regarded as literary elaboration designed to make the event vivid and memorable for Tacitus' readers.

The discovery and publication of the *SCPP* allow us to revisit this question from a new perspective.[174] There are some instances of striking resemblance between the language of Tacitus and the language used by the Senate in the *SCPP*. This is not to infer that Tacitus was directly working from a copy of this very decree, but the similarities are enough to show that Tacitus was influenced by contemporary Tiberian political discourse, which he had seen in accounts of senatorial proceedings.[175] Above all, as discussed above, Tacitus' description of Piso as having been appointed as *adiutor* ('aide') to Germanicus corresponds to the distinctive official language used by the Senate in the *SCPP*.[176] Tacitus also uses the phrase *amicitiam ei renuntiabat* in describing Germanicus' formal rejection of friendship with Piso, paralleled by *amicitiam ei renuntiasse* in the *SCPP*.

---

[170] Momigliano (1990) 110, 112.   [171] Griffin (1982) 405.   [172] Woodman (1979) 154.
[173] Woodman (1979) 152, on *Annales* 1.62.2.   [174] Devillers (2003) 134–35; Eck (1997), (2002).
[175] Lebek (1999) esp. 197–202 insists that Tacitus shows no awareness of the *SCPP* itself, but this does not preclude the possibility that Tacitus consulted the *acta senatus*. Nor does Lebek consider the individual examples raised here. González (2003), by contrast, suggests that Tacitus would not have wanted to follow the biased version of events in the *SCPP*, and so divergence does not necessarily reflect ignorance on the historian's part.
[176] Tac., *Ann.* 3.12.1; *SCPP* lines 29–31.

Alternative expressions for this action were available, including *interdicere domo* and *inimicitias denuntiare*, suggesting that this may be a deliberate echo of the Senate on Tacitus' part.[177] Tacitus further refers to Tiberius as showing unbiased judgement (*integrum iudicium*) in his response to the arrival in Rome of Marcus Piso, and later the adjective recurs when Tiberius sends back the case 'intact' to the Senate (*integramque causam ad senatum remittit*), and makes the request that the Senate judge the case 'with unbiased feelings' (*integris animis*).[178] This insistence upon the impartiality with which Piso's case should be handled is in turn represented at *SCPP* lines 133–36, where Iulia Augusta and Drusus are praised for 'their impartiality in reserving their own judgement intact until the case of Gnaeus Piso Senior was tried' (*aequitatem in servandis integris iudicîs suis*).[179] Although this recurring insistence in Tacitus' narrative upon the fact that Piso's trial is to be judged fairly comes across as ironic, it fits with the official message conveyed by the Senate that the trial was transparent, with all necessary information being made available about the case. Accordingly, right at the start of its decree (*SCPP* lines 15–16), the Senate offers thanks to Tiberius 'because he made available to the Senate everything which was necessary for determining the truth' (*quod earum rerum / omnium, quae ad explorandam veritatem necessariae fuerunt, co/piam senatui fecerit*). Furthermore, both Tacitus and the *SCPP* describe the universal grief felt at Germanicus' death in similar terms, alluding to the fact that he was mourned not only by Romans, but equally by peoples from beyond the boundaries of the Roman empire.[180] Crucially, Tacitus' narrative of Piso's return to Syria tallies with the Senate's interpretation of his actions as provoking civil war: this turns out to be one of the key factors in securing Piso's condemnation.[181]

One of the most unexpected parallels between the *SCPP* and Tacitus is the Senate's reference to Tiberius' 'appearance', his *vultus*: 'for which reason he (Tiberius) should end his grief and regain for his country not only the frame of mind, but also the appearance appropriate to public happiness' (*quo nomine debere eum finire dolorem / ac restituere patriae suae non tantum animum, sed etiam voltum, qui / publicae felicitati conveniret*) (*SCPP* lines 130–32). This is a notable choice of expression on the part of the Senate, since it is precisely Tiberius' *vultus* which is one of the key features of Tacitus' characterisation of Tiberius as secretive and inscrutable. For O'Gorman, 'Tiberius represents the Tacitean narrative, in that the difficulties of reading the princeps are a dramatization of the difficulties

---

[177] Tac., *Ann.* 2.70.2; *SCPP* line 29; alternative expressions in Rogers (1959) 227.
[178] Tac., *Ann.* 3.8.1; 3.11.1; 3.12.1.   [179] Woodman and Martin (1996) 123.
[180] Tac., *Ann.* 2.72.2: *indoluere exterae nationes regesque* ('foreign peoples and kings mourned'); *SCPP* lines 57–58: *cuius in/teritum non p(opulus) R(omanus) modo, sed exterae quoq(ue) gentes luxserunt* ('whose loss not only the Roman people but foreign nations as well mourned').
[181] Tac., *Ann.* 2.76.2; *SCPP* line 45.

3 The SCPP and Tacitus

of reading the Annals.'[182] Moreover, the Senate's request to Tiberius about his appearance occurs in the same context, namely Tiberius' mourning for Germanicus, as Tacitus' analysis of Tiberius' self-imposed absence from public life. Tacitus represents the decision by Tiberius and Iulia Augusta alike to absent themselves from Germanicus' funeral as being the result of their fear that their true feelings about Germanicus might be evident were they to appear in public: 'Tiberius and Augusta kept away from appearing in public, thinking it beneath their dignity if they were to grieve openly, or in fear that they might be understood to be hypocritical once the eyes of all were observing their appearance' (*Tiberius atque Augusta publico abstinuere, inferius maiestate sua rati si palam lamentarentur, an ne omnium oculis uultum eorum scrutantibus falsi intellegerentur*).[183] As Woodman and Martin comment, 'it is ironical that T[acitus] here affects to believe that Tib[erius], the master of pretence, dared not appear in public for fear of revealing his hypocrisy'.[184] The *SCPP* raises the intriguing prospect that Tiberius' *vultus* was the subject of public comment at the time, and that consequently Tacitus' use of this theme may be a genuine echo of contemporary discourse.[185] If Tiberius had been absent from public view until December of AD 20, when the *SCPP* was published, it is perhaps not surprising that the Senate should make this request. Tacitus, however, elaborated upon the theme. Reading and misreading individuals' outward appearances is fundamental to Tacitus' depiction of the relationship between his characters, including Tiberius and Agrippina, and Sejanus and Tiberius, and between Tiberius and the Senate.[186] Tacitus describes, for example, how Tiberius' unchanging expression during their trials in the Senate caused Libo Drusus and Piso in turn to lose hope of being pardoned.[187]

In assessing the historical accuracy of Tacitus' portrayal of the trial of Piso, we now appreciate how some details which were previously considered to be Tacitean inventions have been confirmed to be essentially accurate. Before the discovery of the *SCPP*, it was open to scholars to assume that Tacitus' statement that Plancina was pardoned as the result of intervention by Iulia Augusta was a typical misrepresentation on his part, designed to cast her excessive influence in public affairs in a negative light.[188] Wells, for example, suggested in relation to Plancina's acquittal that 'Tacitus attributes this, **unreasonably**, not to lack of evidence, but to her friendship with Livia.'[189] The Senate's fulsome acknowledgement in the *SCPP* that Plancina's pardon was entirely the result of Iulia Augusta's intervention, therefore, came as something of a surprise. Tacitus' depiction

---

[182] O'Gorman (2000) 78.   [183] Tac., *Ann.* 3.3.1.   [184] Woodman and Martin (1996) 90.
[185] Compare Ovid's allusion to Germanicus' *vultus* in his dedication of the *Fasti*: Ov., *Fast.* 1.3.
[186] O'Gorman (2000) chapter 4.   [187] Tac., *Ann.* 2.29.2; 3.15.2.
[188] Tac., *Ann.* 3.15.1, 3.17.4; L'Hoir (1994), esp. 5, on the theme of Tacitus' depiction of women as 'individuals unduly and inappropriately obsessed with power'.
[189] Wells (1984) 108, my emphasis.

of Iulia Augusta's influence in public affairs can now be seen to be no exaggeration; on the contrary, his description of her intervention is couched in rather more moderate terms than those used by the Senate.[190]

Tacitus was not, of course, totally reliant upon the senatorial records. As Syme asserts, 'never at the mercy of his sources, he can select, omit, postpone'.[191] The absence from the *Annales* of particular details to be found in the *SCPP* cannot be used to suggest that Tacitus was simply unaware of them.[192] Whilst his narrative sometimes closely follows thematic motifs also to be found in the *SCPP*, Tacitus chooses different phrasing.[193] For example, in narrating Piso's response to news of Germanicus' death, both Tacitus and the *SCPP* allude to his performing sacrifices and opening up of temples which had been closed as a sign of mourning for Germanicus. Tacitus (*Ann*. 2.75.2) condenses this into an asyndetic phrase – *caedit uictimas, adit templa* – differing markedly from the Senate's more elaborate account (*SCPP* lines 62–65): *quod nefaria sacrificia ab eo facta, quod naves, quibus vehebatur, ornatae sint, quod recluserit deorum immortalium templa, quae totius imperi Romani constantissuma pietas clauserat* ('that wicked sacrifices were offered by him, that the ships in which he sailed were decorated, that he reopened the temples of the immortal gods which the most unwavering devotion of the whole Roman empire had closed'). This is typical of Tacitus' linguistic restraint, in contrast to the Senate's effusiveness. It was central to the Senate's aims in publishing their judgement on Piso to emphasise his immoral conduct and his isolation from the rest of humanity in behaving in this way, whereas Tacitus draws a more ambivalent picture of Piso's alleged villainy.[194] As Woodman and Martin observe, 'T[acitus] characteristically converts the monument's monotonous confidence into discrepancy and doubt.'[195] Tacitus (*Ann*. 2.78.1) describes Piso as *promptus ferocibus* ('naturally inclined towards insubordination'), whereas the Senate adopts a more extreme turn of phrase, alluding to his 'brutish behaviour' (*feritate morum*) (*SCPP* line 27), thereby dehumanising Piso by using language associated with mythological monsters or uncivilised barbarians.[196] In this way, even though the narrative details may be the same, the emotive language used by the Senate is in stark contrast to Tacitus' compressed style. Both allude to Piso sending a letter to Tiberius in which he criticised Germanicus: Tacitus (*Ann*. 2.78.1) describes this act as *missique ad Tiberium epistulis incusat Germanicum luxus et superbiae* ('Piso accused Germanicus of luxury and arrogance in a letter sent to Tiberius'), whereas the Senate also adds detailed interpretation as to Piso's motivations in doing so (*SCPP* lines 59–61): *libellum, quo eum accusaret, mittere ausus sit oblitus non tantum venerationis caritatisq(ue), quae principis filio debebantur,*

---

[190] *SCPP* lines 109–20.   [191] Syme (1977) 231.   [192] Damon (1999b) 148; contra, Lebek (1999).
[193] Detailed analysis of different versions of events in Tacitus and the *SCPP* in Damon (1999b).
[194] Cooley (1998).   [195] Woodman and Martin (1996) 117.   [196] Cooley (1998) 200.

ceterum humanitatis quoq(ue), quae ultra mortem odia non patitur procedere ('a document in which he made accusations about Germanicus, forgetting not only the respect and affection which were owed to the son of the Princeps, but even common humanity which does not permit feuds to be carried on beyond death'). Another significant difference is that Tacitus (*Ann.* 2.71.1) attributes to the dying Germanicus the fear that he has been poisoned by Piso and Plancina – *nunc scelere Pisonis et Plancinae interceptus* ('now struck down through the crime of Piso and Plancina') – whereas in the *SCPP* (line 28), Germanicus is recorded as mentioning only Piso by name. This does not mean that Tacitus was therefore using a different source, since the *SCPP* as we have it reflects the Senate's view of the situation only after Piso's suicide and Plancina's pardoning, when they would no longer have wished to draw attention to Plancina's alleged involvement.

Overall, then, the balance of evidence suggests that Tacitus did extensively consult senatorial records. He was not the only writer to do so nor the first: Pliny the Younger (*Ep.* 8.6) describes how the outrage provoked by the effusive language used on the epitaph of Claudius' freedman Pallas, which he had recently seen inscribed on his tomb, prompted him to consult the original senatorial decree in order to check exactly what had been said in the Senate, only to find to his horror that the language originally used in the Senate had actually been even more immoderate.[197] Tacitus was not, however, writing as an antiquarian, whose aim would have been to transcribe his source material; as a historian he was constantly engaged in interpreting the evidence he found, and in creating an entertaining and vivid historical narrative that drew upon the full range of literary and rhetorical techniques available to him. Although the suggestion has been made that Tacitus may have read the account of the trial of Piso as it appeared on bronze tablets displayed in the city of Rome, rather than as it was recorded in the senatorial archive,[198] the image of Tacitus as a prototype epigrapher is less plausible than the notion that he may have anticipated to some extent the archival techniques of the modern historian. Finally, Tacitus' narrative includes arguments made in Piso's defence (including a version of Piso's self-justification written before his suicide), which were entirely ignored by the Senate in its decrees, something which points towards his reading more widely than the subjective account of the trial publicised by the Senate in epigraphic form.[199] Other details included in Tacitus, such as the list of penalties proposed against Piso which Tiberius then vetoed, also support the view that Tacitus was not reliant upon the Senate's decrees but drew upon senatorial records more widely.[200] Above all, the major

---

[197] See Potter (2012) 129 on the use of documents in other historians.
[198] Woodman and Martin (1996) 114–16.
[199] On Piso's *codicilli* read out in the Senate, Tac., *Ann.* 3.16.3–4; Zecchini (1999) 331.
[200] Tac., *Ann.* 3.17–18; Lebek (1999) 185–87. On divergences between Tacitus and the *SCPP* in listing penalties imposed upon Piso, see Bodel (1999) and Woodman and Martin (1996) 114–18, 185–88.

difference between Tacitus and the *SCPP* is the result of the texts' quite distinct aims. Whereas Tacitus focuses the trial of Piso on the accusation that Germanicus was murdered,[201] after the end of the trial the Senate was more concerned with documenting why Piso's behaviour should be roundly condemned. Furthermore, whereas Tacitus creates an ambiguous picture of Piso (as secret collaborator with Tiberius or as enemy of the state), the Senate has no doubt about Piso's guilt. Tacitus is therefore more likely to have been working from the senatorial records, which would have been much more wide-ranging in scope, than directly from the document preserved for us as the *SCPP*.[202]

The most vexed interpretative problem raised by comparing the *SCPP* with Tacitus is a fundamental one, namely when exactly the trial took place.[203] Ostensibly there is a major discrepancy between the inscribed decree, which was both passed and drafted by committee on 10 December AD 20, and Tacitus' narrative, which implies that the trial started at some date after 10 April and had come to an end by 28 May. Tacitus' account of the year AD 20 starts dramatically, with Agrippina's wintry voyage back to Rome with the ashes of Germanicus (*Ann.* 3.1.1), delaying mention of the new consuls for the year and confining them to a parenthesis (*Ann.* 3.2.3) in order both to highlight Agrippina's determination and endurance of hardship and to continue with the story of Germanicus leading on from the end of *Annales* 2.[204] The next chronological pointer is a reference to the approach of the *ludi Megalenses* (*Ann.* 3.6.3), which took place 4–10 April.[205] Then follows the narrative of Piso's return to Rome and his trial, the section being rounded off with the celebration of Drusus' *ovatio*, which had been granted jointly to Drusus and Germanicus, but postponed out of respect for Germanicus' recent death.[206] The date of this *ovatio* is given in the *Fasti Ostienses* as 28 May.[207] Furthermore, in the sequence of Tacitus' narrative, the occasion of Germanicus' son Nero assuming his adult toga – likewise independently dated by the *Fasti Ostienses* to 7 June – also occurs after the trial has ended.[208] If the *SCPP* is assumed to represent the

---

[201] Tac., *Ann.* 3.7.1, 3.12.2, 3.18.2–3, 3.19.2; Woodman and Martin (1996) 110.
[202] Coudry (1994) 78 on the wider scope of *acta senatus*, in comparison with documented *senatus consulta*; Flower (1999) 110.
[203] The chronological problem is analysed by Woodman and Martin (1996) 67–77; Eck, Caballos, Fernández (1996) 109–21; Caballos, Eck, Fernández (1996) 143–48; *Hispania Epigraphica* 6 (1996) no.881: 323–25; Griffin (1997) 253–55, 259–60; Yakobson (1998) 207–11; Barnes (1998) 129–35; Potter (1998) 452–54; Champlin (1999) 119–20; Flower (1999) 110–15; Talbert (1999) 90–96; Lebek (1999) 202–09; Zecchini (1999) 322–23; Giua (2000) 255–64; González (2002) 191–97; Mackay (2003) 357–67.
[204] Ginsburg (1981) 17, 58–59; Woodman and Martin (1996) 78, 88.
[205] Degrassi (1963) 435–36.   [206] Tac., *Ann.* 2.64.1, 3.11.1.
[207] Tac., *Ann.* 3.19.3; Bargagli and Grosso (1997) 23 – *Fasti Ostienses* frag. Ce, lines 37–39.
[208] Tac., *Ann.* 3.29.3; Bargagli and Grosso (1997) 23 – *Fasti Ostienses* frag. Ce, lines 40–41. Woodman and Martin (1996) 69 point out, however, that the point at which this notice appears in the year's narrative could be regarded as an 'end-of-year' section summarising non-chronologically some significant events relating to prominent individuals, just before a similar 'obituary' section; cf. Ginsburg (1981) chapter 3, esp. 38–39.

3 The SCPP and Tacitus

senatorial decree passed immediately after the end of Piso's trial, we are faced with a contradiction between the implication of Tacitus' narrative that Piso's trial took place in April/May and the explicit dating of the *SCPP* to 10 December.

Chronological uncertainties are not unparalleled in the *Annales*, given that Tacitus does not always narrate events simply in order within each year: for example, Tacitus announces at the start of his account of the year AD 61 that this was the year of the Boudiccan revolt in Britain, even though his own narrative suggests that it actually took place during AD 60.[209] Indeed, as Ginsburg discusses, Tacitus freely structures events within each year even in the Tiberian books, which are generally considered more annalistic in flavour than the later ones. She concludes:

> Nor was he bound to a chronological framework for the narrative of the year as a whole. Thematic considerations lead the historian to abandon a strictly chronological presentation of material at or near the year's close, and he sometimes goes so far as to postpone an account of early events in order to begin with later ones ... Tacitus rejects chronology as the governing principle of the annual account and with it the notion that it was the historian's task to record events in the order in which they actually occurred.[210]

Tacitus may therefore have knowingly foreshortened his narrative of the trial for dramatic effect, not wishing to delay his account of the trial until the end of AD 20, when it actually took place. Such 'temporal displacement' might be regarded as 'the historian's prerogative', an effective way of associating Piso's trial much more closely with the death of Germanicus than would have been possible had Tacitus preserved chronological niceties.[211] One option, then, is to assume that Tacitus deliberately shifted the chronology of Piso's trial. This is the view firmly espoused by the original editors of the *SCPP*, who argue that Piso did not return to Rome until November, and that his trial and suicide took place relatively quickly over the ten to twelve days immediately preceding the decree being written up on 10 December.[212] They conclude that Tacitus either deliberately changed the chronology of his narrative of the trial of Piso for literary purposes (their preferred option) or made a mistake (a view argued by Barnes), not realising that the trial had not in fact taken place in April/May.[213] The chronological distortion would not have been apparent to an ancient reader, given that it is only our modern tendency to compare different

---

[209] Tac., *Ann.* 14.29.1; Syme (1958) vol.2, 765–66; Potter (2012) 138; contra, Carroll (1979), who supports Tacitus' statement that the revolt began in AD 61. Cf. Ginsburg (1981) 67–72 on Tacitus' reversal of the order of events in his account of AD 15; Goodyear (1981) 393–96 on *Ann.* 2.59–61.
[210] Ginsburg (1981) 96–97; quotation from 97, 99.
[211] Pagán (2012) 4–5; cf. Eck, Caballos, Fernández (1996) 116–19.
[212] Eck (1995b) 7; Eck, Caballos, Fernández (1996) 109–21; cf. Yakobson (1998) 208.
[213] Eck, Caballos, Fernández (1996) 116–17; Barnes (1998) 142–43 concludes, 'The historian's error derives from a faulty correlation of literary and documentary sources.' Cf. Lebek (1999) 202–09, who argues that Tacitus was simply unaware that the decree was passed in December.

types of sources that has revealed the discrepancy between Tacitus, the *fasti Ostienses*, and the *SCPP* in the first place: Tacitus himself mentions only the celebration of Drusus' *ovatio*, and does not name the date on which it occurred.

Talbert, however, argues that this timetable is too tight to allow for the investigations and trial in the Senate to be completed, observing that a time limit would have been applied only to the advocates' speeches in the Senate, and not to the reading of documents and consideration of the evidence from witnesses. Instead of considering the whole process to have taken up just a few days in the Senate towards the end of November/December, Talbert proposes that we should instead consider the possibility that Piso's trial along with the investigation after his suicide may have extended over several months.[214] In this case, the trial did commence in April/May, as implied by Tacitus' narrative structure, but lasted for many weeks, ending only in December with the summing up represented by the *SCPP*.

There is, however, another possible interpretation to explore, which relates to the fundamental question of what type of document we consider the *SCPP* to be. After all, the chronological problem only persists on the assumption that the *SCPP* is tightly connected with the outcome of the trial. If the *SCPP* were a routine senatorial decree, then the usual process whereby senatorial decrees were registered and archived would suggest that the *SCPP* was created in the immediate aftermath of the end of the Senate's session during which the trial was conducted. As far as we can ascertain, normal procedure was for senatorial decrees to be edited after the Senate had ended its plenary meeting by the magistrate who had proposed the subject for discussion along with a small number of other senators who are named in the decree's prescript. The edited version of the decree was then approved, written on wooden tablets, and deposited in the *aerarium* by the urban quaestors.[215] This was an essential step in ensuring the decree's validity. Given that a new procedure was introduced in AD 21 whereby a delay of ten days was imposed between the passing of a decree and its deposit in the *aerarium*, we can assume that the practice in AD 20 was for this process to take place much more quickly.[216]

The *SCPP* is not, however, a typical senatorial decree, in several respects.[217] It is not a straightforward record of the senatorial proceedings containing an account of the trial itself, but is a document drafted only after Piso's suicide and after the trial had ended. The senators involved in drafting the text of the *SCPP* were not concerned with documenting the trial, but with presenting their judgement about the contrasting characters of Germani-

---

[214] Talbert (1999) 90–96.
[215] Bonnefond-Coudry (1989) 570; Coudry (1994); Talbert (1984) 303.
[216] Tac., *Ann.* 3.51.2, with Coudry (1994) 67.   [217] Giua (2000) 256.

3 The SCPP and Tacitus

cus and Piso: *et quo facilius totius actae rei ordo posterorum memoriae tradi posset atque hi scire<nt>, quid et de singulari moderatione Germ(anici) Caesa(ris) et de sceleribus Cn(aei) Pisonis patris senatus iudicasset* ('And in order that the course of the proceedings as a whole might be more easily transmitted to the memory of future generations and so that they might know what the Senate's judgement was concerning the exceptional restraint of Germanicus Caesar and the crimes of Gnaeus Piso Senior') (*SCPP* lines 165–68). There are, in addition, unique features in the phrasing whereby the matter is introduced to the Senate. It is the only decree known to be introduced with the phrase *quod ... ad senatum rettulit* ('whereas he referred to the Senate for decision') rather than the usual *quod ... verba fecit* ('whereas he made a statement'). This change underlines Tiberius' role in delegating discussion to the Senate.[218] Furthermore, the Senate's decision is introduced through a much shorter phrase than normal, with the words *d(e) i(is) r(ebus) i(ta) c(ensuerunt)* ('concerning these matters the Senate decreed as follows'), omitting the first part of the usual formula, *quid de ea re fieri placeret* ('with regard to what it might please the Senate to be done with regard to this matter'), and also using the plural 'concerning these matters' in place of the more normal 'with regard to this matter'. This emphasises that multiple matters were being considered by the Senate on this occasion, rather than a single question. At the end of the *SCPP*, too, we are informed that the decree was passed 'in accordance with a single proposal' (see 173n., *per relationem solum*). The text published by the Senate is to be complemented by the inscribing and display of a speech made by Tiberius: *placere uti oratio, quam recitasset princeps noster, itemq(ue) haec senatus consulta in {h}aere incisa, quo loco Ti(berio) Caes(ari) Aug(usto) videretur, ponere<n>tur* ('the Senate has decided that the speech which our Princeps had delivered and also these decrees of the Senate, inscribed on bronze, should be set up in whatever place seemed best to Tiberius Caesar Augustus') (*SCPP* lines 168–70). This suggests that what the senatorial committee has drawn up was distinct from a standard decree, an interpretation which is reinforced further by the unparalleled personal note from Tiberius himself, written in the first person and appended to the very end of the Senate's document:

Ti(berius) Caesar Aug(ustus) trib(unicia) potestate XXII manu mea scripsi: velle me `h`<oc> s(enatus) c(onsultum), quod e<s>t factum IIII idus Decem(bres) Cotta et Messalla co(n)s(ulibus) referente me, scriptum manu Auli q(uaestoris) mei in tabellis XIIII, referri in tabulas pub<l>icas.

I, Tiberius Caesar Augustus, holder of tribunician power for the twenty-second time, wrote this with my own hand: it is my wish that this senatorial decree, which was passed on 10 December in the year when Cotta and Messalla were consuls on the

---

[218] Talbert (1984) 304 on the standard wording of decrees.

basis of my proposal and was copied by the hand of my quaestor Aulus on fourteen tablets, should be placed in the public archives. (*SCPP* lines 174–76)

Lastly, the detailed instructions about the publication of the *SCPP* demonstrate that the Senate was taking extraordinary measures in order to convey its opinion of Piso around the empire. The publication of senatorial decrees in the form of bronze inscriptions was not standard procedure.[219] Even less so was the Senate's decision to mandate the publication of their decrees concerning Germanicus and Piso beyond Rome. The publication clause of the *SCPP* goes beyond the provision for publishing the *Tabula Siarensis*.[220] Whereas the Senate had mandated the publication of the honours for Germanicus in *coloniae* on whiteboards, the *SCPP* was to be published in permanent monumental form, and to be distributed not only to colonies but also to legionary winter quarters. In short, several features raise the possibility that the fourfold *relatio* of the *SCPP* and the decree it contains are distinct from documentation relating to the original trial of Piso held earlier in the year.[221]

In the light of these unique characteristics in the *SCPP*, therefore, another explanation for the apparent chronological mismatch between the *SCPP* and Tacitus is to suggest that the *SCPP* is connected not with the ending of the original trial, but with an attempt of the Senate, some months after the trial had ended, to revisit the case because of the persistence of rumours at Rome and a continued threat of popular unrest.[222] Even though some scholars have questioned whether it is likely that Tiberius would have wanted to revisit such a sensitive subject six months after the end of the trial,[223] this hypothesis fits the character of the *SCPP*, which is not straightforwardly an account of the trial itself. One chronological detail embedded in Tacitus' narrative may seem to support the view that the trial did occur in April/May. This is the statement in the account of Piso's journey back to Rome that Piso fell in with the Ninth Hispanica Legion as he travelled back through Italy. The legion is described as being in transit in preparation for its summer campaigns against Tacfarinas.[224] Although absolute chronology is still not fixed by this encounter, the requirement for the legion to reach North Africa in time for summer campaigning is perhaps more aligned with the idea that Piso came across the legion in northern Italy during April/May than in June/July. Griffin has further pointed out that it might have seemed insensitive had Drusus celebrated his *ovatio*, which had been granted to him jointly with Germanicus, before the trial of Piso had taken place.[225] For others, however, Drusus'

---

[219] Talbert (1984) 306–08; Cooley (2012).
[220] *Tabula Siarensis* = Crawford (1996) no.37, frag. b, col. II, lines 24–27 = LACTOR 19, J8h.
[221] Giua (2000) 256.   [222] Griffin (1997) 253–55, 259–60.   [223] Yakobson (1998) 208–09.
[224] Tac., *Ann.* 3.9.1; Woodman and Martin (1996) 74; Potter (1998) 453.
[225] Griffin (1997) 259.

celebration of his *ovatio* in May is seen as an attempt by Tiberius to restore normality to public life in Rome following the ending of the official period of mourning for Germanicus,[226] whilst Barnes further argues that the date of Drusus' *ovatio* may have been intended to echo the earlier *ovatio* celebrated by his father Tiberius over Pannonia: if this is correct, it would not perhaps have seemed untimely.[227] Rumours, however, may have persisted in Rome suggesting that Tiberius and Iulia Augusta had been complicit in Germanicus' poisoning. Unrest may have broken out at the time of the first anniversary of Germanicus' death in October, or of the *iustitium* declared on 8 December, prompting the Senate to convene a committee to draw up for publication an official version of events. What is clear, though, is that the final decree was far from an objective account of the trial and its outcomes, but was a rhetorical exercise in propping up the imperial regime. As already discussed above, this explains the radical difference in tone between the *SCPP* and Tacitus, but it also explains a difference in thematic emphasis, with the *SCPP* putting much emphasis upon Piso's crimes in stirring up unrest in Parthia and Armenia whilst Tacitus, by contrast, focuses upon the question of Germanicus' murder.[228] In short, this interpretation sees the *SCPP* not as a documentary account of the trial of Piso, but as a rhetorical explanation of why Piso was uniquely wicked and so why the rest of his family might be pardoned. It was intended to work on the emotions of its readers and secure their loyalty towards the imperial family. The extraordinary reaction to Germanicus' death among the people of Rome has already been described above (§2). On this interpretation, the Senate chose to take this exceptional step of revisiting the trial some months after it had concluded, undertaking to provide a new synopsis of Piso's crimes. In this way, the date of the inscribed decree represented by the *SCPP* would be separate from the actual trial of Piso.[229] It is possible, therefore, that the trial and suicide of Piso did take place in May AD 20, as implied by Tacitus' narrative, even if this does not allow much time for the respective travels of Drusus and Piso between Illyricum and Rome.[230] Without further new evidence, certainty about the chronology of the trial and its aftermath remains elusive, but it now seems clear that Tacitus' narrative of the death of Germanicus and trial of Piso was influenced by contemporary discourse shaped by the Senate, among others (see §5–6).

---

[226] Eck, Caballos, Fernández (1996) 116, followed by Yakobson (1998) 210.
[227] Barnes (1998) 132.
[228] Woodman and Martin (1996) 110; Zecchini (1999) 316.
[229] Compare the delay between the Senate passing decrees in 18 BC and February 17 BC on holding the *ludi saeculares*, which were only incorporated into a dossier of various documents relating to the games on 23 May: *CIL* VI 32323, lines 58–63 = LACTOR 17, L27h; Giua (2002) 127–28.
[230] Eck, Caballos, Fernández (1996) 113–15 consider that the speed of travel this would require for both Drusus and Piso between Illyricum and Rome during April/May makes this scenario unlikely, and suggest (119) that they met instead in June, before Piso had returned to Rome; cf. Barnes (1998) 132.

4 THE INSCRIPTIONS OF THE *SCPP*

The dramatic political circumstances surrounding the death of Germanicus, therefore, dominate much of books 2–3 of Tacitus' *Annales*. Before the 1980s, our appreciation of the political crisis that developed at Rome following the death of Germanicus was largely dependent upon this narrative, but the discovery and publication of the *Tabula Siarensis*, which overlapped with and extended the scope of the text of the *Tabula Hebana*, offered an opportunity to compare Tacitus' narrative in detail with contemporary epigraphic evidence. Together, the *Tabula Siarensis* and *Tabula Hebana* presented details of the honours decreed to Germanicus by the Senate in December AD 19. These were then further complemented by the discovery of bronze inscriptions bearing the *SCPP*. Following publication of various preliminary articles on the new discoveries[231] and detailed discussion at a series of collaborative international workshops, two editions of the *SCPP* were published, in Spanish and German.[232] These editions presented six – or possibly seven – different copies of the inscription, which are the product of at least five previous steps in the transmission of the text.[233] Consequently, there are differences between the two main copies of the text, some of which are the result of the engraver's error, but others of which relate to a deliberate choice, such as the tendency of Copy B to retain more archaisms in orthography.[234]

Copy A (MAS inv. D09579) is believed to have been found by clandestine digging at some point before 1990 in the area of El Saucejo to the south of the province of Seville (variously known as Las Herrizas, Cerro de los Baldíos, and El Diente de la Vieja) in the same location where the *Lex Irnitana* was found in 1981.[235] Structural remains of walls and tiles there suggest that this was the site of the *municipium* of Irni. The bronze tablet was originally held in place by six nails, which were positioned after the engraving had been completed. It may have been displayed on the wall of a public building, or on the base of a monument, perhaps on the side of a base supporting an equestrian statue of Germanicus. It consists of

---

[231] Eck (1993a) = *AE* 1993, 21b; Eck (1993b) = *AE* 1993, 21a; Caballos Rufino, Eck, Fernández Gómez (1994a) = *AE* 1994, 894a; Caballos Rufino, Eck, Fernández Gómez (1994b) = *AE* 1994, 894b.

[232] Caballos, Eck, Fernández (1996) and Eck, Caballos, Fernández (1996) = *AE* 1996, 885. The two editions largely overlap, but the Spanish edition includes additional metallurgical and palaeographical analysis of the inscriptions, whilst the German edition includes a section on the political significance of the *SCPP*. Summary of the key differences between the two editions: Barnes (1998). Copies A–F also published in Caballos (2002).

[233] Eck, Caballos, Fernández (1996) 53.   [234] Eich (2009) 273–75.

[235] Caballos, Eck, Fernández (1996) 15–16; Eck, Caballos, Fernández (1996) 1–3 remain cautious about whether the findspot should also be regarded as the original location of the inscription's display. Summary in Lott (2012) 50–52. EDCS-46400006, with photographs – http://db.edcs.eu/epigr/bilder.php?bild=$SCPisoneA.jpg;$SCPisoneA_1.jpg;$SCPisoneA_2.jpg;$SCPisoneA_3.jpg;$SCPisoneA_4.jpg;$SCPisoneA_5.jpg;$SCPisoneA_6.jpg;$SCPisoneA_7.jpg;$SCPisoneA_8.jpg;pp&nr=10 (accessed 25/08/2019).

4 The Inscriptions of the SCPP

twenty-three fragments of various dimensions of what was originally two bronze sheets fused together,[236] which together preserve the text almost in its entirety. Weighing over 20 kg, Copy A has the following overall dimensions: 46 (left)–43.3 (right) cm high; 118 (above)–118.7 (below) cm wide; 4.7–4.8 mm thick. The letters in the prominent heading are 4–4.5 cm in height, whilst the rest are only 0.5–0.6 cm tall. The text is set out over four columns, with an average overall of sixty-two letters per line, and it includes interpuncts between words. The work of engraving looks to have been shared by two engravers, with one engraving columns I–II, and the other completing columns III–IV. Tiberius' statement at the end of document is visually privileged by consisting of only fifty-four letters per line.[237] A missing fragment from Copy A (4.25 cm x 3.93 cm x 3.3 cm, 4.5 mm thick) was published a little later, having appeared on the American antiquities market. This contains part of lines 25–29, with the result that the whole of Copy A has now been identified.[238]

Copy B (MAS inv. D09479)[239] was at first believed to come from the site of Olaurum, but it was later thought to be more likely that the fragments were found during the construction of the road between Córdoba and Málaga, at El Tejar in the province of Córdoba, where the site of Ad Gemellas seems to have been located.[240] Four fragments of this bronze tablet have been found, which jointly weigh just under 11 kg. There are no traces of holes for fixing the tablet to a wall, so it seems that it must have been incorporated into a frame of some sort. Three of the pieces join together to form a large part of the left-hand side of the tablet, with maximum dimensions of 60.7 cm in height, 52.5 cm in width, and 2–4 mm in thickness. The fourth fragment from the right-hand side of the tablet has the following dimensions: 60.5 cm high, 25.2 cm maximum width. Its original width may have been roughly 91 cm. The text is set out over two columns, with an average overall of seventy-eight letters per line. The first three lines of text are in rather larger letters (line 1, 14–16 mm; line 2, 9–11 mm; line 3, 8–9 mm) than the rest of the inscription (lettering 6–8 mm down to line 11; then 5–6 mm). There are interpuncts only in line 1. Two engravers may have worked on a column of text apiece. The engraving is less regular than on Copy A, and many letters remain incomplete. Copy B also contains more errors than Copy A, including the

---

[236] Caballos, Eck, Fernández (1996) 16; Eck, Caballos, Fernández (1996) 2: twenty-four fragments but on p.7 twenty-three fragments, checked via autopsy.
[237] On the physical characteristics of Copy A, see Caballos, Eck, Fernández (1996) 16–23; Eck, Caballos, Fernández (1996) 7–10.
[238] *AE* 2014, 628 = Gradel (2014).
[239] Also, *CIL* II² V 900. EDCS-46400001, with photographs – http://db.edcs.eu/epigr/bilder.php?bild=$SCPisoneB_1.jpg;$SCPisoneB_2.jpg;$SCPisoneB_3.jpg;$SCPisoneB_4.jpg;$SCPisoneB_5.jpg;$HEp-04_00831.jpg;5/cilii5,00900frg.a-c;5/cilii5,00900frg.d;pp (accessed 25/08/2019).
[240] Caballos, Eck, Fernández (1996) 66–68; Eck, Caballos, Fernández (1996) 3–4.

accidental omission of complete words, but neither Copy A nor Copy B is without error.[241]

No precise information is available about the provenance of Copies C–F, which are thought to have come from the province of Seville.[242] Metallurgical analysis of the composition of these fragments confirms that they all belong to different plaques.[243]

Copy C (MAS inv. CE1990/139) is a small fragment (maximum 3.2 cm high; maximum 3.5 cm wide; 4 mm thick), with remains of four lines of text (letter heights, 0.6–0.7 cm), which can be matched with parts of lines 78–82 of Copy A:[244]

[adfinitateve conti]**ng**[erent, si dedissent operam, si quis eius gentis aut quis eorum, qui cognatus adfinisve Calpurniae fa]**miliae f**[uisset, mortuos esset, lugendus esset, ne inter reliquas imagines, <quibus> exequias eorum funerum celebrare solent, imago C]**n. Pison**[is patris duceretur neve imaginibus familiae Calpurniae imago eius interponeretur; *vacat* utiq(ue) nomen Cn. Pi]**son**[is patris tolleretur]

This would result in lines of about 100 letters, which would result in one or two columns of text that would be rather wider than those on either Copy A or Copy B. Given that this part of the text is also preserved on both Copy A and B, this fragment must represent a third separate copy of the text.[245]

Copy D (MAS inv. CE1990/140) is a small fragment (maximum 3.1 cm high; maximum 3.3 cm wide; 4 mm thick), with remains of three lines of text (letter heights, 0.5–0.6 cm), which can be identified as parts of lines 81–84 of Copy A:[246]

[neve imaginibus familiae Ca]**lpurni**[ae imago eius interponeretur; *vacat* utiq(ue) nomen Cn. Pisonis patris tol]**leretur** [ex titulo statuae Germanicì Caesaris, quam ei sodales Augustales in campo ad a]**ram** [Providentiae posuissent]

This points to a line length of roughly seventy-two letters. This fragment also overlaps with text on Copy A and B, and does not appear to belong to Copy C, given differences in lettering and line length.[247] This therefore presents us with a fourth individual copy of the inscription, probably over four columns.

Copy E (MAS inv. CE1990/134) is an even smaller fragment (maximum 2.7 cm high; maximum 2.1 cm wide; 5 mm thick), with remains of

---

[241] On the physical characteristics of Copy B, see Caballos, Eck, Fernández (1996) 68–72; Eck, Caballos, Fernández (1996) 21–23.
[242] Caballos, Eck, Fernández (1996) 80–82; Eck, Caballos, Fernández (1996) 6.
[243] Caballos, Eck, Fernández (1996) 82, 83, 87–91.
[244] EDCS-46400002, with photograph – http://db.edcs.eu/epigr/bilder.php?bild=$SCPisoneC.jpg;pp (accessed 25/08/2019).
[245] Most likely Copy C contained two columns of text; Eck, Caballos, Fernández (1996) 30–31.
[246] EDCS-46400003, with photograph – http://db.edcs.eu/epigr/bilder.php?bild=$SCPisoneD.jpg;pp (accessed 25/08/2019).
[247] Caballos, Eck, Fernández (1996) 82–83; Eck, Caballos, Fernández (1996) 32.

4 The Inscriptions of the SCPP

three lines of text (letter heights, 0.5–0.6 cm), which can be matched with letters on Copy A, lines 39–42:[248]

[Vononem] **q**[u]**i su**[spectus regi Part(h)orum erat, longius removeri voluerit, ne profugere ex custodia pos]**set, id q**[uod fecit, et conloqui quosdam ex numero Armeniorum malos et audaces cum Vonone passus] **sit** [ut per eosdem]

It has been suggested that this belongs to a fifth, separate copy of the text, given that its text overlaps with Copies A and B, whilst the lettering is distinct from that in Copy C. Its lettering, however, is not dissimilar from that on Copy D in height and style, even though both fragments slightly differ from each other in projected line-lengths and in the thickness of the bronze tablet itself, with Copy E estimated at a line-length of seventy-four letters.[249] Metallurgical analysis supports a distinct origin for this fragment, and so Copy E appears to represent a fifth copy, albeit a very small fragment of it.

Copy F (MAS inv. CE1990/135) is likewise a very small fragment (maximum 2.7 cm high; 2.4 cm wide; 3 mm thick), with remains of three lines (letter heights, 0.4–0.5 cm), which match letters from towards the end of Copy A, lines 165–68:[250]

[et quo facilius totius actae r]**ei** [ordo posterorum memoriae tradi posset atque hi scire<nt>, quid et de singulari mod]**eratio**[ne Germ(anici) Caesa(ris) et de sceleribus Cn(aei) Pisonis patris senatus iudicasset, pl]**acere ut**[i oratio, quam]

Copy F has a line length of sixty-six to sixty-eight letters, which excludes it from belonging to Copy C, whilst the height and shape of its letters also exclude an identification of the fragment as belonging to the same copy of the text as either Copy D or E. Identification with Copy B is excluded by partial overlap of the two texts.[251]

Another bronze inscribed fragment, known as the fragment from Martos (*CIL* II² V 64) (ancient *Tucci Colonia Gemella* in the *Conventus Astiganus*), may represent another copy of the decree: its text could belong to the heading of the decree, as preserved on Copy A, but the letter heights (1.7 cm, compared with 4.7 cm for the heading in Copy A) make this unlikely, since they would be unusually small for a title on a bronze tablet.[252]

At the time of the first edition of the *SCPP*, therefore, the editors considered that they had evidence for six (or less likely seven) separate copies

---

[248] EDCS-46400004, with photograph – http://db.edcs.eu/epigr/bilder.php?bild=$SCPisoneE.jpg;pp (accessed 25/08/2019). Potter (1998) 438 is sceptical that fragments E–F and the Martos fragment should be regarded as copies of the *SCPP*.
[249] Caballos, Eck, Fernández (1996) 83–84; Eck, Caballos, Fernández (1996) 33–34.
[250] EDCS-46400005, with photograph – http://db.edcs.eu/epigr/bilder.php?bild=$SCPisoneF.jpg;pp (accessed 25/08/2019).
[251] Caballos, Eck, Fernández (1996) 84–85; Eck, Caballos, Fernández (1996) 34–35.
[252] Eck, Caballos, Fernández (1996) 35–37; Caballos, Eck, Fernández (1996) 105–06 [Stylow].

of the *SCPP* inscribed on bronze, all of which appeared to come from the region of Baetica.[253] Even on a pessimistic interpretation, there appeared to have been four copies of the inscribed decree found in Baetica alone.[254] As already outlined above, the decision by the Senate to issue instructions for the distribution and display of their decree was a reflection of the seriousness of the political crisis they faced. If their instructions for publication had been followed closely, we would have expected to find one copy of the decree displayed 'in the most frequented city of each province and in the most frequented place in that city' (*SCPP* lines 170–71). In the case of Baetica, the decree would have been displayed prominently in the city of Corduba. The suggestion therefore that Baetica alone may have had at least four copies of the inscribed decree on display in various places – among them comparatively unimportant settlements such as Irni and Ad Gemellas – invites consideration of why Baetica went well beyond the publication requirements imposed by the Senate, not least because the setting up of such weighty bronze tablets would have entailed considerable expense. One explanation for the clustering of copies in Baetica is a practical one, namely the fact that Baetica had an abundance of mineral resources suitable for creating the bronze tablets. Other explanations for the discovery of multiple copies there relate to modern conditions, such as the introduction of deep ploughing, the increasing popularity of metal detecting, and low population levels in the areas where bronzes have been found. These factors have led to the recovery of a strikingly large number of bronze inscriptions from Baetica in general – not just senatorial decrees, but also municipal laws, imperial letters, and municipal decrees.[255]

The initial editors argued that the over-representation of the *SCPP* in Baetica could be attributed directly to the over-enthusiastic intervention of the provincial governor of Baetica, Vibius Serenus, whose name appears prominently in the heading to Copy A (see note on Heading, **N(umerio) Vibio Sereno pro co(n)s(ule)**).[256] They suggested that the dissemination of the decree within Baetica reflected its governor's political ambitions.[257] In AD 16, Vibius Serenus had played a significant role in prosecuting Libo Drusus for *maiestas*, but had subsequently reproached Tiberius for not having rewarded his services adequately.[258] By AD 20 Vibius Serenus was

---

[253] On the dissemination of the *SCPP* in Baetica, see Caballos, Eck, Fernández (1996) 133–41; Eck, Caballos, Fernández (1996) 279–87.

[254] Potter (1998).

[255] Caballos Rufino, Eck, Fernández Gómez (1994b); Caballos Rufino, Fernández Gómez (1999); Caballos Rufino (2009) catalogues 128 public documents on bronze from Baetica, updated in Caballos Rufino (2018).

[256] Eck (1993b) 204–08; Caballos, Eck, Fernández (1996) 135–36, 139–41; Eck, Caballos, Fernández (1996) 284–87; Eck, Caballos, Fernández (1997) 221.

[257] Eck, Caballos, Fernández (1996) 287: 'der auf diese Weise möglicherweise seine Beziehungen zu Tiberius verbessern wollte'.

[258] Tac., *Ann.* 2.30, 4.29.2–3.

4 The Inscriptions of the SCPP

perhaps attempting to curry favour with Tiberius again by arranging for the Senate's decree to be distributed much more widely than instructed, in a desire to improve his relationship with the emperor. Nevertheless, we might question whether Vibius Serenus really believed that setting up multiple bronze copies of the *SCPP* in his province was likely to be helpful in bolstering his political position back at Rome. We might be sceptical whether Tiberius would have been able to appreciate Vibius Serenus' efforts to express his loyalty to the imperial family in this way in distant Baetica. The fact that Vibius Serenus was subsequently condemned *de vi publica* (the unjustified use of force against Roman citizens) certainly suggests that his efforts to appease Tiberius failed, if that is what his aim was in distributing the *SCPP* around Baetica.[259]

In the years since 1996, two new fragments of the text have been found. Copy G, consisting of a small fragment (2.6 cm high, 3 cm wide, 0.5 cm thick) sold on the Spanish antiquities market, was published in 1999.[260] It preserves traces of two lines of letters (0.6–0.7 cm high), which can be mapped onto Copy A, lines 30–34: [transma]**rina**[rum … aut ipsius Ti Ca]**esaris** A[ug]. The only information about its provenance is that it originates from the province of Jaén in southern Spain. Its text overlaps with Copies A and B, whilst its line length differs from Copies C, D, and F. Although it could potentially belong to Copy E in terms of line length and letter heights, its different lettering style excludes this possibility, pointing towards this being a seventh copy of the inscription from Baetica. Nevertheless, the very small dimensions of the fragment urge caution before assuming that this must be the case. Finally, Copy H was published in 2009, having been found during excavations in the cathedral of St Peter in Geneva on 13 March 1992, in a fill layer of fourth-century date.[261] This makes it the only fragment of the *SCPP* to have come from a properly excavated context. It consists of a small fragment (7 cm high, 8 cm wide, 0.3 cm thick), with letters 0.9 cm in height, preserving traces of four lines of text, which correspond to lines 78–80 of Copy A: [cont]**ingerent si de**[dissent operam, si quis eius gentis aut quis eorum] **qui cognatus** [adfinisve Calpurniae familiae fuis]**set** <mortuos esset, lugendus esset> **ne inter rel**[iquas imagines, <quibus> exequias eorum funerum cel]**ebrar<e> solent**. It is, however, unlikely that the *SCPP* was originally displayed in Geneva, since the town was merely a *vicus* of the *Colonia Iulia Augusta Florentia Viennensium* during the first century AD. It is therefore more likely that the inscribed fragment was originally displayed in Nyon (*Colonia Iulia Equestris*), located roughly 20 km to the north-west of the *vicus*,

---

[259] Tac., *Ann.* 4.13.2.
[260] Stylow and Corzo Pérez (1999); EDCS-14700038 (accessed 25/08/2019).
[261] Bartels (2009) = *ILN-Vienne* 869. EDCS-08600752, image: http://db.edcs.eu/epigr/bilder.php?bild=$ILN-05-03_00869.jpg (accessed 25/08/2019).

and that it was among spoliated material removed from Nyon to Geneva during late antiquity.[262]

Although we cannot exclude a role for Vibius Serenus in the enthusiastic display of the decree in Baetica (and certainly the Senate took the unusual move of requiring him, along with all other provincial governors, to set up the *SCPP* on bronze in the most important town in his province), the discovery of a copy of the inscription from a completely different geographical area invites us to reconsider other possibilities. In general, the findspot of Copy H, which points to its display in a comparatively unimportant *colonia* in Gallia Narbonensis supports the idea that people around the empire may have felt motivated to mourn Germanicus and to condemn Piso beyond what they were instructed to do by the Senate. The erasure of Piso's name from a dedication which he had set up in AD 9/10 at Campa Torres (Gijón, Asturias) in Hispania Tarraconensis similarly points to the desire of communities beyond Rome to exceed the instructions from the Senate, which had desired statues of Piso to be removed but had mandated the erasure of his name from just one specific monument in Rome (lines 75–76, 82–84) (see §7).[263] Piso's name had been a prominent feature of the regional landscape, since the substantial inscription (80 cm in height, 162 cm in width) had perhaps originally been part of a lighthouse.[264] The erasure itself, extending over almost two lines, would consequently also have been clearly visible. The monument's prominence, together with the fact that Piso had earlier been governor of Tarraconensis, perhaps explains why this inscription was modified after Piso's condemnation. At any rate, it suggests that someone in Tarraconensis was aware of the penalties imposed upon Piso by the Senate and chose to extend those penalties to the coast of northern Hispania, even though no copy of the *SCPP* has yet been uncovered in the province.[265]

Publication of Roman public documents in permanent epigraphic form in provincial cities could be the result of a number of interconnecting factors, reflecting the desire of the Senate, of provincial governors, and of local elites and their communities to monumentalise events and decisions which they deemed to be important to them.[266] Even in the case of the *Res Gestae*, whose dissemination is often cited as a straightforward example of publication arising from the initiative of the governor of the province of Galatia,[267] the interests of the local elite of Ancyra, Apollonia, and Pisidian Antioch may well have been equally important in explaining the decision to set up the text in distinctive monumental formats in each town.[268] It is worthwhile, therefore, exploring in more detail whether the exceptional

---

[262] Bartels (2009) 5–6.   [263] *CIL* II 2703, with Kajava (1995) 205.
[264] Fernández Ochoa, Morillo Cerdán, Villa Valdés (2005).
[265] Eck, Caballos, Fernández (1996) 280.   [266] Cooley (2012).
[267] For example, by Eck, Caballos, Fernández (1996) 285–86.
[268] Cooley (2009) 18–22; Cooley (2012) 171–79.

4 The Inscriptions of the SCPP

distribution of the *SCPP* in Baetica may reflect the interests of the local elite rather than – or alongside – those of their governor.[269] Despite the insistence in the heading of Copy A upon Piso being the protagonist of the *SCPP*, the display of the *SCPP* was as much concerned with reflecting enthusiasm for and loyalty towards Germanicus and the imperial family as with condemning Piso himself.

The cluster of bronzes in Baetica goes far beyond what the Senate envisaged and could have a number of different explanations: it could reflect local inclination to publish documents on bronze; it could be the result of a popular impulse or of a proconsul's instructions; or it could reflect the desire of local elites to align their interests with those of Rome. If we suppose that the initiative for wider publication came from the towns themselves rather than from their governor, the inclusion of Vibius Serenus' name in the heading to Copy A becomes a dating formula rather than a statement that he was the agent of distribution (see notes on the Heading). This interpretation is reflected in the translation into English of the phrase *s(enatus) c(onsultum) de Cn(aeo) Pisone patre propositum N(umerio) Vibio Sereno pro co(n)s(ule)* as 'Decree of the Senate concerning Gnaeus Piso senior, published in the proconsulship of Numerius Vibius Serenus',[270] whilst the translations into both German and Spanish equating to 'published under' in English leave the question more open.[271] The original editors elaborate upon their interpretation of the heading to make clear that they regard this as equivalent to an indication of agency on the governor's part,[272] arguing that he would in addition have issued an edict explaining the significance of the *SCPP*.[273] At the same time, they propose that the heading must have been added to the decree by authorities at Irni, whilst drawing upon the wording used by Vibius Serenus in his edict.

In looking for alternatives to the hypothesis that the display of the *SCPP* in Baetica can simply be explained by instructions issued by Vibius Serenus, Baetican promotion of the cult of *Providentia Augusti* offers an interesting perspective, which benefits from recent numismatic research.[274] Designs on coinage produced at local mints in the provinces of the Roman empire often reflected local enthusiasms, especially for cults.[275] It is a striking feature of coins minted in all three Hispanic provinces – Baetica,

---

[269] Caballos Rufino, Eck, Fernandez Gómez (1994b) 328–30 track evidence for local Baetican loyalties towards Tiberius and his family.
[270] Potter and Damon (1999) 15; cf. Griffin (1997) 250.
[271] 'Senatsbeschluß über Cn. Piso pater, öffentlich angeschlagen unter dem Prokonsul Numerius Vibius Serenus': Eck, Caballos, Fernández (1996) 39; 'Senadoconsulto de Gneo Pisón padre, expuesto publicamente bajo el proconsul N. Vibio Sereno': Caballos, Eck, Fernández (1996) 128.
[272] Eck, Caballos, Fernández (1996) 126: 'zumindest *propositum N. Vibio Sereno procos.* ist ein Zusatz, der erst die Folge der Publikation durch den Statthalter war'.
[273] Eck, Caballos, Fernández (1996) 126–30.
[274] I am grateful to Suzanne Frey-Kupper for her guidance on this numismatic evidence.
[275] Burnett, Amandry, Ripollès (1992) 43.

Tarraconensis, and Lusitania – that several designs imply enthusiasm for emperor-worship and the imperial family in the age of Tiberius.[276] For example, Germanicus and Drusus are commemorated as honorary magistrates at Carteia.[277] Furthermore, images on coins minted at Italica and Hispalis (Baetica), Tarraco and Turiaso (Tarraconensis), and Emerita (Lusitania) include divus Augustus, Drusus, and Germanicus with military standards, and an altar of *Providentia*.[278]

This last design – an altar of *Providentia Augusti* – offers a clue to understanding what seems to be Baetican obsession with Germanicus (Fig. 2). Bronzes minted at Italica carry on the obverse a bare-headed Tiberius, with the legend IMP TI CAESAR AVGVSTVS PON MAX ('Imperator Tiberius Caesar Augustus, pontifex maximus'), and on the reverse the legend [M]VNIC ITALIC PER DI[VI] AVG ('Municipium of Italica by permission of deified Augustus') together with an image of an altar, inscribed PROVIDENTIAE AVGVSTI ('to the Foresight of Augustus').[279] Similar images of the altar are found on coins of Rome, paired with an image of a radiate divus Augustus.[280] Until recently, the coins minted at Rome were believed to be produced in around AD 22/23 and perhaps later,[281] but

Fig. 2. Bronze coin minted at Italica. Obverse (A): a bare-headed Tiberius, with the legend IMP TI CAESAR AVGVSTVS PON MAX ('Imperator Tiberius Caesar Augustus, pontifex maximus'). Reverse (B): an image of an altar, inscribed PROVIDENTIAE AVGVSTI ('To the Foresight of Augustus') and the legend [M]VNIC ITALIC PER DI[VI] AVG ('Municipium of Italica by permission of deified Augustus'). *RPC* I 64; source: gallica.bnf.fr / Bibliothèque nationale de France).

---

[276] Compare also the recent publication of a statue of divus Augustus, possibly a cult statue, from the forum of Torreparedones (Baena) in Baetica: Márquez (2019).
[277] *RPC* I 123.
[278] Italica *RPC* I 64–65, 70–71; Hispalis *RPC* I 73–75; Tarraco *RPC* I 218–20, 228–30; Turiaso *RPC* I 422–24; Emerita: *RPC* I 20–37.
[279] *RPC* I 64.   [280] *RIC* I² 99, no. 81.
[281] Klein and von Kaenel (2000) 71–77, with review of earlier scholarship.

new metallurgical analysis of the coins has now redated them as minted in three stages, in AD 15–16, 22–23, and 34–37.[282] The earliest date makes sense if the coins are seen as a celebration of Augustus' *consecratio*. The editors of *RPC* I commented on the *Providentia* issues from Italica that they were reluctant to date them to before AD *c.*22/23, when the altar appears on imperial issues (*RIC* I[2] Tiberius 80–81) since it was unlikely that Italica would have anticipated the imperial message, but in the light of the redating of the coins, the way is now clear to date Italica's issues also to the early years of Tiberius. This early date is consistent with the use of the formula 'by permission of deified Augustus', which is later altered to 'by permission of Augustus [i.e., Tiberius]'.[283] The coins demonstrate how during the years from around AD 15/16 the local elite of Baetica were consciously trying to align their communities with the political interests of Rome.[284] Consequently, this numismatic evidence now points towards a celebration of the *ara Providentiae* in Baetica in the years before Piso's trial and conviction.[285] This is important since the *ara Providentiae* was closely linked to the place of Germanicus within the imperial family as likely successor to Tiberius.

The date at which the altar was built in Rome is still disputed (indeed, before the discovery of the Piso inscription mentioning it, it had been argued at some length that it should be associated with the suppression of the conspiracy of Sejanus).[286] It was located on the part of the Campus Martius bequeathed to the Roman people by Agrippa, sited to the east of the via Lata, opposite the Altar of Augustan Peace (see 83–84n, *in campo ad aram Providentiae*). By AD 38, the altar of *Providentia* is attested as being associated with imperial succession, given that the *fasti Arvales* of that year allude to the *ara Providentiae Augustae in campo Agrippae*, with a sacrifice at the altar on 26 June, a significant date, since it recalls the day of Tiberius' adoption by Augustus in AD 4. This date was also that on which Germanicus was adopted by Tiberius. Consequently, the cult of *Providentia* may have been introduced as early as AD 4, but most likely in AD 15, to celebrate Augustus' planning for his successors in the form of Tiberius and Germanicus.[287] The *SCPP* now confirms the close association of Germanicus with the *ara Providentiae*, since one of the penalties imposed upon Piso was for his name to be erased from the base of a statue set up to honour Germanicus by the *sodales Augustales* at the *ara Providentiae*.

---

[282] Barrandon, Suspène, Gaffiero (2010) 161–64, with further discussion of *Providentia Augusta* at 164–67.
[283] Barrandon, Suspène, Gaffiero (2010) 163.   [284] Calomino (2015) 68–69.
[285] Continued enthusiasm for the cult of *Providentia* in Baetica is further suggested by the possible existence of an *ara Providentiae* in the forum at Emerita under Claudius, which featured Agrippa: Nogales Basarrate (2000).
[286] Martin (1982) 110–20.
[287] Barrandon, Suspène, Gaffiero (2010) 166 plausibly suggest that the altar was dedicated on 26 June AD 15; compare Cox (2005) 254–57.

The minting of local coins at Italica imitating imperial issues depicting the *ara Providentiae* at Rome, therefore, suggests that the theme of imperial succession and Germanicus' place within it was close to the hearts of the local elite of the town, and offers a plausible context within which to place the widespread publication of the *SCPP*. Overall, then, although the Senate may have had clear views as to the extent to which they wished to see their decree illustrating the nobility of Germanicus and villainy of Piso disseminated, in the end it was not necessarily the intervention of the Roman governor, Vibius Serenus, that resulted in the over-enthusiastic setting up of the decree on bronze in insignificant towns in southern Spain. Instead, it may be the case that the local elite of those towns had signed up to imperial ideology and emperor-worship, and they associated the cult of *Providentia Augusti* with the succession plans put in place by Augustus, fruitlessly, of course, as it turned out. The towns of southern Hispania – and not in Baetica alone – are notable for the number of coins minted in imitation of Roman imperial issues.[288] The widespread publication of the *SCPP* perhaps makes most sense when viewed against this background of a strong sense of political integration expressed via the coins minted in the region. The local elite of these towns may have perceived that the death of Germanicus had dealt a serious blow to Augustus' plans for dynastic succession. Their response was to set up multiple bronze inscriptions justifying in effect why members of the *domus Augusta* should maintain rule at Rome, having already embraced the idea of *providentia Augusti* on their locally minted coins. Likewise, the *Tabula Siarensis* illustrates a willingness to go beyond what the Senate required, with the decrees being published on bronze rather than on whiteboards, and in Siarum rather than (or presumably in addition to) in the provincial capital at Cordoba. The key to understanding the multiple copies of the *SCPP* is, then, to set them in the wider context of evidence for a regional pattern of reflection upon and support for the idea of the imperial family's political dominance at Rome extending over different generations.

5 THE SENATE AND ITS RELATIONSHIP WITH THE IMPERIAL FAMILY

As is the case with the senatorial decree concerning the honours for Germanicus of the previous year (see §2),[289] the *SCPP* gives a detailed picture of how the Senate sought to forge a role for itself in the evolving political context under Tiberius. The *SCPP* illustrates the challenges which the Senate met in dealing with Tiberius and in justifying its actions relating to the imperial family. The *maiestas* trial of Piso posed particular problems, not

---

[288] Calomino (2015) 69; Ripollès (2005) 90–91.
[289] On the political and ideological significance of this decree, see González and Arce (1988); Corbier (1994), (2001a), (2006) chapter 7; González (1999), (2002); Severy (2000).

least since his case concerned offences towards members of the imperial family – notably divus Augustus, Tiberius, and Germanicus – alongside more traditional charges of sedition and abuse of power.[290] The language used by the Senate and the ways in which its decree was framed, together with its instructions about publishing the decree throughout the empire, reveal the Senate's desire to assert its own authority, as well as its awareness that it was obliged to act as it believed Tiberius wanted. Overall, the Senate made a distinctive contribution to a more general debate about the place of the imperial family in Roman society, which can be seen in other contemporary texts too.

The Senate's role as a court for hearing *maiestas* trials involving members of its own order was a relatively new innovation.[291] Previously, cases had been heard in the *quaestiones* presided over by a praetor: the Senate's involvement now boosted its own status but created challenges for its members to negotiate. In Piso's case, Tiberius himself acted as convenor (*relator*), bringing the case before the senatorial court.[292] He did so by virtue of his tribunician power, which gave him the right to summon the Senate, to bring matters for discussion before it, and to interpose his veto.[293] In this way, Tiberius directed the proceedings and was present as all the evidence from witnesses was heard. The Senate found itself in the position of trying to anticipate what Tiberius wished in dealing with the case: it was not expected to exercise its own independent judgement.[294] It is important to recognise that the *SCPP* does not give us details of how the original case was brought before the Senate, but only of how Tiberius instructed the Senate to proceed in the aftermath of Piso's suicide.[295] We do not have, therefore, the Senate's original decree of judgement against Piso, but only a version edited especially for audiences in provincial capitals and in legionary winter quarters.[296] Although it would have been entirely possible for the trial to have come to an end when the accused committed suicide,[297] Tiberius wanted to give Piso's sons the chance to speak before the Senate.[298] This illustrates neatly the Senate's difficulties in handling the situation: on the one hand, the Senate allows no room for doubt that Piso had been guilty as charged – *cum manufestissuma sint Cn(aei) Pisonis patris scelera* ('although the crimes of Gnaeus Piso Senior are most flagrant', *SCPP* line 18) – and yet it states that Piso's sons were being encouraged to speak in defence of their father, mother, and the younger son Marcus. The elder son Gnaeus had not been involved in Piso's crimes at all, but the younger

---

[290] Charges against Piso reviewed by Castro-Camero (2000) 44–50.
[291] Talbert (1984) 461; Rowe (2002) 42–43.   [292] *SCPP* lines 4–11; Tac., *Ann.* 3.12.
[293] *SCPP* lines 5, 174; Rowe (2002) 43, 46–59.
[294] Talbert (1984) 479.   [295] Ermann (2002).
[296] Severy (2000) 327: 'the aim of the decree is to communicate to provincial governors and their soldiers what has happened to a governor who has rebelled'.
[297] Compare the case of C. Licinius Macer in Val. Max. 9.12.7; Chilton (1955) 79.
[298] *SCPP* lines 20–22.

son Marcus had been accompanying his father in the East at the time. The line of defence developed for Marcus, excusing his actions on the grounds that he had only been obeying his father, appears to have given Tiberius (and ostensibly the Senate) the opportunity to display clemency, in returning virtually all of Piso's confiscated property to his heirs.[299] This was a striking contrast to normal procedure, whereby a quarter of the accused's property would have been given to his prosecutors,[300] and was all the more unpredictable because Roman law (albeit preserved in the words of the third-century jurist Marcianus) laid down that such an action would only occur if the heirs had proven the innocence of the deceased during the continuation of the trial after his death.[301] Indeed, only four years later, Tiberius vetoed a proposal to abolish the rewards for prosecutors in cases of *maiestas* where the defendant committed suicide.[302]

One of the challenges faced by the Senate, then, was the unpredictability of the application of the *lex maiestatis* in general, and Tiberius' unpredictability in particular.[303] Whereas one type of charge might be thrown out of court in one case, the Senate could not be confident that this would create a firm precedent for how to act in later cases. For example, whereas Tiberius began by rejecting cases involving alleged offences against divus Augustus, such cases were later admitted.[304] Tacitus' representation of a Senate anxious about its ability to anticipate Tiberius' wishes in its decisions and which fundamentally deferred to Tiberius rings true in the light of the language of the *SCPP* and *Tabula Siarensis*, as discussed below within the present section.[305] Whereas it was usual practice for the convenor (*relator*) of the original meeting to chair the meeting of the drafting committee drawing up the official version of the decree after it had been agreed upon in the Senate, this task was not undertaken by Tiberius in the case of the *SCPP*.[306] The committee of senators needed to choose the right words in describing the Senate's response to the behaviour of Piso, and given that this closely concerned members of the imperial family, this was a matter of some delicacy. The Senate's solution in AD 19 had been to consult an advisory board made up of members of the imperial family in order to decide upon the honours deemed appropriate for the dead Germanicus. This advisory board included imperial women – Iulia Augusta, Antonia, and Agrippina (if she were to have returned to Rome in time) – in what appears to be unprece-

---

[299] *SCPP* lines 90–105; Tac., *Ann.* 3.16.3; Dowling (2006) 170–77.
[300] In the case of Libo Drusus, however, it seems that all of his property was handed over to his prosecutors: *bona inter accusatores diuiduntur*, Tac., *Ann.* 2.32, with Goodyear (1981) 280, ad loc.
[301] *Dig.* 48.21.3.8 [Marcianus].
[302] Tac., *Ann.* 4.30.2–3. By AD 34, however, it seems that suicide did protect an estate: Woodman (2018) 167, ad loc.
[303] On the inherent danger of the *maiestas* law being used for political purposes, see Levick (1999) 183–94; Castro-Camero (2000) 33–38.
[304] Contrast Tac., *Ann.* 1.73 and *SCPP* lines 68–70 for offences against the *numen* of Augustus.
[305] On Tacitus' representation of this relationship, see O'Gorman (2000) 82–83.
[306] Mommsen (1891) 199; Coudry (1994) 71–72.

5 The Senate and its Relationship with the Imperial Family 47

dented dependence of the Senate upon non-senators for advice.[307] Even so, the Senate still appears hesitant about determining some details, leaving the decision about the location of the arch in Syria open to change.[308] It also defers to Tiberius about the location of the inscription recording his speech on the death of Germanicus delivered before the Senate.[309] Similarly, in the *SCPP* (lines 168–70), the Senate leaves it to Tiberius to decide upon the location in Rome where the bronze inscriptions containing Tiberius' speech in the Senate and its own decree should be put on display. Above all, the Senate could not rely on precedent in order to decide on the penalties to be imposed. The lack of consistency in penalties applied for *maiestas* under Tiberius has inspired much discussion about what the penalties actually were, but such discussion risks missing the point that the penalties were flexible, and that one of the Senate's key tasks was precisely to determine what the penalties should be in Piso's case.[310]

A consideration of the *SCPP* from a paratextual perspective illustrates further the problems faced by the Senate in navigating its relationship with Tiberius and the rest of the imperial family.[311] This approach is inspired by the work of Gérard Genette, who in 1987 published *Seuils*, which was translated into English in 1997 with the title *Paratexts: Thresholds of Interpretation*. In this study, Genette developed a paradigm for the paratextual reading of texts which was focused upon literary texts (and specifically, modern novels) published in book form.[312] Genette explored two paratextual dimensions. Firstly, he defined peritext as material conventionally included within a book, framing the text itself in the form of what he termed 'liminal devices' on its thresholds both front and back. These include features such as titles, signs of authorship, dedications, prefaces, notes, and epilogues. Secondly, he studied public and private epitext, in the form of additional elements that exist separately from a book itself, such as interviews, reviews, correspondence, and diaries. The idea of peritext is particularly useful as an analytical tool for understanding Latin epigraphy.[313] Arguably, inscriptions are an excellent example of paratexts since they bear meaning through their physical appearance and context as well as through their actual words. They are therefore suitable for analysis of the ways in which the meaning of texts may be influenced by how they are physically presented. The *SCPP* displays a rich paratextual space: features include its physical appearance, prominent title, prescript, concluding statement of senatorial procedure, and striking first-person intervention

---

[307] *Tabula Siarensis* = Crawford (1996) no.37, frag. a, lines 6–8 = LACTOR 19, J8a; Severy (2000) 321.
[308] *Tabula Siarensis* = Crawford (1996) no.37, frag. a, lines 22–24 = LACTOR 19, J8c; Potter (1987).
[309] *Tabula Siarensis* = Crawford (1996) no.37, frag. b, col. II, lines 11–13 = LACTOR 19, J8g.
[310] Chilton (1955); Allison and Cloud (1962); Levick (1979); Castro-Camero (2000) 53–139. On Piso's punishments, see §7.
[311] For a detailed analysis see Cooley (2014).
[312] Genette ([1987] 1997); on an overview of paratexts in Roman contexts, see Jansen (2014).
[313] See also Cooley (2015) on paratextual aspects of the *Res Gestae*.

of Tiberius himself at the very end. These peritextual features cluster at the start and end of the inscription, fulfilling the possibility that liminal features – *seuils* ('thresholds') in Genette's original French – can contribute to the ways in which meaning is generated by the text. Paragraphing by extending text into the left margin (see Fig. 5), leaving lines partially blank, and differentiation in lettering size and spacing (see Figs 3–4) also guide readers towards being able to distinguish between different parts of the text. All of these features represent modes of structuring meaning for readers of the inscription, but not all of them resulted in increasing clarity of interpretation for readers. Indeed, the committee of senators who drafted it is not entirely successful in maintaining control over its decree: paratextual elements inadvertently throw doubt upon the integrity of the Senate's central message of support for Tiberius and his family. As Genette commented, 'it does not necessarily follow that the paratext always fulfils its function well'.[314]

The decision to inscribe the decree upon bronze (*SCPP* lines 170–72) was itself a paratextual statement of the perceived status of the text. There was no requirement for senatorial decrees to be published in this way.[315] By mandating the decree of 10 December to be displayed as a monumental inscription in provincial capitals and in legionary winter quarters,

Fig. 3. Heading of *SCPP* on Copy A (photograph: A.E. Cooley) (by kind permission of the Museo Arqueológico de Sevilla, Colección Museística de Andalucía, Junta de Andalucía: MAS inv. D09579).

[314] Genette ([1987] 1997) 409. [315] Coudry (1994).

Fig. 4. Prescript of Copy B (photograph: A.E. Cooley) (by kind permission of the Museo Arqueológico de Sevilla, Colección Museística de Andalucía, Junta de Andalucía: MAS inv. D09479).

Fig. 5. Paragraphing on Copy B at line 84 (photograph: A.E. Cooley) (by kind permission of the Museo Arqueológico de Sevilla, Colección Museística de Andalucía, Junta de Andalucía: MAS inv. D09479).

the Senate was declaring that this decree was of exceptional importance. Another option would have been to require the decree to be disseminated to the provinces and displayed in public on whiteboards (as seems to have been the case with the decree concerning honours for Germanicus), but the Senate specified that it required the *SCPP* to be published on bronze tablets. By doing so, the Senate implicitly imbued its decree with an air of sanctity and inviolability,[316] and endeavoured to lend weight to its decree by non-textual means, enhancing the status and meaning of its text.

The first paratextual element in the inscribed text appears only in Copy A: a prominent title that summarises the content of the inscription: *s(enatus) c(onsultum) de Cn(aeo) Pisone patre propositum N(umerio) Vibio Sereno pro co(n)s(ule)* ('Decree of the Senate concerning Gnaeus Piso senior, published in the proconsulship of Numerius Vibius Serenus') (Fig. 3). Including a heading of this sort above the text of a senatorial decree was far from customary, although there are a few parallels.[317] The title runs across virtually the whole width of the tablet, in letters 4–4.5 cm high, whereas the rest of the text is inscribed in letters only 0.5–0.6 cm high. In this way, Piso's name becomes a prominent element in the title. This is perhaps surprising, given that the Senate had taken considerable pains to suppress his memory at Rome (see §7). This reflects the Senate's self-contradiction in desiring both to abolish the memory of Piso at Rome, and yet to transmit a report of the affair *posterorum memoriae* ('to the memory of future generations') (*SCPP* lines 165–66). Piso's prominence potentially even undercuts the main message of the decree, which was not concerned simply with listing the penalties imposed upon Piso himself but with justifying the fundamental role played by Tiberius and his family in maintaining Rome's welfare.

By contrast, the inclusion of a prescript before the start of the decree itself (*SCPP* lines 1–4) is a standard feature. In Copy B, which lacks a separate heading, these lines appear in larger letters than the rest of the text (see §4) (Fig. 4). The prescript's commonplace appearance does not diminish its potential significance, however. It contains the usual information about which senators were present at the drafting of the decree, where they met, and when. The standard practice was for the committee to convene in the same venue straight after the plenary senatorial meeting on which they were reporting.[318] The meeting-place used by the senatorial committee on this occasion – the library in the Temple of Palatine Apollo – provides an early clue as to the likely contents of this decree (see 1n: *in Palatio in porticu, quae est ad Apollinis*). This meeting-place was part of the complex on the Palatine recently constructed by Augustus, and it was also the location where the Senate had met a few months earlier to discuss the honours to be granted to Germanicus after his death towards the end of AD 19. These earlier decrees of the Senate were then inscribed on bronze tablets and displayed there as well.[319] By re-assembling in the very location where they had previously praised Germanicus, and where their decrees honouring him were now on display, the senators would have been sensitive to the accusations against Piso of having been insubordinate towards

---

[316] Williamson (1987).   [317] Eck, Caballos, Fernández (1996) 127–28.
[318] Mommsen (1891) 199–200.
[319] *Tabula Siarensis* = Crawford (1996) no.37, frag. b, col. II, lines 20–21 = LACTOR 19, J8h.

5 The Senate and its Relationship with the Imperial Family

Germanicus. Even if the accusation that Piso had murdered Germanicus had been officially dropped, there is no doubt that it would still have lingered in the minds of the senators meeting in this particular location. The Senate's aim of praising Germanicus and vilifying Piso would have been reinforced by their choice, or – perhaps better – Tiberius' choice, of meeting-place. The prescript could have reminded some readers that they were not about to read a word-for-word account of a debate held in the Senate, but an approved version of the discussion written by committee. Ostensibly, the committee of senators was in charge of approving the text, but, as we shall see, final words from Tiberius give the lie to this impression, revealing who was really in charge of approving the wording of the decree.

The Senate's central message conveyed in its decree is clear (*SCPP* lines 12–15):

senatum populumq(ue) Romanum ante omnia dis immortalibus gratias agere, / quod nefaris consilis Cn(aei) Pisonis patris tranquillitatem praesentis status / r(ei) p(ublicae), quo melior optari non pote\<st\> ⌐e⌐t quo beneficio principis nostri frui contigit, / turbar⌐i⌐ passi non sunt

that the Senate and people of Rome give thanks above all to the immortal gods because they did not allow the tranquillity of the current state of affairs in the republic – something better than which it is not possible to desire and which it has fallen to our lot to enjoy, thanks to the beneficence of our Princeps – to be disturbed by the wicked plans of Gnaeus Piso Senior.

This statement is given syntactical prominence in the text, as the first element following on from *censuerunt* ('they decreed'), which governs the listing of the Senate's resolutions made in response to Tiberius' *relatio*. This verb then controls the majority of the text, from line 12 down to line 172.[320] Visually, too, the phrase stands out: in Copy A, there is a substantial blank space occupying about half a line after the abbreviated formula introducing the Senate's decision *d(e) i(is) r(ebus) i(ta) c(ensuerunt)*, whilst the initial S in *senatum* is twice the size of the other letters and encroaches upon the left margin. In Copy B, there is only a short blank space before the phrase, but this still serves to bring the start of the judgement into focus (Fig. 4). In the version edited for the benefit of the provinces and army, the Senate takes pains to frame the formal content of its decree, which contained a report of its judgements upon Piso, his son Marcus, Plancina, and two equestrian members of his staff, with effusive statements of loyalty towards the emperor and his family, delivering an unequivocal message that the safety of the Roman state depended upon Tiberius and his family (*SCPP* lines 159–63). In this way the final decree was not simply a report on judicial proceedings at the trial of Piso held in the Senate, but was transformed into an opportunity to rally the whole of Roman society

---

[320] See structural analysis by Damon and Takács (1999) 5.

behind the current regime. If readers were led to expect from the title that the decree solely concerned Piso *pater*, then they were in for a surprise.

Following the main body of the decree, the Senate's shift towards end-material is marked clearly by a sudden surge in the use of main verbs. Having had well over 150 lines of text in Copy A dependent upon the single verb *censuerunt* in line 11, we suddenly find four main verbs in quick succession: 172–73 *censuerunt*, 173 *fuerunt*, 173 *factum est*, 174 *scripsi*.[321] This rapid sequence of verbs effectively reframes the centre text paratextually and then adds new paratextual elements upon the final threshold of the Senate's text. After the end of the decree itself, we first of all find a statement about voting procedure in the Senate (*SCPP* lines 172–73). This is followed by one of the most surprising features of the *SCPP*, a *subscriptio* of Tiberius himself appended after the end of the actual decree (*SCPP* lines 174–76). This is so unexpected that it has been suggested that the *subscriptio* was included in error.[322] The *subscriptio* is clearly separated from the main body of the Senate's text by the standard form of paragraphing in inscriptions, with the opening letters being inscribed further to the left of the rest of the text. Furthermore, in Copy A, the lines containing the *subscriptio* include only 54 letters, fewer than the rest of the text, visually drawing attention to the final section on the inscription.[323] Not only is the format of the *subscriptio* noteworthy, but also its content. First of all, it offers a rare glimpse of Tiberius' own voice, and confirms that he represented his tribunician power as being the key to his dealings with the Senate: it was by virtue of this power that he was permitted to summon the Senate and put a motion before it. Furthermore, Tiberius here instructs one of the two quaestors in post during December AD 20 to see to the archiving of the decree, referring to him simply as 'Aulus' (see 175–76n, *scriptum manu Auli q(uaestoris) mei in tabellis XIIII*). This informal form of address seems at odds with its context at the end of an official document. For the original editors, Tiberius' use of the *praenomen* on its own was a reflection of the high level of trust between emperor and *quaestor*, but it might also be suggestive of the way in which the emperor took for granted this senator's services.[324] Arguably, therefore, Tiberius' real relationship with the Senate is revealed and to some extent the lengthy professions of loyalty and thanks delivered by the Senate in the decree itself become even more hollow-sounding.

Returning to Genette's insistence upon the functionality of paratext, we may ask what readings of its decree the Senate was seeking to promote through its paratextual properties: what 'destiny' did the Senate desire for its text?[325] It is clear that the text's intended readership was twofold, both civil and military, and that it was based in the provinces. The overall

---

[321] Damon and Takács (1999) 5. [322] Eck, Caballos, Fernández (1996) 272.
[323] Eck, Caballos, Fernández (1996) 8. [324] Eck, Caballos, Fernández (1996) 103.
[325] Genette ([1987] 1997) 407.

5 The Senate and its Relationship with the Imperial Family

paratextual structure of the *SCPP* served as a socio-political form of communication between the Senate at Rome and its provincial subjects. The unusual instruction that the decree was to be engraved upon bronze was intended to imbue the decree with particular solemnity, giving it status akin to laws passed by the Roman people. Together with the senatorial decree of honours for Germanicus, the publication of the *SCPP* reflects the virtual usurpation of legislative power by the Tiberian Senate. Although its decrees had no actual legal force, the Senate was strongly suggesting that its decrees were in fact equally important as laws and statutes formally passed by the assembly at Rome.[326] The paratextual elements added by the Senate, which frame the text, namely the prescript to the decree and the final record of voting procedure at the Senate's meeting, were intended to emphasise the official nature of the decree as well as to create the impression of a Senate unified in its praise of Tiberius and his family. The Senate did its best to create an impression of unanimity amongst its members.

Nevertheless, the *SCPP* presents us with a struggle between paratext and text, something akin to Genette's formulation of dysfunctional paratext: 'the paratext sometimes tends to go beyond its function and to turn itself into an impediment'.[327] Paratextual elements, especially the way in which Tiberius frames the text, and particularly his first-person utterance recorded in the subscript, suggest that the Senate is not the ultimate authority. It is unclear whether or not this is an intentional effect, but the impression emerges that the Senate is acting under imperial instructions and that its words have been vetted by the *princeps*. All this means that the Senate's eagerness to praise the *princeps* and his family and to thank Tiberius for intervening in this affair starts to sound rather artificial. Tiberius' subscript in effect invites the reader to reconsider possible reasons for the Senate's obsequious language towards the imperial household in the central text of the decree. The game is given away, perhaps, unintentionally by one small detail: 'There were 301 present in the senate' (see 172–73n., *censuerunt. in senatu fuerunt CCCI*).[328] The fact that the concluding statement of the senatorial decree reveals that only roughly half of the total possible number of senators (or around sixty per cent of senators not abroad on official business) were actually present at the discussion might appear to undermine the claims to universal consensus so emphatically claimed earlier on in the text. This is not very convincing as a testimony to the universal consensus of support for the *princeps* which the Senate is so keen to proclaim in the decree. Paratextual elements framing the decree work to the detriment of the central text itself, supporting the notion that the senators did not keep control over their words, and perhaps reflecting a mounting sense of crisis at Rome. Even though not all of the paratextual phenomena were created

---

[326] Rowe (2002) 43, 64–66.   [327] Genette ([1987] 1997) 409–10, quotation from 410.
[328] On a total membership of *c.*600 in this period, see Talbert (1984) 131–34.

intentionally by the text's authors with a view to plotting meaning, they jointly add considerably to our appreciation of the creation of a text whose contradictory messages may well reflect the turbulent political realities of Tiberian Rome.

Two features of the language adopted by the Senate in its decree appear to reveal anxiety in its dealings with the imperial family. Firstly, the Senate makes use of hyperbolic language, both positively and negatively, revealing how the Senate felt the need to respond emotionally to this case.[329] This is atypical of the measured style usually displayed in senatorial decrees: not even in the case of the honours decreed to Germanicus had the Senate used such extreme language. Indeed, it is only in later decrees of the mid-first century that the Senate indulged in similar hyperbole, and it is significant that the closest parallel is in the language used to honour Claudius' freedman Pallas, which offended the Younger Pliny so much.[330] This later example calls to mind the dangers of using hyperbole, since as a rhetorical device it risks either making a phrase seem false or, at best, 'difficult to decide its truth value because of the additional emotive content'.[331] In the course of the *SCPP*, the drafting committee of senators uses no fewer than twenty-one superlative adjectives and adverbs (leaving aside *pontifex maximus* and the formula about displaying the inscription in the most frequented places). Hyperbolic language is a feature of the Senate's judgement about Piso right from the start of its resolution (from *SCPP* line 12), where it describes the state as having been protected from Piso's 'wicked plans' (*nefaris consilis*), whilst Piso's crimes are considered to have been 'most flagrant' (*SCPP* line 18: cum **manufestissuma** sint Cn(aei) *Pisonis patris scelera*). Piso's character is condemned on the grounds that he acted with 'the worst frame of mind and example' (*SCPP* line 48: **pessumo** *et animo et exemplo*) in leaving his province, and as having behaved with 'unparalleled cruelty' (*SCPP* line 50: *crudelitate* **unica**) in his treatment of some of his soldiers. Piso's behaviour towards Germanicus, Tiberius, and even his own men is depicted as uniquely wicked. The Senate's choice of wording, describing him as demonstrating 'brutish behaviour' (*SCPP* line 27: *feritate morum*), even dehumanises him, since the word *feritas* is used commonly to describe wild beasts or barbarians, and alienates him

---

[329] Hyperbole designed to elicit emotion: Nemesi (2004) 354.
[330] Plin., *Ep.* 8.6, citing the Senate's decree: *ut Pallas, cui se omnes pro virili parte obligatos fatentur,* **singularis fidei singularis industriae** *fructum meritissimo ferat … cum senatui populoque Romano liberalitatis gratior repraesentari nulla materia posset, quam si* **abstinentissimi fidelissimique custodis** *principalium opum facultates adiuvare contigisset* ('that Pallas, to whom everyone duly professes themselves to be obliged, may most deservedly bear the fruit **of his unique loyalty, his unique diligence** … since no more pleasing opportunity for generosity might present itself to the Senate and people of Rome, than if it had succeeded in supporting the means **of the most abstemious and most loyal guardian** of the *princeps'* wealth').
[331] Nemesi (2004) 353.

5 The Senate and its Relationship with the Imperial Family 55

from the possibility of any sympathy from fellow Romans.[332] Indeed, the Senate's description of how Piso alone, not just among Romans, but even among non-Romans beyond the boundaries of the empire, did not mourn Germanicus' death isolates him and condemns him for a lack of humanity. This was also shown by Piso allegedly pursuing his vendetta against Germanicus even after the latter's death, 'forgetting … even common humanity which does not permit feuds to be carried on beyond death' (*SCPP* lines 60–61: *oblitus … humanitatis quoq(ue), quae ultra mortem odia non patitur procedere*).[333]

Conversely, the Senate uses positive hyperbolic language generously in relation to Tiberius and other members of his family (Fig. 1). Tiberius is described as Germanicus' 'most excellent and most forbearing parent' (*SCPP* lines 58–59: *patri **optumo** et **indulgentissumo***), and as having exceeded all others in demonstrating his *pietas* after Germanicus' death: 'Likewise, since it was the judgement of the Senate that Tiberius Caesar Augustus our Princeps has surpassed all parties in his devotion to duty' (*SCPP* lines 123–24: *item cum iudic<ar>et senatus omnium partium pietatem antecessisse Ti(berium) Caesarem Aug(ustum) principem nostrum*). The Senate extends its hyperbole to other members of the imperial family, especially Agrippina, 'whom the memory of deified Augustus, by whom she was most highly approved, and of her husband Germanicus, with whom she had lived in unique harmony, and the many children born of their most fortunate union, who survived, commended to the Senate' (*SCPP* lines 137–39: *quam senatui memoria{m} divi Aug(usti), qu<o>i fuisset **probatissuma**, et viri Germanici, cum quo **unica concordia** vixsisset, et tot pignora edita partu **felicissumo** eorum, qui superessent, commendare<nt>*). This extensive use of hyperbole is a high-risk strategy, since such inflated language can raise questions about its sincerity, given the 'reduced truth value of hyperbole'.[334] Over-use of superlatives may also reflect a sense of anxiety, and a need to over-compensate in order to persuade an audience of a particular point of view.[335] This can be illustrated in the Senate's description of the willingness of the lynch-mob to moderate its impulses: 'That the Senate praises the *plebs* as well … although with its unrestrained enthusiasm it had roused itself to the point of itself carrying out the punishment of Gnaeus Piso Senior, it allowed itself, nevertheless, to follow the example of the equestrian order and be governed by our Princeps' (*SCPP* lines 155–58: *plebem quoq(ue) laudare senatum … cum **effusissumis studis** ad repraesentandam poenam Cn(aei) Pisonis patris ab semet ipsa accensa esset, regi tamen exemplo equestris ordinis a principe nostro se passa sit*). The

---

[332] Cooley (1998) 200; cf. De Monte (1999) 128–29 on Velleius' depiction of barbarians in these terms.
[333] For more detailed discussion of this theme, see Cooley (1998).
[334] Fónagy (2001) 218.   [335] Nemesi (2004) 355.

56   *Introduction*

hyperbole here raises questions over just how close the situation had come in reality to tipping over into mob violence. Overall, the Senate's tone is highly subjective and emotional, bearing more similarity to the 'effusive, superlative-filled, highly rhetorical prose style'[336] of fellow-senator Velleius Paterculus rather than to the customary style of public documents, even though the decree does share some formal characteristics with juridical texts,[337] such as archaic spellings (see §6 for more on echoes of Velleius).

The second main feature of the decree is its syntactical complexity.[338] The Senate piles up subordinate clauses – concessive, causal, temporal, comparative, purpose, consecutive, and descriptive – in an attempt to cope with the complexities and contradictions it faces in this case, not the least of which was the fact that Piso's sons were encouraged to offer a defence for their father even though his crimes were 'most flagrant'. One of the most multi-layered sections is that which relates to the Senate's granting of pardon for Plancina, which contains as many as five levels of subordination,[339] as may be illustrated from the following break-down of the clauses.

quod ad Plancinae causam pertineret,
    qu<o>i pluruma et gravissuma crimina obiecta essent,
        quoniam confiteretur se omnem spem in misericordia{m} principis nostri et senatus habere,
        et saepe princeps noster accurateq(ue) ab eo ordine petierit,
            ut contentus senatus Cn(aei) Pisonis patris poena uxori ˹e˺ius
                sic uti M(arco) filio parceret,
        et pro Plancina rogatu matris suae depreca˹tus˺ s˹it˺ et,
            quam ob rem ˹id˺ mater sua inpetrari vellet,
        iustissumas ab ea causas sibi expositas acceperit,
senatum arbitrari
    et Iuliae Aug(ustae),
        optume de r(e) p(ublica) meritae non partu tantum modo principis nostri,
            sed etiam multis magnisq(ue) erga cuiusq(ue) ordinis homines beneficis,
        quae,
            cum iure meritoq(ue) plurumum posse in eo,
                quod a senatu petere<t>
            deberet,
        parcissume uteretur eo,
    et principis nostri summa<e> erga matrem suam pietati suffragandum indulgendumq(ue) esse
    remittiq(ue) poenam Plancinae
placere;

That as regarded the case of Plancina,
    against whom very many extremely serious charges had been brought,

---

[336] Rowe (2002) 44; cf. Woodman (1975a) 13–14 on Velleius' style.   [337] Calboli (1998).
[338] Detailed analysis can be found in schematic form in Suerbaum (1999) 215–26.
[339] Rowe (2002) 16.

5 The Senate and its Relationship with the Imperial Family

       since she was now admitting that she placed all her hope in the mercy of our Princeps and the Senate,
       and since our Princeps has often and pressingly requested from this body
             that the Senate be satisfied with the punishment of Gnaeus Piso Senior and spare his wife
                   as it was sparing his son Marcus,
       and since he pleaded himself for Plancina at the request of his mother and had very just reasons presented to him by her for wanting to secure her request,
the Senate considers that to Iulia Augusta,
       who has served the state superlatively
             not only in giving birth to our Princeps
             but also through her many great favours towards men of every rank,
       who rightly and deservedly ought to have supreme influence
             in what she asked from the Senate,
       but used that influence sparingly,
and to the supreme piety of our Princeps towards his mother, support and indulgence should be accorded
and has decided that the punishment of Plancina should be waived.

This illustrates how this section constantly embeds subordinate clauses, as it attempts to explain why Plancina, 'against whom very many extremely serious charges had been brought', should not be punished. Even more awkwardly, though, the Senate cannot explain on what grounds Plancina should be pardoned, other than the fact that this is due to Tiberius' *pietas* towards his mother, whose 'very just reasons' in Plancina's favour remain unspecified. The phrase 'since our Princeps has often and pressingly requested from this body' betrays the unease felt by the Senate, since Tiberius needed to make the case to it on multiple occasions. This seems to be a prime example of Tiberius' potential to veto proposals made by the Senate lurking in the background, which results in the Senate following his lead even though with evident reluctance. The Senate's pardon for Marcus Piso a few lines earlier (*SCPP* lines 100–01) is similar in tone, with the Senate feeling compelled to follow Tiberius' suggestion that Marcus should be unpunished. In this way, Tiberius 'could exert informal influence and control proceedings under tacit threat of a veto'.[340] The syntactical awkwardness of the whole clause seems to reflect the awkwardness with which the Senate dealt with requests made to it by Tiberius. As Boatwright sums up, 'Ambiguous phrasing and ponderous, indirect grammatical structure are characteristic of this document as the senate struggles both to evoke its traditional autonomy while conveying suitable deference, and to express appropriate outrage at the alleged insults against Tiberius and the imperial house.'[341]

---

[340] Rowe (2002) 51–52.   [341] Boatwright (2021) 44.

The publication clause towards the end of the *SCPP*, however, implies a new claim to authority and influence on the part of the Senate. The Senate gives detailed instructions for its decree to be disseminated around the empire and put on display in different contexts.[342] It orders for the *SCPP* to be inscribed on bronze and displayed in the most frequented city of each province and in military legionary winter quarters. This would have resulted in roughly fifty copies of the inscription on display around the empire at a minimum, given the multiple copies in Baetica alone (see §4).[343] These instructions differ from the Senate's arrangements for the publication of the decree of honours for Germanicus at the end of the previous year, when it had agreed that two senatorial decrees relating to honours for Germanicus should be inscribed and displayed in Rome in the Temple of Apollo on the Palatine; that the consuls should see to the dissemination of the decree throughout Italy; and finally, that provincial governors should arrange for the decree to be set up in colonies in the provinces.[344] There was no requirement for the senatorial decree to be inscribed on bronze beyond Rome, and so it is more likely that the Senate envisaged its publication on whiteboards. Of course, the discovery of the bronze *Tabula Siarensis* from a small town rather than colony illustrates that provinces could exceed the minimum mandated to them.[345] In AD 20, however, the Senate states that the *SCPP* should be engraved upon bronze, and also extends publication to army winter quarters, reflecting the perception that Piso had tested the loyalty of the army towards the imperial family. This publication was intended to reinforce the consensus. Such publication clauses on the part of the Senate were far from the norm. Previously, the Senate had given instructions for its decrees to be disseminated only rarely, such as in the case of the *SC de Bacchanalibus*.[346] In other cases where senatorial decrees are found published in monumental form, the initiative for this comes from other individuals or groups, and not from the Senate itself. It is a distinctive trait only of the Tiberian Senate that it starts to order publication of its decrees around the empire.[347] As was shown above (see §4), even then the implementation of the Senate's instructions appears to reflect provincial enthusiasm. Nevertheless, publication of its decrees reflects a new sphere of influence for the Senate and an implicit claim about the Senate's importance in the state.[348]

From the *SCPP*, then, we form an impression of some of the challenges which the Senate faced in dealing with Tiberius and the rest of the imperial family. At the same time, we witness the Senate seizing the opportunity to

---

[342] On the publication of the Honours for Germanicus and *SCPP*, see Hurlet (2006).
[343] Calculation by Suerbaum (1999) 213; Hurlet (2006) 56 n.28 suggests fifty-five in total.
[344] *Tabula Siarensis* = Crawford (1996) no.37, frag. b, col. II, lines 20–27 = LACTOR 19, J8h.
[345] Bartels (2009) 9.
[346] *CIL* X 104; see Takács (2000) on the political significance of the senatorial decree.
[347] Cooley (2007) 203–10; (2012) 159–71.   [348] Rowe (2002), chapter 1; Giua (2002) 103–15.

5 The Senate and its Relationship with the Imperial Family

assert its own importance by publishing its decrees concerning the imperial family. In AD 20, Roman society was still working out how to define the role of the imperial family, and the Senate made a distinctive contribution to a more general debate about what that was.

Firstly, the Senate creates a parallelism between Augustus and Tiberius that successfully aligns the two *principes* and yet preserves a differentiation between them. At *SCPP* lines 46–47, the Senate alludes to the fact that 'all the evils of civil war had long since been buried through the divine power of deified Augustus and the virtues of Tiberius Caesar Augustus …' (*iam pridem numine divi Aug(usti) virtutibusq(ue) Ti(beri) Caesaris Aug(usti) omnibus civilis belli sepultis malis*). Similarly, at *SCPP* lines 52–53, we read that Piso 'had damaged the military discipline which had been established by deified Augustus and maintained by Tiberius Caesar Augustus' (*qui militarem disciplinam a divo Aug(usto) institutam et servatam a Ti(berio) Caesare Aug(usto) corrupisset*). At the same time, the Senate maintains the special status now held by Augustus in charging Piso with offences against Augustus' *numen* (*SCPP* lines 68–70): 'it was also the opinion of the Senate that the divine spirit of deified Augustus had been violated by him in that every sign of honour was removed which was being accorded either to his memory or to those portraits which had been [set up] to him before he was entered into the number of the gods' (*numen quoq(ue) divi Aug(usti) violatum esse ab eo arbitrari senatum omni honore, qui aut memoriae eius aut imaginibus, quae, antequam in deorum numerum referre{n}tur, ei r[eddi]tae erant, habeba{n}tur, detracto*). The *SCPP* therefore consistently asserts that the deified Augustus and Tiberius perform a special role in preserving the prosperity and tranquillity of the Roman state. Similar sentiments can be found in Valerius Maximus, for whom Augustus and Tiberius are the 'two divine eyes of the state' (4.3.3: *duobus rei publicae divinis oculis*).[349]

One of the most important developments of the late Augustan and early Tiberian period, first found in Ovid's exile poetry, was the formulation of the imperial family as the *domus Augusta*.[350] This reflected the need to embrace the special position in Roman social and political hierarchy of Tiberius' family members, both male and female, adults and children. In AD 20 the Senate develops the significance of the *domus Augusta* still further in the *SCPP*, by representing members of the *domus Augusta* as leaders of Rome by virtue of their distinctive moral qualities.[351] The Senate relates how its own behaviour has been guided by virtues which it has learned from Augustus and Tiberius: 'Likewise the Senate, mindful of its clemency, justice, and generosity of spirit, virtues which it had inher-

---

[349] Compare also Velleius Paterculus' description of Tiberius at 2.99.1 as *uere alterum rei publicae lumen et caput* ('truly the second light and head of the republic').

[350] Millar (1993); Pani (2000); Corbier (2001b); Lott (2012) 15–18; Seager (2013).

[351] On the paradigmatic role of the imperial family, see further Cooley (1998) 207–10; Potter (1999) 76–78.

ited from its ancestors, then learned in particular from deified Augustus and Tiberius Caesar Augustus, its Principes' (*SCPP* lines 90–92: *item senatum, memorem clementiae suae iustitiaeq(ue) <atq(ue)> animi magnitudinis, quas virtutes {quas} a maioribus suis accepisset, tum praecipue ab divo Aug(usto) et Ti(berio) Caesare Aug(usto) principibus suis didicisset*). It then also describes Iulia Augusta and Drusus as imitating Tiberius' virtues: 'likewise, the Senate offers abundant praise of the restraint of Iulia Augusta and Drusus Caesar as they imitate the justice of our Princeps …' (*SCPP* lines 132–33: *item senatum laudare magnopere Iuliae Aug(ustae) Drusiq(ue) Caesaris moderationem imitantium principis nostri iustitiam* …). The next generation too – Germanicus' sons – is also presented as having learnt its *moderatio* from the older generation: 'the Senate judges that it ought primarily to be traced back to the training of their grandfather and uncle and of Iulia Augusta, but nonetheless accords them praise in their own right' (*SCPP* lines 148–50: *iudicare senatum referendum quidem esse acceptum maxume discipulinae avi ⌐e⌐orum et patrui et Iuliae Aug(ustae), sed tamen ipsorum quoque nomin⌐e⌐ laudandum existumare{t}*). In this way, a model is established by which virtues are initially to be found in Augustus himself, but are then passed down through senior members of the *domus Augusta* to the rest of the imperial family.[352] This pattern then extends implicitly to the equestrian order and Roman army, and explicitly to the Senate and the plebs of Rome, which has 'allowed itself, nevertheless, to follow the example of the equestrian order and be governed by our Princeps' (*SCPP* line 158: *regi tamen exemplo equestris ordinis a principe nostro se passa sit*). This didactic view of the imperial family as exemplars had already been encouraged by Tiberius himself, who had offered a eulogy of Germanicus in order to inspire future generations. This was delivered in the Senate orally and then inscribed on bronze.[353] Fundamentally, therefore, Tiberius according to the Senate acts together with Augustus as the ultimate role model for the rest of Roman society, something which finds echoes in other contemporary texts, discussed below (see §6). Imperial women have a part in this. It is no surprise to find Iulia Augusta named, but other imperial women – namely Antonia, Agrippina, and Livi(ll)a – are also all praised for their moral qualities, which are represented as justifying their promotion by marriage within the imperial family first by Augustus, then by Tiberius.

In its decree, the Senate continues to redefine who might be properly regarded as belonging to the *domus Augusta* (Fig. 1). Divus Augustus, Tiberius, and Iulia Augusta are, naturally, the senior members of the household, but the Senate goes out of its way to justify why Agrippina, Antonia, and Livi(ll)a should also be regarded as members of the *domus*

---

[352] See further Cooley (1998) 203–07 for how this fits into traditional Roman ideas about inherited family characteristics.
[353] *Tabula Siarensis* = Crawford (1996) no.37, frag. b, col. II, lines 11–17.

5 The Senate and its Relationship with the Imperial Family 61

(*SCPP* lines 136–46). In two of the three cases, their special status is defined in terms of their having met with approval from divus Augustus for their high moral characters: Agrippina, 'whom the memory of deified Augustus, by whom she was most highly approved ... commended to the Senate' (*quam senatui memoria{m} divi Aug(usti), qu<o>i fuisset probatissuma ... commendare<nt>*); Antonia, 'who, through the excellence of her moral character, proved herself to deified Augustus worthy of so close a relationship' (*quae ... sanctitate morum dignam se divo Aug(usto) tam arta propinquitate exhibuerit*). Livi(ll)a's case is justified in even more detail, with reference to her approval by Livia and Tiberius, 'whom her grandmother and her father-in-law, who is also her uncle, our Princeps, held in the highest esteem, whose esteem, even if she did not belong to their family, she could deservedly vaunt, all the more as she is a woman attached by such family ties' (*de qua optume et avia sua et socer idemq(ue) patruos, princeps noster, iudicaret, quorum iudicis, etiam si non contingere{n}t domum eorum, merito gloriari posset, nedum tam coniunctis necessitudinibus inligata femina*). In this way, the Senate positions members of the *domus Augusta* as the leaders at Rome by virtue of their exemplary ethical roles, something which Valerius Maximus echoes in dedicating his work to Tiberius, whom he describes as offering security for Rome through his encouragement of virtues and punishment of vices (see further §6). The natural consequence of this elevation of the *domus Augusta* is the Senate's statement in the *SCPP* that only Tiberius or his sons Germanicus and Drusus are suitably qualified to carry out certain roles for the state (*res publica*). Tiberius and his sons are acknowledged to be the only ones fit to undertake delicate negotiations in the East, particularly perhaps in representing the Roman state in discussing with the Parthians how to settle the disputed succession in the kingdom of Armenia, with the Senate describing them as 'affairs which called for the presence either of Tiberius Caesar Augustus himself or of one of his two sons' (*SCPP* lines 31–32: *desiderantium praesentiam aut ipsius Ti(beri) Caesaris Aug(usti) aut filiorum alterius utrius*). Further, the Senate considers that the entire safety of the state depends upon the protection of Tiberius and his family, praising the soldiers who 'knew that the safety of our empire depends on the protection of that House' (*SCPP* lines 162–63: *cum scirent salutem imperi nostri in eius domˊuˋ<s> custodia posita<m> esse{t}*).

As well as bringing more members of the imperial family into public view, the Senate introduces a new concept – the *maiestas* of the *domus Augusta* – in what is the first known attestation of this expression. In the *SCPP* lines 32–33, the Senate accuses Piso of having offended against the *maiestas* of the *domus Augusta*, of having acted 'without regard for the majesty of the House of Augustus, without regard even for public law' (*neˊgˋlecta maiestate domus Aug(ustae), neˊgˋlecto etiam iure publico*). This is the first time this phrase is known to be used in this way. The specific context in which the *maiestas domus Augustae* is referred to is significant here, namely

Germanicus being voted *imperium* formally by the *populus Romanus* and being sent out to the East on his mission as a proconsul. In this way, the Senate is not being revolutionary in attributing *maiestas* to a member of the *domus Augusta* who is also an official of the *populus Romanus*. It does, however, open up the possibility of *maiestas* now also being applicable to other members of the *domus Augusta* as well. Although Piso's offences are framed as concerning primarily Germanicus, who is simultaneously a member of the *domus Augusta* and an official appointed by the state,[354] the relevance of the concept to the *domus Augusta* is an additional element. It did not displace its applicability to more traditional representatives of *maiestas*, as can be seen in the senatorial decree of AD 19 from Larinum, where the Senate is concerned with protecting the *maiestas* of its own order.[355] This finds a parallel in Velleius Paterculus' list of Tiberius' achievements (2.126.2), which include the restoration of *maiestas* to the Senate, a passage which in turn echoes his earlier account of the benefits of the ending of the civil wars by Augustus (2.89.3) (see further on *maiestas* below, §6).[356] By AD 20, then, the Senate has both extended the membership of the *domus Augusta* and increased its dignity and authority. As Beth Severy observes, the new concept of the *domus Augusta* as leaders of society adds up to nothing less than a 'new structure of the state',[357] and what we find in the *SCPP* is contemporary evidence illustrating how the Senate went about trying to define what the membership and role of the *domus Augusta* now was, and what its own relationship should be with it.

6 THE *SCPP* AND THE CREATION OF TIBERIAN POLITICAL DISCOURSE

Until fairly recently, Tiberius has often been considered simply to have followed in Augustus' footsteps, taking over his new political system and continuing his priorities.[358] Augustus and Tiberius were naturally bracketed together in Tiberian sources, as briefly discussed above. Most notably, Strabo supports the view that Tiberius modelled his rule upon that of Augustus, a view which Lasserre argues had its origins in a statement made

---

[354] On the scope of the *lex maiestatis*, see Castro-Camero (2000) esp. 25–27.
[355] *AE* (1978) 145, (1983) 210.   [356] Woodman (1975b) 290–91 on this panegyrical motif.
[357] Severy (2000) 328.
[358] A general expression of this view can be found in Hellegouarc'h (1980) 180: 'Cette attitude s'explique par la conception même que Tibère a du principat et qui est conforme, en principe tout au moins à l'esprit du système qu'Auguste a voulu instituer.' Compare Levick (1999) 82: 'Repeatedly Tiberius declared his intention of maintaining one or other Augustan precedent or institution. It was a principle with him – no doubt one that was sometimes convenient to cite'; Seager (2005) 147–50: 'slavish adherence to the policies of Augustus' (149). The long shadow cast by this idea can be seen from the fact that although Martin (1982) esp. 120–22 emphasises Tiberius' innovative approach to *Providentia*, elsewhere, at 125, he states that Tiberius 'ne faisait que suivre l'exemple de son prédécesseur'.

6 The SCPP and the Creation of Tiberian Political Discourse 63

to the Senate in September AD 14 by Tiberius.[359] Whether or not that is true, it certainly shows that this was one possible contemporary perception. In addition, epigraphic evidence, such as the requisitioning edict of Sex. Sotidius Strabo Libuscidianus from Sagalassos, illustrates clearly how important Augustus' authority was to the legitimacy of Tiberius and of his governors in the provinces in the immediate aftermath of Augustus' demise.[360] Coins commemorating *divus Augustus pater* also kept in view both the newly deified *princeps* and Tiberius' inheritance of his father's role, especially since this theme featured not only on precious metal but also on prolific base metal issues.[361] In regarding Tiberius as basically trying to continue along the same track as Augustus, therefore, some modern scholars have taken their cue from contemporary sources.

In the last decade or so, however, the picture has become more nuanced. The idea that Augustus handed down a new political system to Tiberius has been questioned.[362] This opens up the possibility that the years immediately after Augustus' death witnessed further debate about how politics at Rome should function and what the place of the imperial family was in this (see above §5). Furthermore, Cowan has demonstrated that Tiberius was not consistently represented as simply imitating Augustus. She has analysed how imitation of Augustus is a prominent theme in Tacitus' account of Tiberius, which has subsequently been influential on how later historians viewed Tiberius. Even so, Tacitus shows Tiberius selectively interpreting and modifying as much as imitating Augustan precedent. Furthermore, she argues for a clear distinction between the Tacitean depiction of Tiberius' responses to Augustan precedent and how contemporary sources instead emphasise Tiberius' virtues as legitimising his rule. Given that Tiberius is represented as inheriting these virtues from Augustus, however, his predecessor's spectre continues to float around in the background.[363]

The publication of the great bronze inscriptions of Baetica has made it clearer than ever that a distinctive political discourse emerged during this period, and this can be also illuminated by analysis of contemporary texts. Whereas previous studies of Tiberian discourse focused upon the evidence of coins and later writers – notably Tacitus, Suetonius, and Cassius Dio – we can now use epigraphic evidence originating with the Senate along with

---

[359] Lasserre (1983) 885–86. Compare the parallelism between Tiberius and Augustus created by Velleius' verbal echoes in 2.89.3 and 2.126.2 (with Woodman 1975b: 290–91 on this as a panegyrical motif), and the depiction of Tiberius making it his priority to follow Augustus' handwritten instructions about the *comitia* in one of his first actions after Augustus had been deified – 2.124.3.
[360] In his edict, the governor Sex. Sotidius Strabo Libuscidianus alludes to 'the Augusti – the one the greatest of gods, the other of leaders' (*Augusti alter deorum alter principum maximus*): *AE* (1976) 653 = *SEG* XXVI 1392 = S. Mitchell (1976), esp. 113.
[361] *Aurei*, struck at Lugdunum: *RIC* I², Tiberius nos 23–24; *aes* at Rome: *RIC* I², Tiberius nos 70–73, AD c.15–16.
[362] Cooley (2019).   [363] Cowan (2009a).

the contemporary texts of Valerius Maximus and Velleius Paterculus in order to uncover both the distinctiveness of Tiberian discourse and how it was developed and debated.[364] The *SCPP*, together with the decrees commemorating Germanicus from the previous year, is one of our most valuable sources for illustrating the distinctiveness of political discourse under Tiberius. Whereas in other instances – notably coinage – we may wonder about the extent to which the emperor was personally involved in the development of political discourse,[365] the fact that Tiberius seals the whole *SCPP* (lines 174–76) with a first-person statement of his approval allows us to be confident that the Senate's words were checked by him. Similarly, in the case of the *Tabula Siarensis*, the involvement of members of the imperial family as advisors to the Senate allows us to assume that what the Senate promulgates was in accordance with their wishes.[366] In the *SCPP*, therefore, we can trace the Senate's role in creating and developing a distinctive Tiberian political discourse, but other mechanisms and agents also contributed to this discourse, shaping and challenging it in different contexts.

The qualities of *clementia*, *moderatio*, and *providentia* have long been recognised as characteristics promoted by the Tiberian regime.[367] The fact that these are ethical values does not diminish their political significance:[368] far from it, Roman political discourse had long existed within a moralising framework articulated by exemplarity,[369] and this became all the more closely monopolised by members of the imperial family as the *domus Augusta* emerged as a distinctive feature of the early Tiberian era (as explored above, see §5).[370] In publishing its decrees on Germanicus and Piso, the Senate took the initiative to advertise the qualities shared by members of the imperial family, which justified their position of influence in Roman politics and society.[371] Tiberius similarly emerges as the ultimate exemplary figure in the works of both Velleius Paterculus and Valerius Maximus, both of whom were writing soon after Piso's trial.[372] For Velleius (2.126.5), 'the best *princeps* teaches his citizens to act correctly by so acting himself, and although he is greatest in power, he is greater through example' (*facere recte ciues suos princeps optimus faciendo docet, cumque sit imperio*

---

[364] Contrast Rogers (1943) 1–88 and Levick (1999) chapter 6, who are largely dependent upon non-contemporary texts and coins, with Gowing (2005) chapter 2 on the distinctiveness of the *res publica Tiberiana*.
[365] Whatever the system for designing Roman 'imperial' coins, they did, however, constitute an official medium of communicating simple messages: Noreña (2011).
[366] *Tabula Siarensis* = Crawford (1996) no.37, frag. a, lines 6–8 = LACTOR 19, J8a.
[367] Rogers (1943) on *liberalitas, providentia, clementia*, and *moderatio*; Martin (1982) on *providentia*.
[368] Wallace-Hadrill (1981) on the evolving importance of imperial qualities.
[369] On exemplarity in Roman ethical and political thought, see Langlands (2008), (2018) esp. chapter 11, building on David (1998); Roller (2018) esp. chapter 1. Compare also Lobur (2008) chapter 6, although his discussion focuses upon *exempla* as generating consensus rather than debate.
[370] Severy (2000), (2003) chapter 9.   [371] Cooley (1998).
[372] Velleius completed his work in AD 30: Sumner (1970) 284–88; Rich (2011) 84–86. Valerius Maximus wrote at roughly the same time, AD 27–31, since his work alludes to the downfall of Sejanus: Briscoe (2019) 2–4, contra Bellemore (1989).

6 *The* SCPP *and the Creation of Tiberian Political Discourse* 65

maximus, exemplo maior est). Velleius has been criticised for deliberately misleading his readers about certain recent historical episodes,[373] a trait that is closely related to his unremittingly positive attitude to Tiberius.[374] Nevertheless, his work gives insight into the values of an individual who prospered under Tiberius, first serving under his command in the army, then enjoying military and then political advancement, ending up as praetor in AD 15 (2.124.4).[375] In Velleius' view, Tiberius' moral qualities – his *virtutes* – permeated through the rest of society and thus underpinned the welfare of Rome. As Woodman has observed, the motif of ruler as exemplar was nothing new at this date,[376] but the exemplarity of Tiberius and the rest of his family emerges with fresh importance during the first fifteen years or so of his rule. In Valerius Maximus, for instance, members of the imperial family – Augustus, Agrippa, Iulia Augusta, Tiberius, Drusus, and Antonia – are almost the only positive *exempla* to be cited for the period after the triumvirate. This reflects a new monopoly on exemplarity compared with the wider variety of families whose members were represented as exemplary in Roman society during the Republic, and gave credit to members of the *domus Augusta* for their exceptionally virtuous behaviour.[377]

Valerius Maximus goes further still in his preface to his work on exemplary ethics, *Memorable Doings and Sayings*, dedicating his work to Tiberius, whom he describes as offering security to Rome through his encouragement of virtues and punishment of vices, stating: 'Therefore I invoke you to this undertaking, Caesar, to whom the consensus of gods and men has desired to give the control of land and sea, surest salvation of the fatherland, by whose heavenly foresight the virtues of which I am about to tell are most kindly fostered and the vices most sternly punished' (*te igitur huic coepto, penes quem hominum deorumque consensus maris ac terrae regimen esse uoluit, certissima salus patriae, Caesar, inuoco, cuius caelesti prouidentia uirtutes, de quibus dicturus sum, benignissime fouentur, uitia seuerissime*

---

[373] Velleius' factual distortions in Tiberius' favour are catalogued by Syme (1978), whose view finds support from Lobur (2008) 115 – 'a mixture of truths and untruths'; compare Lana (1952), who views Velleius as a propagandist for the Tiberian regime.

[374] Sumner (1970) 270 on reasons for Velleius' positive account of Tiberius, dubbed 'triumphal history' by De Monte (1999); Woodman (1975b) 288–96 on Velleius as fulfilling literary conventions of panegyric; Balmaceda (2014) 360–63 on the Tiberian era for Velleius as the culmination of Roman history and the summit of Roman virtue.

[375] Velleius' career: Sumner (1970) 265–79. Velleius' usefulness as a gauge of contemporary political discourse: Hellegouarc'h (1980); Schmitzer (2000); Gowing (2005) chapter 2, (2007); Lobur (2007); Cowan (2011b); Balmaceda (2014), (2017) chapter 4. Velleius' importance in the development of historiography is explored by Woodman (1975a); Jacquemin (1998).

[376] Woodman (1975b) 292, with note 1 for a list of precedents; cf. Kuntze (1985) 120–23.

[377] Gunderson (2014) 133. 4.3.3, conjugal fidelity of Drusus and Antonia; 4.7.7, Agrippa as friend of gods (*deorum alter maximum amicum*); 5.5.3, brotherly love of Tiberius and Drusus; 6.1.praef., invocation of *Pudicitia* and the 'marriage bed of Iulia' (Augusta); 7.6.6, Augustus' rule as *cura* and *tutela*; 7.7.3–4, Augustus intervening in disputes about inheritance, exercising his role as *pater patriae*; 7.8.6, Augustus excluded from the will of T. Marius of Urbinum.

uindicantur). Nevertheless, as has become increasingly clear from recent studies, by Rebecca Langlands in particular, exemplarity was not a straightforward system of communicating unproblematic models of behaviour for imitation.[378] Discourse about exemplarity did not simply involve depicting role models to be imitated, but debating what behaviour should be considered exemplary in different contexts and exploring ethical problems. Building upon this insight, this section aims to explore the ways in which virtues were not simply disseminated from the top – despite the fact that the Senate in the *SCPP* may appear to imply that this is indeed how exemplarity works – but how a variety of individuals was actively involved in shaping expectations and engaging in debate about the conduct of the *princeps*, his family, and the rest of Roman society. Just as the four virtues named on the golden shield awarded by the Senate to Augustus in 27 or 26 BC (*virtus, iustitia, clementia, pietas*) never achieved canonical status in defining essential imperial qualities,[379] so the expectation of what behaviour should result from individual imperial virtues could likewise be up for debate. Even later on, there was no fixed set of imperial virtues which *principes* were obliged to demonstrate. All the more, therefore, might we reasonably expect there to have been under Tiberius debate about how to define imperial virtues. Exactly what the qualities of *clementia, moderatio*, and *providentia* entailed was not fixed. We can trace how different texts explored what these should be in different contexts. As Clark observes in relation to divine qualities, 'Divine qualities were not simply "received" by those the emperor ruled. They were rather communicative elements enabling exchanges between rulers and ruled.'[380]

It has long been recognised that the virtues of *clementia* and *moderatio* are distinctive traits of Tiberian political discourse, not only because of their striking appearance on the coinage of the time,[381] but also because they were prominent in contemporary texts and inscriptions, as well as in later historical accounts of the period.[382] Attempts have been made to pin down the political contexts in which *clementia* and *moderatio* were promoted through coin issues, associating them for example with the trial of Libo Drusus in AD 16 or with the Senate's decree in recognition of Tiberius' '*clementia*' towards Agrippina in AD 33.[383] An examination of inscriptions, coins, and literature alongside each other, however, reveals a flexibility in the meaning of these concepts, and an ongoing exploration of why *clementia* and *moderatio* were important elements in political

---

[378] Langlands (2011), (2018).
[379] Augustus' virtues: *Res Gestae* 34.2, with Cooley (2009) 266–71; Wallace-Hadrill (1981) 298–307 questions the idea of a fixed canon of virtues, an idea developed further by Classen (1991) and Noreña (2001), esp. 152–53, 156–57.
[380] Clark (2007) 273.   [381] Rogers (1943) 35–88; Levick (1975).
[382] Overview of Tiberius' *moderatio*, with further references: Woodman and Martin (1996) 367 on Tac., *Ann.* 3.50.2.
[383] Possibilities proposed by Levick (1975) 131; Gesche (1971) 51, arguing from Suet., *Tib.* 53.2.

6 The SCPP and the Creation of Tiberian Political Discourse

discourse. *Clementia* and *moderatio* did not have some fixed significance, relevant only to specific political situations, but their meanings were creatively developed by a variety of voices. This moves us away from a model of centralised top-down distribution of ideological values towards a more dynamic process whereby different constituents interacted to explore the workings of political power.

Perhaps the most famous coin issues under Tiberius are the matching *dupondii* issued with the legends CLEMENTIAE S C ('To clemency, by decree of the Senate') and MODERATIONI S C ('To moderation, by decree of the Senate') along with a male portrait framed within a shield (*imago clipeata*) (Figs 6–7).[384] The chronology of these issues has been much debated, with proposals including AD 16, 22/23, or 33/37.[385] There has been a similar lack of consensus about the identity of the busts depicted within the shields, with some seeing them as Tiberius himself, Germanicus and Drusus, and even Gemellus and Gaius.[386] The portraits themselves are on too small a scale for identification to be certain. Such uncertainty also reflects the continuing importance of *clementia* and *moderatio* throughout the Tiberian era, but the depiction specifically of *imagines clipeatae* appears to associate them with Germanicus and Drusus, given that Germanicus

Fig. 6. *Dupondius*. Obverse (A): Laureate head of Tiberius, facing left, with the legend TI CAESAR DIVI AVG F AVGVST IMP VIII ('Tiberius Caesar Augustus, son of the deified Augustus, imperator for the eighth time'). Reverse (B): male portrait framed within a shield with the legend CLEMENTIAE S C ('To Clemency, by decree of the Senate'). *RIC* I² Tiberius no.38. Münzkabinett, Staatliche Museen zu Berlin, 18211825. Photograph by Dirk Sonnenwald. Courtesy of Dr Karsten Dahmen (Münzkabinett, Staatliche Museen zu Berlin).

---

[384] *RIC* I², Tiberius nos 38–39.
[385] Dates reviewed by Sutherland (1979), who concludes that the coins must date from the first decade of Tiberius' rule, with 22/23 being plausible.
[386] Options reviewed by Galimberti (1998) 177.

Fig. 7. *Dupondius.* Reverse: male portrait framed within a shield with the legend MODERATIONI S C ('To Moderation, by decree of the Senate'). *RIC* I² Tiberius no.39. American Numismatic Society: 1944.100.39284, available at numismatics.org/collection/1944.100.39284.

was granted an *imago clipeata* in the Palatine Library by the Senate in AD 19 as part of the bundle of honours decreed to him after his death, and it seems likely that Drusus was granted the same in AD 23 on his death.[387] Furthermore, a context of AD 22/23 seems most likely on the grounds that the coins commemorating *clementia* and *moderatio* are thematically linked with *dupondii* depicting *iustitia*, *pietas*, and *salus Augusta*, all of which belong to AD 22/23.[388] This hypothesis is supported by a recently published pseudo medallion struck on an oversized *sestertius* flan with the *dupondius* die of the *clementia* issue.[389] This close connection with *sestertii* would imply a date of production in AD 22/23, when *sestertius* production was resumed briefly before lapsing again until AD 34/35.[390] If Sutherland is correct in interpreting such medallions as non-monetary imperial gifts,[391] then this raises the possibility of Tiberius' own endorsement of this imagery. Some have worried that there is a mismatch between text and image on these coins, on the assumption that there is a lack of

---

[387] 'And it was agreed that on the Palatine, in the portico which is near Apollo's temple, in the consecrated space in which the Senate usually meets, [among the *imagines*] of men of distinguished talent, *imagines* should be set up of Germanicus Caesar and of Drusus Germanicus, his natural father [and the brother] of Tiberius Caesar Augustus, inasmuch as he too was of fertile talent, above the capitals of the columns of [the roof] by which the statue of Apollo is covered' – *Tabula Hebana* lines 1–4 = Crawford (1996) no.37 = LACTOR 19, J8j; on its format as *clipeus*, see Tac., *Ann.* 2.83.3. For Drusus, this is the inference from Tac., *Ann.* 4.9.2, 'the same things were decreed to the memory of Drusus as had been for Germanicus'.

[388] Woytek (2017) 86.

[389] Woytek (2017); *RIC* I², Tiberius no.38; for a definition of 'pseudo medallions' or 'medallised coins', see Toynbee (1944) 24–25.

[390] Woytek (2017) 89.

[391] *RIC* I² p.8; compare Toynbee (1944) 5, 15–16.

6 The SCPP and the Creation of Tiberian Political Discourse 69

connection between *moderatio* and *clementia*, which are intimately associated with the figure of Tiberius himself, and the clipeate portraits, which may depict other members of the imperial family.[392] But what the iconography on the coins suggests is that *clementia* and *moderatio* are not to be regarded as virtues monopolised by Tiberius himself, but were also shared by both Germanicus and Drusus. This fits neatly with the political message of the *SCPP*, as explored above (see §5), in which the Senate promotes the idea that members of the *domus Augusta* all share similar virtues.

Clementia had previously appeared on coinage associated with Iulius Caesar in 44 BC, to commemorate the Senate's decree of a temple to *Clementia Caesaris* ('Clemency of Caesar') during the previous year in recognition of his restrained attitude towards opponents defeated in civil war.[393] This was an innovation in the Roman understanding of *clementia* that was promoted by Cicero.[394] In this way, the Senate also articulated the shift by which *Clementia* could be formally regarded as a divine quality.[395] It is unclear whether or not the temple was actually built, but, in the aftermath of the Ides, *clementia* became closely attached to the assassinated dictator, especially by Cicero, and remained a prominent theme in later historians' characterisation of him, even though Caesar himself may have preferred to use other words to describe his actions.[396] In this way, *clementia* was closely associated with a specific individual – Caesar – and foreshadowed later 'August(an)' qualities which were also given state cult, the first of which was *Pax Augusta* ('Augustan Peace') in 9 BC.[397] At the time that the *dupondii* were minted under Tiberius, then, *Clementia* may not yet have been in receipt of public cult in Rome, despite the earlier decree for a temple of *Clementia Caesaris*. The possibility that *Clementia* could evoke a divine quality, though, must already have been recognised, given that the Senate decreed an altar to *Clementia* only a few years later, in AD 28.[398]

Clementia became a central prop for Augustus, featuring on the golden shield awarded to him by the Senate,[399] and acquiring new resonance. As Dowling has argued, *clementia* under Augustus gradually became associated with peacetime rather than with war, as a benefit to be enjoyed on a global scale by Roman citizens and foreigners alike.[400] Tiberian *clementia* was not, however, a carbon copy of either the Augustan virtue or of Cae-

---

[392] Woytek (2017) 84.
[393] *RRC* I 491, no.480/21; App. *B Civ.* 2.106; Plut., *Vit. Caes.* 57.3; *LTUR* 1, 'Clementia Caesaris, aedes' = Palombi (1993a). I follow Clark (2007) chapter 1 in distinguishing between *clementia* (the virtue) and *Clementia* (the divine quality in receipt of public cult at Rome).
[394] Weinstock (1971) 239; Griffin ([2003a] 2018) 573.
[395] On the expression 'divine quality', see Clark (2007), with 247–50 on Caesar's *clementia*.
[396] On Caesar's *clementia*, see Weinstock (1971) 236–43; Griffin ([2003a] 2018) 571–74; Konstan (2005) argues that *clementia* was always regarded as a positive trait.
[397] On imperial divine qualities, see Clark (2007) 263–69.   [398] Tac., *Ann.* 4.74.
[399] *RGDA* 34.2.
[400] Dowling (2006) chapters 2–4 on Augustan *clementia*, with summary of main conclusions on 166–68.

sar's, nor is it to be expected that a virtue such as *clementia* should remain unchanged over time.[401] *Clementia* had a variety of resonances – political, military, and legal – including being merciful towards fellow citizens or defeated foreign enemies, and being lenient in the lawcourts. Different elements of the divine quality could come to the fore at different times. Whereas Iulius Caesar was primarily associated by others with *clementia* in times of civil war, Augustus himself alludes to his exercise of *clementia* in both civil and external wars, whilst the Senate's grant of the civic crown to him in 27 BC also related to his saving of citizen lives.[402]

Just as the meaning of *clementia* gradually changed and expanded under Augustus, being developed and debated in contemporary visual and literary representations, so too did Tiberian *clementia* and other virtues not hatch fully developed into political discourse, but rather were moulded by a variety of voices and in different contexts over time.[403] There has been a consensus that Tiberius was represented above all as exercising *clementia* in the lawcourts, particularly in relation to trials for *maiestas*, and that this was a new feature of his rule.[404] We might therefore expect this theme to be prominent in the *SCPP*. In the *SCPP* (lines 90–100), the Senate claims that its proposal to alleviate the penalties imposed upon Piso's elder son was inspired by its own sense of *clementia*, justice, and generosity of spirit, which it had learned from its ancestors and from Tiberius and Augustus. Superficially, this might seem to fit neatly into the standard template of *clementia* exercised in a judicial context. Closer consideration, however, reveals that referring specifically to *clementia* here is rather jarring, given that *clementia* should be exercised towards someone who is guilty, whereas on all accounts Cn. Piso *filius* had not been involved in his father's misdeeds to any extent at all. By contrast, where we might have expected an allusion to Tiberius' *clementia* – in remitting the penalties imposed upon Marcus Piso (*SCPP* lines 100–01), who had been associated with his father's crimes – we instead find reference to Tiberius' *humanitas* and *moderatio*. Furthermore, although Plancina is described as relying upon Tiberius' *misericordia* (*SCPP* line 110), a synonym for *clementia*, her pardon is not actually attributed to his *clementia* but to his *pietas* towards his mother (*SCPP* line 119). The Senate's single explicit reference to *clementia*, therefore, occurs in an unexpected context. This illustrates the complex inter-weaving of imperial virtues in the Senate's decree, and the fluidity with which they were invoked.

Likewise, the presentation of *clementia* in Valerius Maximus does not fit neatly into what we might expect given the work's Tiberian context.

---

[401] Griffin (2003a).
[402] *RGDA* 3; 34.2, with Sen. *Clem.* 1.26.5 for the civic crown's association with *clementia*, as the culmination of Book 1 of the treatise.
[403] Cowan (2016) on 'contesting *clementia*'.   [404] Rogers (1943) 35–59; Levick (1975).

6 The SCPP and the Creation of Tiberian Political Discourse

The author's decision to pair *clementia* with *humanitas* (5.1.praef.) has the effect of diluting the distinctiveness of acts of *clementia*, and of making it less prominent overall, since the episodes narrated in this section can illustrate either quality. In fact, where Valerius explicitly links an *exemplum* with either *humanitas* or *clementia*, the former *exempla* far outnumber the latter (by fourteen to eight). He also states at the start of the section that *clementia* is demonstrated in cases of doubtful Fortune (*ancipiti Fortunae praestatur*) and judges that *humanitas* is more commendable (5.1.praef.). *Clementia* itself does not actually seem to accomplish much in one of the first *exempla*: the fact that Marcus Marcellus is depicted weeping over the capture of Syracuse (5.1.4) does nothing to mitigate the fact that the city has been destroyed. The limited impact of *clementia* in this instance is emphasised by the very next *exemplum*, which describes a parallel situation. In this case, though, the *humanitas* of Quintus Metellus at the siege of Centobriga (5.1.5) does prove useful to the town, since he lifts the siege rather than expose the sons of Rhoetegenes to harm. Further examples of *clementia* also illustrate respect for a dead enemy, as in the case of Iulius Caesar towards Pompey (5.1.10, although Valerius avoids using the word *clementia* here, instead describing his actions as showing his *mansuetus animus*), and in Hannibal's behaviour towards leading Romans (5.1.ext.6): both leaders see to the decent burial of their fallen foes. Valerius Maximus does not include *exempla* illustrating the exercise of *clementia* in judicial affairs. This may reflect the fact that this was a new Tiberian feature. Consequently, if he had focused upon something that was an innovation, this might have worked against his overall attempts to trace continuities between Rome's past and present. He therefore restricts himself to illustrating the quality of *clementia* that was a traditional feature of Roman history in the sphere of warfare.[405] In this way, Valerius Maximus invites reflection upon the ethical qualities whose *exempla* he presents and is not trying to pin down a single interpretation of *clementia*.[406]

The other context in which we might confidently expect Tiberius' *clementia* to be prominent is in Velleius Paterculus. The absence of the term from passages featuring Tiberius is a striking feature, all the more so since the altar of *Clementia* voted by the Senate in AD 28 is likely to have overlapped with the period of composition. Instead, the idea of *clementia* remains only implicit in Velleius' account of Tiberius,[407] even though he uses the word of other Roman leaders, such as Scipio Africanus (1.12.5), Iulius Caesar (2.55.2), Brutus and Cassius (2.69.6), and Augustus in particular (2.83.2, 86.2, 100.4). Kuntze argues that this omission reflects the

---

[405] Contrast the slightly different reading of *clementia* in Valerius Maximus in Dowling (2006) 181–84.
[406] Compare Langlands (2008) on *severitas* in Valerius Maximus.
[407] Balmaceda (2014) 357.

political crisis of AD 29/30 in the lead-up to the fall of Sejanus, while Tiberius absented himself from Rome, and hints at uneasiness on the part of Velleius as to the extent to which *clementia* continued to be exercised at this time.[408] This interpretation is consistent with the view that Velleius' final prayer also betrays his sense of unease about what the immediate future might bring, in the wake of Sejanus' meteoric promotion.[409] *Clementia*, then, is not a prominent part of the positive picture of Tiberius which Velleius presents.

Therefore, consensus about the contexts in which *clementia* should be exercised is far from evident. In the *SCPP*, *clementia* is invoked, but not in the circumstances where it is expected, namely in giving mercy to those who are guilty. Nevertheless, the Senate alludes to *clementia* in order to align itself with an imperial quality associated with Augustus and Tiberius. Velleius does not even include *clementia* as a feature of his account of Tiberius' rule, whilst *clementia* in Valerius Maximus is comparatively underplayed and lacking in clarity, playing second fiddle to *humanitas*. All this points to a continuing debate about how *clementia* ought to operate that went beyond a simple acceptance of the idea that imperial *clementia* should be shown in judicial cases above all.

The decision to feature the other quality commemorated alongside *clementia* on Tiberian coinage, *moderatio*, was an innovation.[410] Although paired with *clementia* iconographically, *moderatio* was not a divine quality in the sense of receiving official cult at Rome. *Moderatio* later became a quality to be praised in honorific or funerary inscriptions, but did not also become the recipient of dedications in the same way as other divine qualities.[411] Augustus had not been publicly honoured for his *moderatio*, even though his references to refusing various powers and offices in the *Res Gestae* might be regarded as implicitly staking a claim to *moderatio*.[412] The only reference to Augustus showing *moderatio* as a ruler comes in Ovid (for example, *Tristia* 2.41–42), where the poet is more concerned with encouraging Augustus' *moderatio* in the context of recalling him from exile than with outlining any more general characteristic of his rule: 'nor could anyone ever hold the reins of his power more moderately than you' (*nec te quisquam moderatius umquam / imperii potuit frena tenere sui*).[413]

---

[408] Kuntze (1985) 136–46.
[409] Vell. Pat. 2.131, with Balmaceda (2017) 137–39. Compare the edgy description of Sejanus at 2.127.3-4, with Woodman (1975b) 296–303.
[410] On *moderatio* under Tiberius, see especially Rogers (1943) chapter 3; Hellegouarc'h (1980); Kuntze (1985) 130–36; Christes (1994); Galimberti (1998); Lucarelli (2007) 264–80; Lobur (2008) chapter 6; Cowan (2009b); Westphal (2015).
[411] Praise for *moderatio* is a feature of inscriptions of a much later date, such as *CIL* VI 41222, epitaph for Pompeia Apa, Rome, third century; *CIL* VI 32051, statue for Vulcacius Rufinus, Rome, fourth century. Cult for divine qualities discussed in detail by Clark (2007).
[412] *RGDA* 5–6.
[413] Ingleheart (2010) ad loc.: Ovid repeats this theme at *Tr.* 1.9.25, 5.2.55, *Pont.* 2.9.77, 3.6.23.

6 *The* SCPP *and the Creation of Tiberian Political Discourse* 73

By contrast, *moderatio* was a prominent and distinctive part of Tiberius' persona, playing a fundamental role in defining Tiberius' position as successor to Augustus. As Cowan has argued, '*moderatio* played a specific and important role in Tiberius' ability to construct a role for himself as the successor of Augustus. It was through *moderatio* that Tiberius' principate accommodated and explained succession, continuity and even change.'[414] In a phrase that finds clear resonance in the *SCPP*, Velleius Paterculus (2.122.1) highlighted Tiberius' *singularis moderatio* in turning down triumphs that were his due. This sphere of *moderatio* – declining honours – was something that Tiberius shared with Augustus, but Tiberian *moderatio* was more wide-ranging than this particular example suggests and, as with the case of *clementia*, pinning down exactly in what contexts *moderatio* was considered typical of imperial exemplary behaviour is not straightforward.

Many scholars have sought to define the characteristics of Tiberius' *moderatio*. Levick concludes that *moderatio* above all relates to Tiberius' restraint in the use of his powers.[415] There are two contexts in which this *moderatio* is displayed: firstly, in declining honours for himself and members of his family and in disliking displays of flattery,[416] and secondly in participating in the trials of senators. Tiberius' *clementia* and *moderatio* are most often associated with his appearances in judicial cases.

It comes as no surprise, then, to find that *moderatio* features in the *SCPP*, where the Senate mentions the *moderatio* shown by Germanicus, Tiberius, Iulia Augusta, Drusus, Agrippina, Antonia, Livi(ll)a, the sons of Germanicus, and his brother Claudius.[417] The majority of these instances belong to the Senate's long passage in praise of the *moderatio* of members of the *domus Augusta*, specifically in the context of attempting to check the excess of mourning shown throughout Roman society at the death of Germanicus,[418] by setting before them the admirable restraint of his family members in drawing a line under their grief. The Senate begins the list (*SCPP* line 132) by praising the *moderatio* of Iulia Augusta and Drusus, who are said thereby to be imitating the *iustitia* of Tiberius. Curiously, the Senate does not praise Tiberius for his *moderatio* here, because in the previous few lines the Senate has taken pains to implore Tiberius to put an end to his grief, devote his energies to the one son remaining, and restore himself to public view. It would seem that in this very specific instance the Senate feels it appropriate to imply that Tiberius needs encouragement to adopt his usual *moderatio*. In this way, it is possible that the Senate is publicly supporting Tiberius' stance on the need to cease mourning Germanicus,

---

[414] Cowan (2009b) 480.
[415] Levick (1975) 130; Nakagawa (2002) 223 tracks four main categories of *moderatio*, plus a fifth category for 'altri casi generici'.
[416] Balmaceda (2014) 356.
[417] Nakagawa (2002) 224–25 on the different uses of *moderatio* in the *SCPP*.
[418] Versnel (1980).

74 *Introduction*

as expressed in his edict issued in May, in the face of public dissatisfaction at the restrained level of ceremonial mourning that had accompanied the burial of his ashes in the Mausoleum.[419] The specific context of *moderatio* as pertaining to grief is then attributed (*SCPP* line 145) to Agrippina, Antonia, and Livi(ll)a, with the Senate approving of them 'in equal measure for their most loyal grief and their moderation in that grief' (*quarum aeq(ue) et dolor ̂e ̂m fidelissumum et in dolore moderatione<m> senatum probare*), whilst Germanicus' sons and brother are praised (*SCPP* line 148) for not exceeding the proper limit of grief. The appearance of *moderatio* here has a specific point, given that Tiberius' undemonstrative behaviour following Germanicus' death appears to have been one of the problems which the Senate sought to settle in issuing its decree (see §2).

This is not the only use of *moderatio* in the *SCPP*. Towards the start of its decree (*SCPP* lines 26–27), the Senate also refers to Germanicus' unique *moderatio* and *patientia* in a phrase that echoes that used of Tiberius by Velleius, as discussed earlier: 'the Senate wonders at the fact that the exceptional restraint and patience of Germanicus Caesar …' (*<senatum> admirari singularem moderationem patientiamq(ue) Germanici Caesaris …*). In this case, the Senate is referring to Germanicus' behaviour towards Piso, and indeed this is in the end the main message of the decree, since it summarises its intention towards the very end of the inscription (*SCPP* lines 165–67) as being to illustrate to future generations Germanicus' unique *moderatio* and Piso's crimes: 'And in order that the course of the proceedings as a whole might be more easily transmitted to the memory of future generations and so that they might know what the Senate's judgement was concerning the exceptional restraint of Germanicus Caesar (*de singulari moderatione Germ(anici) Caesa(ris)*) and the crimes of Gnaeus Piso Senior …'. Since in the earlier passage (*SCPP* lines 28–29) the Senate proceeds to allude to Germanicus' fear that he was being poisoned by Piso, it seems that Germanicus may have been showing his *moderatio* in this case by his decision merely to renounce his friendship with Piso rather than to pursue vengeance in a more direct manner.

Finally, the Senate also mentions Tiberius' *moderatio*, along with his *humanitas*, in a different context (*SCPP* line 100), in which the Senate defers to Tiberius' *humanitas* and *moderatio* in pardoning Piso's younger son Marcus for his involvement in his father's misdeeds. As mentioned earlier, the absence of *clementia* is surprising here, and raises the question of how interchangeable *moderatio* and *clementia* were considered to be.[420] Imperial virtues therefore were not confined to a fixed interpretation. In the course of the *SCPP*, the Senate alludes to different types of *moderatio* shown by all the members of the imperial family in remitting punishment

---

[419] Potter (1999) 72, with Tac., *Ann.* 3.6 for Tiberius' edict.
[420] Rogers (1943) 60 argues that *moderatio* is a distinct virtue, separate from *clementia*.

6 The SCPP and the Creation of Tiberian Political Discourse 75

for Marcus, restraining their grief at Germanicus' death, and in Germanicus not taking drastic action against Piso, even though he believed he was being poisoned by him. In the case of *moderatio*, then, we can see how the Senate in the *SCPP* tries to use its fluidity to the advantage of the imperial family.

Further light on the shifting understanding of *moderatio* can be found in Valerius Maximus, who dedicates a whole section of his work at the start of Book 4 to *exempla* of *moderatio*. This virtue is thus even more brilliantly spotlighted than even *clementia*. In introducing the subject of *moderatio* (4.1.praef.), Valerius Maximus characterises the virtue as proof against impulsiveness: 'I shall pass over to the most wholesome part of the soul, moderation, which does not allow our minds to be borne along turned aside by the assault of a lack of control and rashness' (*transgrediar ad saluberrimam partem animi, moderationem, quae mentes nostras impotentiae <et> temeritatis incursu transuersas ferri non patitur*). Nevertheless, the first few *exempla* which he then cites from Rome all relate to the virtue of *moderatio* in the context of exercising *imperium*. This aligns *moderatio* much more closely with the virtue as exercised by Tiberius.[421] Valerius starts with P. Valerius Publicola (4.1.1), who, following the ejection of the kings from Rome, took on all their power and insignia under the title of consul, but still avoided unpopularity by showing *moderatio* and sharing half of his power with a colleague. His second example (4.1.2) is Furius Camillus, who waited until his powers had been legally established before proceeding to Veii to take command of the army against the Gauls. He then moves on (4.1.3) to the case of Marcius Rutilus Censorinus, whom he characterises as being concerned about the people's desire to give him too much power. Similarly, L. Quinctius Cincinnatus is depicted (4.1.4) as turning down the chance to retain his powers as consul, whilst Fabius Maximus is described (4.1.5) as trying to dissuade the people from electing his son as consul, so as to prevent the highest power from remaining in a single family. With Scipio Africanus (4.1.6), the emphasis shifts towards him declining excessive honours, but this is mentioned alongside his refusal to hold a permanent consulship and dictatorship, which links to the previous examples of restraint in the retention of *imperium*. The following two *exempla* relate to an individual in a position of power who does not allow his personal feelings to interfere with his treatment of those hostile to him. M. Marcellus (4.1.7) is celebrated for 'new degrees of moderation towards our allies' (*nouis gradibus moderationis aduersus socios usus est*), in his respectful treatment of Sicilians who had come to Rome to lodge complaints against him before the Senate. Valerius couples his *moderatio* with *clementia* in observing that he 'received them mildly when they prayed and beseeched that they should be accepted by him as

[421] Lobur (2008) 201.

his clients' (*supplices et orantes ut ab eo in clientelam reciperentur clementer excepit*). Tiberius Gracchus follows (4.1.8), for not allowing his personal hostility to flavour his dealings with Scipio Asiaticus as one of the college of tribunes. At 4.1.9, C. Claudius Nero is presented as showing restraint in accepting public honours, specifically a triumph, on the grounds that although the Senate had voted for him to share equally in the triumph of Livius Salinator, Claudius Nero considered that the fact that the triumph had been awarded for success in Salinator's *provincia* should strictly speaking exclude him from participating in the triumph as an equal partner. It is worth noting here the coincidence of a Claudius Nero being cited for having refused a triumph and Velleius' praise of his descendant, Tiberius, for doing the same (2.122.1). This suggests that the contemporary world of Tiberian Rome is not forgotten even when recalling *exempla* from the Republican past. The *moderatio* of Scipio Africanus is then illustrated in the context of him holding censorial powers (4.1.10).

Having established in this way a whole series of *exempla* relating to the exercise of *moderatio* in public life by holders of official magisterial positions, Valerius only then turns to *exempla* that seem better to fit his description of *moderatio* at the start of the section. His postponement of such *exempla* draws readers' attention to alternative interpretations of *moderatio* in an effective manner. Having included a single *exemplum* of the exercise of *moderatio* by Q. Scaevola as witness in a lawsuit (4.1.11), Valerius pauses to acknowledge that his coverage of *moderatio* has been rather limited in scope (4.1.12): 'I realise what citizens are these, what acts and sayings of theirs, and in how narrow a verbal compass I am embracing them. But since I have to tell in brief so many tales of greatness, my pen, surrounded by an infinite number of persons and affairs, could not do both offices for men of outstanding renown' (*sentio quos ciues quaeue facta eorum ac dicta quam angusto ambitu orationis amplectar. sed cum magna mihi atque permulta breuiter dicenda sint, claritate excellentibus infinitis personis rebusque circumfusus <stilus> utrumque praestare non potuit*).[422] This draws further attention to the potential wider scope of *moderatio*.[423] Valerius' next two Roman *exempla* relate much more clearly to the theme of emotional control, with Metellus Macedonicus honouring the deceased Scipio Africanus despite personal enmity (4.1.12), and Metellus Numidicus displaying no signs of emotion on receiving a letter informing him that the Senate and people had granted him return to Rome from exile (4.1.13). But immediately afterwards, an *exemplum* of Cato the Younger reverts once again to the theme of observing correct electoral procedure (4.1.14). Finally, in his

---

[422] Trans. Shackleton Bailey (2000), following his textual emendations of this passage.
[423] Westphal (2015); Lucarelli (2007) 264–80 traces how *exempla* in other sections may add further to the diversity of contexts in which *moderatio* is presented in Valerius, but the *exempla* discussed do not allude to the term *moderatio* or cognate words.

6 The SCPP and the Creation of Tiberian Political Discourse

last Roman *exemplum*, Valerius marks the shift to foreign *exempla* by citing the case of M. Bibulus' restraint in his dealings with Cleopatra (4.1.15), but again what is at stake is his strict observance of the limits of his powers, in refusing to kill prisoners handed over to him 'saying that the power to punish them ought to belong not to him but to the Senate' (*dicendo potestatem huius uindicatae non suam sed senatus esse debere*).

When turning to his foreign *exempla*, however, Valerius brings into the foreground *exempla* that fit his initial definition of the virtue, as being able to control one's feelings. He cites a series of *exempla* of individuals who resist the urge to give way to anger, personal animosity, greed, and vanity. But even in the case of the foreign *exempla*, he still includes examples of *moderatio* in the wielding of political power, by citing Thrasybulus' granting of an amnesty to the Thirty Tyrants (4.1.ext.4). His final two *exempla* invite his readers to draw parallels between foreigners and Rome. Firstly, he compares the checks put upon the powers of kings at Sparta by Theopompus' introduction of ephors with the role of Roman plebeian tribunes in acting as a balance for consular power (4.1.ext.8). Finally, the section on *moderatio* ends with a reflection of the importance of *moderatio* for sustaining power, as King Antiochus affirms that he is happy for the size of his empire to be reduced by Rome, given that he has been freed from too large a responsibility (4.1.ext.9). This recalls Scipio's *moderatio* in conducting the *lustrum* as censor (4.1.10a), when instead of praying for the gods to increase and improve Rome's fortunes, he preferred to pray for the gods merely to protect Rome as it was, on the grounds that Rome's affairs were already 'sufficiently good and great' (*satis bonae et magnae sunt*). In this way, the political context for the exercise of *moderatio* bookends the presentation of the virtue, inviting reflection on *moderatio* primarily as a political rather than personal virtue.

What we see, then, in the case of *clementia* and *moderatio* in the Tiberian age is an exploration of what these virtues might mean. We may contrast this with the confident reaffirmation in the decrees passed by the Senate in AD 19 and 20 that members of the *domus Augusta* are all to be characterised by sharing in the same virtues, whether this be *humanitas*, *pietas*, *clementia*, or *moderatio*. Their possession of such virtues contributes to the Senate's perception that it is now appropriate to talk of the *maiestas* of the *domus Augusta* and of the imperial family's crucial role in safeguarding the Roman state (see above, §5).[424] Although *clementia* and *moderatio* are most prominent in Tiberian discourse, imperial virtues extend beyond these, and there is a striking overlap between what the Senate promotes in the *SCPP* and what is explored in other sources. But whereas the Senate might present an 'exposition' of imperial virtues,[425] other sources might

---

[424] *SCPP* lines 150–63; Potter (1999) 70–72.
[425] Potter (1999) 65 on public decrees 'as an important venue for the exposition of state ideology'.

offer more of an exploration. The very virtues highlighted as belonging to the imperial family in the *SCPP* – *moderatio, clementia, providentia, patientia, humanitas* – also feature in Valerius Maximus, as do other Tiberian themes such as *consensus, maiestas*, and military discipline, but Valerius' work on *exempla* engages with the ethical and moral debates that can be traced in his contemporary world, and makes a distinctive contribution to this discourse. As we have seen, Valerius does not simply reproduce existing *exempla*, but juxtaposes them in new ways.[426] Nor does Velleius just reproduce an official version of Tiberius' qualities, omitting the key virtue of *clementia* from his account. Contemporary sources illustrate that there was scope to debate what specific type of behaviour these virtues promoted. The importance of *clementia* and *moderatio* might be promoted across different media, but there could still be active discussion about what these virtues really signified. As Cowan has observed, the Principate did not 'arrive fully-formed in terms of either its political structures or its ideological or iconographical messages'.[427] Consequently, political discourse around imperial virtues shares similarities with the negotiation of the meaning of divine qualities, which allowed different constituencies to make sense of their own place in Roman society and to help to shape how their rulers might act.[428]

The same pattern of debating rather than replicating political discourse can also be traced in the case of *maiestas*. Like *clementia* and *moderatio*, the theme of *maiestas* looms large in accounts (both ancient and modern) of Rome under Tiberius.[429] Tacitus gives the sinister impression in his Tiberian books of the *Annales* of *maiestas* as an organic growth that reached maturity during these years, commenting in AD 17 that 'meanwhile, the law of *maiestas* was reaching maturity' (*Ann.* 2.50.1: *adolescebat interea lex maiestatis*).[430] But the idea that *maiestas* was distinctive under Tiberius is not just a perception building on the benefits of hindsight. Contemporary texts illustrate how *maiestas* appeared in new guises during this period. As discussed earlier (see §5), the Senate speaks of the *maiestas* of the *domus Augusta* in what is the first known attestation of this expression (*SCPP* lines 32–33). It was not just the Senate, though, that contributed to the transformation of *maiestas*, which remained an ambiguous concept.[431] Other Tiberian authors also engaged in the gradual morphing of the notion of *maiestas*. Ovid's celebration in AD 16 of the elevation of C. Pomponius Graecinus to the consulship represents Graecinus' dignity as derived from Tiberius' support for his election as consul (*Pont.* 4.9.68–69): 'the weightiness of its proposer multiplies this honour and the gift has the

---

[426] Illustrated by Langlands (2008); Gowing (2005) 59–62. [427] Cowan (2011a) xii.
[428] Clark (2007) 266.   [429] Levick (1999) chapter 10; Seager (2005) 125–37.
[430] As Goodyear (1981) 344 comments, ad loc.: 'This is no hackneyed metaphor but full personification.'
[431] Yakobson (2003).

6 *The SCPP and the Creation of Tiberian Political Discourse* 79

majesty of the giver' (*multiplicat tamen hunc grauitas auctoris honorem, / et maiestatem res data dantis habet*).[432] In this way, *maiestas* is associated with the person of Tiberius, whilst the *maiestas* of other officeholders – in this case a consul – is depicted in turn as drawing upon his quality. By contrast, for the freedman Phaedrus, writing his fables during the Tiberian era,[433] Tiberius' *maiestas* can be humorously invoked in describing his put-down of an obsequious slave (2.5.23): 'then the so great majesty of the leader joked in this way' (*tum sic iocata est tanta maiestas ducis*).

More curious, though, is the way in which Valerius Maximus thwarts our expectations in his section of *exempla* relating to *maiestas* at 2.10. Book 2 purports to relate to Rome's 'ancient and memorable institutions' (2 praef., *priscis ac memorabilibus institutis*), leading us to expect that the *exempla* in this section will illustrate *maiestas* as pertaining to the dignity of the *populus Romanus* and its office-holders. Instead of presenting *maiestas* as a quality to be protected in Roman office-holders by virtue of their role as representatives of the Roman state (*res publica*) – in other words with *maiestas* being by definition a public quality – Valerius offers a series of *exempla* that show how it is the behaviour of individuals which itself imbues public office with *maiestas*. He paradoxically introduces his section on the topic with the words (2.10.praef.), 'There is as well a sort of private censorship, the majesty of distinguished men, powerful in retaining its greatness without the rank of public office, without the service of public servants .... Someone would say rightly that it is a long and happy honour without the honour of office' (*est et illa quasi priuata censura, maiestas clarorum uirorum, sine tribunalium fastigio, sine apparitorum ministerio potens in sua amplitudine obtinenda .... quam recte qui dixerit longum et beatum honorem esse sine honore*). This is despite the fact that in various *exempla* that appear in the work before the section explicitly devoted to *maiestas*, Valerius Maximus includes prime examples of the traditional use of the concept. For instance, we find P. Vatienus being punished for being in contempt of the Senate's *maiestas* (1.8.1b). Then, at 2.2.2, magistrates are described as taking pains to retain their own *maiestas* and that of the *populus Romanus* through their behaviour in insisting on the use of Latin in discussions with Greeks. The *maiestas* of magistrates then recurs at 2.2.8 before we reach the section on *maiestas* at 2.10.

Having introduced the topic in an unexpected way, Valerius continues to his first *exemplum* of Metellus, accused of extortion. *Maiestas* itself is not mentioned in this paragraph, which concerns the jury's unwillingness to look at evidence since it considered that Metellus' own life-history should be enough to prove his integrity. The subsequent cluster of *exempla* all relate in turn to individuals whose *maiestas* was noted by non-Romans,

---

[432] Millar (1993) 14.
[433] For Phaedrus' chronology, see Henderson (2001) 11, contra Grimal (1980).

starting with respect shown to Scipio Africanus by King Antiochus and by pirate chiefs (2.10.2). This is followed (2.10.3) by Macedonian leaders paying their respects at the funeral of Aemilius Paullus at Rome and by Carthaginians and King Masinissa honouring the young Scipio Aemilianus, who had been sent as envoy to them (2.10.4). The *exempla* chosen demonstrate how individuals can be regarded as possessing *maiestas* even after they have left public office, as in the *exemplum* of Scipio Africanus in his retirement at Liternum (2.10.2b). The last two *exempla*, relating to Marius and Cato, similarly illustrate *maiestas* as a relatively woolly concept, relating to an individual's presence and virtuous reputation. Marius' *maiestas* saves him from being assassinated by a Cimbrian slave who was dazzled by his fame (2.10.6), whilst Cato's *maiestas* led to the crowd at the *Floralia* being ashamed of enjoying the antics of naked mime-actresses (2.10.8). In this way, the *exempla* devoted to illustrating the workings of *maiestas* among Romans unexpectedly explore the ways in which famous individuals' charismatic presence has an impact upon Romans and non-Romans alike.

Given that the technical meaning of *maiestas* is ignored in the Roman examples, we might therefore expect the subsequent section of external *exempla* to proceed in a similar vein. Only two external *exempla* follow (2.10.ext.1–2) – Harmodius / Aristogeiton, and Xenocrates – both from Athens. The word *maiestas* is not used: rather, *veneratio* is invoked in relation to the tyrannicides, whilst Xenocrates is honoured for his *sinceritas*. Despite Valerius' decision to eschew *exempla* demonstrating *maiestas* in its more traditional contexts in his Roman section, the implication remains, therefore, that *maiestas* is characteristic of Rome alone (compare the complete absence of external *exempla* in the sections on the exclusively Roman legal sphere of wills).[434]

Consequently, readers may be forgiven for becoming confused about what constitutes *maiestas* during the section explicitly devoted to the topic. This is despite the fact that in the rest of the work, Valerius reverts to more traditional uses of the term, with *maiestas* being used of the Senate (3.4.6 and 9.5.1), the *populus Romanus* (4.8.5), *imperium* (6.3.3a), and the *res publica* (6.4.2a and 9.2.3), whilst *maiestas publica* (6.5.4) is at stake when a tribune abuses his sacrosanctity by not paying his debts. Above all, in his section on witnesses, he draws vignettes of law cases concerning *maiestas* from 95 or 94 BC (8.5.2) and also 66 BC (8.5.4).[435] This tendency towards contradiction is typical of the work; it is not a sign of incompetence, but is intended to challenge readers to make sense of the ethical issues being presented to them.[436] As explored above, Valerius' ordering of *exempla* is also designed to stimulate ethical reflection among his readers. The shifting significance of *maiestas* from being a quality that is inseparable from public

---

[434] 7.7 *de testamentis quae rescissa sunt*; 7.8 *quae rata manserunt cum causas haberent cur rescindi possent*.
[435] Briscoe (2019) 117, 118 for these dates.   [436] Langlands (2008); (2018) chapter 12.

6 The SCPP and the Creation of Tiberian Political Discourse 81

office to being intrinsically a private quality mirrors the transition in contemporary society from an emphasis upon the ability of any member of the elite to attain the quality of *maiestas* through holding public office towards an awareness that members of the *domus Augusta* now might claim *maiestas* through simply belonging to the ultimate exemplary family.[437]

Similarly, in Velleius Paterculus' account of Tiberius' succession (2.124.1), it is precisely Tiberius' *maiestas* which is highlighted by Augustus. What we find, then, is that a through-reading of Valerius Maximus implicitly opens up a debate about how *maiestas* functions in a similar way to how he encourages discussion and debate about ethics.[438] The unexpected use of *maiestas* seen in the specific section on the topic, as encapsulating the inherent dignity and status of an individual, does recur once more later in the book. Valerius uses *maiestas* in this sense to refer to Iulius Caesar in relating (9.8.2) that Caesar chose to make a rash sea voyage in 47 BC, disguising his *maiestas* with the garb of a slave. This recalls the earlier cases of Marius and Scipio, with *maiestas* being a personal quality rather than one associated with *imperium*, and sets the scene for the possibility of this quality becoming characteristic of the Julio-Claudians who claimed descent from Caesar.

In this way, although the vast majority of his *exempla* are drawn from Republican times, Valerius also incorporates glimpses of the new political reality, in particular recognising that the *princeps* and his family occupy a unique place as exemplary figures for the rest of society.[439] In relating *exempla* from his own times, his inclusion of members of the *domus Augusta* as exemplary figures almost to the exclusion of any other is complemented by the way in which the Senate in the *SCPP* sets up the imperial family as playing a uniquely exemplary role for the rest of Roman society. This combination of the idea of the *domus Augusta* and its exemplarity might be taken to justify why members of the *domus Augusta*, whatever their gender or age, could be regarded as possessing *maiestas* because of their exemplary behaviour rather than as a result of their role as representatives of the state (*res publica*). The exceptional character of the whole of the *domus Augusta* makes sense within the context of Roman belief in the family as the unit within which virtues (and vices) might be passed down.[440]

Whereas previous studies have focused upon the role of the Senate in creating a new language of power in collaboration with Tiberius,[441] we may

---

[437] Compare Bloomer (1992) 22–23.
[438] On reading Valerius Maximus sequentially, see Morgan (2007) 264. Ethical debate illustrated by Langlands (2008); (2018) chapter 13; Wardle (1997).
[439] Bloomer (1992) 3, 9, 11–12.
[440] Cooley (1998) 205–09. Compare also Velleius' focus on patterns of behaviour shared by fathers and sons, and the idea of the ancestral *imagines* on display in the *atrium* as an inspiration to later generations, as expressed in Val. Max. 5.8.3.
[441] See, for example, Corbier (2006) chapter 7, for the new political formulas devised by Senate and emperor.

also trace how other parts of society explored the values to be wished for in their leaders. Even if we accept the premise that the Senate intended to influence public opinion by publishing its decrees,[442] other texts suggest that the Senate's views were not simply digested and replicated without further thought. The political discourse that emerges in the age of Tiberius, therefore, reveals a complex picture of negotiation and discussion whereby the dominance of Tiberius and the imperial family in Roman politics and society is justified. In this way, it fits into the pattern outlined by Cowan whereby the Tiberian era can be especially characterised as one in which ethical and moral issues were keenly debated.[443] The joint development of the *domus Augusta* and of *maiestas*, along with the ethical view that Tiberius and his family were to be regarded as moral exemplars, illustrates a distinctive feature of Tiberian political discourse.

7 THE PUNISHMENTS OF PISO

One of the most detailed sections of the *SCPP* is the passage in which the Senate sets out the additional penalties to be imposed upon Piso after his death (*SCPP* lines 71–108; see also commentary on 'Posthumous punishments for Piso').[444] It seems likely that the statutory penalty for someone convicted under the *lex Iulia maiestatis* at this time was interdiction.[445] This involved confiscation of property and exile,[446] as was pronounced against Piso's accomplices, Visellius Karus and Sempronius Bassus (*SCPP* lines 120–23). By committing suicide before being convicted, however, Piso was endeavouring to protect his property.[447] As Griffin observes, the treatment of Piso was a 'foreshadowing of the later legal situation ... whereby the general rule regarding concessions to death (including suicide) will regularly be waived in cases where it is held that the accused was aware of his guilt and was seeking to avoid the proper penalty by suicide'.[448] This explains why the Senate is so insistent upon Piso's manifest guilt, as a way of justifying both their confiscation of his property (even though this was then mostly restored to Piso's heirs by the Senate and Tiberius) and their imposition of further penalties. Flexibility in imposing penalties had been previously shown in the case of Libo Drusus, whose entire property had been distributed to his prosecutors.[449] One of the many problems with

---

[442] Giua (2002) 103–15 on the Senate's emerging communicative strategies in this period.
[443] Cowan (2016) esp. 79.
[444] Flower (1998); (2006) 132–38; Bodel (1999); Castro-Camero (2000) 129–39; G.P. Kelly (2006) 25–39.
[445] Contra, Levick (1979) argues that *maiestas* entailed the death penalty.
[446] Chilton (1955); Allison and Cloud (1962) 723; Bauman (1996) 21; Castro-Camero (2000) 53–139.
[447] For the legal principle, cf. Tac., *Ann.* 6.29.1 (AD 34).   [448] Griffin (1997) 263.
[449] Tac., *Ann.* 2.32.1, with Goodyear (1981) 280 ad loc., who observes that the implication that the whole of Libo's property was disposed of in this way is not standard procedure, however: 'possibly the whole was divided because the estate was impoverished'.

the implementation of the *maiestas* law, therefore, was the way in which there was flexibility for the Senate to recommend further penalties. In the case of Piso, the Senate sets out a whole series of tailor-made sanctions against him, in recognition that by his suicide he was considered to have escaped the severe penalties which would otherwise have been inflicted upon him. These include the following measures: Piso's death was not to be mourned by the women of his household; statues and portraits representing Piso, wherever they exist, should be removed; Piso's *imago* should not be included at any funeral of a member of his family nor displayed in any *atrium*;[450] Piso's name should be removed from beneath the statue of Germanicus set up by the *sodales Augustales* next to the altar of *Providentia* on the Field of Mars;[451] a woodland in Illyricum, which Augustus had given to Piso, should be returned to Tiberius. The initial recommendation by the Senate that the rest of Piso's property should be publicly confiscated was immediately modified, so that between them, Piso's two sons and his daughter (or granddaughter: see 104–05n., *n(ummum) (decies centena milia) dotis nomine Calpurniae Cn(aei) Pisonis filiae*) were instead granted the property 'in the name of the *Princeps* and the Senate'. This was provisional upon Gnaeus Piso *filius* changing his *praenomen*. Lastly, an extension to Piso's house which he had built above the Fontinal Gate was to be destroyed. In this way, the Senate targeted Piso *pater* individually, but did not punish his family. Tacitus also adds further details about potential penalties which were proposed in the Senate but turned down by Tiberius. These included erasing Piso's name from the *fasti*, and dedicating a golden statue in the Temple of Mars the Avenger and an altar of Vengeance (*Ann.* 3.17.4–18.2). Tacitus' statement that 'many aspects of the proposal were modified by the *princeps*' (3.18.1: *multa ex ea sententia mitigata sunt a principe*) fits with the hint of Tiberius' intervention in the *SCPP* (lines 90–92), where the Senate describes that its proposal for Gnaeus *filius* reflects the fact that it is 'mindful of its clemency, justice, and generosity of spirit, virtues which it had inherited from its ancestors and also learned in particular from deified Augustus and Tiberius Caesar Augustus, its Principes' (*memorem clementiae suae iustitiaeq(ue) <atq(ue)> animi magnitudinis, quas virtutes {quas} a maioribus suis accepisset, tum praecipue ab divo Aug(usto) et Ti(berio) Caesare Aug(usto) principibus suis didicisset*). This especially applies where the Senate explains that in its treatment of Marcus, it is acting 'in agreement with the humanity and restraint of its Princeps' (*SCPP* lines 100–01: *humanitati et moderationi principis sui adsensus*). These hints from the Senate that its clemency towards the sons of Piso is inspired by Tiberius are later transformed in Tacitus' account of the penalties, which is designed to draw attention to Tiberius' alleged favouritism towards Piso.[452]

---

[450] Flower (1996) 23–31.   [451] Östenberg (2019).   [452] Woodman and Martin (1996) 187.

The penalties selected by the Senate and approved by Tiberius were individually tailored for Piso and were intended to dishonour him in far-reaching and long-lasting ways.[453] The penalties appear in a unique combination, suggesting that the Senate had particular aims in mind in imposing these specific punishments. This selectivity can be made clear by comparing Piso's penalties and those imposed upon M. Scribonius Libo Drusus a few years earlier, the most recent comparable case and the first major case of *maiestas* under Tiberius.[454] In AD 16, Libo Drusus had been accused of plotting against the state. Although Tacitus characterises Libo Drusus as a 'thoughtless man prone to idle illusions' (*iuuenem inprouidum et facilem inanibus*),[455] whilst the Younger Seneca reinforces this with his description of him as 'a young man as stupid as he was noble' (*adulescentis tam stolidi quam nobilis*),[456] the serious charges against him included consulting astrologers and speculating about the life spans of members of the imperial family and Senate. On being tried in the Senate, Libo Drusus anticipated a guilty verdict by committing suicide, after which Tiberius declared that he had intended to pardon him. Tacitus records that the following penalties were proposed in the Senate: his property was to be confiscated and distributed to his prosecutors; his *imago* banned from family funerals;[457] his *cognomen* Drusus banned among the Scribonii; a day of thanksgiving prayers to be held; gifts to be made to Jupiter, Mars, and Concordia; and finally, the date of his suicide to be celebrated. As observed above in the case of Piso, we cannot be certain which of these penalties were actually imposed, but the *Fasti Amiterni* for 13 September confirm the celebration of the suppression of Libo Drusus' wicked plans (*nefaria consilia* – anticipating the same language used by the Senate for Piso, *SCPP* line 13) against the welfare of Tiberius, his children, and other leading figures in the state (*de salute Ti. Caes. liberorumque eius et aliorum principum ciuitatis*).[458] Apart from the ban on his *imago*, the penalties against Libo Drusus differ from those imposed on Piso, whilst even the ban relating to his personal name is different in character. Whereas Piso's *praenomen* was removed from his family, in Libo Drusus' case, it was his *cognomen* that was banned for future Scribonii. This is likely to reflect the Senate's desire

---

[453] On the flexibility of sanctions against an individual's memory, Flower (1998) 156; (2006) chapters 1, 4, 6; Roller (2010) 120 n.9; Östenberg (2019) 331–32.

[454] *PIR*² S268; Tac., *Ann.* 2.27–32; Velleius moves rapidly from the *scelerata consilia* of Drusus Libo to Piso, 2.130.3; for the seriousness of the case, see Pettinger (2012).

[455] Tac., *Ann.* 2.27.2, trans. Goodyear (1981) 265 ad loc., who points out that *iuuenem* indicates 'no stripling perhaps, since he was ready for a praetorship'.

[456] Sen., *Ep.* 70.10.   [457] Pettinger (2012) 39–40.

[458] *Fasti* from *Amiternum* = *Inscr.It.* XIII.2, 193, no.25: 'Holiday in accordance with a decree of the Senate, because on this day the wicked plans begun by Marcus Libo concerning the safety of Tiberius Caesar and his children and other leaders of the state and concerning the state, were exposed' (*fer(iae) ex s(enatus) c(onsulto) q(uod) e(o) d(ie) nefaria consilia quae de salute Ti. Caes(aris) liberorumq(ue) eius et aliorum principum civitatis deq(ue) r(e) p(ublica) inita ab M. Libone erant in senatu convicta sunt*).

7 *The Punishments of Piso*

to remove the *cognomen* Drusus specifically because this name was shared by members of the imperial family.[459] The penalty on Piso's *praenomen*, as explored below, was quite different in aim.

At the same time, each of Piso's penalties recalled those imposed on earlier disgraced individuals, inviting comparison between them and Piso. The ban on mourning (see 73–74n., *ne quis luctus mortis eius causa a feminis*) may have brought to mind the ban on women from the families of Gaius Gracchus and his followers from mourning the deceased, but parallels between Piso and Gracchus were complicated, and penalties inflicted against Gracchus extended to his supporters and families too.[460] On the one hand, comparing Piso and Gracchus could have heightened the sense that Piso had posed a serious threat to the stability of Roman society, and that he had become alienated from the rest of Rome's senatorial elite. On the other hand, it seems unlikely that Piso had enjoyed widespread support among the plebs that had mourned the death of Germanicus so effusively. In fact, there seems to be a fundamental mismatch between the two cases, with sanctions against Gaius Gracchus trying to forestall the possibility of a resurgence of popular support for his political agenda. The Senate's phrasing (*SCPP* lines 73–75), 'that no mourning for his death be undertaken by the women by whom he should have been mourned, in accordance with ancestral custom, had this decree of the Senate not been passed' (*ne quis luctus mortis eius causa a feminis quibus {e}is more maiorum, si hoc senatus consultum factum non esset, lugendus esset, susciperetur*), understandably avoids drawing attention to Piso's widow, the co-accused Plancina, and has the effect of excluding Piso from membership of his family.[461] It seems more likely therefore that the ban on mourning Piso was not primarily intended to recall the similar sanction imposed on Gaius Gracchus. Instead, the fact that Piso is condemned by the Senate on the grounds that he alone had not mourned the death of Germanicus (*SCPP* lines 57–68) must have made the idea that he in turn would not be mourned seem appropriate in the context.

The ban on mourning is complemented by the ban on Piso's *imago* (see 75–76n., *utiq(ue) statuae et imagines Cn(aei) Pisonis patris, quae ubiq(ue) positae essent, tollerentur*). The wax mask of an office-holding member of Rome's senatorial class would normally have been created during his lifetime and displayed in the *atrium* of houses belonging to members of his family, along with the *imagines* of past generations.[462] These played a prominent role at funerals of that family's members. The famous passage in Polybius (6.53–54) describing aristocratic Roman funerals illustrates how

---
[459] Solin (1995) 198.
[460] It is unclear whether Plut., *Vit. C. Gracc.* 17 refers to just the widows or the women in the family more widely: ἀπεῖπαν δὲ πενθεῖν ταῖς γυναιξί; Bodel (1999) 46. On the extensive penalties against Gracchus, Flower (2006) 76–81.
[461] Flower (1998) 159.   [462] Plin., *HN* 35.6–8; Flower (1996) 2.

the younger generation was to be inspired by their ancestors' deeds: at an aristocratic funeral, actors donned the *imagines* of the ancestors and were part of the audience at the eulogy, which not only praised the life of the recently deceased, but also renewed the memory of his ancestors. An *imago* therefore was intended to spur on future generations to emulate the virtues of their forebears. The repetition of this thematic motif in Sallust's *Jugurtha* (4.5–6) illustrates that this continued to be perceived as the impact of gazing upon the *imagines* of one's ancestors. By banning his *imago*, therefore, the Senate was also preventing Piso's life history from being passed down via eulogies at funerals of his family members. The potential role of ancestral *imagines* in encouraging dangerous ambitions features in Tacitus' account of Libo Drusus: one of the ways in which Firmius Catus is represented as framing his 'friend' is by reminding him of his 'house filled with *imagines*' (*Ann.* 2.27.2, *plenam imaginibus domum ostentat*). Banning an *imago* from a family's funeral, however, was not guaranteed to secure the individual's absence from memory: Tacitus observes that the *imagines* of Brutus and Cassius 'shone out' (*praefulgebant*) all the more brightly through their absence from the funeral of Iunia, wife of Cassius and sister of Brutus, in AD 22.[463] The Senate does not mandate the destruction of Piso's *imago*, but prohibits it from being displayed in private or public.[464] It is unusual for the Senate to intervene in what would normally be a family affair: its awareness that it is over-stepping its traditional sphere of influence is perhaps reflected in the wording, whereby the Senate advises the family that by removing Piso's *imago* from the family's repertoire of *imagines*, it would be acting 'rightly and properly' (*SCPP* line 76: *recte et ordine*).[465]

The Senate also extends its sanctions beyond the specific medium of the wax *imago*, which was primarily associated with an individual's family, in instructing that all statues and portraits of Piso (*statuae et imagines*) should be destroyed.[466] This relates to portrait statues and busts set up in domestic or public spaces by Piso himself, his family, and his clients or dependents, or as public honours. This sanction was potentially much more political in its significance than the other measures discussed so far, reflecting the way in which an individual's portrait could remind viewers of a political agenda.[467] This had been clearly illustrated at the trial of the plebeian tribune Sextus Titius in 98 BC, who was accused of keeping a portrait (*imago*) of the radical tribune L. Appuleius Saturninus in his house, despite being no relation.[468] This was taken as an indicator of Titius' revolutionary intent,

---

[463] Tac., *Ann.* 3.76. [464] Flower (1998) 161. [465] Bodel (1999) 48.
[466] *Imagines* here refers to portrait busts in other materials (bronze, marble), distinct from the wax masks of the previous sanction.
[467] The political significance of *imagines* is emphasised by Gregory (1994) 90–93, but their ethical implications were just as significant.
[468] Flower (2006) 81–85.

explained by Cicero (*Rab. Post.* 9.24) in the way in which he 'either honoured his death, or stirred up with compassion the regrets of the ignorant, or made known his own desire to imitate his wickedness' (*aut mortem eius honestaret, aut desideria imperitorum misericordia commoueret, aut suam significaret imitandae improbitatis uoluntatem*). Valerius Maximus (8.1.damn.3) even suggests that Titius was innocent, but that the *imago* of Saturninus was enough to turn the whole assembly against him, in its anxiety that memories of the tribune could stir up resistance and unrest. This demonstrates that the sentiment that a portrait could send out a strong political message was present in the Tiberian thought-world of Valerius. The destruction of Piso's statues also explains the Senate's claim that Piso had escaped penalties worse than death by his suicide. By this the Senate may have been alluding to Piso's avoidance of execution, as well as even the mutilation of his corpse. Tacitus narrates how a lynch-mob, which had congregated outside the Senate-house during Piso's trial, had already started toppling Piso's statues, dragging them towards the Tiber for a symbolic traitor's death: 'they had dragged down Piso's likenesses onto the Gemonian steps and were ripping them apart, had they not been protected and put back in place by the *princeps'* command' (*effigiesque Pisonis traxerant in Gemonias ac diuellebant, ni iussu principis protectae repositaeque forent*).[469] The Gemonian steps were the location where the bodies of executed criminals would be left exposed. Tacitus' syntax here is ambiguous as to what actually happened: the sentence starts with indicative pluperfect and imperfect tenses, so that the reader thinks that this is an account of what really took place, only suddenly to change direction with a shift to the subjunctive mood, which then implies that the statues were not in fact dismantled. The syntax thus emphasises the violence of the mob and their grim determination to punish Piso, recalling the fate of Gaius Gracchus' body, which had been unceremoniously dumped into the Tiber, and foreshadowing Sejanus' fate just a few years later.[470] In this way, Piso's statues become a kind of proxy for his person, showing how the plebs had started to anticipate the death penalty by attacking Piso's statues even whilst the trial was still in session.[471] The Senate's measures against Piso's statues after his death may represent an attempt by the Senate to control reactions in the streets of Rome, by making attacks on the statues an official policy, thereby forestalling further popular violence.

Having mandated the removal of all statues and likenesses of Piso, the Senate adds instructions about erasing his name from one specific inscription (see 82–83n., *utiq(ue) nomen Cn(aei) Pisonis patris tolleretur ex titulo*

---

[469] Tac., *Ann.* 3.14.4.
[470] Vell. Pat. 2.6.7 (Gaius Gracchus' body cast into the Tiber); Cass. Dio 58.11.3–5 (attacks on Sejanus' statues closely followed by similar attacks on his person).
[471] Gregory (1994) 96–97.

statuae Germanici Caesaris). Whereas the destruction of Piso's statues may also have entailed destroying any inscribed bases associated with them, together with his name, the Senate does not undertake a wider erasure of his name from other inscriptions, even though as Tiberius' co-consul in 7 BC Piso's name appeared on monuments set up at Rome and elsewhere. The Senate does not insist that Piso's name should be erased from every inscription that it appears in – after all, the *SCPP* itself contains Piso's name over twenty times – but requires his name to be removed from beneath a statue set up in honour of Germanicus by the *sodales Augustales* (*SCPP* lines 82–84). The reason for targeting this monument is likely to have been the hostility between the two men, which resulted in Germanicus formally renouncing his friendship with Piso (*SCPP* lines 26–29), along with the social context of the *sodales*, whose members comprised leading representatives of the senatorial elite and imperial family alike (see §2).[472] This would have made it incongruous for Piso's name to appear on this statue base, which must have been set up relatively recently, in the period after Augustus' death in AD 14 and before Germanicus left for the East in AD 17, and so is likely to have been fresh in the minds of senators in AD 20.[473] Tacitus does not mention any of this, but records instead (*Ann.* 3.17.4–18.1) a proposal in the Senate for Piso's name to be erased from the *fasti*, which Tiberius rejects on the grounds that Augustus had set a precedent for not deleting names from the *fasti* in his treatment of Antony.[474] In this way, Tacitus continues to create the impression of favouritism on the part of Tiberius towards Piso, as mentioned earlier.

Other inscriptions allow us to track a variety of responses to the Senate's sanctions against Piso, revealing a willingness in some cases to go beyond the penalties decreed by the Senate.[475] Having served as consul jointly with Tiberius in 7 BC, Piso's name appeared as part of official dating formulae on some public monuments. It is erased, for example, from an inscribed base commemorating votive games for Augustus' return to Rome in 7 BC, where Piso's name appears alongside that of Tiberius as co-consul.[476] As is usually the case with memory sanctions, the process does not appear to have been systematic, since Piso's name is retained alongside that of Tiberius on another inscription from 7 BC relating to the presentation of a golden crown to an individual whose name is erased.[477] Piso's name

---

[472] See above, §2, for discussion of Piso's possible erasure from the Arval *acta* in Rome, a context which would similarly have integrated Piso with leading members of the imperial family.
[473] Flower (1998) 162.
[474] On the over-hasty deletion and then reinscription of Antony's name from the *fasti*, see Östenberg (2019) 333–38; cf. Flower (2006) 116–21 on Antony's name in inscriptions more widely.
[475] Flower (1998) 162–63.   [476] *CIL* VI 385; Kajava (1995) 202.
[477] *CIL* VI 7461: ------ /⟦[---]⟧*ex d(ecreto) d(ecurionum) et populi sc[itu] / corona aurea h(onoris) c(ausa) data est Ti(berio) Nerone Cn(aeo) Pi[sone co(n)s(ulibus)]*, found in the vigna Amendola along the via Appia. The possibility should not be excluded that the inscription had been reused already by AD 20.

7 The Punishments of Piso

is equally unaffected on the inscribed *fasti* of a set of *magistri vici*. This includes a list of consuls from 43 BC to AD 3 and a list of *magistri vici* from 7 BC (when they were founded, which just happens to be the year of the joint consulship of Piso and Tiberius, and so is therefore fairly prominent on the stone at the top of a column) down to AD 21.[478] The latest addition in AD 21 shows that the inscription was still on display at the time of Piso's trial, so we might have expected his name to be erased, especially given the cult's close associations with Augustus, who 'gave the *Lares Augusti* to the neighbourhood magistrates', a phrase immediately preceding the consular names of Tiberius and Piso on the inscription. The unexplained erasure of the names of the suffect consuls for 2 BC, L. Caninius and C. Fufius, shows that the inscription was not immune from such alteration. This inconsistent pattern regarding Piso's name on inscriptions in Rome suggests that erasure could be carried out on private initiative, reflecting a sensitivity towards Piso that went beyond instructions issued by the Senate. The same pattern can be seen in the provinces, where sometimes the initiative is taken to go beyond the sanctions imposed by the Senate.[479] The most prominent example of the erasure of Piso's name is a highly visible dedication to Augustus which Piso had set up in AD 9/10 at Campa Torres (Gijón, Asturias) in Tarraconensis (see above, §4), which may originally have been part of a lighthouse.[480] The monument's prominence, its association with Augustus, and the fact that Piso had earlier been governor of Tarraconensis perhaps explain why this inscription was modified after Piso's condemnation. By contrast, a large inscription set in the paving of the Old Forum of Lepcis Magna in AD 4/5 or 5/6 not only retained Piso's name – possibly a practical measure given the type of lettering, set into the paving – but was even preserved and relocated during the Claudian era.[481] Piso's name remained in view despite the fact that the inscription was close to the Temple of Rome and Augustus, founded in AD 14–19 by members of the local elite, with its statues of Roma, Augustus, Tiberius, Iulia Augusta, Germanicus, Drusus, Antonia, and Agrippina.[482] This might have seemed indelicate following Germanicus' death, but it seems that the local elite of Lepcis were either unaware of or unconcerned about the juxtaposition of honours for the imperial family next to a monumental inscription put in place by Piso himself.

The Senate gives detailed instructions about demolishing only part of Piso's house, targeting 'the structure which Gnaeus Piso Senior had built above the Fontinal Gate to connect private residences' (*SCPP* lines 105–08: *Cn(aeus) Piso pater supra portam Fontinalem quae inaedificasset iungendarum domum privatarum causa*) (see Figs 9–10). Various reasons for

---

[478] Liverani (2012) = *CIL* VI 10286–87. [479] Kajava (1995).
[480] *CIL* II 2703, with Kajava (1995) 205; Fernández Ochoa, Morillo Cerdán, Villa Valdés (2005).
[481] *IRT2009* 520; Di Vita-Évrard (1990). [482] Jongeling (2008) 23 Labdah N14.

this have been presented. One possibility is that this structure was demolished because it had been built illegally on top of a public structure, the Fontinal Gate in the Servian Wall.[483] This would be consistent with the premise articulated in the *Digest* by the third-century jurist Ulpian that if an individual builds a structure on top of another one belonging to someone else, the additional structure then becomes the property of whoever also owns both the ground surface and original structure ('because what is on the surface belongs to the owner of the ground', *quod superficies ad dominum soli pertinent*).[484] On this interpretation, Piso's additional structure would become public property because it had been built on top of a public structure, and so liable to demolition by the Senate. The sanction imposed by the Senate thus becomes the solution to a legal dispute over property ownership. Another possibility is that this was the only structure built by Piso himself, and so this is why it was targeted and not other parts of the house as well.[485] It seems likely, however, that any mention of demolishing even part of a house would summon the ghosts of infamous individuals from Rome's past – notably, Sp. Cassius, Sp. Maelius, and M. Manlius Capitolinus – accused of aiming for kingship, who had been penalised by the demolition of their houses. As Roller suggests, 'the sanction may still have caused a Roman reader to recall the tradition of kingship-aspirants'.[486] In addition, M. Fulvius Flaccus and L. Saturninus had been penalised in this way more recently following their stirring up of civil disturbance at Rome.[487] The vivid vignette painted by Tacitus of Piso's house lit up for partying on his return to Rome before his trial also draws attention to the way in which Piso may have used his house as a focal point for rallying support to his cause.[488] This would also have recalled the activities of ambitious individuals in the past, who had used their houses to increase their political power via strengthening their social networks and for practical activities like gathering together weaponry.[489] Livy's account of Sp. Maelius, for instance, puts his house firmly in the limelight: 'weapons were being brought together into Maelius' house, he was holding assemblies at home, and there were certain plans for kingship' (4.13.9: *tela in domum Maeli conferri, eumque contiones domi habere, ac non dubia regni consilia esse*). This echo of past would-be kings takes on even more resonance given the topographical context of Piso's house and its extension. The detail in the *SCPP* about the Fontinal Gate, described by Tacitus as 'looming over the forum' (*domus foro imminens*), narrows down its location further. As Bodel summarises it, 'The Porta Fontinalis spanned the road known as the Clivus Argentarius (Lautumiarum) where it crossed the shoulder of the Arx on the east side of the Capitoline and formed the principal access

---

[483] Eck, Caballos, Fernández (1996) 207–10; Flower (1998) 169; Castro-Camero (2000) 133–34.
[484] *Dig.* 9.2.50 [Ulpian].   [485] Flower (1998) 169–70.   [486] Roller (2010) 174 n.139.
[487] Bodel (1999) 59–60.   [488] Tac., *Ann.* 3.9.3.   [489] Roller (2010) 125–33, 137.

7 The Punishments of Piso

through the Servian Wall from the Campus Martius via the via Flaminia to the Forum.'[490] In other words, it seems likely that one of the structures being joined up by Piso was located upon the Capitoline Hill.[491] If this is correct, then this would have given the Senate another good reason to demolish the structure because, since the downfall of Manlius Capitolinus in 384 BC and the destruction of his house on the Capitol, patrician families had been forbidden from owning a house on the Capitoline.[492] Piso's building-work encroaching on the Capitol may therefore have seemed all the more criminal if it is correct that Piso's family had become patrician in 29 BC.[493] Although, therefore, it is possible to give a sober legalistic interpretation of the demolition of Piso's house in terms of its encroachment upon public space, this sanction is also likely to have recalled crimes of sedition, treason, and kingly aspirations that may have contributed to the Senate's depiction of Piso as uniquely wicked (see also 106n., *supra portam Fontinalem* and 106–07n., *quae inaedificasset iungendarum domum privatarum causa*).

The figure of Manlius Capitolinus also lurks in the background of the instruction by the Senate that Piso's elder son should change his *praenomen* (see 99–100n., *recte atque ordine facturum, si praenomen patris mutasset*), since as well as demolishing his house a ban had also been self-imposed by the Manlii ('by decree of the *gens*') on using the *praenomen* Marcus following his condemnation in 384 BC.[494] The sanction reflects the gravity of the charges against the erstwhile hero of the Gallic siege in 390 BC. Livy narrates how Manlius Capitolinus had been accused of being motivated by an overblown sense of his own importance and personal jealousy towards Camillus to aspire towards personal power by cosying up to the plebs and stirring them up against the Senate.[495] The Claudii had also decided to avoid the *praenomen* Lucius on their own initiative as a family following two individuals of that name being convicted of murder and brigandage.[496] More recently, though, the same penalty had been imposed by senatorial decree rather than on the initiative of a family, when the Antonii were forbidden from using the *praenomen* Marcus after Antony's final defeat at Alexandria in 30 BC.[497] In the case of Piso, the Senate advises his elder son Gnaeus to change his *praenomen* so as to allow him to distance himself

---

[490] Bodel (1999) 58.
[491] Recent evidence relating to houses on the Capitol presented by Tucci (2019) 76–77, 91–92.
[492] Livy 6.20.13; Val. Max. 6.3.1a.
[493] Rüpke (2008) 593 n.3; cf. *RGDA* 8.1 and for a list of the new patrician families created in 29 BC, including the Calpurnii Pisones, Scheid (2007) 39. Eck, Caballos, Fernández (1996) 72 are sceptical that Augustus raised the family to patrician rank.
[494] Cic., *Phil.* 1.32; Livy 6.20.14. Aulus Gellius cites the explanation of this phenomenon by Herodes Atticus at *NA* 9.2.11 as being a move by patrician families to cancel out the name of a family member executed for treasonous activity.
[495] Livy 6.11, 14–20; Roller (2010) 128. Name changes among Rome's elite discussed by Solin (1989) and in more detail (1995).
[496] Suet., *Tib.* 1–2.   [497] Plut., *Vit. Cic.* 49.4; Cass. Dio 51.19.3; Flower (2006) 116–17.

from his disgraced father. The Senate expresses the view that Piso's son has already 'made it possible to hope that he would turn out very different from his father' (*SCPP* line 97: *sperari posset, dissimillumum eum patri suo futurum*), on the basis of his impeccable behaviour to date. The significance of the change demanded of Piso's elder son therefore lies in the idea that he will be all the more able to shake off any temptation to imitate his father's moral failings in this way. The hope expressed by the Senate that he will be 'very different' (*dissimillumum*) from his father contrasts starkly with the language in which Gaius Caesar was lamented by the Pisans a few years earlier on his death in AD 4. Their comment that he was 'already designated as a leader most just and most like his father in his virtues' (*iam designatu[m i]ustissumum ac simillumum parentis sui virtutibus principem*)[498] pinpoints the stark contrast between Pisones and Caesares: whereas Augustus was regarded as the positive exemplar for the younger generations of his family, Piso was to be remembered only as a negative *exemplum*. The fact that Piso's elder son went on to enjoy a high-flying political career (see §8) shows that he successfully distanced himself from his father's fate.[499] Although the Senate's decree mentions only the son changing his *praenomen*, the absence of Gnaeus in future generations of Calpurnii Pisones implies that the avoidance of Gnaeus became general family policy.[500] The change of *praenomen* was even in time projected retrospectively onto Piso himself: in the customs law of Asia, of AD 62, Gnaeus Piso himself is listed as Lucius alongside Tiberius as consul for 7 BC.[501] The fact that this text from Ephesos was explicitly copied and certified from official documents kept in the archives of the curators of public revenues in the *basilica Iulia* (lines 1–3) illustrates how thorough the removal of the *praenomen* Gnaeus was at Rome at least. By contrast, a fragment of the municipal *fasti* from Teanum Sidicum in Campania, where the name of Piso as co-consul with Tiberius in 7 BC is inscribed as C. Calpurn[ius Piso] rather than Cn., more likely reflects a stonecutter's error than a conscious change of *praenomen*.[502] Although the *fasti Ostienses* were recarved after Domitian's assassination so as to allow his name to be recut in a new format as simply Domitianus, omitting his imperial titles, to reflect his downfall and to detract from his imperial status,[503] it seems unlikely that the *fasti* at Teanum would be recarved just for Piso's name to be modified in 7 BC, particularly since the *praenomen* recorded is Gaius rather than Lucius.

In order to understand why this particular set of penalties was imposed on Piso, therefore, we need to consider both what the Senate writes about its motivations and what deductions can be drawn from parallel cases. On the one hand, the Senate does not actually declare that it is its aim to erase Piso from the collective memory of Roman society; rather, the Senate attempts

---

[498] *CIL* XI 1421.   [499] *PIR*² C293.   [500] Solin (1986) 72.   [501] *AE* (2008) 1353, line 109.
[502] Camodeca (2008) 327–29 = *AE* (2008) 387.   [503] Flower (2006) 249–52.

7 The Punishments of Piso

to modify how Piso was remembered.[504] The Senate summarises its decree at the start as aiming to display 'how the case of Gnaeus Piso Senior had been regarded and whether he was regarded as having taken his own life deservedly', and introduces the section on penalties with the words that 'it was the opinion of the Senate that he had not undergone the punishment he deserved but had saved himself from the harsher one which he inferred from the devotion to duty and the strictness of the judges was threatening him; therefore it adds to the punishments which he had inflicted on himself'. In its concluding remarks, the Senate states that its aim in publishing the decree is to hand down memory of Germanicus and Piso. The apparent contradiction has often been commented on, between on the one hand the Senate's desire to erase memory of Piso and, on the other, to publish details of his crimes and wicked behaviour.[505] Sanctions against memory are often contradictory, but in this case the Senate's overall aim is clear, namely to perpetuate the memory of Piso as a negative *exemplum*.[506] Alongside the wider penalty imposed upon Piso's statues and portraits in general, some of the other penalties inflicted on Piso are remarkably specific: the Senate singles out an individual inscription from which Piso's name should be erased; a specific estate is confiscated; a particular part of Piso's house is to be demolished. Above all, the penalties are directed towards removing Piso from his family and are focused upon rituals and monuments in the city of Rome.[507]

The Senate appears, therefore, to have precise aims in its choice of penalties. Above all, the Senate was not intending to 'expunge the memory of the condemned', but to abolish his memory in specific ways. First of all, memory of Piso is removed from his family context by banning mourning, his *imago*, and his *praenomen*. The overall impact of these sanctions altering family behaviour was effectively to remove memory of Piso from his family. This was important given the attitude among the elite that normally a son would be expected to inherit his father's character. By emphasising that Gnaeus Piso *filius* had already behaved in a way most unlike his father, having worked amicably with Germanicus, the Senate opened up the possibility that he was likely to continue behaving in a manner most unlike his father for the future too. Changing his *praenomen* was designed to reinforce this tendency. The Senate was not trying to ensure that Piso *pater* was forgotten by Roman society more generally – on the contrary, he was to be vigorously remembered as a villain whose behaviour isolated him from the rest of decent society – but it was concerned to remove him from family history in order to remove potential contamination from his uniquely vicious character. Secondly, Piso's former close relationship with the imperial family is to be forgotten. His name upon the base beneath

---

[504] See Nikulin (2015) for useful summary of theoretical approaches to social memory.
[505] Bodel (1999) 44.   [506] Compare Val. Max. books 8–9 for the presentation of negative *exempla*.
[507] Bodel (1999) 45.

a statue of Germanicus and the property in Illyricum given to him by Augustus could have been reminders of just how close Piso had been to the imperial family: belonging to the *sodales Augustales* was a reflection of the imperial favour enjoyed by Piso in the aftermath of Augustus' death, whilst his provincial estate had been a personal gift from Augustus. Given that the friendship between Iulia Augusta and Plancina remained lurking in the background, it was perhaps all the more important to remove any hint of good relations between Piso and Tiberius, and thus any hint of skulduggery behind the death of Germanicus.

The penalties imposed by the Senate upon Piso after his suicide did not belong to a template of fixed penalties, but reflected a selection of penalties chosen for their particular ability to isolate Piso from his own family and from the imperial family. The fact that the Senate thanks Tiberius for providing full access to all information relevant to Piso's case (*SCPP* lines 15–17) implies that Tiberius was eager to project an objective stance during the trial. The Senate was concerned to hold out the promise that Piso's criminal behaviour had not infected the younger generation, and that his criminal activities had been the aberration of one individual alone, who was so morally corrupt as to be beyond the pale of Roman society. Piso's lack of *humanitas* is underlined by his rejoicing at Germanicus' death, which distanced him from normal decent behaviour, and by his sending a letter of complaint to Tiberius regarding Germanicus' actions. The Senate observes that pursuing hatred beyond death reflects Piso's singularity:

he dared, after the death of Germanicus Caesar, whose loss not only the Roman people but foreign nations too mourned, to send to Germanicus' most excellent and most forbearing parent a document in which he made accusations about Germanicus, forgetting not only the respect and affection which were owed to the son of the Princeps, but even common humanity which does not permit feuds to be carried on beyond death.

qui post mortem Germanici Caesaris, cuius interitum non p(opulus) R(omanus) modo, sed exterae quoq(ue) gentes luxserunt, patri optumo et indulgentissumo libellum, quo eum accusaret, mittere ausus sit oblitus non tantum venerationis caritatisq(ue), quae principis filio debebantur, ceterum humanitatis quoq(ue), quae ultra mortem odia non patitur procedere. (*SCPP* lines 57–61)

It even makes clear that Piso was not only isolated from the rest of Roman society, which was united in its overwhelming grief at Germanicus' death, but that non-Romans too had even mourned Germanicus' demise. In this way, Piso's treasonous actions could be condemned and contained, on the understanding that he was uniquely wicked, that he had been found guilty of the most serious charges of non-Roman and inhuman behaviour, and that he had only won support from soldiers through bribery and corruption.

8 LATER PISONES

The punishments inflicted upon Piso, therefore, were calculated to isolate Piso from his family and to allow his family to retain its wealth and social importance. A survey of later Pisones reveals the extent to which this was a successful strategy. An examination of later Pisones raises the question of the extent to which its members might be regarded somehow as congenital conspirators, naturally inclined to challenge imperial authority: a striking number of the Pisones and their near relations did in fact conspire or were represented as conspiring against emperors as diverse as Gaius Caligula, Nero, Vespasian, Nerva, Trajan, and Hadrian. Challenging imperial authority appears to have been a consistent pattern of behaviour, regardless of whether the ruling emperor of the time might be judged 'good' or 'bad'. This repeated pattern is elaborated upon by Tacitus in particular, so one problem is to disentangle reality from historiographical representation.[508] Nevertheless, contemporary reference to family patterns of behaviour in the *SCPP*, with the Senate's expectation that Piso's elder son will turn out 'very different from his father' (see §7), suggests that this theme was not entirely a Tacitean invention (*qui complura modestiae suae posuisset pignora, ex quibus sperari posset, dissimillumum eum patri suo futurum*, 'who had given many indications of his restraint, which made it possible to hope that he would turn out very different from his father', *SCPP* lines 95–97).

Of Piso's immediate family, his elder son, now Lucius, went on to enjoy a long and successful career following his father's condemnation.[509] His behaviour had been unimpeachable during his father's dubious activities, based as he was in Rome.[510] The *SCPP* records that he had served as Tiberius' quaestor and enjoyed a good relationship with Germanicus himself (*qui principis nostri q(uaestor) fuisset, et quem Germanicus <Caesar> quoq(ue) liberalitate sua honorasset*, 'who had served as quaestor of our Princeps, and whom Germanicus Caesar also had honoured with his liberality', *SCPP* lines 94–95). He became *consul ordinarius* only a few years after Piso's trial, in AD 27, and this was followed by further promotion by the end of Tiberius' lifetime to the office of *praefectus urbi*, and then as proconsul of Africa.[511] He enjoyed a long life into at least his mid-70s, and similar political success was enjoyed by his son, who also became both *consul ordinarius* in AD 57 and then proconsul of Africa (see further below on the abrupt end to his career, however).[512] By contrast, Piso's younger son, Marcus, does not resurface in the historical record after AD 20, either for his own part or via his descendants, leaving us to speculate whether he

---

[508] O'Gorman (2006) explores Tacitus' delineation of an alternative 'Pisonian dynasty'.
[509] *PIR*² C293; Hofmann-Löbl (1996) 269–73; Flower (1998) 173. [510] Tac., *Ann.* 3.16.5.
[511] Joseph., *AJ* 18.169; Cass. Dio 59.20.7.
[512] Plin., *Ep.* 3.7.12; Sherwin-White (1966) 229.

suffered an early death by natural causes or whether he chose a low profile or was marginalised from public life despite having been pardoned.[513] Piso's brother, Lucius Calpurnius Piso Augur (consul in 1 BC), described by Tacitus as 'noble and fierce' (*nobili ac feroci uiro*), died whilst being tried on a charge of *maiestas* in AD 24.[514] The two brothers – Gnaeus and Lucius the Augur – are characterised by their fierce outspokenness, their *ferocia* inherited from their father (*insita ferocia a patre Pisone*), Gnaeus Calpurnius Piso, the consul of 23 BC.[515] Cn. Piso is described as speaking out fearlessly in the Senate, whilst his brother the Augur had similarly expressed uncompromising views on the Senate's role in government and had even challenged Iulia Augusta's ability to protect her friends by prosecuting the indomitable Urgulania.[516] His defence of his brother in AD 20 may have reflected his willingness to express unpalatable opinions as much as his fraternal obligation to undertake the defence.[517] The augur's son, L. Piso, appears to have inherited his family's fierce spirits, ending up just the year after his father's death, AD 25, being assassinated for his cruelty in Spain where he was serving as legate.[518] It is probably this tendency towards *ferocia* that the Senate deprecates in Piso's son. Piso's grandson, also named Lucius, continued the family tradition of occupying high political office, as consul alongside Nero in AD 57, and then *curator aquarum* and proconsul of Africa in 69/70.[519] Imperial favour is suggested by his membership of the pontifical college and Arvals.[520] His own nobility was complemented by his marriage to Licinia Magna, who was descended from both Pompey and Crassus. His successful career came to an abrupt end in AD 70, though, when he was believed to have held back grain supplies from Africa deliberately in opposition to the new regime, and so was murdered on the command of Valerius Festus, legionary legate in Africa (see further, below).[521]

Several later Pisones who were direct descendants of Cn. Piso were suspected or accused of conspiracy, but this trope also goes back to earlier generations. Cn. Piso's grandfather had been suspected of supporting Catiline's attempts to undermine the establishment. Sallust's vignette of his character shares some features with the later generations, mentioning his *nobilitas* and his spirited behaviour (*summae audaciae*), but is also quite

---

[513] *PIR*² C296; Syme (1986) 375–78 reviews the careers of Piso's two sons and nephew in the context of family characteristics.
[514] *PIR*² C290; Tac., *Ann.* 4.21.1–2; Flower (1998) 174–75.   [515] *PIR*² C286; Tac., *Ann.* 2.43.2.
[516] On Cn. Piso's outspokenness in the Senate, see Tac., *Ann.* 1.74.5, 2.35. For L. Piso's threat to leave Rome and his prosecution of Urgulania, Tac., *Ann.* 2.34.
[517] Tac., *Ann.* 3.11.2.
[518] Tac., *Ann.* 4.45, a passage echoing Sallust's account (*Cat.* 19) of the earlier death of his great-grandfather Cn. Piso, thus foregrounding the idea of repeated family behaviour: Syme (1956) 20–21, (1958) vol.2, 729, (1986) 377–78; Woodman (2018) 237–38; contra, *PIR*² C292, suggesting he is the son of Piso Pontifex.
[519] *PIR*² C294.   [520] Rüpke (2008) 593 no.1054.   [521] Tac., *Hist.* 4.38, 48–50.

8 Later Pisones

different in focusing upon his poverty as a reason for his support for Catiline.[522] As with Cn. Piso in AD 20, though, Sallust comments negatively upon his bad character (*mali mores*), and his revolutionary or seditious disposition (*factiosus*). After him, Cn. Piso's father backed Brutus and Cassius and was chosen by Augustus to replace him as consul in 23 BC precisely because his fierce independence was clear, according to Tacitus.[523] As discussed above, Piso's elder son, Lucius, went on to enjoy a long and successful career; even so, he is represented as arousing the suspicions of the (admittedly irrational) Gaius Caligula. According to Cassius Dio, Lucius Piso was suspected by Gaius Caligula of being prone to revolt as a result of his 'arrogance' (ὑπὸ μεγαλαυχίας). Consequently, the emperor changed arrangements for command of the legions in Africa, the province to which Piso was being sent as governor, by reassigning them from the command of the proconsul, who was instead confined to administrative rather than military duties, to the command of a propraetorian legate.[524] The fact that Dio explicitly identifies this Piso as the 'son of Plancina and Gnaeus Piso' shows the strength of the historiographical tradition (discussed further below) that developed concerning the Pisones as potential rivals for imperial power. By contrast, in discussing the same measure taken by Gaius Caligula, in divorcing the proconsular governorship of Africa from control of troops, Tacitus in the *Histories* attributes Caligula's fears to another individual altogether, M. Iunius Silanus (consul, AD 19).[525] This alternative tradition may have a simple explanation, if the measure was introduced towards the end of Silanus' term in office (AD 38/39) and at the beginning of Piso's (AD 39/40). It is also possible that Tacitus deliberately introduces Silanus since the context of the passage is to cast doubt upon the validity of fears that the next generation of Pisones, represented by Lucius Piso (consul AD 57), had been plotting a revolution in AD 70. As a result of this, he was killed by Valerius Festus, who was eager to prove his loyalty to the

---

[522] Broughton (1952) 159, 163; Sall., *Cat.* 18.4, with Ramsey (2007) 112 on *factiosus*: *erat eodem tempore Cn. Piso, adulescens nobilis, summae audaciae, egens, factiosus, quem ad perturbandam rem publicam inopia atque mali mores stimulabant* ('There was at the same time Cn. Piso, a noble youth, of the utmost temerity, lacking financial resources, seditious, whom his poverty and bad character incited to throw the state into disorder').

[523] Tac., *Ann.* 2.43.2.

[524] Cass. Dio 59.20.7: ἐπειδή τε Λούκιος Πίσων ὁ τῆς τε Πλαγκίνης καὶ τοῦ Γναίου Πίσωνος υἱὸς ἄρξαι τῆς Ἀφρικῆς ἔτυχεν, ἐφοβήθη μὴ νεωτερίσῃ τι ὑπὸ μεγαλαυχίας, ἄλλως τε καὶ ὅτι δύναμιν πολλὴν καὶ πολιτικὴν καὶ ξενικὴν ἕξειν ἔμελλε, καὶ δίχα τὸ ἔθνος νείμας ἑτέρῳ τό τε στρατιωτικὸν καὶ τοὺς Νομάδας τοὺς περὶ αὐτὸ προσέταξε· καὶ ἐξ ἐκείνου καὶ δεῦρο τοῦτο γίγνεται ('Also, when Lucius Piso, the son of Plancina and Gnaeus Piso, was allotted to govern Africa, he was a source of fear lest he revolt in some way on account of his arrogance, especially as he was about to have a large force consisting both of citizens and foreigners, and having divided the province into two, he gave command to someone else of the army and the local tribesmen around about: and since that time until now this is still the case').

[525] Humphrey (1976) 203–08; Tac., *Hist.* 4.48.1, with Chilver and Townsend (1985) 59–60; *PIR*² I 839 (which thinks that Tacitus is mistaken in this).

new regime given that he was related to Vitellius.[526] Tacitus may not have wanted to remind his readers of the Pisones' reputation for insurrection, given his keenness to dismiss any suspicion of Piso's loyalty. Ironically, L. Piso, the grandson of Cn. Piso, is depicted by Tacitus as not actually wanting power for himself despite rumours that he was seeking to overthrow the Flavians:

> Meanwhile Vespasian for the second time and Titus entered upon the consulship in absentia, whilst Rome was downcast and anxious because of numerous fears. It had adopted unfounded anxieties in addition to the evils which pressed upon it, fearing that Africa had revolted, as Lucius Piso was striving for a revolution as its proconsul. He was by no means a violent character; but since the ships were being held up by the ferocity of the winter, the people, accustomed to purchase their food from day to day and whose one concern for the state was the grain supply, were afraid because they believed that the shoreline had been shut off and food supplies were being held back. The Vitellians were fanning the rumour inasmuch as they had not yet jettisoned the interests of their side, whilst the rumour was not even unpleasing to the winning side, whose desires – unfulfilled by foreign wars too – no victory in civil war ever satisfied.[527]

In this passage, Tacitus attributes rumour-mongering to both Vitellian and Flavian supporters, resulting in the Roman populace panicking in response to a grain shortage. The idea that Piso himself was blameless is supported by Pliny the Younger, who describes Piso's death as perpetrated 'through the worst crime' (*per summum facinus*).[528] Both Piso's son and grandson, therefore, are associated with conspiracy in historiographical accounts, even though both of them are at the same time explicitly exculpated from any revolutionary intent. That there may have been continuing nervousness about the Pisones in reality, however, may be reflected in the way in which later Pisones are not known to have been active in the Greek East, the scene of Cn. Piso's 'civil war', but are associated most with the Spanish peninsula and Africa.[529]

The depiction of the Pisones as being on the fringes of imperial power extends beyond Cn. Piso's immediate family. A continuum of resistance and conspiracy – or alleged conspiracy – is apparent among both the Calpurnii Pisones and the closely related Licinii Crassi.[530] M. Licinius Crassus Frugi, who had shared the consulship of AD 27 with Cn. Piso's elder son and was honoured for his role in Claudius' conquest of Britain,

---

[526] Tac., *Hist.* 4.49–50.
[527] Tac., *Hist.* 4.38: *interea Vespasianus iterum ac Titus consulatum absentes inierunt, maesta et multiplici metu suspensa ciuitate, quae super instantia mala falsos pauores induerat, desciuisse Africam res nouas moliente L. Pisone. is pro consule prouinciae nequaquam turbidus ingenio; sed quia naues saeuitia hiemis prohibebantur, uulgus alimenta in dies mercari solitum, cui una ex re publica annonae cura, clausum litus, retineri commeatus, dum timet, credebat, augentibus famam Vitellianis, qui studium partium nondum posuerant, ne uictoribus quidem ingrato rumore, quorum cupiditates externis quoque bellis inexplebilis nulla umquam ciuilis uictoria satiauit.* Cf. O'Gorman (2006) 284–85.
[528] Plin., *Ep.* 3.7.12. [529] Flower (1998) 175. [530] Flower (1998) 175; O'Gorman (2006).

was killed by Claudius in AD 46 along with his wife Scribonia and eldest son (of four) Cn. Pompeius Magnus (Claudius' son-in-law).[531] In his satirical *Apocolocyntosis*, Seneca makes a pointed remark that Claudius and Crassus were as alike as two eggs, and that the latter was consequently also stupid enough to have been able to rule.[532] Their second son, M. Licinius Crassus Frugi, consul in AD 64, was executed in AD *c*.67 for alleged conspiracy against Nero,[533] whilst their third son, L. Calpurnius Piso Frugi Licinianus, came close to imperial power, being adopted by Galba in AD 69, only to be murdered with him just five days later.[534] Finally, their remaining son, Licinius Crassus Scribonianus, was likewise executed in 70, following rumours that he had been urged to seek power for himself by Antonius Primus, even though Scribonianus had apparently shown no inclination to do so.[535] By AD 70, therefore, all four sons of Crassus Frugi and Scribonia had been executed for sedition. In addition, their only daughter, Licinia Magna, was the wife of Cn. Piso's grandson, Lucius, who was executed in AD 70. The precise family relationships of C. Calpurnius Piso, the figurehead of a conspiracy against Nero in AD 65, are unclear,[536] but his son Calpurnius Piso Galerianus is described as both cousin and son-in-law of L. Piso (*consobrinum eius generumque*), the grandson of Cn. Piso.[537] Although his description as *consobrinus* should probably be interpreted broadly, rather than as indicating the relationship of first cousin, it is important to note that Tacitus wanted to bring into focus Galerianus' connections with the grandson of Cn. Piso. Allegations of conspiracy in the early years of the Flavians, therefore, caused the downfall of the son of the Neronian conspirator, Calpurnius Piso Galerianus; the grandson of Cn. Piso, L. Calpurnius Piso;[538] and the son of M. Licinius Crassus Frugi, Licinius Crassus Scribonianus. Similar charges were made in AD 101 against Libo Frugi (probably son of M. Licinius Crassus Frugi, consul AD 64), who was banished,[539] and finally C. Calpurnius Piso Crassus Frugi Licinianus (suffect consul in AD 87) was suspected of conspiring against Nerva, Trajan, and Hadrian and eventually killed in exile on suspicion of plotting insurrection.[540] In this way, the Pisones continued for

---

[531] M. Licinius Crassus Frugi: *PIR*² L190; Suet., *Claud.* 17. Pompeius Magnus: *PIR*² P630; Cass. Dio 60.5.7–9; 61.29.6a.
[532] Sen., *Apocol.* 11: *Crassum vero tam fatuum ut etiam regnare posset ... hominem tam similem sibi quam ovo ovum.*
[533] *PIR*² L191.
[534] *PIR*² C300; Tac., *Hist.* 1.14–19, 43, 48; Chilver (1979) 74 has a useful stemma (but note the error of labelling M. Crassus as consul in 44 rather than 64).
[535] Licinius Crassus Scribonianus: *PIR*² L192; Tac., *Hist.* 4.39.13.
[536] *PIR*² C284; *OCD*⁴, s.v. Calpurnius (*RE* 65) Piso (2), Gaius (R.L. James; G.E.F. Chilver; M.T. Griffin).
[537] Tac., *Hist.* 4.49; *PIR*² C301. [538] *PIR*² C294.
[539] *PIR*² L166; Plin., *Ep.* 3.9.33, with Sherwin-White (1966) 238.
[540] *PIR*² C259; Cass. Dio (Xiphilinus) 68.3.2, 68.16.2; SHA, *Hadr.* 5.6.

decades to attract the reputation for being eager for imperial power, even in cases where the individuals concerned appear innocent of such a desire.

More specifically, Tacitus' account of the career and downfall of Cn. Piso in *Annales* books 1–3 takes on a distinctive flavour in light of the careers of other Pisones as related in the *Historiae*.[541] Although these Pisones lived later than Cn. Piso, Tacitus' composition of history in reverse chronological order (with the *Annales* covering an earlier period, but being composed later than his *Historiae*) allowed his account of the Tiberian Cn. Piso to be coloured by the narrative which Tacitus had already composed about the same man's descendants. The powerful Roman idea of family inheritance of character (as discussed earlier in §2) would have made it seem valid to Tacitus to retroject characteristics of the later Pisones as if they had been inherited from earlier representatives of their family. O'Gorman argues that Tacitus goes so far as to construct a virtual history of an alternative, Pisonian dynasty.[542] We might take for granted the succession of Julio-Claudian and then Flavian emperors, but generations of Calpurnii Pisones might be forgiven for harbouring an expectation that their turn to rule Rome might in due course come around.[543] The idea that Cn. Calpurnius Piso might have been both willing and able to succeed Augustus is conjured up near the start of the *Annales*, as an alternative name allegedly mulled over by Augustus in his assessment of those he deemed *capaces imperii* ('capable of ruling').[544] Cn. Piso is one of the only individuals identified in this way as both willing and capable of doing so. One of the constant themes in Tacitus' narratives, therefore, is the way in which the Pisones were dogged by rumours about their intentions of seizing power. Such rumours alone were enough to result in their deaths.

9 'SOME JUSTICE': PISO IN ROBERT GRAVES' *I, CLAUDIUS* AND JACK PULMAN'S BBC PRODUCTION

The poet Robert Graves (1895–1985) published the acclaimed historical novels *I, Claudius* and *Claudius, the God* in May and November of 1934. The novels ostensibly comprised the lost autobiography of the emperor Claudius, written in Greek. Studies of the work to date have focused upon the circumstances of the novels' composition,[545] Robert Graves' affinities with the character of Claudius,[546] the impact of Graves' contemporary world upon his representation of imperial Rome,[547] and the scene in the novel which portrays a debate between Asinius Pollio and Livy about the

---

[541] O'Gorman (2006) 281–92.   [542] O'Gorman (2006).   [543] Suspène (2010) 850–51.
[544] Tac., *Ann.* 1.13.3.   [545] Seymour (1995) chapter 18; Firla (2000).
[546] Seymour-Smith (1982) 231; Seymour (1995) 215; Koelb (2000); Furbank (2004) 101; Bennett (2015) 31.
[547] Burton (1995); Hopkins (1999); Joshel (2001) 124–26; Furbank (2004).

9 'Some Justice'

writing of history.[548] After briefly reviewing these themes, this section will focus upon the depiction of Piso, as a means of further exploring Graves' compositional technique.

The writing of the novels was intricately connected to Graves' personal life in many ways.[549] In 1929, he and fellow-writer Laura Riding moved to Mallorca, no longer content with their increasingly complicated life in England and following a tempestuous episode that had ended in Laura jumping out of a fourth-floor window and Graves subsequently being grilled by the police on suspicion of attempted murder. They left behind Graves' wife Nancy Nicholson to start a new life with Geoffrey Phibbs, former admirer of Riding.[550] Many contemporaries commented upon the intensity of the relationship between Graves and Riding, with the latter's infallibility and 'holiness' being a major principle.[551] In their new surroundings, Graves and Riding invested in plans for large-scale property and road development around their newly built house, Canellún, into which they moved in 1932. This led to such severe financial pressures that in 1933 Graves wrote to fellow-poet and First World War veteran Siegfried Sassoon (whom he had earlier offended deeply in *Goodbye to All That*) requesting a loan of £1,000, whilst Riding concocted various unrealistic money-making plans.[552] Graves considered that he was at risk of financial ruin, writing to Sassoon, 'If the money does not turn up before the end of the summer it means spectacular financial ruin.'[553] On being rebuffed by Sassoon, Graves decided to write his way out of trouble. This was not feasible via his poetry. As he declared in an interview in 1970, 'People say there's no money in poetry: but on the other hand there's no poetry in money.'[554] In the same interview, Graves declared that his poetry only produced enough cash to buy cigarettes, although given that Laura Riding was smoking sixty Cuban cigarettes a day by 1933 this is perhaps not quite so little as it sounds.[555] So he resumed ideas for a novel (a 'historical romance' or 'interpretative biography', as he called it) about Claudius, which he had first noted in his 'Journal of Curiosities' on 5 September 1929.[556] The eventual novel differed in some important ways from these initial thoughts, in which Claudius was to have committed suicide and to have been the author of the *Apocolocyntosis*, but the fundamental basis of the novel remained the same. Claudius was to remain 'an idealistic enemy of Caesardom', who

---

[548] Kennedy and O'Gorman (2015).   [549] Seymour (1995) chapter 18.
[550] Seymour-Smith (1982) chapters 12–15.   [551] Seymour-Smith (1982) chapter 15.
[552] Seymour-Smith (1982) 191–200 on Sassoon's reaction to *Goodbye to All That*. R.P. Graves (1990) 198–99; letters from Robert Graves to Siegfried Sassoon, between May and July 1933: O'Prey (1982) 220–23.
[553] Letter from Robert Graves to Siegfried Sassoon, 8 June 1933: O'Prey (1982) 220–21.
[554] Edwin Newman, 1970: 'Speaking freely', pp.109–27 from *Difficult Questions, Easy Answers* (Garden City, NY: Doubleday 1973) 190–213, reprinted in Kersnowski (1989) 116.
[555] R.P. Graves (1990) 203.
[556] Transcribed in Seymour-Smith (1982) 226–28; R.P. Graves (1990) 187; Seymour (1995) 214.

deliberately tried to bring an end to rule by the Caesars.[557] Graves wrote the novels rapidly, in a matter of months, spurred on, as he stated in an interview in 1969, by the fact that he was £4,000 in debt.[558] Fortunately, he was given a year's extension on his loans from the summer of 1933, allowing him in the meantime to pay back interest only.[559] This gave him just enough time to get the first novel written and published. Its instant success started to solve his financial worries. Indeed, in a letter to Edward Marsh (a high-ranking civil servant and patron of the arts) written on 12 May 1935, Graves reveals that '*Claudius* has been an extraordinary relief to me: I had been let down by a friend in a business affair and was about 4000 pounds in the red. I wrote the book to clear off part of this; but by midsummer I shall be absolutely clear.'[560]

Graves, however, maintained a disparaging attitude to the novels as 'potboilers', regarding only his composition of poetry as his real work. In letters to T.E. Lawrence ('Lawrence of Arabia') written at the time he was composing the novels, he lamented that 'I agree it is a pity that Claudius books have to be written because people won't pay a living wage for the essential works' and that 'Claudius is only the most stupid side-activity, like eating and dressing & going up & down stairs for fire-wood for the stove.'[561] He continued to reiterate this: in an interview in 1969, for example, he declared 'I will say, moreover, that I am a poet and I put very little value on my prose work.'[562] Despite this, Graves clearly took care over his Claudius novels, asking T.E. Lawrence and Eirlys Roberts (a recent Classics graduate from Cambridge) to fact-check the works. His approach is revealed in a letter to T.E. Lawrence: 'I don't want any too great howlers. The book is largely guess-work and imagination but I want it to hold water and have done a great deal of reading to get it passable.'[563] He had earlier given an impression of great industry in a letter dated 22 July 1933 to Julie Matthews: 'I have to read so many classical authorities to get it anything like historical that it's been a beastly job.'[564] It seems likely that to some extent Graves modified the impression of historical effort in letters to different correspondents. Whereas he was relatively disparaging about

---

[557] Seymour-Smith (1982) 226–27.
[558] Peter Buckman and William Fifield, 1969: 'The art of poetry XI: Robert Graves', pp.92–108 from *The Paris Review* 47 (1969), reprinted in Kersnowski (1989) 99.
[559] As revealed in a letter dated 22 July 1933 to Julie Matthews: O'Prey (1982) 224.
[560] O'Prey (1982) 244–45.
[561] A.W. Lawrence (1962) 111–12, letter from Robert Graves to T.E. Lawrence, Nov./Dec. 1933.
[562] Juan Bonet, 1969: 'A conversation with Robert Graves', pp.77–80 from *La Estafeta Literaria* 426–28 (15 Sept 1969) 39–40 trans. by Richard D. Woods, reprinted in Kersnowski (1989) 78.
[563] A.W. Lawrence (1962) 108–09, letter from Robert Graves to T.E. Lawrence, autumn 1933. Compare his letter dated 24 November 1932 to Julie Matthews, that he has been writing 'with the help of three large volumes of a Classical Dictionary, an encyclopedia, a Latin Dictionary, four Latin historians, one Greek, and a lot of other books, the story of the Emperor Claudius': O'Prey (1982) 218–19.
[564] O'Prey (1982) 224.

historical accuracy in writing to T.E. Lawrence, in writing to Julie and Tom Matthews in the hope that Tom (who wrote for *Time* magazine) might write a review of *I, Claudius*, he gave a more positive impression of his efforts, noting that 'I attach some time-saving historical notes to indicate what twists I have put in the story as it came to me from Suetonius, Tacitus, Dio Cassius, Josephus (the main authorities) and the forty or fifty lesser ones. I did not use any History of Rome by any English or foreign modern author, because I didn't want my sense of the originals obscured.'[565] He claimed further that 'The point is that I have nowhere, so far as I know, *gone against* history; but wherever authors have disagreed, or there has been a gap or confusion or mystery or they were obviously lying I have felt free to invent, in the spirit of the story, what made sense of the story.'[566] Finally, in writing to Edward Marsh on 5 November 1934, he asserts that 'I am so glad that you liked *Claudius the God*: it meant a lot of work for me because I was never a Classical scholar of any accuracy or distinction and stopped dead off when the war broke out; and you know how careful one has to be even in fiction.'[567]

Despite the letters, Graves' private view of his novels is difficult to uncover. Laura Riding's view is only too clear: she was utterly scornful of historical novels as a genre (although she subsequently wrote one on Troy, with Graves' help), and was implacably hostile towards the Claudius books, even ripping up the press reviews which Graves had collated.[568] Given that Graves subscribed to the view that Riding was infallible, it should be no surprise to find that Graves also adopted her negative attitude towards his books. That is not to imply, however, that Graves was in reality quite so dismissive of them.[569] He observed wryly in a letter to John Buchan, that the award of the James Tait Black Memorial Prize bestowed on both novels in March 1935 was 'My first prize since my preparatory school days'.[570] In addition, he had collected press reviews of the novels until Laura Riding tore them up.

Graves' presentation of the novel as the lost autobiography of Claudius offers up a double authorship to his readers.[571] Narrating it in the first person, Claudius explains why he has decided to compose in Greek, on the assumption that with the fall of the Roman empire, Latin too will disappear: 'As you see, I have chosen to write in Greek, because Greek, I believe, will always remain the chief literary language of the world, and if Rome rots away as the Sibyl has indicated, will not her language rot away with

---

[565] O'Prey (1982) 236–37, letter from Robert Graves to Julie and Tom Matthews, 1 May 1934.
[566] O'Prey (1982) 349.   [567] O'Prey (1982) 240–41.
[568] Seymour-Smith (1982) 232; Seymour (1995) 213.   [569] Firla (2000) 33–34.
[570] Perry (2015) 255–56, citing an unpublished letter from Robert Graves to John Buchan dated 27 March 1935.
[571] On the tensions within historical fiction between history and literature, see Bennett (2015).

her?' (*I, Claudius*, 14).[572] The front material of the novel describes it as 'I, Claudius from the autobiography of Tiberius Claudius emperor of the Romans. Born 10 B.C. murdered and deified A.D. 54'. What purports to be Claudius' autograph signature in Greek appears alongside this, but the mirage of this actually being Claudius' lost autobiography is not kept up with much intensity: Robert Graves is listed as the author, whilst the use of 'B.C.' and 'A.D.' gives the modern context away immediately. Anachronistic annual dates in this vein (rather than genuine Roman annual dates, which would refer to the year's consuls) also continue in the margins as the novels progress, reminding us of modern authorial intervention in the text at regular intervals, even though Claudius claims 'I shall be careful with dates (which you see I am putting in the margin)' (*I, Claudius*, 14).[573] Although Graves offers us an analysis of the decisions on translation which he has apparently made in presenting us with the text, the fact that these are offered within an 'Author's Note' rather than 'Translator's Note' likewise shows a lightness of touch.[574]

Graves wrote in a modern style, similar to the one he had already used in his autobiography *Goodbye to All That* (1929), and he included anachronisms liberally.[575] According to Graves' prefatory 'Author's Note', this supposedly reflects the more conversational style in which Claudius composed his account in Greek, and excuses Graves from having to try to reconstruct the notoriously clunky Latin handed down to us as typical of Claudius in texts such as the Lugdunum Tablet. Even terms related to the Roman army with which a modern audience would be familiar, like legion and tribunes, are updated as 'regiment' and 'captains'. In addition, he invented some personal names purely to stop the modern reader unfamiliar with the complex Julio-Claudian family tree from becoming confused by homonyms. In place of two Agrippinas (usually dubbed the 'Elder' and 'Younger'), we find instead Agrippina and Agrippinilla, and even more drastically the Younger Drusus becomes 'Castor' (as explained in the Family Tree at the back of the novel). Graves was not trying to recreate an entirely authentic Roman world, but to appeal to a contemporary twentieth-century audience. For T.E. Lawrence, invited by Graves to comment upon a draft of the work, this was a major strength of the novel: 'You have made the scenes your own, and there is little parade of research: the tone is deliberately modern, and I like that.'[576] Claudius explains that he wants his words to be read 1,900 years hence, as if written by a contemporary: 'my hope

---

[572] Du Pont (2005) on 'pseudotranslation' in the Claudius novels.
[573] Robert Graves as author intrudes still further in *Claudius the God*, by including footnotes signed R.G. and at one point even interrupting the narrative flow at the end of chapter 27 to include translations of 'Two documents illustrating Claudius' legislative practice, also his epistolary and oratorical style'.
[574] Du Pont (2005) 334–35.   [575] Burton (1995) 198–207.
[576] Letter from T.E. Lawrence to Robert Graves, 12 November 1933: A.W. Lawrence (1962) 174. Cf. letters from Robert Graves to T.E. Lawrence in A.W. Lawrence (1962) 108–14.

is that you, my eventual readers of a hundred generations ahead or more, will feel yourselves directly spoken to, as if by a contemporary' (*I, Claudius*, 11).[577] Graves' adoption of the narrative technique of pseudo-translation, then, allowed him 'to combine a modern writing style with an eyewitness account of a historical figure'.[578]

One of the most analysed sections of the novel is the discussion in the Palatine Library between Livy and Pollio, in Claudius' presence, of the correct way to write history, with Livy championing a vivid, readable style – as Claudius puts it, 'He makes the people of Ancient Rome behave and talk as if they were alive now' – and Pollio insisting on a dry factual narrative, which Claudius defends 'because he had a love of literal truth, amounting to pedantry' (*I, Claudius*, 102–13 [chapter 9]).[579] Despite the fact that Claudius adjudicates in favour of Pollio, and despite the fact that Graves himself was aware of his own family inheritance as great-nephew of Leopold von Ranke, regarded as the 'inventor of modern historiography', with his insistence that history should relate events as they really were,[580] the Claudius novels themselves steer more towards the vivid Livian style. As Burton has remarked,

Pollio's insistence that history 'is a true record of what happened' recalls the oft-quoted dictum of Graves's great-uncle the historian Leopold von Ranke that history is a record of what happened as it actually happened ('wie es eigentlich gewesen ist'). But at the same time Graves does credit his characters with motives and habits and speeches which are aggressively, if not impossibly, modern.[581]

Graves regarded himself as immersed in the world of Claudius, and as finding affinities with the character of Claudius. In a letter to T.E. Lawrence, written after he had completed a draft of *I, Claudius* in November/December 1933, he claimed that 'I wrote the most popular book I could write while keeping within the limits of personal integrity … I identify myself with him as much as with any other historical character I know about.'[582] Both Graves and Claudius were isolated from a contemporary world whose disintegration they felt they were witnessing; both were subject to the influence of forceful women; both were bookish introspects,

---

[577] On the anachronistic style, see R.P. Graves (1990) 189; cf. Furbank (2004) on the characteristics of modernising historical novels.

[578] Du Pont (2005) 339. [579] Burton (1995) 209; Kennedy and O'Gorman (2015).

[580] Robert Graves himself stated in an interview of 1969, 'My granduncle was Leopold von Ranke, the so-called "father of modern history." He was always held up to me by my mother as the first modern historian who decided to tell the truth in history': Peter Buckman and William Fifield, 1969: 'The art of poetry XI: Robert Graves', pp.92–108 from *The Paris Review* 47 (1969), reprinted in Kersnowski (1989) 101. Cf. Hopkins (1999) 131–32.

[581] Burton (1995) 209.

[582] A.W. Lawrence (1962) 111, letter from Robert Graves to T.E. Lawrence, Nov./Dec. 1933. Cf. interview with Robert Graves recorded by Peter Buckman and William Fifield, 1969: 'The art of poetry XI: Robert Graves', pp.92–108 from *The Paris Review* 47 (1969), reprinted in Kersnowski (1989) 100.

who suffered from a stammer.[583] Graves' representation of forceful women was based on personal experience. It was a point of principle that Laura Riding was infallible. Consciously or not, however, Graves' Claudius seems to reflect a desire to break free from women's tyrannical rule.[584] Indeed Seymour, Graves' biographer, goes so far as to assert that '*Claudius* is about a man, who, surrounded by powerful women, achieves the position of ultimate authority without their realizing it.'[585] Graves describes his sense of self-identification with Claudius in a later poem (1936), 'To Bring the Dead to Life':[586]

> To bring the dead to life
> Is no great magic.
> Few are wholly dead:
> Blow on a dead man's embers
> And a live flame will start.
>
> Let his forgotten griefs be now,
> And now his withered hopes;
> Subdue your pen to his handwriting
> Until it prove as natural
> To sign his name as yours.
>
> Limp as he limped,
> Swear by the oaths he swore;
> If he wore black, affect the same;
> If he had gouty fingers,
> Be yours gouty too.
>
> Assemble tokens intimate of him –
> A ring, a hood, a desk:
> Around these elements then build
> A home familiar to
> The greedy revenant.
>
> So grant him life, but reckon
> That the grave which housed him
> May not be empty now:
> You in his spotted garments
> Shall yourself lie wrapped.

Furthermore, his short story (1960) 'The Tenement: A Vision of Imperial Rome', told as a first-person narrative of a day in the life of an individual called Egnatius, has an unexpected narrative shift at the end, as Graves himself re-embodies the central character, who is killed in the collapse of his tenement block but reanimated to watch Queen Victoria's Diamond

---
[583] Seymour (1995) chapter 18 tracks parallels between Graves and Claudius.
[584] R.P. Graves (1990) 190–91.   [585] Seymour (1995) 213.
[586] First published in *The Faber Book of Modern Verse*, edited by Michael Roberts: Higginson (1987) 218 (B23).

Jubilee procession as a young child (one of the earliest memories claimed by Graves at the start of his autobiography, *Goodbye to All That*).[587] As Koelb observes, the collapsed tenement is transformed into the graves of the victims, whilst 'the central idea is really the role of the author as a modern dwelling place for these ancient ghosts'.[588] Nevertheless, the direction of travel is more complicated than this, since Egnatius relates the playing of a game sounding suspiciously like rugby at the baths: 'The most popular sport is bladder-ball: anyone may join in and try to keep the bladder off the floor. Personally, I prefer *harpastum*: you grab the heavy pigskin ball, full of sand, and carry it hither and thither until robbed – dodging, feinting, leaping, handing off' ('The Tenement', 277). As Robert Graves commented in an interview in 1969, 'I got so close to him [i.e. Claudius] that I was accused of doing a lot of research that I had never done at all', and he continued:

I didn't think I was writing a novel. I was trying to find out the truth of Claudius. And there was some strange confluent feeling between Claudius and myself. I found out that I was able to know a lot of things that happened without having any basis except that I knew they were true. It's a question of reconstructing a personality.[589]

Graves was not just writing a novel for financial reward, but fully immersing himself in the world of early imperial Rome.

Graves, of course, did not know of the *SCPP*. Given his willingness to draw upon documentary sources, such as Claudius' Letter to the Alexandrians and his edict concerning the Anauni, there is no doubt that he would have incorporated it somehow into his novel, perhaps enjoying the proof that Livia's intervention in the case of Plancina was 'as it actually happened'. The suggestion that Plancina 'counted on Livia, with whom she had been on intimate terms, to get her off' (*I, Claudius*, 244) no longer seems like an exaggeration. The account of Germanicus' death and the trial of Piso occupies a prominent place in Claudius' narrative, naturally enough since Claudius was Germanicus' brother. Graves drew heavily upon Tacitus' *Annales*, but was well aware of the challenges of establishing an accurate historical narrative. In fact, Graves adapted Tacitus' reflections (*Ann.* 3.19.2) on the difficulty of discerning the truth, which Tacitus made specifically in the context of the death of Germanicus, as a prologue to the novel as a whole:

A story that was the subject of every variety of misrepresentation, not only by those who then lived but likewise in succeeding times: so true is it that all trans-

---

[587] In the book of Graves' short stories edited by L. Graves ([1995] 2008) 271–79; Koelb (2000).
[588] Koelb (2000) 34.
[589] Peter Buckman and William Fifield, 1969: 'The art of poetry XI: Robert Graves', pp.92–108 from *The Paris Review* 47 (1969), reprinted in Kersnowski (1989) 99–100.

actions of pre-eminent importance are wrapt in doubt and obscurity; while some hold for certain facts the most precarious hearsays, others turn facts into falsehood; and both are exaggerated by posterity.

Nevertheless, we can surmise that Tacitus' account of Piso created a major problem for Graves since the central point of his novels is the idea that Claudius deliberately tried to bring down the imperial system, in order to allow the Republic to be restored.[590] Similarly, Augustus, Drusus the Elder, Agrippa Postumus, and Germanicus are represented as not wishing Rome to be ruled by emperors.[591] Tacitus, by contrast, hints at a revolutionary tendency in Piso, his father, and brother (see above, §2). Replicating this would have undermined the distinctiveness of Claudius' character in the novels. Graves therefore introduces a new element in his characterisation of Piso, attributing many of his actions in the East to financial embarrassment: 'He was deeply in debt and the hint that he could behave how he liked in Syria, so long as he provoked Germanicus, seemed an invitation to make another fortune to replace the one he had made in Spain and had long since run through' (*I, Claudius*, 230). One wonders whether Robert Graves felt any empathy for Piso's financial situation or was inspired by his own problems to pursue this theme. In Tacitus (*Ann.* 2.53.3, 55.1–2), Piso is provoked by what he sees as Germanicus' lack of dignity in using only a single lictor in Athens, so as to condemn the Athenians as degenerate successors to their glorious ancestors. Graves, however, attributes Piso's antagonism towards the Athenians as a sordid matter of financial gain. Piso's hostility is explained as being the result of the Athenians' refusal to pardon the brother of one of Piso's creditors, which in turn would have released Piso from this debt (*I, Claudius*, 230). Piso's changes to the army are likewise presented as motivated by the desire to make a quick profit: 'Instead of removing slack, bullying captains, he reduced to the ranks every officer who had a good record and appointed scoundrelly favourites of his own in their places – with the understanding that a commission of half whatever they succeeded in making out of their appointments should be paid to him, and no questions asked' (*I, Claudius*, 231). Consequently, Piso's corruption of army discipline is not attributed to any treasonous intent, but is simply explained as a route towards making a quick profit. This theme continues in explaining Piso's support for Vonones, which is inspired by the prospect of financial gain (*I, Claudius*, 232), elaborating upon a comment in Tacitus that Vonones had made very many gifts to Plancina (*Ann.* 2.58.2; cf. *SCPP* line 45 for the Senate's accusation of bribery of Piso by Vonones).

The idea that Piso was financially embarrassed is absent from the ancient sources. As explored above (§2), Tacitus instead emphasises his independ-

---

[590] Joshel (2001) 122–23.   [591] Joshel (2001) 148.

ent and proud character, and his reluctance to regard Germanicus as a superior, hinting at a family tradition of 'republicanism'. Graves retains the emphasis upon the personality clash which is so clear not just in Tacitus but also in the *SCPP*, but transforms Germanicus' character: 'He disliked Germanicus for his seriousness and piety and used to call him a superstitious old woman; and he was also extremely jealous of him' (*I, Claudius*, 230). Of course, Germanicus' character in Graves is represented through the lens of his brother Claudius, so it is no surprise to find a more positive picture emerge of his 'seriousness'. At the same time, Graves' emphasis upon his superstitious nature is clearly designed to fit with the later reports of Germanicus' panicky response to the black magic deployed against him, and his loss of all hope on the inexplicable disappearance of his protective charm of Hecate (*I, Claudius*, 236–39).

It has often been observed that the women – Livia, Agrippina the Elder, Messalina, Agrippina the Younger – are the most powerful agents in the novels.[592] In the husband–wife relationships depicted in the novel, the wives are dominant. This is true of Germanicus, for instance, who is described as having 'followed blindly' his wife (*I, Claudius*, 220). This theme has specific relevance to the Piso episode. As well as depicting strong female characters in it (Livia, Agrippina, Plancina), Graves continuously gives Livia a greater role in the action than is warranted by the sources. For example, Piso is appointed governor of Syria not just by Tiberius but also by Livia, who jointly 'told him in private that he could count on their support if Germanicus tried to interfere with any of his political or military arrangements' (*I, Claudius*, 230). In Graves' version, it is Plancina, rather than Piso himself, who is given the central role in the murder of Germanicus, under instructions from Livia and in collaboration with Martina and (as is revealed later) Caligula (*I, Claudius*, 244–48). Plancina, we read, 'had the reputation of being a witch', making Germanicus fear that she was practising witchcraft against him (*I, Claudius*, 237). Whereas in Tacitus (*Ann.* 2.69.3) Germanicus suspects Piso of poisoning him, in *I, Claudius* Piso shares this charge with his wife.

In his narration of the death of Germanicus and trial of Piso, Graves can be detected to have made a factual error, in representing Lucius Calpurnius Piso Augur as the nephew rather than brother of Piso (*I, Claudius*, 230). This weakens the sense of the two brothers sharing a family trait in their similar outspokenness in standing up to Tiberius (as discussed above, §8), but strengthens the parallel between Tiberius and Gnaeus Piso. This then plays a key narrative role in allowing a letter from Germanicus in which he condemns Piso as an 'incompetent, avaricious, bloody-minded sexagenarian debauchee' (*I, Claudius*, 232) to be interpreted by Tiberius as actually

---

[592] Koelb (2000) 44; Joshel (2001) 123. Seymour (1995) 213, however, suggests that both Graves and Claudius may in reality have developed strategies to survive their apparent subordination.

referring to himself, thus heightening his hostility towards Germanicus. Graves' prosopographical error is, however, entirely understandable since neither Tacitus nor Cassius Dio ever explicitly identifies the two men as brothers: sorting out the identity of the different Pisones in Tacitus was only gradually effected by Syme after the Claudius novels had been published.[593]

By 1935, the Claudius novels were already being adapted for a blockbuster film, and shooting of some key scenes had already taken place before the project was abandoned in 1937, after Merle Oberon (Messalina) was injured in a car crash.[594] This film in any case was not intended to cover the early life of Claudius, but to start with Caligula.[595] A further effort to film the novels in 1956, starring Alec Guinness as Claudius, did not take off either,[596] but finally a BBC television series was produced to great acclaim in 1976. With a script written by Jack Pulman, a complete episode, 'Some Justice', was devoted to the trial of Piso. This version differed from the original novel by removing any hint that Piso's activities had been motivated by financial hardship, putting the emphasis squarely upon Piso and Plancina being commissioned by Tiberius and Livia (in Piso's words) 'to harass and provoke Germanicus into showing his hand'. In a heated discussion with his wife, Piso further claimed that it had been Plancina's idea to go so far as to murder Germanicus. Pulman retained the final plot twist, with Piso being murdered by Plancina, but made Livia's involvement even more prominent, adding a new scene in which she dines with Germanicus' poisoner Martina, whom her agents have intercepted. In Graves, by contrast, Martina is discovered by Sejanus' agents and smothered (*I, Claudius*, 243). This allows Pulman to develop an unforgettable scene where Livia displays her keen interest in and knowledge of different types of poison, eliciting the dramatically ironic comment from Martina, 'it's a pity in a way you don't get the chance to practise: you'd be very good'.

---

[593] Syme (1956); (1986) chapter 26. [594] Gibson (2015) 275–87, esp. 284.
[595] Graves' letter to Julie and Tom Matthews, 10 February 1935: O'Prey (1982) 242–43.
[596] Seymour-Smith (1982) 473–76; Gibson (2015) 287–89.

TEXT AND TRANSLATION

THE *SENATUS CONSULTUM DE CN. PISONE PATRE*

Text and Translation

EXPLANATORY NOTE

The following text is based upon Eck, Caballos, Fernández (1996) 38–50, a composite text derived from the different copies of the inscription, and upon autopsy of the inscriptions in the Museo Arqueológico de Sevilla. The apparatus following the text and translation presents differences on the inscriptions, including engraving errors, and highlights differences between this edition and Eck, Caballos, Fernández (1996). Copy A is primarily followed, but Copy B is used where it offers a better reading (see, for example, Copy A line 7).

The following standard symbols are used:

[abc]   Letters which have been lost where the inscription has been damaged, but which the editor has supplied.
<abc>   Letters omitted by mistake from the original inscription, which the editor has added.
{abc}   Letters included by mistake in the original inscription, and which should be deleted.
⌜abc⌝   Letters corrected by the editor, in place of an error in the original inscription.
a(bc)   An abbreviated word, which the editor has written out in full.
ì   i *longa*.

HEADING

s(enatus) c(onsultum) de Cn(aeo) Pisone patre propositum N(umerio) Vibio Sereno pro co(n)s(ule)

LINES 1–4 PREAMBLE (*PRAESCRIPTIO*)

[1] a(nte) d(iem) IIII eid(us) Dec(embres) in Palatio in porticu, quae est ad Apollinis. scribendo / [2] adfuerunt M(arcus) Valerius M(arci) f(ilius) Lem(onia tribu) Messallinus, C(aius) Ateius L(uci) f(ilius) Ani(ensi tribu) Capito, Sex(tus) Pomp(eius) / [3] Sex(ti) f(ilius) Arn(ensi tribu), M(arcus) Pompeius M(arci) f(ilius) Teret(ina tribu) Priscus, C(aius) Arrenus C(ai) f(ilius) Gal(eria tribu) Gallus, L(ucius) Nonius L(uci) f(ilius) / [4] Pom(ptina tribu) Asprenas q(uaestor), M(arcus) Vinucius P(ubli) f(ilius) Pob(lilia tribu) q(uaestor). *vacat*

LINES 4–11 FOUR ITEMS FOR DISCUSSION IN THE SENATE, INTRODUCED BY TIBERIUS (*RELATIO*)

[4] quod Ti(berius) Caesar divi Aug(usti) f(ilius) Aug(ustus) / [5] pontifex maxumus, tribunicia potestate XXII, co(n)s(ul) III, designatus IIII, ad sena/tum rettulit qualis causa Cn(aei) Pisonis patris visa esset et an merito sibi mor/tem conscisse videretur et qualis causa M(arci) Pisonis visa esset, cui relationi ad/iecisset, uti precum suarum pro adulescente memor is ordo esset, <et> qualis cau/sa Plancinae visa esset, pro qua persona, quid petisset et quas propter causas, / [10] exposuisset antea, et quid de Visellio Karo et de Sempronio Basso, comitibus / [11] Cn(aei) Pisonis patris, iudicaret senatus, d(e) i(is) r(ebus) i(ta) c(ensuerunt): /

LINES 12–22 THANKS TO THE GODS FOR THWARTING PISO, AND TO TIBERIUS FOR FACILITATING HIS TRIAL

[12] senatum populumq(ue) Romanum ante omnia dìs immortalibus gratias agere, / [13] quod nefaris consilìs Cn(aei) Pisonis patris tranquillitatem praesentis status / [14] r(ei) p(ublicae), quo melior optari non pote<st> ⌈e⌉t quo beneficio principis nostri frui contigit, / [15] turbar⌈i⌉ passi non sunt; deinde Ti(berio) Caesari Augusto, principi nostro, quod earum rerum /

The Senatus Consultum de Cn. Pisone Patre [1–22]   115

HEADING

Decree of the Senate concerning Gnaeus Piso senior, published in the proconsulship of Numerius Vibius Serenus.

LINES 1–4   PREAMBLE (*PRAESCRIPTIO*)

[1] On 10 December on the Palatine in the portico at the Temple of Apollo. Present at the drafting of the decree were Marcus Valerius Messallinus, son of Marcus, of the Lemonian voting-tribe; Gaius Ateius Capito, son of Lucius, of the Aniensian voting-tribe; Sextus Pompeius, [3] son of Sextus, of the Arnensian voting-tribe; Marcus Pompeius Priscus, son of Marcus, of the Teretinan voting-tribe; Gaius Arrenus Gallus, son of Gaius, of the Galerian voting-tribe; Lucius Nonius Asprenas, son of Lucius, of the Pomptinan voting-tribe, quaestor; Marcus Vinucius, son of Publius, of the Poblilian voting-tribe, quaestor.

LINES 4–11   FOUR ITEMS FOR DISCUSSION IN THE SENATE, INTRODUCED BY TIBERIUS (*RELATIO*)

[4] Whereas Tiberius Caesar Augustus, son of deified Augustus, [5] supreme pontiff, holding tribunician power for the twenty-second time, consul for the third time, consul designate for the fourth time, referred to the Senate for decision:

how the case of Gnaeus Piso Senior had been regarded and whether he was regarded as having taken his own life deservedly;

and how the case of Marcus Piso had been regarded, to which item he had added the request that this body be mindful of his pleas on behalf of the young man;

and how the case of Plancina had been regarded, on behalf of which individual he had earlier set out what he had requested and for what reasons;

and what the Senate's judgement was concerning Visellius Karus and Sempronius Bassus, members of the staff [11] of Gnaeus Piso Senior;

concerning these matters the Senate decreed as follows:

LINES 12–22   THANKS TO THE GODS FOR THWARTING PISO, AND TO TIBERIUS FOR FACILITATING HIS TRIAL

[12] that the Senate and people of Rome give thanks above all to the immortal gods [13] because they did not allow the tranquillity of the current state of affairs [14] in the republic – something better than which it is not possible to desire and which it has fallen to our lot to enjoy, thanks to the beneficence of our Princeps – to be disturbed by the wicked plans

[16] omnium, quae ad explorandam veritatem necessariae fuerunt, co/piam senatui fecerit, cuius aequitatem et patientiam hoc quoq(ue) nomine / [18] admirarì senatum, quod, cum manufestissuma sint Cn(aei) Pisonis patris scelera / [19] et ipse de se supplicium sumpsisset, nihilominus causam eius cognosci volue/rit filiosque eius arcessitos hortatus sit, ut patris suì causam defenderent, ita ut / [21] eum quoq(ue), qui ordinis senatori nondum esset, ob eam rem ìntroducì in senatum vellet et / [22] copiam utriq(ue) dicendi pro patre et pro matre ipsorum et pro M(arco) Pisone faceret.

LINES 23–70 DESCRIPTION OF THE CIRCUMSTANCES THAT LED TO PISO'S PROSECUTION:

Lines 23–37 Piso's relationship with Germanicus

[23] ìtaque, cum per aliquot dies acta causa sit, ab accusatoribus Cn(aei) Pisonis patris et ab ipso / [24] Cn(aeo) Pisone patre recitatae epistulae recitata exemplaria codicillorum, quos / [25] Germanicus Caesar Cn(aeo) Pisoni patri scripsisset, producti testes cuiusq(ue) ordinis sint, / [26] <senatum> admirari singularem moderationem patientiamq(ue) Germanici Caesaris evic/tam esse feritate morum Cn(aei) Pisonis patris atq(ue) ob id morientem Germanicum Cae/sarem, cuius mortis fuisse causam Cn(aeum) Pisonem patrem ipse testatus sit, non inme/rito amicitiam ei renuntiasse, qui – cum deberet meminisse adiutorem se datum / [30] esse Germanico Caesari, qui a principe nostro ex auctoritate huius ordinis ad / [31] rerum transmarinarum statum componendum missus esset desiderantium / [32] praesentiam aut ipsius Ti(beri) Caesaris Aug(usti) aut filiorum alterius utrius, neˊgˊlecta / [33] maiestate domus Aug(ustae), neˊgˊlecto etiam iure publico, quod adleˊcˊt(us) pro co(n)s(uli) et ei pro co(n)s(uli), de quo / [34] lex ad populum lata esset, ut, in quamcumq(ue) provinciam venisset, maius ei imperium / [35] quam ei qui eam provinciam proco(n)s(ul) optineret, esset, dum in omni re maius imperi/um Ti(berio) Caesari Aug(usto) quam Germanico Caesari esset, tamquam ipsius arbitri et potestatis omnia / [37] esse deberent, ita se, cum in provincia Syria fuerit, gesserit –

of Gnaeus Piso Senior; then to Tiberius Caesar Augustus, our Princeps, because he made available to the Senate everything which was necessary for determining the truth – whose impartiality and patience the Senate wonders at on this count too, that, although the crimes of Gnaeus Piso Senior are most flagrant [19] and although he had inflicted the death penalty on himself, nonetheless our Princeps wanted a formal enquiry into Piso's case to be held [20] and, having summoned his sons, urged them to defend their father's case, to the extent that [21] he wished even the son who was not yet a member of the senatorial body to be brought into the Senate for this purpose, and [22] gave them both the opportunity to speak on behalf of their father, on behalf of their mother, and on behalf of Marcus Piso.

LINES 23–70 DESCRIPTION OF THE CIRCUMSTANCES THAT LED TO PISO'S PROSECUTION:

23–37 *Piso's relationship with Germanicus*

[23] That therefore, when the case was pleaded over a number of days, by the prosecutors of Gnaeus Piso Senior and by Gnaeus Piso Senior himself letters were read out, and copies of the memoranda were read out, which [25] Germanicus Caesar had written to Gnaeus Piso Senior, when witnesses of each order were brought before the court, [26] the Senate wonders at the fact that the exceptional restraint and patience of Germanicus Caesar was exhausted by the brutish behaviour of Gnaeus Piso Senior, and that for this reason, when dying, Germanicus Caesar, [28] of whose death he himself bore witness that Gnaeus Piso was the cause, renounced his friendship with him, not without good cause: this man, although he should have kept in mind that he had been assigned as an aide [30] to Germanicus Caesar, who had been dispatched by our Princeps in accordance with the authority of this body to put overseas affairs in order, affairs which called for [32] the presence either of Tiberius Caesar Augustus himself or of one of his two sons, without regard for the majesty of the House of Augustus, without regard even for public law in that he, inasmuch as he had been assigned to a proconsul, and indeed to a proconsul concerning whom [34] a law had been passed by the people to the effect that into whatever province he entered he would have greater *imperium* [35] than the person who was governing this province as proconsul, with the proviso that in every respect Tiberius Caesar Augustus had greater *imperium* than Germanicus Caesar, conducted himself while he was in the province of Syria as if everything ought to be a matter for his decision and authority;

Lines 37–45 Piso and Vonones

bellum {cum} Armeniacum / [38] et Parthicum, quantum in ipso fuerit, moverit, quod neq(ue) ex mandatis principis / [39] nostri epistulisq(ue) frequentibus Germanici Caesaris, cum is abesset, Vononem, qui sus/pectus regi Part(h)orum erat, longius removeri voluerit, ne profugere ex custodia / [41] posset, id quod fecit, et conloqui quosdam ex numero Armeniorum malos et / [42] audaces cum Vonone passus sit, ut per eosdem tumultus in Armenia excita/retur ac Vonone<s> vel occiso vel expulso rege Armeniae, quem Germanicus / [44] Caesar ex voluntate patris sui senatusq(ue) ei genti regem dedisset, <eam> occuparet, / [45] eaq(ue) magnis muneribus Vononis corruptus fecerit;

Lines 45–57 Piso's stirring up of civil war

bellum etiam civile ex/citare conatus sit, iam pridem numine divi Aug(usti) virtutibusq(ue) Ti(beri) Caesaris Aug(usti) / [47] omnibus civilis belli sepultis malis, repetendo provinciam Syriam post / [48] mortem Germanici Caesaris, quam vivo eo pessumo et animo et exemplo re/liquerat, atq(ue) ob id milites Romani inter se concurrere coacti sunt, perspecta etiam / [50] crudelitate unica, qui, incognita causa, sine consili sententia plurimos ca/pitis supplicio adfecisset neq(ue) externos tantummodo, sed etiam centurionem / [52] c(ivem) R(omanum) cruci fixsisset; qui militarem disciplinam a divo Aug(usto) institutam et / [53] servatam a Ti(berio) Caesare Aug(usto) corrupisset, non solum indulgendo militibus, <ne> / [54] his, qui ipsis praesunt, more vetustissumo parerent, sed etiam donativa suo / [55] nomine ex fisco principis nostri dando, quo facto milites alios Pisonianos, a/lios Caesarianos dicì laetatus sit, honorando etiam eos, qui post talis nominis / [57] usurpationem ipsi paruisse<n>t;

Lines 57–70 Piso's response to Germanicus' death

qui post mortem Germanici Caesaris, cuius in/teritum non p(opulus) R(omanus) modo, sed exterae quoq(ue) gentes luxserunt, patri optumo et / [59] indulgentissumo libellum, quo eum accusaret, mittere ausus sit oblitus non / [60] tantum venerationis caritatisq(ue), quae principis filio debebantur, ceterum / [61] humanitatis quoq(ue), quae ultra mortem odia non patitur procedere, et cuius / [62] mortem gavisum esse eum hìs argumentis

Lines 37–45 Piso and Vonones

he stirred up war with Armenia [38] and Parthia, as far as lay within his power, because he was unwilling, in accordance with the instructions of our Princeps [39] and with the many letters of Germanicus Caesar when he was away, that Vonones, who was an object of suspicion to the king of the Parthians, be moved further away, so that he might be unable to escape from custody [41] (something which he actually did), and because he allowed some evil and reckless persons from the body of the Armenians to converse with Vonones to the end that disorder might be provoked through those same individuals in Armenia [43] and that, once the king of Armenia, whom Germanicus Caesar had assigned as king to that people in accordance with the wishes of his father and of the Senate, had been killed or expelled, Vonones might occupy Armenia, [45] and these things he did, corrupted by large bribes from Vonones;

Lines 45–57 Piso's stirring up of civil war

he also tried to foment civil war, even though all the evils of civil war had long since been buried through the divine power of deified Augustus and the virtues of Tiberius Caesar Augustus, by trying to regain, after [48] the death of Germanicus Caesar, the province of Syria, which he had abandoned, demonstrating both the worst frame of mind and example, while Germanicus was still alive, [49] and on that account Roman soldiers were forced into conflict with each other, when he had also manifested his [50] unparalleled cruelty inasmuch as he had inflicted the death penalty on very many without hearing their cases, without consulting his council, and had crucified not only foreigners but also a centurion, [52] a Roman citizen; he had damaged the military discipline which had been established by deified Augustus and [53] maintained by Tiberius Caesar Augustus, not only by allowing soldiers not to obey [54] in the traditional manner those in command of them, but also by giving donatives [55] in his own name from the treasury of our Princeps; once this was done he was pleased to see some soldiers being called 'Pisonians', [56] others 'Caesarians', by going on to confer distinctions on those who, after usurping such a name, had shown him obedience;

Lines 57–70 Piso's response to Germanicus' death

he dared, after the death of Germanicus Caesar, whose [58] loss not only the Roman people but foreign nations too mourned, to send to Germanicus' most excellent and most forbearing parent a document in which he made accusations about Germanicus, forgetting not [60] only the respect and affection which were owed to the son of the Princeps, but even [61] common humanity which does not permit feuds to be carried on beyond death; that he rejoiced in Germanicus' death

senatui apparuerit: quod nefaria / [63] sacrificia ab eo facta, quod naves, quibus vehebatur, ornatae sint, quod reclu/serit deorum immortalium templa, quae totius imperi Romani constantissuma / [65] pietas clauserat, eiusdemque habitus animi argumentum fuerit, quod dedisset congi/arium ei, qui nuntiaverit sibi de morte Germanici Caesaris, probatum<q(ue)> sit frequen/ter{q(ue)} convivia habuisse eum ˊhˋis ipsis diebus, quibus de morte Germanici Caesaris ei / [68] nuntiatum erat; numen quoq(ue) divi Aug(usti) violatum esse ab eo arbitrari senatum / [69] omni honore, qui aut memoriae eius aut imaginibus, quae, antequam in / [70] deorum numerum referre{n}tur, eì r[eddi]tae erant, habeba{n}tur, detracto; *vacat*

LINES 71–123 SENATE'S RECOMMENDATIONS ON THE FOUR ITEMS UNDER DISCUSSION

Lines 71–90 Posthumous punishments for Piso

[71] quas ob res arbitrari senatum non optulisse eum se deˊbˋitae poenae, sed maiori / [72] et quam inminˊeˋre sibi ab pietate et severitate iudicantium intellegeba{n}t / [73] subtraxsisse; *vacat* itaq(ue) iis poenis, quas a semet ipso exegisset, adicere: ne quis luc/tus mortis eius causa a feminis quibus {e}is more maiorum, si hoc senatus consultum factum / [75] non esset, lugendus esset, susciperetur; utiq(ue) statuae et imagines Cn(aei) Pisonis / [76] patris, quae ubiq(ue) positae essent, tollerentur; recte et ordine facturos, qui qu/andoq(ue) familiae Calpurniae essent, quive eam familiam cognatione / [78] adfinitateve contingerent, si dedissent operam, si quis eius gentis aut quis eo/rum, qui cognatus adfinisve Calpurniae familiae fuisset, mortuos esset, lugen/dus esset, ne inter reliquas imagines, <quibus> exequias eorum funerum celebrare solent, / [81] imago Cn(aei) Pisonis patris duceretur neve imaginibus familiae Calpurniae i/mago eius interponeretur; *vacat* utiq(ue) nomen Cn(aei) Pisonis patris tolleretur / [83] ex titulo statuae Germanicì Caesaris, quam ei sodales Augustales in campo ad / [84] aram Providentiae posuissent; *vacat* utiq(ue) bona Cn(aei) Pisonis patris publicarentur / [85] excepto saltu, qui esset in Hillyrico; eum saltum placere Ti(berio) Caesari Augusto prin/cipi nostro, cuius a patre divo Aug(usto) Cn(aeo) Pisoni patri donatus erat, reddi, cum / [87] is idcirco dari eum sibi desiderasset, quod <civitates>, quarum fines hos saltus contin/gerent, frequenter de iniuris Cn(aei) Pisonis patris libertorumq(ue) et servorum / [89] eius questae essent, atq(ue) ob id providendum putaret, ne postea iure meritoq(ue) / [90] soci p(opuli) R(omani) queri possent; *vacat*

was obvious to the Senate from the following evidence: that wicked [63] sacrifices were offered by him, that the ships in which he sailed were decorated, that he [64] reopened the temples of the immortal gods which the most unwavering devotion of the whole Roman empire had closed; evidence of the same attitude was to be found in the fact that he had given a [66] gift of money to the man who informed him of the death of Germanicus Caesar; and it was also proven that [67] on several occasions he had held banquets during those very days on which the announcement had been made to him about the death of Germanicus Caesar; it was also the opinion of the Senate that the divine spirit of deified Augustus had been violated by him [69] in that every sign of honour was removed which was being accorded either to his memory or to those portraits which had been [set up] to him before he was entered into the number of the gods.

LINES 71–123 SENATE'S RECOMMENDATIONS ON THE FOUR ITEMS UNDER DISCUSSION

Lines 71–90 Posthumous punishments for Piso

[71] That for these reasons it was the opinion of the Senate that he had not undergone the punishment he deserved but had saved himself from the harsher one which he inferred from the devotion to duty and the strictness of the judges was threatening him; therefore it adds to the punishments which he had inflicted on himself: that no mourning for his death be undertaken by the women by whom he should have been mourned, in accordance with ancestral custom, had this decree of the Senate not been passed; and that the statues and portraits of Gnaeus Piso [76] Senior, wherever they had been placed, be removed; that whoever shall at any time belong to the Calpurnian family or be connected to the family by blood or marriage will have acted rightly and properly if they take care, when anyone who belongs to that *gens* or who is one of those who is connected by blood or marriage to the Calpurnian family dies and is [80] to be mourned, that [81] the portrait of Gnaeus Piso Senior should not be brought out with the rest of the portraits with which they customarily solemnise the processions at their funerals nor placed among the portraits of the Calpurnian family; and that the name of Gnaeus Piso Senior be removed [83] from the inscription on the statue of Germanicus Caesar which the *sodales Augustales* had erected to him in the Field of Mars next to the [84] Altar of Foresight; and that the property of Gnaeus Piso Senior be declared public property [85] with the exception of the woodland in Illyricum. This woodland, it is decided, should be returned to Tiberius Caesar Augustus [86] our Princeps, by whose father deified Augustus it had been given to Gnaeus Piso Senior, since [87] he had expressed the wish that it be given to him because the communities whose territory bordered that of the woodland had often complained of injuries from Gnaeus Piso Senior, his freedmen and slaves, and for this reason he thought that care should be taken that allies of the Roman people should no longer be able to complain with just cause.

Lines 90–108 Decisions about Piso's property

item senatum, memorem clementiae suae ius/titiaeq(ue) <atq(ue)> animi magnitudinis, quas virtutes {quas} a maioribus suis acce/pisset, tum praecipue ab divo Aug(usto) et Ti(berio) Caesare Aug(usto) principibus suis didicisset, / [93] ex bonis Cn(aei) Pisonis patris publicatis aequom humanumq(ue) censere, filio eius / [94] Pisoni maiori, de quo nihil esset dictum, qui principis nostri q(uaestor) fuisset, et quem / [95] Germanicus <Caesar> quoq(ue) liberalitate sua honorasset, qui complura modestiae / [96] suae posuisset pignora, / [97] ex quibus sperari posset, dissimillumum eum patri suo futurum, donari / [98] nomine principis et senatus bonorum partem dimidiam eumq(ue), cum tan/to benificio obligaretur, recte atque ordine facturum, si praenomen patris / [100] mutasset; *vacat* M(arco) etiam Pisoni, qu<o>i inpunitatem senatus humanitati et mode-/rationi principis sui adsensus dandam esse{t} arbitraretur, quo facilius / [102] inviolatum senatus benificium ad eum pervenire<t>, alteram partem dimi/diam bonorum paternorum dari, ita ut ex omnibus bonis, quae decreto / [104] senatus publicata et concessa iis essent, n(ummum) (decies centena milia) dotis nomine Calpurniae / [105] Cn(aei) Pisonis filiae, item peculi nomine n(ummum) (quadragies centena milia) daretur. *vacat* item / [106] placere, uti Cn(aeus) Piso pater supra portam Fontinalem quae inaedificasset / [107] iungendarum domum privatarum causa *vacat*, ea curatores locorum publico/rum iudicandorum tollenda dimolienda curarent. *vacat*

Lines 109–20 Pardon for Plancina

[109] quod ad Plancinae causam pertineret, qu<o>i pluruma et gravissuma crimina / [110] obiecta essent, quoniam confiteretur se omnem spem in misericordia{m} / [111] principis nostri et senatus habere, et saepe princeps noster accurateq(ue) ab / [112] eo ordine petierit, ut contentus senatus Cn(aei) Pisonis patris poena uxori ⌜e⌝ius / [113] sic uti M(arco) filio parceret, et pro Plancina rogatu matris suae depreca⌜tus⌝ s⌜it⌝ et, / [114] quam ob rem ⌜id⌝ mater sua inpetrari vellet, iustissumas ab ea causas sibi ex/positas acceperit, senatum arbitrari et Iuliae Aug(ustae), optume de r(e) p(ublica) meritae non / [116] partu tantum modo principis nostri, sed etiam multis magnisq(ue) erga cui/usq(ue) ordinis homines beneficis, quae, cum iure meritoq(ue) plurumum posse in eo, quod / [118] a senatu petere<t> deberet, parcissume uteretur eo, et principis nostri summa<e> erga / [119] matrem suam pietati suffragandum indulgendumq(ue) esse remittiq(ue) / [120] poenam Plancinae placere;

Lines 90–108 Decisions about Piso's property

Likewise, the Senate, mindful of its clemency, [91] justice, and generosity of spirit, virtues which it had inherited from its ancestors, then learned in particular from deified Augustus and Tiberius Caesar Augustus, its Principes, [93] has deemed it fair and humane that from the confiscated goods of Gnaeus Piso Senior half of the property be given, in the name of the Princeps and the Senate, to his son the elder Piso, about whom nothing had been said, who had served as quaestor of our Princeps, and whom [95] Germanicus Caesar also had honoured with his liberality, and who had given many indications of his restraint, which made it possible to hope that he would turn out very different from his father; and that he, since he was put under obligation by so great a favour, would be behaving rightly and appropriately, if he changed his first name, that of his father; [100] and that to Marcus Piso, to whom the Senate, in agreement with the humanity and restraint of its Princeps, thought that impunity should be given, so that the favour of the Senate might more easily accrue to him unspoiled, the other half [103] of his father's property should be given, and in such a way that from the whole of the estate which had been declared public property by senatorial decree and conceded to them, one million sesterces be given to Calpurnia, [105] the daughter of Gnaeus Piso, as dowry and likewise four million sesterces as her *peculium*. Likewise [106] the Senate has decided that the superintendents responsible for adjudicating public places should see to it that the structure which Gnaeus Piso Senior had built above the Fontinal Gate to connect private residences be removed and destroyed.

Lines 109–20 Pardon for Plancina

[109] That as regarded the case of Plancina, against whom very many extremely serious charges [110] had been brought, since she was now admitting that she placed all her hope in the mercy [111] of our Princeps and the Senate, and since our Princeps has often and pressingly requested from [112] this body that the Senate be satisfied with the punishment of Gnaeus Piso Senior and spare his wife [113] as it was sparing his son Marcus, and since he pleaded himself for Plancina at the request of his mother and [114] had very just reasons presented to him by her for wanting to secure her request, the Senate considers that to Iulia Augusta, who has served the state superlatively not [116] only in giving birth to our Princeps but also through her many great favours towards men [117] of every rank, who rightly and deservedly ought to have supreme influence in what [118] she asked from the Senate, but used that influence sparingly, and to the supreme piety of our Princeps towards [119] his mother, support and indulgence should be accorded and has decided that the punishment of Plancina should be waived.

Lines 120–23 Penalties for Visellius Karus and Sempronius Bassus

Visellio Karo et Sempronio Basso, comitibus Cn(aei) / [121] Pisonis patris et omnium malificiorum socis ac ministris, aqua et igne interdici oportere / [122] ab eo pr(aetore), qu⌐i⌐ lege{m} maiestatis quaereret, bonaq(ue) eorum ab pr(aetoribus), qui aerario / [123] praeesse<n>t, venire et in aerarium redigi placere; *vacat*

LINES 123–51 PRAISE FOR MEMBERS OF THE IMPERIAL FAMILY

Lines 123–32 Exhortation of Tiberius

item cum iudic<ar>et senatus / [124] omnium partium pietatem antecessisse Ti(berium) Caesarem Aug(ustum) principem nostrum / [125] tant⌐i⌐ et ⌐t⌐am aequali<s> dolor⌐i⌐<s eius indicis> totiens conspectis, quibus etiam senatus ve/hementer motus sit, magnopere rogare et petere, ut omnem curam, quam / [127] in duos quondam filios suos partitus erat, ad eum, quem haberet, converteret, / [128] sperareq(ue) senatum eum, qui supersit, ⌐tanto maior⌐i⌐ curae dis immortalibus / [129] fore, quanto magis intellegerent, omnem spem futuram paternae pro / [130] r(e) p(ublica) stationis in uno repos[i]ta<m>, quo nomine debere eum finire dolorem / [131] ac restituere patriae suae non tantum animum, sed etiam voltum, qui / [132] publicae felicitati conveniret;

Lines 132–36 Praise of Iulia Augusta and Drusus

item senatum laudare magnopere Iuliae Aug(ustae) / [133] Drusiq(ue) Caesaris moderationem imitantium principis nostri iustitiam, quos / [134] animadvertere{t} hunc ordinem non maiorem pietatem in Germanicum / [135] quam aequitatem in servandis integris iudicìs suis, donec de causa Cn(aei) Pisonis / [136] patris cognosceretur, praestitisse;

Lines 120–23 Penalties for Visellius Karus and Sempronius Bassus

On Visellius Karus and Sempronius Bassus, members of the staff of Gnaeus [121] Piso Senior and his associates and allies in all his misdeeds, the Senate has decided that the penalty of interdiction from water and fire should be imposed by the praetor presiding over cases under the law of *maiestas*, and that their goods should be sold and the profits consigned to the public treasury by the praetors in charge of the public treasury.

LINES 123–51 PRAISE FOR MEMBERS OF THE IMPERIAL FAMILY

Lines 123–32 Exhortation of Tiberius

Likewise, since it was the judgement of the Senate [124] that Tiberius Caesar Augustus our Princeps has surpassed all parties in his devotion to duty, [125] after witnessing so often the signs of his grief, so great and of such intensity, by which the Senate has also [126] been deeply moved, it makes a strong plea and requests that he devote all the care which [127] he previously divided between his two sons to the one whom he still has, [128] and the Senate hopes that the immortal gods will devote all the more care to the one who remains, [129] the more they realise that all hope for the position which his father holds to the benefit [130] of the state has rested for the future on one person alone; for which reason he should end his grief [131] and regain for his country not only the frame of mind, but also the appearance [132] appropriate to public happiness;

Lines 132–36 Praise of Iulia Augusta and Drusus

likewise, the Senate offers abundant praise of the restraint of Iulia Augusta [133] and Drusus Caesar as they imitate the justice of our Princeps; [134] this body recognises that they have equalled their devotion towards Germanicus [135] with their impartiality in reserving their own judgement intact until the case of Gnaeus Piso Senior was tried;

Lines 136–46 Praise for Germanicus' wife, mother, and sister

ceterorum quoq(ue) contingentium Germanicum / [137] Caesarem necessitudine magnopere probare: Agrippinae, quam senatui memoria{m} / [138] divi Aug(usti), qu<o>i fuisset probatissuma, et viri Germanici, cum quo unica concordia vixsis/set, et tot pignora edita partu felicissumo eorum, qui superessent, commendare<nt>; / [140] itemq(ue) Antoniae, Germanicì Caesaris matris, quae unum matrimonium Dru/si Germ(anici) patris experta, sanctitate morum dignam se divo Aug(usto) tam arta propin/quitate exhibuerit; et Liviae, sororis Germ(anici) Caesar(is), de qua optume et avia sua et / [143] socer idemq(ue) patruos, princeps noster, iudicaret, quorum iudicis, etiam si non contin/gere{n}t domum eorum, merito gloriari posset, nedum tam coniunctis necessitu/dinibus inligata femina: quarum aeq(ue) et dolorʿeʾm fidelissumum et in dolore / [146] moderatione<m> senatum probare; *vacat*

Lines 146–51 Praise for Germanicus' sons and brother

item quod filiorum Germanici puerilis et / [147] praecipue in Nerone{m} Caesare{m} iam etiam iu<v>enis dolor amisso patre tali / [148] itemq(ue) <Ti(beri) Germanici> fratrʿiʾs {Ti(beri)} Germ(anici) Caesar(is) non excʿeʾsserit modum probabilem, iudicare sena/tum referendum quidem esse acceptum maxume discipulinae avi ʿeʾorum et / [150] patrui et Iuliae Aug(ustae), sed tamen ipsorum quoque nominʿeʾ laudandum existu-/ mare{t}; *vacat*

LINES 151–54 PRAISE FOR THE EQUESTRIAN ORDER

item equestris ordinis curam et industriam unicʿeʾ senatui probari, / [152] quod fideliter intellexsisset, quanta res et quam ad omnium salutem pie-tatemq(ue) / [153] pertinens ageretur, et quod frequentibus adclamationi-bus adfectum animi sui / [154] et dolorem de principis nostri filiq(ue) eius iniurìs ac pro r(ei) p(ublicae) utilitate testatus sit;

LINES 155–58 PRAISE FOR THE PLEBS OF ROME

[155] plebem quoq(ue) laudare senatum, quod cum equestre ordine consenserit pietatemq(ue) / [156] suam erga principem nostrum memori-amq(ue) fili eius significaverit, et cum / [157] effusissumis studis ad repraesentandam poenam Cn(aei) Pisonis patris ab semet ipsa / [158] accensa esset, regi tamen exemplo equestris ordinis a principe nostro se passa sit;

Lines 136–46 Praise for Germanicus' wife, mother, and sister

likewise, of the others related by kinship to Germanicus [137] Caesar, the Senate greatly approves: of Agrippina, whom the memory [138] of deified Augustus, by whom she was most highly approved, and of her husband Germanicus, with whom she had lived in unique harmony, and the many children born of their most fortunate union, who survived, commended to the Senate; [140] and further the Senate greatly approves of Antonia, the mother of Germanicus Caesar, whose only marriage was to Drusus the father of Germanicus, and who, through the excellence of her moral character, demonstrated herself to deified Augustus worthy of so close a relationship; and of Livia, the sister of Germanicus Caesar, whom her grandmother and her [143] father-in-law, who is also her uncle, our Princeps, held in the highest esteem, whose esteem, even if she did not [144] belong to their family, she could deservedly vaunt, all the more as she is a woman attached by such family ties: the Senate greatly approves of these ladies in equal measure for their most loyal grief and their moderation in grief.

Lines 146–51 Praise for Germanicus' sons and brother

Likewise the fact that the child's grief felt by the sons of Germanicus [147] at the loss of such a father and especially the grief which is, in the case of Nero Caesar, already that of a young man, [148] and similarly the grief of Tiberius Germanicus, the brother of Germanicus Caesar, has not exceeded the proper limits, the Senate judges that it ought primarily to be traced back to the training of their grandfather and [150] uncle and of Iulia Augusta, but nonetheless accords them praise in their own right.

LINES 151–54 PRAISE FOR THE EQUESTRIAN ORDER

Likewise the Senate particularly approves of the conscientious efforts of the equestrian order [152] in that it had loyally understood how important a matter and how relevant to the safety and devotion of all was at stake, and because it declared with repeated acclamations its sentiments [154] and its grief for the wrongs against our Princeps and his son and did this to the advantage of the state.

LINES 155–58 PRAISE FOR THE PLEBS OF ROME

[155] That the Senate praises the plebs as well because it joined with the equestrian order in demonstrating its devotion [156] towards our Princeps and the memory of his son and, although [157] with its unrestrained enthusiasm it had roused itself to the point of itself carrying out the punishment of Gnaeus Piso Senior, it allowed itself, nevertheless, to follow the example of the equestrian order and be governed by our Princeps.

LINES 159–65 PRAISE FOR THE ARMY

[159] item senatum probare eorum militum fidem, quorum animi frustra sollicita/ti essent scelere Cn(aei) Pisonis patris, omnesq(ue), qui sub auspicìs et imperió principis / [161] nostri milites essent, quam fidem pietatemq(ue) domui Aug(ustae) par⌐a⌐rent, eam sperare / [162] perpetuo praestaturos, cum scirent salutem imperi nostri in eius dom⌐u⌐<s> custo-/ dia posita<m> esse{t}; senatum arbitrari eorum curae atq(ue) offici esse, ut aput eos ii, / [164] qui quandoq(ue) e⌐i⌐<s> praessent, plurumum auctoritatis <haberent>, qui fidelissuma pietate / [165] salutare huic urbi imperioq(ue) p(opuli) R(omani) nomen Caesarum coluissent;

LINES 165–72 INSTRUCTIONS FOR PUBLICATION OF THE DECREE

et quo facilius / [166] totius actae rei ordo posterorum memoriae tradi posset atque hi scire<nt>, quid et / [167] de singulari moderatione Germ(anici) Caesa(ris) et de sceleribus Cn(aei) Pisonis patris / [168] senatus iudicasset, placere uti oratio, quam recitasset princeps noster, / [169] itemq(ue) haec senatus consulta in {h}aere incisa, quo loco Ti(berio) Caes(ari) Aug(usto) vide/retur, ponere<n>tur, item hoc s(enatus) c(onsultum) {hic} in cuiusque provinciae celeberruma{e} / [171] urbe eiusque i<n> urbis ipsius celeberrimo loco in aere incisum figere/tur; item(que) hoc s(enatus) c(onsultum) in hibernis cuiusq(ue) legionis at signa figeretur.

LINES 172–73 SENATORIAL PROCEDURE

censu/erunt. in senatu fuerunt CCCÌ. hoc s(enatus) c(onsultum) factum est per relationem solum.

LINES 174–76 ADDENDUM (SUBSCRIPTIO) BY TIBERIUS

[174] Ti(berius) Caesar Aug(ustus) trib(unicia) potestate XXII manu mea scripsi: velle me ⌐h⌐<oc> s(enatus) c(onsultum), quod / [175] e<s>t factum IIII idus Decem(bres) Cotta et Messalla co(n)s(ulibus) referente me, scri/ptum manu Auli q(uaestoris) mei in tabellis XIIII, referri in tabulas pub<l>icas.

LINES 159–65 PRAISE FOR THE ARMY

[159] That likewise the Senate approves of the loyalty of those soldiers whose hearts had been tempted in vain [160] by the criminal activity of Gnaeus Piso Senior and hopes that all who were soldiers under the auspices and command of our Princeps will continue to manifest the same loyalty and devotion to the Imperial House which they used to deliver, since they knew that the safety of our empire depends on the protection of that House. The Senate believes that it belongs to their concern and duty that, among those [164] who commanded them at any time, the greatest authority with them belonged to those who had with the most devoted loyalty [165] cultivated the name of the Caesars, which gives protection to this city and to the empire of the Roman people.

LINES 165–72 INSTRUCTIONS FOR PUBLICATION OF THE DECREE

And in order that the course of the proceedings as a whole might be more easily transmitted to the memory of future generations and so that they might know what the Senate's judgement was [167] concerning the exceptional restraint of Germanicus Caesar and the crimes of Gnaeus Piso Senior, the Senate has decided that the speech which our Princeps had delivered [169] and also these decrees of the Senate, inscribed on bronze, should be set up in whatever place seemed best to Tiberius Caesar Augustus and that likewise this decree of the Senate, inscribed on bronze, should be set up in the most frequented city of each province and in the most frequented place in that city; [172] and that likewise this decree of the Senate should be set up in the winter quarters of each legion where the standards are kept.

LINES 172–73 SENATORIAL PROCEDURE

Decree passed. [173] There were 301 present in the Senate. This senatorial decree was passed in accordance with a single proposal.

LINES 174–76 ADDENDUM (*SUBSCRIPTIO*) BY TIBERIUS

[174] I, Tiberius Caesar Augustus, holder of tribunician power for the twenty-second time, wrote this with my own hand: it is my wish that this senatorial decree, which [175] was passed on 10 December in the year when Cotta and Messalla were consuls on the basis of my proposal and was copied [176] by the hand of my quaestor Aulus on fourteen tablets, should be placed in the public archives.

NOTES ON VARIATIONS BETWEEN COPIES OF THE TEXT

Initial line numberings are from Copy A. The fragment in the top left corner of Copy B, shown in the photograph in Eck, Caballos, Fernández (1996) Tafel 11, is not on display with the rest of the inscription in Seville. Copy A marks the beginning of paragraphs by shifting the start of the line further to the left, and has regular interpuncts. In Copy B, the accuracy of engraving is less secure in column 1 than in column 2 (Eck, Caballos, Fernández 1996: 57); there is also a tendency not to complete the letter A with the cross-bar. Copy B lacks interpuncts, save for line 1, but has similar paragraphing. Readings and comments that differ from the *editio princeps* (Eck, Caballos, Fernández 1996) are indicated in **bold**. For analysis of possible reasons for divergences between the copies, see Eich (2009), 273–75.

- Heading: Copy A only; the abbreviation pro co(n)s(ule) could also be expanded as pro co(n)s(uli) as suggested by Alicia M. Canto in *Hispania Epigraphica* 6 (1996) no.881, p.307
- Line 1: new paragraph marked by shifting A to the left in Copies A and B; quae [A1]; qua<e> [B1]
- Line 2: Valerius [A2]; Valer(ius) [B2]; Messallinus [A2]; Messal<l>inus [B2]
- Line 3: Pompeius [A3]; Pomp(eius) [B3]; f(ilius) [A3]; E [B3] = ⌜f⌝(ilius); Teret(ina) [A3]; Ter(etina tribu) [B3]
- Line 4: Asprenas [A4]; **A<sp>re[nas] [B3] [following *CIL* II, rather than ARN with underdotted N in Eck, Caballos, Fernández 1996: 23]**; Vinucius [A4]; Vinicius [B4]; Caesar divi Aug(usti) f(ilius) [A4]; Caesar <divi> Aug(usti) f(ilius) [B4]
- Line 5: tribunicia potestate [A5]; tribunic(ia) potest(ate) [B4]
- Line 6: patris [A6]; <patris> [B5]
- Line 7: rel{l}ationi [A7]; relationi [B6]
- Line 8: <et> [supplied both to A8 and B7 by Eck, Caballos, Fernández 1996: 57]
- **Line 9: visa esset [A9]; visa e<s>set [B7, with a blank space where the first S should be; E[.]SET Eck, Caballos, Fernández 1996: 24, but no damage to the surface of the bronze is visible**
- **Line 10: exposuisset [A10; [ex]/posuisset B8] [EXPOSVISET, A10: Eck, Caballos, Fernández 1996: 11 in error, since exposuisset is clearly visible on Copy A]**
- Line 12: new paragraph marked with taller S, shifted to the left in Copy A; senatum populumq(ue) Romanum (A12); senatus populusq(ue) [B9] = senatu⌜m⌝ populu⌜m⌝q(ue)
- Line 13: status **[crossbar of first T is incomplete to the right, B10]**
- Line 14: optari [A14]; <optari> [B10]; pote ut [A14; B10–11] = **non pote<st> ⌜e⌝t [following Griffin, rather than the archaising pote**

Notes on Variations between Copies of the Text 131

⸢et⸣ or pote⸢s⸣t in Eck, Caballos, Fernández 1996: 57–58; quo beneficio [A14]; quod benificio = quo{d} ben⸢e⸣ficio [B11]
- Line 15: turbare [A15; B11 – error on both copies] = turbar⸢i⸣ [Eck, Caballos, Fernández 1996: 38]; sunt [correction to s⸢i⸣nt suggested by Lebek and Salomies: Eck, Caballos, Fernández 1996: 58]; Caesare [A15] = Caesar⸢i⸣; Caesari [B12]; principi suo [A15; Eck, Caballos, Fernández 1996: 38]; **principi nostro [following B12; González 2002: 360, 382]**
- Line 17: senatui [A17]; senatus [B13] = senatu⸢i⸣
- Line 18: admirari [A18]; **admirarì {se} [B13: the engraver may have duplicated se, having started to engrave the word senatum, only to run out of space, restarting the complete word on the next line]**; quod cum manufestissuma [A18]; quod <cum> manufestissum<a> *vacat* [B14: there is blank space where the A should be engraved]
- Line 19: causam [A19]; causa<m> [B15]
- Line 20: filiosq(ue) [A]; filiosque [B15]; hortatus [A20]; <h>ortatus [B15]; defenderent [A20]; defenderet [B16, Eck, Caballos, Fernández 1996: 24]; **deffnderf<n>t [B16; not all the letter Es are completely engraved, cf. González 2002: 360]**
- Line 21: **esse[t] <ob eam rem> [A21]: since the bronze is damaged at this point, the T might have been engraved originally, rather than assuming the error esse<t ob eam rem>; esset ob eam rem [B16]**
- Line 22: utriq(ue) [A22]; utr<i>q(ue) [B17]; Pisone [A22]; Pisonim [B17] = Pison⸢e⸣; facerft [A22: E incompletely engraved]
- Line 23: new paragraph marked by shifting I to the left in Copy A; itaq(ue) [A23]; itaque [B18]; aliquot (A23); aliquod [B18] = aliquo⸢t⸣; accus{s}atoribus [Copy A]; accusatoribus [B18]. See further the commentary for a discussion of alternative interpretations dependent upon different punctuation.
- Line 24: Pisone patre [A24]; <patre> [B18]; exemplaria [A24]; exemp{u}laria [B19]; **codicillorun [A24: Eck, Caballos, Fernández 1996: 12, but possibly faint traces visible of the final upright for an M] = codicilloru⸢m⸣**; codicllorum [B19] = **codic⸢i⸣llorum** [Eck, Caballos, Fernández 1996: 24]
- Line 25: cuiusq(ue) ordinis [A25]; quoiusque ii ordinis [B20: Eck, Caballos, Fernández 1996: 24, 58]; **quoiusque ll ordinis [engraver's error may be the result of the fact that LLORD is engraved a little beneath LLOR of CODICILLORVM in the previous line – the two uprights are not the letter I but L]**
- Line 26: <senatum> admirari [A26; B20; retained by González, 2002: 360, 384] cf. Gil 1999: 218; alternative emendations reviewed by Eck, Caballos, Fernández 1996: 58 – <senatum> a⸢rb⸣i<t>rari

- [Eck]; a⸢rb⸣i<t>rari <senatum> [Jones, Lebek]; <senatum?> a⸢rbit⸣rari [*CIL* II² 900]; <senatui> a⸢pp⸣ar⸢ere⸣ [Reeve]
- Lines 26–27: evictam [A26–27]; evicta<m> [B21]
- Line 28: cuius [A28]; quoius [B22]; fuisse *vacat* [B22]; **causam Cn. [A28: cf. Gradel 2014], updating c[ausam Cn] Pisonem [Eck, Caballos, Fernández 1996: 12]**; caussam Cn. Pisonem [B22]; caussam Cn. Pisonem [Eck, Caballos, Fernández 1996: 40]
- Line 29: renuntiasse [A29 – letters damaged; only partially legible]
- Line 31: conponendum [A31]; componendum [B25]
- Lines 32–33: neclecta / maiestate [A32–33]; neclecta *vacat* maiestate{m} [B26]; **ne⸢g⸣lecta [following González 2002: 384]**
- Line 33: neclecto **[ne⸢g⸣lecto, following González 2002: 384]**
- Line 33: quo<d> adleg pro cos [A33]; quod adlegt *vacat* pro cos [B 27: **the T has an additional lower stroke, like an E without cross-bar] = quod adle⸢c⸣t<us> pro cos; pro co(n)s(uli) et ei proco(n)s(uli) [Caballos, Eck, Fernández 1996: 123, followed by González 2002: 385]**; Eck, Caballos, Fernández (1996) 40 n.41 argue that pro co(n)s(ule) should be understood as dative case in both instances here, but do not actually print pro co(n)s(uli). De Martino, 1996: 479 suggests that some words may have accidentally dropped out here, such as *obsequium deberet* in front of *ei proconsuli*.
- Line 34: quamcumq(ue) provinciam [A34]; qua<mcum>q(ue) / [–3?–] provinciam [B27–28]
- Lines 34–35: maius ei imperium / quam ei [A34–35]; minus ei imperium quam sibi [B28] = m⸢ai⸣us ei imperium quam ⸢ei⸣
- Line 35: procos A35 and B28 [Eck, Caballos, Fernández 1996: 40 expand as proco(n)s(ule); **following González 2002: 385 who expands as proco(n)s(ul)]**; maius [A35]; minus [B29] = m⸢ai⸣us
- Line 36: Ti Caesari <Augusto> [A36]; Ti Cae<s>are Aug [B29, with a blank space for the missing S in CAE ARE] = Cae<s>ar⸢i⸣; Germ(anico) Caesar(i) [A36]; Germanico Caesari [B29]; potestatis omnia [A36]; potestatis <omnia> [B30]
- Line 37: cum in provincia Syria fu<er>it [A37: fuerit printed by Eck, Caballos, Fernández 1996: 40 in their reconstructed text, although they prefer fuit (59)]; <cum> in provincia{m} Syria{m} fuerit [B30]
- Lines 37–38: cesserit bellum {cum} Armeniacum / et Parthicum [A37–38] = ⸢g⸣esserit bellum {cum} Armeniacum et Parthicum; [bell]um Armeniacum et Part<h>icum [B31: **there seems no need to assume that the engraver of Copy B replicated the error of cum from Copy A – the underdotted C printed in Eck, Caballos, Fernández 1996: 25 is far from certain**]; bellum cum Armeniacum / ⸢tum⸣ Parthicum [Lebek in Eck, Caballos, Fernández 1996: 59; Gil 1999: 218]; <ut> bellum {cum} Armeniacum (González 2002: 361); i[p]so [A38]

- Line 39: epistuli[s]q(ue) [A39]; Germ(anici) Caesar(is) [A39]; Germanici Caesaris [B32]
- Line 40: Pahrtorum [A40]; **Part(h)orum [B33]**; Parthorum [Eck, Caballos, Fernández 1996: 40]
- Line 41: start of column 2 in Copy A; quod [A41]; qu<od> [B33: **the engraver runs out of space for the last two letters at the end of the line**]
- Line 42: Armenia [A42]; Armenia{m} [B35]
- Line 43: Vonone<s> vel occiso vel expulso [A43]; Vonone<s> vel oc<c>iso vel inpulso [B35] = Vonone<s> vel oc<c>iso vel ˹ex˺pulso
- Line 44: senatusq(ue) ei genti regem [A44]; senatus<q(ue)> regem ei genti [B36]; <eam> [A44; B36 – direct object of verb occuparet omitted from both copies]; <eam> or <regnum> [Reeve, Heinrichs, Jones in Eck, Caballos, Fernández 1996: 59; Gil 1999: 218]
- Line 45: corruptus [A45]; corruptis [B37] = corrupt˹u˺s; bellum etiam civile{m} [A45]; bellum etiam civile [B37]
- Line 46: numine [A46]; numini [B38] = numin˹e˺; Caesaris Auc [A46] = Au˹g˺; Caesaris Aug(usti) [B38]
- Line 47: civilis belli [A47]; civibus bellis [B38] = civi˹li˺s belli{s}; provinciam Syriam [A47]; provinciam <Syriam> [B39]
- Line 49: milites R(omani) inter se concurrere coacti sint [A49]; militem Romani inter se concucurre conati sunt [B40] = milite˹s˺ Romani inter se con{cu}curre<re> co˹ac˺ti s˹i˺nt [Eck, Caballos, Fernández 1996: 60]; coacti sunt [Damon in Potter and Damon 1999: 20]
- Line 50: crudelitate [A50]; crudelitate{m} [B41]; causa [A50]; caussa [B41]; sententia [A50]; sententia{m} [B41]; plurimos [A50]; plurumos [B41]
- Line 51: tantum<m>odo [A51]; tantummodo [B42]
- Line 52: fixsisset [A52]; fixi/[sset] [B42–43]; discipulinam a divo [A52]; disciplinam ab divo [B43]
- Line 53: a Ti(berio) Caesar(e) [A53]; ab Ti(berio) Caesare [B43]
- Lines 53–54: militibus <ne> / his [A53–54: **ne is omitted at the end of the line, although there is empty space available**]; militibus <ne h>is [B44] – ne supplied by Eck, Caballos, Fernández (1996) 60
- Line 54: parere<n>t [A54]; parerent [B44]
- Line 55: facto [A55]; facti [B45] = fact˹o˺
- Line 56: eos [A56]; eo<s> [B 46]; post talis [A56]; <t>alis [B46]
- Line 57: paruisse<n>t {ut} qui [A57]; paruisse<n>t qui [B47] – Eck, Caballos, Fernández (1996) 60; cuius [A57]; quoius [B47]
- Lines 57–58: interitum [A57–58]; interiium [**second T lacks crossbar: B47 = interi˹t˺um**]
- Line 58: non p R [A58]; <non> p R [B47]; luxerint [A58]; luxserunt [B48: Eck, Caballos, Fernández 1996: 60]

- Line 59: ausus est [A59]; ausus sit [B49]
- Line 60: debeba‹n›tur [A60]; [debe]bantur [B50]
- Line 61: odia non patitur [A61]; ‹odia› non pati{un}tur [B50]
- Line 62: his argumentis senatui apparuerit [A62]; is argumentis senatus apparaverit [B51] = ‹h›is argumentis senatu ͡i ͡ appar{a}uerit
- Line 63: vehebatur ornatae sint [A63]; veheba{n}tur ‹ornatae› sint [B52]
- Lines 63–64: reclu/serit [A63–64]; recluserunt [B52] =recluser ͡i ͡ t
- Line 64: imperi R(omani) [A64]; imperi{i} Romani [B53]
- Line 65: que habitus [A65: these letters were omitted in error, and later squeezed in between lines 64–65, above eiusdem animi]; e‹iu›sdemq(ue) [B53]; quod dedisset [A65]; quod dedisse‹t› [B54]; quod eum dedisse [Jones, Lebek in Eck, Caballos, Fernández 1996: 60; González 2002: 387–88]
- Line 66: Germanici ‹Caesaris› [A66]; Germanici Caesaris [B54]
- Lines 66–67: probatum‹q(ue)› sit frequen/ter{q(ue)} [A66–67]; [pro]-batum‹q(ue)› sit frequenter{q(ue)} [B54–55] – emendation to Copies A and B by Reeve, Salomies in Eck, Caballos, Fernández (1996) 60; probatum sit frequenterq(ue) – González (2002) 387–88
- Line 67: iiis [A67, with H lacking the crossbar]; iis [B55]; Germanici ‹Caesaris› [A67 and B55]
- Line 69: aut imaginibus [A69: T lacks crossbar]; aut imagines [B57] = imagin ͡ ibu ͡ s
- Line 70: refferentur habebantur [A70]; referretur ei r[eddi]/tae erant habeba{n}tur [B57–58]; referre{n}tur, eì r[eddi]tae erant, habeba{n}tur – Eck, Caballos, Fernández (1996) 61. Other restorations include r[e-cep]tae and r[ela]tae (see discussion in Eck, Caballos, Fernández 1996: 186]
- Line 71: new paragraph marked by shifting Q to the left in Copy A; optulissi [A71: final E lacks crossbar]; optulisse [B58]; deditae [A71; B59] = de ͡ b ͡ itae [emended by Eck, Caballos, Fernández 1996: 61]
- Line 72: in minore [A72]; in minorem [B59] = inmin ͡ e ͡ re [emended by Eck, Caballos, Fernández 1996: 42, who observe that this mistake presumably stems from the exemplar text from which both Copy A and B were produced]; intellegeba{n}t [A72; B60] [emended by Eck, Caballos, Fernández 1996: 42]
- Line 73: subtraxsisse [A73]; subtraxisse [B60]; his [A73]; iis [B60]
- Line 74: causa [A74]; caussa [B61]; {e}is more maiorum [A74]; {e}is more ‹maiorum› [B61]; quibus is [Reeve in Eck, Caballos, Fernández 1996: 61]; quibus e ͡ x ͡ more maiorum [Jones in Eck, Caballos, Fernández 1996: 61]; e ͡ x ͡ s [Gil 1999: 218]; s(enatus) c(onsultum) [A74]; senatus consultum [B61]
- Line 77: cognatione{m} [A77]; cognatione [B64]

- Line 78: gentis [A78]; genti<s> [B64]
- Lines 78–79: cognatus adfinisve ... fuisset [A78–79]; cognati adfinesve ... fuissent [Haensch in Eck, Caballos, Fernández 1996: 61]
- Line 79: esset [A79]; esse<t> [B65]; {esset} [Reeve, Lebek in Eck, Caballos, Fernández 1996: 62]; mortuos esset, <et> lugen/dus esset [Suerbaum 1999: 215; cf. Gil 1999: 218]
- Column 2 of Copy B begins at B65 [---]ae fuisset mortuos; a large number of letters is missing from the start of each line, down to B76
- Line 80: imagines <quae> exequias [A80]; imagines <quae> ex/[equias] [B65–66] – quae supplied by Eck, Caballos, Fernández (1996) 62; **imagines <quibus> [following Griffin, Jones in Eck, Caballos, Fernández 1996: 62 and Potter 1998: 440]**
- Line 81: imaginibus familiae Calpurniae [A81]; imaginibus <familiae> Calpurnia<e> [B66: **the final E is omitted at the end of the line, where there is no more space available**]
- Line 82: nomen on [A82] = nomen ˋCˊn(aei) [O for C, emended by Eck, Caballos, Fernández 1996: 15]; [uti(que) Cn(aei) Pisonis p]atris nomen [B67]
- Line 83: Caesaris [A83]; Caesari<s> [**B67, where the final S is omitted at the end of the line, where there is no more space available**]
- Line 85: start of column 3 in Copy A; eum saltum placeret Caesari Augusto [A85]; [---]e saltum placere Ti(berio) Caesari Aug(usto) [B69]
- Line 87: pari eum [A87] = ˋdˊari eum; dari eum [B70]; desiderasset quod <civitates> quarum fines [A87]; desideras<s>et, quod <civitates>, quarum <fines> [B70] – emended by Eck, Caballos, Fernández (1996) 62; <gentes> rather than <civitates> [Reeves, Jones in Eck, Caballos, Fernández 1996: 62; Gil 1999: 218]
- Line 88: final M in servorum incompletely engraved at the end of the line, like an A lacking cross-bar [A88]; servorum [B71]
- Line 89: questae essent atq(ue) [A89]; quae sita esset adq(ue) [B71] = qu{a}es{i}ta<e> esse<n>t aˋtˊq(ue)
- Line 90: possent [A90]; [po]sse<nt> [B72]; iustitiaeq(ue) [A90–91]; **iustitiae<q> [B73: engraver runs out of space at line end]**
- Line 91: <atq(ue)> animi magnitudinis [A91 – emended as <atq(ue)> by Jones, Lebek or <et> by Correa, Ferrary in Eck, Caballos, Fernández (1996) 62; quas virtutes {quas} a maioribus [A91]; virtutes quˋomˊ or quˋumˊ, balancing tum in the next clause [Jones in Eck, Caballos, Fernández 1996: 62, followed by Potter and Damon 1999; Lott 2012: 148, 290]; {quas} emended by Reeve in Eck, Caballos, Fernández (1996) 62; [atq(ue) animi magnitudinis, quas virtutes {qu]as} ab maioribus [B73], including atq(ue) rather than assuming that the engraver of Copy B necessarily duplicated the error of Copy A here, although Copy B does then seem to have repeated the mistake of duplicating the word quas

- Line 93: humanumq(ue) censere [A93]; humanumq(ue) censep [H lacks crossbar; R incompletely engraved, as P: B74] = cense⌈r⌉[e]
- Line 94: fuisset quem [A94]; **fuisset et quem [B75, following González 2002: 365 in prioritising Copy B here]**
- Line 95: Germanicus <Caesar> [A95; B75 – Eck, Caballos, Fernández 1996: 62 note that the word Caesar must have been omitted in error from the original text copied into A and B]; modest{est}iae corrected by Lott (2012) 290 – but unclear where this reading has come from
- Lines 96–97: pignora {quem Germanicus quoq(ue) liberalitate sua honorasset} ex quibus [A96–97: phrase repeated in error]; pignora ex quibus [B76]
- Line 97: dissimillumum [A97]; dissimillum<um> [B76]
- Line 98: bonorum partem dimidiam eumq(ue) [A98]; [part]em dimidiam bonorum eumq(ue) [B77]
- Line 100: mutas<s>et [A100]; mutasset [B78]; qu<o>i inpunitatem senatus [A100]; qu<o>i inpunitate<m> *vacat* senatus [B78 – both emended by Eck, Caballos, Fernández 1996: 62]; Mackay 2003: 348 n.91 suggests that we should retain qui, as equivalent to cui; hum[anitati...] – [B79] H lacks crossbar
- Line 101: esse{t} [A101 and B79, both emended by Eck, Caballos, Fernández 1996: 44]
- Line 102: pervenire<t> [A102, emended by Eck, Caballos, Fernández 1996: 44]
- Line 105: Pisonis filiae [A105]; Pisonis f(iliae) [B81]
- Line 106: quam = qua⌈e⌉ [A106]; quae [B82]
- Line 109: new paragraph marked by shifting Q to the left in Copies A and B84; qu<o>i [A109, emended by Eck, Caballos, Fernández 1996: 63; Mackay 2003: 348 n.91 suggests that we should retain qui, as equivalent to cui]
- Line 110: misericordia{m} [A110, emended by Eck, Caballos, Fernández 1996: 46]; miseridocordia{m} [transcription error in González 2002: 366]
- Line 111: habere{t} [A111]; habere [B85]
- Line 112: pius [A112: **reading not clear, but first letter does not appear to be P; instead, there appear to be two letters superimposed, perhaps an incomplete E and D**] = ⌈e⌉ius [emended by Eck, Caballos, Fernández 1996: 63]; [ei]us [B86]
- Line 113: uti M(arco) filio [A113]; uti M(arco) f(ilio) [B86]; suae deprecari se et [A113] = suae depreca⌈tus⌉ s⌈it⌉ et [Hinz, Jones]; sua<e> / deprecasetq[---] [B86–87] = suae depreca⌈tus⌉ s⌈it⌉q(ue); deprecari se <veniam testatus sit> [Reeve]; deprecari se <testatus sit> [Lebek]; deprecari se <dixerit> et [Correa] – all in Eck, Caballos, Fernández (1996) 63
- Line 114: et mater [A114], Eck – **but more like E without cross-bar followed by P** = ⌈id⌉ mater [emended by Eck, Caballos, Fernández

1996: 63]; eˈaˈ [Lebek, Salomies in Eck, Caballos, Fernández 1996: 63; followed by Potter and Damon 1999: 32]; iustissumas [A114]; [iustis]suma<s> ae ea sibi causas [B87: B in ab incompletely engraved] = [iustis]suma<s> aˈbˈ ea sibi causas [Eck, Caballos, Fernández 1996: 28]

- Line 115 acceperit [emended to adiecerit by Salomies in Eck, Caballos, Fernández 1996: 63]
- Line 117: **posse** [A117, B89, governed by deberet; posse<t> emended by Eck, Caballos, Fernández 1996: 63]
- Line 118: petere [A118, B89]; **petere<t> [emended by Jones, Lebek, Salomies in Eck, Caballos, Fernández 1996: 63; cf. Potter 1998: 440; Gil 1999: 218]**
- Line 118: summa<e> [A118, emended by Eck, Caballos, Fernández 1996: 46]
- Line 121: maleficiorum <socis ac ministris> aqua [A121]; maleficiorum socis ac minis/tris aqua [F engraved without central bar, B91–92]
- Line 122: qul lege{m} [A122] = quˈiˈ lege [emended by Eck, Caballos, Fernández 1996: 18]; pr(aetoribus) qui [A122]; pr oui [B92: Q is engraved lacking its tail] = pr(aetoribus) ˈqˈui [emended by Eck, Caballos, Fernández 1996: 29]
- Line 123: prae<e>sse<n>t [A123]; praeesse<n>t [B92] – both emended by Eck, Caballos, Fernández (1996) 63; praeesset (Mackay 2003: 352 n.97), supplying pr(aetore) rather than pr(aetoribus) at end of 122; iudic<ar>et [A123, emended by Jones in Eck, Caballos, Fernández 1996: 64]
- Line 124: par<en>tium [A124, emended by Jones, Reeve in Eck, Caballos, Fernández 1996: 64]; pa{r}tˈrˈum [Gil 1999: 219]; [par]tium [B93]; antecessise [A124]; antecess<iss>e [B93]; Ti(berium) Caesar(em) Aug(ustum) [A124]; Ti(berium) Caesarem Aug(ustum) [B93]; principem [A124]; principim [B93 – incompletely engraved E] = principˈeˈm
- Line 125: tantum et iam aequali dolore totiens conspectis [A125] = tantˈiˈ et ˈtˈam aequali<s> dolorˈiˈ<s eius indicis> totiens conspectis [Eck, Caballos, Fernández 1996: 64]; tantˈiˈ et ˈtˈam aequali<s> dolorˈiˈ<s indiciis> totiens conspectis [Jones]; <tantis lacrimis civium non patienter> tantum <sed> et iam aequali dolore totiens conspectis [Lebek] – both in Eck, Caballos, Fernández 1996: 64; t[---] [B94]; tanto et tam aequali dolore, totiens conspectis <et fletibus> Bodel in Potter and Damon (1999) 32; tantum <per tempus oculis eius umentibus perpetuo> et iam aequali [Lebek 1999: 189]
- Line 126: magnopere [A126]; magnopepe [B94, incompletely engraved R] = magnopeˈrˈe
- Line 128: **qui supersit [A128, following diplomatic text in Eck, Caballos, Fernández 1996: 18 – the bronze is damaged here on**

Copy A, but the traces look like QVI rather than QVPI]; qui (Lebek 1999: 189–90, who notes that this is given by Eck, Caballos, Fernández in their diplomatic transcription of the text); qu{p}i [su]persit [emended in composite text by Eck, Caballos, Fernández 1996: 46]; qu⸢i⸣ [González 2002: 367]; quanto maiore curae dis = ⸢t⸣anto maior⸢i⸣ curae [Eck, Caballos, Fernández 1996: 46]
- Line 129: futuram [A129]; futura⸢e⸣ [Lebek 1999: 189]
- Line 130: repos[i]ta<m> [A130, supplied by Eck, Caballos, Fernández 1996: 46]
- Line 131: start of column 4 in Copy A; voltum [A131 – Eck, Caballos, Fernández 1996: 18 note that Copy A might appear to have VOTTVM engraved here, given that the engraver has carved an extended lower bar on the L together with an extended cross-bar on the T to the left]
- Line 132: senatum laudare magnopere [A132]; senatum magnopere laudare [B98]
- Line 134: animadvertere{t} [A134 and B99 – emended by Eck, Caballos, Fernández 1996: 64]; hunc [A134]; iiunc [B99: H lacks crossbar]
- Lines 136–37: Germanic(um) / Caesar(em) [A136–37]; [Germ]anicum Caesarem [B101]
- Line 137: **quam senatui memoria{m} [A137, following González 2002: 368]**; memoria{m} [Salomies in Eck, Caballos, Fernández 1996: 64]; probare <animum> Agrippinae [Reeve in Caballos, Eck, Fernández 1996: 119]
- Line 138: <aui> divi Augusti [A138, emended by Lebek 1999: 190]; qu<o>i fuisset probatissum(a) [A138: emended by Eck, Caballos, Fernández 1996: 64]; [prob]atissuma [B102]
- Line 139: com<m>endare [A139]; commendare [B103]; commendare<t> González (2002) 368; **commendare<nt> [following Salomies in Eck, Caballos, Fernández 1996: 64]**
- Line 143: idem<q>(ue) [A143]; idemq(ue) [B105]; iudicaret [A143]; iudicare<n>t [emended by Lebek 1999: 190]
- Lines 143–44: contin/gere{n}t [A143–44, emended by Eck, Caballos, Fernández 1996: 48]
- Line 145: dolorum [A145, followed by González 2002: 368] = dolor⸢e⸣m [emended by Eck, Caballos, Fernández 1996: 48]
- Line 146: moderatione<m> [A146; B107, emended by Eck, Caballos, Fernández 1996: 48]
- Line 147: in Nerone{m} Caesare{m} [A147; B108, emended by Eck, Caballos, Fernández 1996: 48]; iu<v>enis [A147, emended by Eck, Caballos, Fernández 1996: 48, commenting that iu<v>en<il>is is also possible; cf. Lebek 1999: 190]

Notes on Variations between Copies of the Text

- Line 148: itemq(ue) fratres Ti(beri) Germ(anici) Caesar(is) non excusserit [A148 – diplomatic text in Eck, Caballos, Fernández 1996: 19 prints FRATRIS, with an underdotted I, whereas the diplomatic text in Caballos, Eck, Fernández 1996: 31 prints FRATRES, which appears confirmed from autopsy] = fratrˈiˈs; [---e]xcusserit [B109] = itemq(ue) <Ti(beri) Germanici> fratris {Ti(beri)} Germ(anici) Caesar(is) non excˈeˈsserit [emended by Eck, Caballos, Fernández 1996: 65]; fratris Ti. Germ. {Caesar} [emended by Lebek 1999: 190]
- Line 149: morum [A149] = ˈeˈorum [emended by Eck, Caballos, Fernández 1996: 19, 65]
- Line 150: tamen [A150]; tam<en> [B110]
- Lines 150–51: nominum laudandum existu/maret [A150–51, Eck, Caballos, Fernández 1996: 19, diplomatic text, emended as existu-/mare{t}, 65]; = nominˈeˈ laudandum existumare{t}; no[---] B110
- Line 151: unici [A151; B111] = unicˈeˈ [emended by Eck, Caballos, Fernández 1996: 65 – crossbar missing from E]
- quod [A152]; ouod [B111 – Q engraved lacking tail: Eck, Caballos, Fernández 1996: 29]
- Line 155: new paragraph marked by shifting P to the left in Copy A; **equestre [A155]** = equestrˈiˈ [emended by Eck, Caballos, Fernández 1996: 65; **following Potter and Damon 1999: 38, who retain equestre**]
- Line 157: repraesentandam poenam [A157]; [re] *vacat* praesentandam <poenam> [B115]
- Line 158: se passa [A158]; <se passa> [B116]
- Line 159: new paragraph marked by shifting I to the left in Copy A
- Line 160: sub [A160]; <sub> [B117]
- Line 161: parerent [A161] = pˈraestaˈrent [emended by Jones, Lebek in Eck, Caballos, Fernández 1996: 66]; **parˈaˈrent [following Bodel in Potter and Damon 1999: 38]**
- Lines 162–63: domo custo/dia posita esset [A162–63] = domˈuˈ<s> custodia posita<m> esse{t} [emended by Eck, Caballos, Fernández 1996: 48]
- Line 164: et praessent plurumum auctoritatis qui [A164] = eˈiˈ<s> praessent plurumum auctoritatis <haberent> qui [emended by Griffin, Jones in Eck, Caballos, Fernández 1996: 66]
- Line 165: facelius [A165] = facˈiˈlius [emended by Eck, Caballos, Fernández 1996: 20]
- Line 166: atque hi scire<nt> [A166, emended by Jones, Lebek, Vollmer in Eck, Caballos, Fernández 1996: 66]; ato iì{s} sci/[rent] [B121–22 = Q lacks tail] = atˈqˈ(ue) ii sci/[rent]
- Line 169: in haere [A169] = in {h}aere [emended by Eck, Caballos, Fernández 1996: 50]

- Line 170: poneretur item hoc s(enatus) c(onsultum) hic n [A170]; poneretur utiq(ue) hoc s(enatus) c(onsultum) in [B123, in – N lacks left-hand vertical stroke] = ponere<n>tur item hoc s(enatus) c(onsultum) {hic} in [emended by Eck, Caballos, Fernández 1996: 50]; poneretur [retained by González 2002: 370]; celeberruma{e} [A170, emended by Eck, Caballos, Fernández 1996: 50]
- Lines 171–72: i<n> urbis [A171, emended by Eck, Caballos, Fernández 1996: 50]; figere/tur item [A171–72]; [figere]{n}tur itemq(ue) [B124]; in hiber/[---] [B124: N engraved without left upright stroke]
- Line 174: new paragraph marked by shifting T to the left in Copy A; velle me h(oc) s(enatus) c(onsultum), Eck, Caballos, Fernández 1996: 50: diplomatic text of Copy A174 – VELLE MEI SC, emended by Eck, Caballos, Fernández 1996: 21, 66 as velle me{i} ʽhʼ(oc) or vellem h(oc); h<oc> s(enatus) c(onsultum) [Potter and Damon 1999: 40]; **velle me ʽhʼ<oc> s(enatus) c(onsultum) emending I at end of MEI to H and supplying OC for hoc**
- Line 175: e<s>t factum [A175, emended by Eck]; *vacat* between Decem and Cotta [A175]; [M]essa<l>la [B126]
- Line 176: pub<l>icas [A176, emended by Eck, Caballos, Fernández 1996: 21]

COMMENTARY

Commentary

HEADING

Copy A starts with an unusual feature for this kind of inscription: a prominent heading which identifies the main topic of the senatorial decree and the circumstances in which it is being published (Eck, Caballos, Fernández, 1996: 126–28, with discussion of the few parallels that exist; Lott, 2012: 257). The contemporary senatorial decree from Larinum of AD 19, by contrast, simply has the lettering S C as a heading (*AE* 1978, 145 / *AE* 1983, 210 = LACTOR 19, Q1). It is likely that the heading was added by the authorities at Irni who set up the inscription, perhaps imitating wording used by the governor (Eck, Caballos, Fernández, 1996: 126–29). A good parallel is the heading of the *Res Gestae* at Ancyra, which documents the provincial initiative to set up the inscription (Cooley, 2009: 102–04).

s(enatus) c(onsultum) de Cn(aeo) Pisone patre / Decree of the Senate concerning Gnaeus Piso senior It is unclear whether there was a system for naming senatorial decrees, but they were apparently more often identified by the name(s) of the presiding consul(s) or emperor than by subject-matter (Talbert, 1984: 304–05, 435–36). A later exception under Vespasian is the *SC Macedonianum*, named after Macedo, a notorious usurer, who encouraged sons to take out loans in expectation of their fathers' deaths (*Dig.* 14.6.1.pr. [Ulpian]; Talbert, 1984: 305; Malloch, 2013: 214 on chronology). The prominence given here to Piso's name (even though unlikely to have been the Senate's decision: Eck, Caballos, Fernández, 1996: 130) reflects the fact that the Senate wanted his behaviour to be displayed as a deterrent, and only to abolish memory of him in specific circumstances (see §7). Flower (1999: 100) suggests that 'the penalties imposed on Piso reflect a tension between the desire to remember the villain, by holding him up as an example to warn others, and the desire to erase his memory, since being forgotten is integral to his punishment', and that the contradiction inherent in displaying his name prominently at the top of the decree is typical of Roman sanctions against memory more widely.

propositum / published   This is the technical term used for setting up an inscribed text in public, usually on whiteboards (*TLL* s.v. 'propono', IA: *quae palam exhibentur, ostenduntur*). For example, Livy (9.46) uses this verb to describe the publication in the Forum on whiteboards of a calendar of court-days in 304 BC by aedile Cn. Flavius (*fastosque circa forum in albo proposuit*), an act which was celebrated as giving people access to essential information for the first time (cf. Cic., *Mur.* 25). For the language of official publication, see also the edicts organising the *ludi saeculares* in 17 BC (*CIL* VI 32323 = LACTOR 17, L27: *edictum propositum est*); the Anauni edict of Claudius, AD 46 (*CIL* V 5050 = LACTOR 19, M19: *edictum Ti(beri) Claudi Caesaris Augusti Germanici propositum fuit id quod infra scriptum est*); and the edict of the urban praetor at Rome recorded on a wooden tablet at Herculaneum in AD 62 (*AE* 2006, 305, Tab. III: *descriptum e[t recognitum ex] edicto L. Seru[eni Gall]i pr(aetoris) quod propositum erat Ro[mae]*).

N(umerio) Vibio Sereno pro co(n)s(ule) / in the proconsulship of Numerius Vibius Serenus   N. Vibius Serenus (*PIR*² V575) (whose *praenomen* was confirmed for the first time by this heading) was proconsul of Baetica in AD 20/21 or 21/22, but was called to stand trial at Rome in AD 23 on a charge of the arbitrary use of force against Roman citizens (*vis publica*) and exiled (Tac., *Ann.* 4.13, with Woodman, 2018: 121; Eck, Caballos, Fernández, 1996: 101–03). Only a year later he was brought back from exile to stand trial for *maiestas* and once again exiled. In AD 16 he had played a role in prosecuting Libo Drusus (Tac., *Ann.* 4.28–30; see §2). The naming of the governor appears here simply as a dating clause (see §4). Other cases where *proponere* is used with an agent also include the preposition *a/ab* (*Dig.* 21.2.31 [Ulpian]: *quae ab aedilibus proponitur*; Suet., *Calig.* 16.1: *rationes imperii ab Augusto proponi solitas sed a Tiberio intermissas publicavit*). Alternatively, the abbreviation might be expanded as *pro co(n)s(uli)* rather than *pro co(n)sul(e)* (as suggested by Canto in *Hispania Epigraphica* 6 (1996) no.881), which would result in a dative of agent: 'by Numerius Vibius Serenus, proconsul'. The use of the verb would then imply that the inscription was created in accordance with instructions contained in an edict issued by the governor in the provincial capital at Corduba (Grelle, 2000: 224). This would fit with the publication instructions of the *SCPP*, which deal with the distribution of the decree from Rome to provincial governors (*SCPP* lines 165–72; but see further discussion in §4).

LINES 1–4 PREAMBLE (*PRAESCRIPTIO*)

The opening of the decree is conventional in listing the date and place of the Senate's meeting, along with details of who was witness to the editing of the decree (Talbert, 1984: 304). This consisted of five senators who had a particular interest in the matter in hand plus the two urban quaestors (Volterra, 1993: 217; for doubts about the members having special interest, see Eck, Caballos, Fernández, 1996: 134, depending upon Tacitus' account of the debate). Once the wording of the decree was approved, it was validated by being deposited in the archive of the treasury at the Temple of Saturn (*aerarium Saturni*) by the urban quaestors (see 176n., **referri in tabulas pub<l>icas**) (Bonnefond-Coudry, 1989: 570; Coudry, 1994: 66).

Line 1: a(nte) d(iem) IIII eid(us) Dec(embres) / On 10 December The decision to call the Senate to meet on 10 December may be significant, as Potter (1998: 441–42) observes, given that this is the day on which new tribunes entered office each year. Tiberius may have chosen this date on which to bring the matter before the Senate as it was traditionally the day on which legislation was brought forward by these new tribunes, given that he was summoning the Senate in virtue of his tribunician power (see 5n., **tribunicia potestate XXII**). Alternatively, the date simply reflects the fact that this was when the proceedings against Piso had ended in the Senate (Eck, Caballos, Fernández, 1996: 130; see §3 for further discussion of the chronological problems posed by the decree). The date usually refers to the date of the senatorial meeting rather than of the drafting process, although they may have been the same (Volterra, 1993: 218). In both Copy A and Copy B, the beginning of this line is extended to the left of the main body of text, in order to designate a new paragraph. In Copy B only, the first three lines are engraved in larger lettering, perhaps to compensate for the lack of a heading. The first line in Copy B also contains triangular interpuncts between words, making it stand out visually.

Line 1: in Palatio in porticu, quae est ad Apollinis / on the Palatine in the portico at the Temple of Apollo The Senate met in the complex of the Temple of Palatine Apollo, which had been vowed by Augustus in 36 BC after his victory at Naulochus against Sextus Pompeius and dedicated on 9 October 28 BC (Gros, 1993). Its close connection to Augustus was emphasised by its being built on land allocated to it from Augustus' house, which had been struck by lightning (Suet., *Aug.* 29, who also attests to its use for meetings of the Senate). The portico adjacent to it was part of a library complex, of which the Latin library was consecrated as a *templum* and used for meetings of the Senate (Bonnefond-Coudry, 1989: 179–82; Corbier, 1992: 893–98; Palombi, 1993b; Coarelli, 2003: 65–66; Wiseman, 2019: 132–39). On display there were shield-portraits (*imagines clipeatae*) depicting famous orators (with one of Germanicus himself and his father Drusus added by the Senate as part of the honours decreed to him following his death: *Tabula Hebana*, lines 1–4 = Crawford, 1996: 519 = LACTOR 19, J8j), and a statue of Augustus in the guise of Apollo (Pseudo-Acron on Hor. *Epist.* 1.3.17; Servius on Verg.

Ecl. 4.10; Corbier, 1992: 901–12). In December AD 19 the Senate had also met here to determine what honours to bestow upon the deceased Germanicus (*Tabula Hebana* = Crawford, 1996: no.37, line 1 = LACTOR 19, J8j), and the bronze inscription recording these was on display here (*Tabula Siarensis* = Crawford, 1996: no.37, frag. b, col. ii, 21–22 = LACTOR 19, J8h). This meeting-place was not used by the Senate exclusively for discussing matters closely related to the imperial family, given that the senatorial decree from Larinum prohibiting upper-class participation in public performances was also passed in the same venue (*AE* 1978, 145 / *AE* 1983, 210 = LACTOR 19, Q1). Nevertheless, the venue's display of honours for members of the imperial household, its proximity to houses belonging to Augustus, Tiberius, and Germanicus himself (Joseph., *AJ* 19.117), and its recent hosting of the Senate when it had met to discuss how best to honour the deceased Germanicus must have fostered an emotionally charged atmosphere within which to discuss Piso's crimes against Germanicus (Eck, 1995b: 7). Although Tacitus appears to indicate that Piso's trial took place in the *curia Iulia* rather than on the Palatine (*Ann.* 3.14.4: *simul populi ante curiam uoces audiebantur*), the word *curia* can be used of any meeting-place consecrated for senatorial meetings and so may actually refer to the portico on the Palatine (cf. Tac., *Ann.* 2.37.2: *igitur quattuor filiis ante limen curiae adstantibus, loco sententiae, cum in Palatio senatus haberetur*; Eck, Caballos, Fernández, 1996: 131; Polleichtner, 2003: 297).

Lines 1–2: scribendo adfuerunt / Present at the drafting of the decree were The editing of a decree was not simply a straightforward clerical task of transcribing what had been said at the meeting (Coudry, 1994: 73), but required the senators on the committee to compile a synopsis of the discussion held and decisions reached (Polleichtner, 2003: 292–95). Normally, the individual who had introduced the matter for discussion to the Senate would preside over the editing process (Bonnefond-Coudry, 1989: 570; Coudry, 1994: 71–72), but Tiberius is not named here, despite having been the convenor (*relator*) (hence, the addition of the *subscriptio*, 174–76). This must have made the editing task all the more challenging, as the committee was charged with the high-profile task of drafting a coherent summary of the views expressed about the case of Piso and his accomplices for distribution around the empire (Corbier, 2001b: 157). It seems likely that the drafting committee met immediately after the meeting, in the same place where the Senate had held its discussions (Volterra, 1993: 217). The names of the senators are listed in hierarchical order, according to what office they had held and when, starting with three ex-consuls (or a current consul – see 2n., **M(arcus) Valerius M(arci) f(ilius) Lem(onia tribu) Messallinus**), then two otherwise unknown senators, and ending with the two urban quaestors.

Line 2: M(arcus) Valerius M(arci) f(ilius) Lem(onia tribu) Messallinus / Marcus Valerius Messallinus, son of Marcus, of the Lemonian voting-tribe This individual has been identified as M. Valerius Messalla Messallinus (*PIR*² V146), consul in 3 BC, on the grounds that his name appears in the list before that of Ateius Capito, who was consul in AD 5 (Eck, Caballos, Fernández, 1996: 88–89, 132; Lebek, 1999: 184), thus adhering to hierarchical order in naming the most senior consular first in the list of witnesses. Tacitus (*Ann.* 3.18.2, with Woodman and Martin, 1996: 189) relates that he gave a view on how Piso should be punished, proposing extravagant penalties which Tiberius rejected. In that case he spoke second after his much younger brother M. Aurelius Cotta Maximus Messallinus, one of the current consuls, in his capacity as the most senior ex-consul. This fits his overall depiction in Tacitus as an individual who several times tried to flatter the *princeps*, but who failed to anticipate Tiberius' wishes accurately (Syme, 1986: 233–34). His appearance also fits the hypothesis that members of the drafting committee might be individuals who had shown particular interest in the matter under discussion (a hint of this appears in the senatorial decree from Larinum (*AE* 1978, 145 / *AE* 1983, 210 = LACTOR 19, Q1), in which two of the senators listed as members of the drafting committee had taken an active part in an earlier debate in AD 16 on similar moral issues (Sensi, 1982: 520). His son, M. Valerius Messalla (Messallinus? – it is not clear whether or not he shared precisely the names of his father), consul in AD 20 (*PIR*² V145), was charged, with his fellow-consul at the end of the *Tabula Siarensis* (Crawford, 1996: no.37, frag. b, col. ii, 27–30 = LACTOR 19, J8h), with putting the proposals concerning honours for the dead Germanicus before the people for them to be passed formally as a *lex*. They were given this task as the incoming consuls for AD 20, since the proposals in the *Tabula Siarensis* were only put together right at the end of AD 19, on 16 December (see 175n., ***Cotta et Messalla co(n)s(ulibus)***).

Line 2: C(aius) Ateius L(uci) f(ilius) Ani(ensi tribu) Capito / Gaius Ateius Capito, son of Lucius, of the Aniensian voting-tribe The famous jurist C. Ateius Capito (*PIR*² A1279) was appointed to a suffect consulship by Augustus in AD 5 (testimonia of his career and fragments of his juristic writings recorded in Strzelecki, 1967). He also appears at the top of the list of witnesses for the senatorial decree from Larinum (*AE* 1978, 145 / *AE* 1983, 210 = LACTOR 19, Q1; Sensi, 1982). He had played a leading role in determining the procedure for celebrating the *ludi saeculares* of 17 BC (Zos. 2.4.2 = LACTOR 17: L23). He therefore had experience in providing guidance in both religious and legal affairs and was staunchly loyal to the Imperial House, winning the scorn of Tacitus (*Ann.* 3.70, 75), who concluded, in comparing Ateius Capito with Antistius Labeo, that 'Capito's obsequiousness won more approval from his rulers' (Tac., *Ann.* 3.75: *Capitonis obsequium dominantibus magis probatur*). He had worked closely with members of the imperial family: his name is listed as a member of Augustus' council receiving an embassy from Alexandria in AD 13 after Tiberius, Drusus, and Valerius Messalinus Corvinus (*P.Oxy.* no.2435 reverse = LACTOR 17: M14). His misplaced obsequiousness towards Tiberius is further illustrated in an anecdote related by Suetonius (*Gram. et rhet.* 22) and Cassius Dio (57.17.2), but he appears overall to have played an important role in shaping the political discourse and powers of both Augustus and Tiberius (Bauman, 1989: 28–31, 50–51, 59–62; Pani, 2000: 692). He was from a socially mobile family possibly from Castrum Novum in Etruria, his father having been a praetor and his grandfather a centurion. He died in AD 22 (Tac., *Ann.* 3.75 for his 'obituary notice'; Sensi, 1982: 516; Eck, Caballos, Fernández, 1996: 90, n.159 express doubts about his family's *origo*).

Lines 2–3: Sex(tus) Pomp(eius) Sex(ti) f(ilius) Arn(ensi tribu) / Sextus Pompeius, son of Sextus, of the Arnensian voting-tribe Consul of AD 14, Sex. Pompeius (*PIR*² P584; Eck, Caballos, Fernández, 1996: 91) appears second in the list of witnesses for the senatorial decree from Larinum (*AE* 1978, 145 / *AE* 1983, 210 = LACTOR 19, Q1; Sensi, 1982). Tacitus (*Ann.* 3.11.2) relates that Sex. Pompeius had declined to take on the role of defence for Piso at his trial, whilst Ovid depicts Pompeius as having great respect for Germanicus (*Pont.* 4.5.25–26: *tempus ab his vacuum Caesar Germanicus omne / auferet: a magnis hunc colit ille deis*). He later enjoyed advancement to the post of proconsul of Asia in AD *c.*25, but then died at some time before AD 31 (Val. Max. 2.6.8; 4.7.ext.2b; Bloomer, 1992: 1).

Line 3: M(arcus) Pompeius M(arci) f(ilius) Teret(ina tribu) Priscus, C(aius) Arrenus C(ai) f(ilius) Gal(eria tribu) Gallus / Marcus Pompeius Priscus, son of Marcus, of the Teretinan voting-tribe; Gaius Arrenus Gallus, son of Gaius, of the Galerian voting-tribe It seems likely that M. Pompeius Priscus (*PIR*² P638) and C. Arrenus Gallus were of praetorian rank (although they could in principle be of any rank between praetor and quaestor), since they are sandwiched between men of consular status and quaestors (Eck, Caballos, Fernández, 1996: 91), but neither of them is known from any other source. Pompeius Priscus may have originated from Arles (affiliated with the Teretinan voting-tribe), which would make him one of the earliest members of the Senate to be admitted from Narbonensis (Eck, Caballos, Fernández, 1996: 92).

Lines 3–4: L(ucius) Nonius L(uci) f(ilius) Pom(ptina tribu) Asprenas q(uaestor) / Lucius Nonius Asprenas, son of Lucius, of the Pomptinan voting-tribe, quaestor The two urban quaestors were in charge of depositing and looking after public documents in the archive of the treasury at the Temple of Saturn (*aerarium Saturni*). They are therefore included in the drafting committee in that capacity. Two urban quaestors are also named at the end of the list of witnesses for the senatorial decree from Larinum (*AE* 1978, 145 / *AE* 1983, 210 = LACTOR 19, Q1; Sensi, 1982). Nonius Asprenas (*PIR*² N119) subsequently enjoyed a speedy career progression, as praetor in AD 26 and suffect consul in AD 29, possibly even marrying Piso's granddaughter (see 104–05n., **n(ummum) (decies centena milia) dotis nomine Calpurniae Cn(aei) Pisonis filiae**; Eck, Caballos, Fernández, 1996: 95–96). According to Tacitus (*Ann.* 3.18.3), Nonius Asprenas had intervened in the senatorial debate on Piso in order to request clarification from Valerius Messallinus, whose list of members of the imperial family to be thanked for avenging the death of Germanicus had excluded Claudius (Lott, 2012: 260; see 148n., **fratrꞌiꞌs {Ti(beri)} Germ(anici) Caesar(is)**). This is probably not the quaestor, however, but his homonymous father, consul of AD 6 (*PIR*² N118; Woodman and Martin, 1996: 191; Eck, Caballos, Fernández, 1996: 97), given that Nonius Asprenas would only have entered office as urban quaestor on 5 December.

Line 4: M(arcus) Vinucius P(ubli) f(ilius) Pob(lilia tribu) q(uaestor) / Marcus Vinucius, son of Publius, of the Poblilian voting-tribe, quaestor The spelling of this name differs between Copy A (Vinucius) and Copy B (Vinicius), but this urban quaestor is to be identified as M. Vinicius (*PIR*² V661), who went on to achieve the rare distinction of becoming consul twice, in AD 30 and in 45. His family came from Cales in Campania. His consulship of AD 30 was celebrated in Velleius Paterculus, who dedicated his historical work to him. He married Iulia Livilla, the youngest daughter of Germanicus, in AD 33 (*Ann.* 6.15.1), and died in AD 46, allegedly poisoned by Messalina (Cass. Dio 60.27.4).

LINES 4–11 FOUR ITEMS FOR DISCUSSION IN THE SENATE, INTRODUCED BY TIBERIUS (*RELATIO*)

As is standard practice for a senatorial decree, this first section presents the topics for discussion, here in the format of a sequence of indirect questions. Tiberius invites the Senate to consider four questions. This is the first example of an imperial *relatio* preserved for us at the opening of its senatorial decree (Eck, Caballos, Fernández, 1996: 135). The first three topics, dealing with Piso, his younger son, and his wife share the same unusual, distinctive form of phrasing (6, **qualis causa Cn(aei) Pisonis patris visa esset**). By contrast, the final question concerning Piso's subordinates takes the more customary format (10, **quid de Visellio Karo et de Sempronio Basso**; Eck, Caballos, Fernández, 1996: 138; Ermann, 2002; Ruiz Castellanos and Lomas Salmonte, 2002). This difference in phrasing clearly distinguishes between the Senate being invited to express its opinion on the behaviour of Piso and his family but to pass judgement on the two named members of his staff. Although there has been some discussion concerning the relationship between Tacitus' account of Tiberius' opening speech in the Senate and the *relatio* as recorded here in the *SCPP* (Damon 1999a, comparing Tac., *Ann.* 3.12 and the *SCPP*; Eck, Caballos, Fernández, 1996: 135–36; see 26n., **singularem moderationem patientiamq(ue) Germanici Caesaris**), it is crucial to recognise that Tacitus and the *SCPP* are dealing with different occasions. Tiberius in Tacitus is speaking at the start of the trial, whereas Tiberius in the *SCPP* is addressing the Senate only after Piso has already committed suicide (6–7, **an merito sibi mortem conscisse videretur**, Giua, 2000: 256). By this stage too Tiberius has already spoken on behalf of Marcus Piso and Plancina (Eck, Caballos, Fernández, 1996: 136; cf. Tac., *Ann.* 3.17.1). After Piso's suicide, the whole character of the trial shifted away from a need to establish what had happened to a desire to pass moral judgement on what he had done (Ruiz Castellanos and Lomas Salmonte, 2002: 408–09), which helps to explain the characteristic intermingling in the *SCPP* of technical legal language and moralising judgement. The Senate's decisions on these four issues take up lines 71–123.

Line 4: Ti(berius) Caesar divi Aug(usti) f(ilius) Aug(ustus) / Tiberius Caesar Augustus, son of deified Augustus Since politically sensitive trials for *maiestas* had been moved to the Senate by Augustus (Chilton, 1955: 75; Levick, 1979: 374; Castro-Camero, 2000: 174), it was possible for Tiberius to preside over proceedings, and to establish the terms of reference for discussion. The description of the items for discussion outlined here indicates that the *SCPP* is not recording the initial introduction of the case to the Senate, but a new set of instructions for them to debate Piso's character rather than to establish the facts of the case. This opening statement gives us valuable contemporary evidence for Tiberius' official titles, as used by the Senate in a public document and as also used by Tiberius himself at the end of the decree (see 174n., ***Ti(berius) Caesar Aug(ustus) trib(unicia) potestate XXII manu mea scripsi***). Whereas Suetonius (*Tib.* 26, stating that Tiberius only used the title Augustus in writing to foreign kings: *ac ne Augusti quidem nomen, quanquam hereditarium, nullis nisi ad reges ac dynastas epistulis addidit*) and Cassius Dio (57.8.1) both suggest that Tiberius did not generally adopt the title Augustus, as part of their wider depiction of Tiberius' hesitation to take over after Augustus' death, the *SCPP* shows this not to be the case (Griffin, 1997: 257). It supports other contemporary evidence from AD 14/15, including the edict of the governor of Galatia Sex. Sotidius Strabo Libuscidianus ('propraetorian legate of Tiberius Caesar Augustus': *AE* 1976, 653 = LACTOR 19, M61) and coins of all denominations (*RIC* I² Tiberius 1–2, 33–37), that on the contrary, Tiberius did from the start use this title, which he had inherited in the terms of Augustus' will (Levick, 1999: 247 n.11).

Line 5: pontifex maxumus / supreme pontiff Tiberius took up this office on 10 March AD 15. As elsewhere in the *SCPP*, archaising spelling (*maxumus* for *maximus*) is used, as is typical of juridical documents (Calboli, 1998: 128; see also 18, *manufestissuma*; 48, *pessumo*; 54, *vetustissumo*). Copy B has additional examples of archaisms, with *quoiusque* (B20), and *quoius* (B22, B47: Moralejo, 2009; Eck, Caballos, Fernández, 1996: 55–56).

Line 5: tribunicia potestate XXII / holding tribunician power for the twenty-second time It is by virtue of his holding of tribunician power that Tiberius could formally summon a meeting of the Senate and present it with matters for discussion (*relatio* – cf. Tac., *Ann.* 1.7.3 for Tiberius' summoning of the Senate following Augustus' death; Rowe, 2002: chapter 1 on the importance of tribunician power for Tiberius' relations with the Senate). Tiberius' twenty-second year of tribunician power began on 26 June AD 20.

Line 5: co(n)s(ul) III, designatus IIII / consul for the third time, consul designate for the fourth time Tiberius was consul for the third time in AD 18 and was designated to assume office for the fourth time at the start of AD 21.

Lines 5–6: quod ... ad senatum rettulit / whereas ... referred to the Senate for decision This wording diverges from the conventional formula with which a senatorial decree usually started with an explanation justifying why the proposal was being put to the Senate, in the format of a clause 'whereas he stated' (*quod ... verba fecit*: Talbert, 1984: 304). This variation emphasises Tiberius' delegation of the discussion to the Senate.

Line 6: qualis causa Cn(aei) Pisonis patris visa esset / how the case of Gnaeus Piso Senior had been regarded This wording is not found in any other senatorial decree (Ruiz Castellanos and Lomas Salmonte, 2002). Tiberius is inviting discussion not about the facts of the matter, but about how the matter should be viewed. This direction helps to explain the moralising flavour of the *SCPP*, since the Senate is explicitly requested by Tiberius to offer a judgement on the type of behaviour displayed by Piso rather than upon what facts indicate his guilt. This reflects the fact that after Piso committed suicide the Senate was no longer judging whether he was guilty or innocent as charged (Ermann, 2002: 382).

Lines 6–7: et an merito sibi mortem conscisse videretur / and whether he was regarded as having taken his own life deservedly Piso committed suicide before the end of his trial, after the first or second day of the case for the defence had been presented (Tac., *Ann.* 3.15.2–3). This should have automatically put an end to his trial and prevented the confiscation of his property (Griffin, 1997: 261–63), but this did not happen in this case (see 20n., *filiosque eius arcessitos hortatus sit, ut patris suì causam defenderent* and 102–03n., *alteram partem dimidiam bonorum paternorum dari*). The Senate expresses its view on this question at lines 71–73.

Line 7: qualis causa M(arci) Pisonis visa esset / how the case of Marcus Piso had been regarded   Marcus Calpurnius Piso (*PIR*² C296) was Piso's younger son, who had accompanied him on his tour of duty in Syria (Eck, Caballos, Fernández, 1996: 80–82). He had perhaps benefited from his father's influence to be entrusted with commanding troops (*Ann.* 2.57.1: Germanicus requested that either Piso or his son should lead troops into Armenia), perhaps as a military tribune, even before he had reached the usual age for this, given that he was not yet a member of the Senate (see 21n., *qui ordinis senatori nondum esset*). Tacitus represents him as trying to dissuade his father from returning to Syria by force after Germanicus' death (*Ann.* 2.76.2–3, 3.16.3), but as subsequently throwing himself into the military conflict (*Ann.* 2.78.2). He was finally sent ahead by Piso to Rome to try to put his case before Tiberius (*Ann.* 3.8). The Senate's response to this question is given at lines 100–03 (see 100–01n., *M(arco) etiam Pisoni, qu<o>i inpunitatem senatus humanitati et moderationi principis sui adsensus dandam esse{t} arbitraretur*).

Line 8: uti precum suarum pro adulescente memor is ordo esset / that this body be mindful of his pleas on behalf of the young man   This reveals that Tiberius has already spoken in the Senate on behalf of Marcus Piso, perhaps pointing to a speech made by him following Piso's suicide. Had the Senate chosen not to grant Tiberius' 'pleas', he would have been able to interpose his veto (see 100–01n., *M(arco) etiam Pisoni, qu<o>i inpunitatem senatus humanitati et moderationi principis sui adsensus dandam esse{t} arbitraretur*).

Lines 8–9: qualis causa Plancinae visa esset / how the case of Plancina had been regarded   Munatia Plancina (*PIR*² M737; Raepsaet-Charlier, 1987: no.562), the granddaughter (or less likely daughter) of L. Munatius Plancus (*PIR*² M728), was Piso's wife (probably his second wife or at any rate much younger than her husband, to judge from the ages of their children: Syme, 1986: 369) (see §2). Tacitus (*Ann.* 2.43.3) notes Plancina's high-ranking and wealthy family background. He vividly depicts the clash of personalities between Plancina and Agrippina, by commenting upon their mutual animosity (*Ann.* 2.43.4), and by creating parallel narratives in which both women demonstrate non-feminine behaviour, with Agrippina giving commands to her husband's soldiers and Plancina watching military exercises (*Ann.* 1.69.4; 2.55.6). Plancina may also have borne a grudge against Germanicus on behalf of her brother L. Munatius Plancus (consul AD 13: *PIR*² M729), who was almost killed in the Rhine uprisings as a result of Germanicus' ineffectual actions in controlling his restless troops (*Ann.* 1.39). Her behaviour whilst she accompanied Piso on his tour of duty in Syria was perceived as so problematic that it may have prompted the Senate to discuss just the following year whether governors ought to be allowed to take their wives abroad with them (*Ann.* 3.33). A connection with Plancina's behaviour seems likely, given that the matter was raised in the Senate by A. Caecina Severus, who had served under Germanicus (Shotter, 1974: 241–43). In Tacitus' account of the debate, at any rate, Caecina Severus clearly alludes to Plancina's disreputable behaviour (3.33.3: 'a woman had recently presided over cohorts' training and legions' manoeuvring', *praesedisse nuper feminam exercitio cohortium, decursu legionum*). The Senate's view of her case is set out at lines 109–20.

Lines 9–10: pro qua persona, quid petisset et quas propter causas, exposuisset antea / on behalf of which individual he had earlier set out what he had requested and for what reasons As with Marcus Piso, Tiberius alludes to the fact that he has already spoken in the Senate on behalf of Plancina. It would have been likewise possible for Tiberius to interpose his veto had the Senate not followed his lead in pardoning Plancina. See further below on lines 109–20.

Lines 10–11: quid de Visellio Karo et de Sempronio Basso, comitibus Cn(aei) Pisonis patris, iudicaret senatus / what the Senate's judgement was concerning Visellius Karus and Sempronius Bassus, members of the staff of Gnaeus Piso Senior Neither Visellius Karus nor Sempronius Bassus is otherwise known (Eck, Caballos, Fernández, 1996: 98–100). Their description as *comites* refers to their positions as members of Piso's staff as governor of Syria. This final matter for discussion is introduced by Tiberius in different terms from the earlier questions relating to Piso and his family. The use of the verb 'to judge' (*iudicare*) suggests that the Senate is invited to make a judgement in the cases of Visellius Karus and Sempronius Bassus, in contrast to the cases of Piso and his family on which it is asked instead to express its opinion (Eck, Caballos, Fernández, 1996: 138). This seems to imply that the Senate is being asked to judge not the facts of their case – whether or not Visellius Karus and Sempronius Bassus are guilty as charged – but to express their evaluation of the behaviour of Piso and his family (Griffin, 1997: 256: this 'marks the difference between expressing a senatorial view and passing legal judgement'). A similar contrast can be seen in how the Senate later responds to the question of Piso's associates (see below, lines 120–23). There remains a problem, though, in the way in which the Senate in the *SCPP* slips between technical legal language and non-technical expressions: *iudicare* can mean 'to give a legal judgement' in a legal case (*OLD* s.v. 'iudico', 3) but can equally well mean 'to judge / consider / express an opinion' more generally (*OLD* s.v. 'iudico', 6, 8–9) (Lott, 2012: 362). For example, the Senate uses the phrase *optume iudicare* in referring to the opinion on the character of Germanicus' sister Livi(ll)a held by Iulia Augusta and Tiberius ('and of Livia, the sister of Germanicus Caesar, whom her grandmother and her father-in-law, who is also her uncle, our Princeps, held in the highest esteem', *et Liviae, sororis Germ(anici) Caesar(is), de qua* **optume** *et avia sua et / socer idemq(ue) patruos, princeps noster,* **iudicaret**, lines 142–43). Similarly, the Senate 'judges' Tiberius' character ('Likewise, since it was the judgement of the Senate that Tiberius Caesar Augustus our Princeps has surpassed all parties in his devotion to duty', *item cum* **iudic<ar>et** *senatus / omnium partium pietatem antecessisse Ti(berium) Caesarem Aug(ustum) principem nostrum*, lines 123–24; compare also lines 148–50, 167–68). This allows Richardson (1997: 516) to challenge the view that *iudicare* in this context means 'to issue a legal judgement' (cf. Griffin, 1997: 256). In this case, the Senate should instead be viewed as merely making recommendations to the court, not as itself passing judgement. It remains possible, however, that Tiberius' shift in language indicates that he is deliberately inviting the Senate to pass legal judgement. By making a recommendation to the praetor overseeing the lawcourt (*quaestio maiestatis*), the Senate would informally bypass the lawcourt, even though that court may still have heard the cases of Visellius Karus and Sempronius Bassus (Richardson, 1997: 517, 'the senate is the effective *locus* of decision about the case under the *lex maiestatis* but not the formal *locus*') (further discussion of these problems in Richardson, 1997: 514–18; G.P. Kelly, 2006: 45 n.112; see below, lines 120–23). There are two reasons why the relationship between the roles of the Senate and the lawcourt (*quaestio*) is not clear: firstly, this case was heard at a time of transition, as the Senate's judicial functions were still developing (Williamson, 2016: 340); secondly, the decree as a whole is fundamentally more concerned with the political than legal optics of the cases it is reporting (Eck, Caballos, Fernández, 1996: 55).

Line 11: d(e) i(is) r(ebus) i(ta) c(ensuerunt) / concerning these matters the Senate decreed as follows This change in formula from the customary 'concerning this matter the Senate decreed as follows' (*d(e) e(a) re i(ta) c(ensuerunt)*), as illustrated in the decree concerning the *ludi saeculares* of 17 BC: *CIL* VI 32323) reflects the fact that the Senate is being requested by Tiberius to deal with four different questions. It may also be an indication that the current decree has been put together as a summary of several previous decrees (Eck, Caballos, Fernández, 1996: 138; Griffin, 1997: 254; contra, Mackay, 2003: 311–22 who argues that the *SCPP* is not a composite decree, but a collection of decisions all made at the same time; see 169n., **itemq(ue) haec senatus consulta in {h}aere incisa**).

LINES 12–22 THANKS TO THE GODS FOR THWARTING PISO, AND TO TIBERIUS FOR FACILITATING HIS TRIAL

Before turning to address the matters introduced by Tiberius for discussion, the Senate prefaces its analysis of Piso's behaviour with an effusive outpouring of thanks to the gods for stopping Piso in his tracks and to Tiberius for allowing the Senate access to all materials relevant to Piso's trial and for allowing the trial to continue after Piso's suicide. This illustrates the Senate's tendency to introduce additional eulogistic elements into the decree, going beyond the framework for debate which Tiberius sets out in his introductory statement (*relatio*) (Damon, 1999a: 336; see also §5). Eck, Caballos, and Fernández (1996: 141) consider that this passage, along with lines 123–51, corresponds to the proposal of Valerius Messallinus recorded by Tacitus (*Ann.* 3.18.1–3), split into two separate sections. This interpretation risks under-playing differences between the *SCPP* and Tacitus. In the *Annales*, Tacitus focuses upon the theme of Germanicus' murder: Valerius Messallinus is presented as proposing thanks 'on account of the vengeance of Germanicus' (*ob uindictam Germanici grates*), whereas the Senate concentrates upon the potential threat to the state which Piso's military activities had presented. (See also below on lines 123–51 for an analysis of how that passage also differs from the presentation of Messallinus' proposal in Tacitus.)

Line 12: senatum populumq(ue) Romanum ante omnia dìs immortalibus gratias agere / that the Senate and people of Rome give thanks above all to the immortal gods This clause starts a whole sequence of indirect statements dependent upon 'they decreed' (*censuerunt*), by which the Senate's views on the matters in hand are expressed. This lasts all the way down to line 172. Consequently, all subordinate clauses are in the subjunctive mood, except for those which offer an authorial comment (for example, at 41, ***id quod fecit***). The phrase 'the Senate and people of Rome' sets a suitably formal tone, since this is the standard wording used of Rome's two political bodies, but the Senate is arguably speaking out of turn by claiming to express views on behalf of the Roman people without the matters having first been debated in the popular assemblies (contrast 34n., ***lex ad populum lata esset***). This mirrors the way in which during this period the Senate implicitly usurps the legislative function of the *populus Romanus* by publishing its decrees without waiting for ratification by the people (Rowe, 2002: 43, 64–66): in the case of the honours decreed for Germanicus as preserved on the *Tabula Siarensis*, for instance, the text is published and distributed in the form of a bill (*rogatio*) even before it is formally ratified before the people as a law (*lex*), probably because of the urgency felt by the Senate to be seen to respond to the crisis caused by the death of Germanicus (Lott, 2012: 238). The start of this section is marked visually on Copy A by SE at the start of *Senatus* sticking out into the left margin of the inscription, and S appearing as a letter that is twice as tall as the others around it. On Copy B, the paragraphing is indicated by leaving a blank space in front of the word *senatus*.

One of the key shifts in political discourse that emerges in the late Augustan and Tiberian eras is the idea that the *princeps* plays a unique role in protecting Rome because of his special relationship with the gods (Cooley, 2019: 78–79, 81–82). That idea is extended in the *SCPP* beyond the *princeps* to encompass members of the *domus Augusta* (lines 160–63). A similar belief can be understood to lie behind the closing prayer in Velleius Paterculus (2.131.1), who calls upon Jupiter, Mars, Vesta, and other gods to protect Rome's current peace and prosperity along with – and as dependent upon – Tiberius as *princeps*: 'Capitoline Jupiter, Mars Gradivus the originator and defender of the Roman name, and Vesta guardian of the everlasting fires, and whatever god has extended this mighty Roman empire over the highest point on earth, with public voice I call upon you and pray that you protect, preserve, and defend this state of affairs, this peace, this *princeps*' (*Iuppiter Capitoline, et auctor ac stator Romani nominis Gradiue Mars, perpetuorumque custos Vesta ignium, et quicquid numinum hanc Romani imperii molem in amplissimum terrarum orbis fastigium extulit, uos publica uoce obtestor atque precor, custodite, seruate, protegite hunc statum, hanc pacem, <hunc principem>*) (on *status*, see 13–14n., **tranquillitatem praesentis status r(ei) p(ublicae)**). It also underpins the annual vows on behalf of the welfare of the *princeps* undertaken by the Arvals on the Capitol (such as *CFA* 7a col. 2, 11–23 = *CIL* VI 2025, AD 36).

Line 13: nefaris consilìs Cn(aei) Pisonis patris / by the wicked plans of Gnaeus Piso Senior
This is the first statement about Piso's manifest guilt (see also lines 18, 71, 167). The same language is used in the *Fasti Amiterni* (13 September) to describe the 'wicked plans' made by Libo Drusus in AD 16 against the safety of Tiberius, his children, and other leading men in the state (*Inscr.It.* XIII.2, 193, no.25 = LACTOR 19, P1a: 'Holiday in accordance with a decree of the Senate, because on this day the wicked plans begun by Marcus Libo concerning the safety of Tiberius Caesar and his children and other leaders of the state and concerning the state, were exposed' – *fer(iae) ex s(enatus) c(onsulto) q(uod) e(o) d(ie) nefaria consilia quae de salute Ti. Caes(aris) liberorumq(ue) eius et aliorum principum ciuitatis deq(ue) r(e) p(ublica) inita ab M. Libone erant in senatu conuicta sunt*). It was also used to describe a plot against Gaius Caligula in the Arval records of 27 October AD 39: 'on account of the detection of the wicked plans of Gnaeus Lentulus Gaetulicus against Gaius Germanicus' (*ob detecta nefaria con[silia in C(aium) Germa/ni]cum Cn(aei) Lentuli Gae[tlici]*, *CIL* VI 32346 / *CFA* 13fgh, lines 17–19 = LACTOR 19, A39e). It thus illustrates

the development of official terminology to refer to conspiracies against the state (Eck, Caballos, and Fernández, 1996: 142).

Lines 13–14: tranquillitatem praesentis status r(ei) p(ublicae) / the tranquillity of the current state of affairs in the republic Rule by Tiberius is considered to be a guarantor against the recurrence of civil wars (Lott, 2012: 264). In addition to the evolution of official language to allude to conspiracies against the state (see 13n., *nefaris consilis Cn(aei) Pisonis patris*), set phrases also emerge to refer to the current enjoyment of peace and prosperity. The practice of referring to the 'current state of affairs in the republic' (*status rei publicae*) in a political sense goes back to Cicero (Köstermann, 1937: 225, tracing the evolution of the term), who used it to refer to the state of public affairs, their organisation, their stability, and the established order of government (definitions explored by Turcan, 2011: 626; Wirszubski, 1954: 5), especially when these seemed under threat. Augustus, however, seems to have adopted it as a term to refer to the general condition of the state rather than to a specific constitutional form, and promoted the idea that under his guidance Rome was enjoying 'a most fortunate state of affairs' (Gell. *NA* 15.7.3 = LACTOR 17, J57). Attributing the existing prosperous state of affairs to the *princeps* personally was also presented in official media, such as the coins issued by Mescinius Rufus in 16 BC, which commemorated a vow made in 16 BC by the Senate and Roman people for Augustus' safety, 'because through him the state is in a more expansive and peaceful condition' (*quod per eu(m) r(es) p(ublica) in amp(liore) atq(ue) tran(quilliore) s(tatu) e(st)*: *RIC*² Aug. 358 = LACTOR 17, L10). The phrase's Tiberian context emerges most clearly in the final prayer to the gods by Velleius Paterculus (see 12n., *senatum populumq(ue) Romanum ante omnia dis immortalibus gratias agere*), where the author both expresses his appreciation of the current stable state of affairs and betrays some anxiety about how long it was likely to last (Balmaceda, 2017: 138). The principle that Rome's stability and peace depended upon the person of the *princeps* also became embedded in public ritual, as revealed in the annual vows made by the Arvals on behalf of Tiberius' welfare, which hope that 'Tiberius himself shall be preserved in the same state as now or better' (*eumque in eodem statu qui [nunc es]t aut eo meliore seruaueris*, *CFA* 7a col. 2, 22; Eck, Caballos, and Fernández, 1996: 142).

Line 14: quo melior optari non pote\<st\> ʿeʾt quo beneficio principis nostri frui contigit / something better than which it is not possible to desire and which it has fallen to our lot to enjoy, thanks to the beneficence of our Princeps The idea that Tiberius personally was a guarantor of Rome's wellbeing (see 13–14n., *tranquillitatem praesentis status r(ei) p(ublicae)*) is similarly expressed in other contemporary authors. In his section 'On Old Age', in which he expresses hope for Tiberius to enjoy the longest possible life, Valerius Maximus (8.13) writes of the 'tranquillity of our age, than which there never was a happier' (*tranquillitas saeculi nostri, qua nulla umquam beatior fuit*). The striking similarities in sentiment between the *SCPP*, Valerius Maximus, and Velleius Paterculus bear witness to the emergence of a specific Tiberian political discourse (see §6; Cooley, forthcoming). This expression is also reminiscent of Augustus' desire to be 'the originator of the best state of affairs' (*optimi status auctor*), as he proclaimed in an edict (Suet., *Aug.* 28.2; Cooley, 2019: 72–73). The language of *beneficium* used here of Tiberius is echoed later in the Senate's description of Iulia Augusta (see 116–17n., **sed etiam multis magnisq(ue) erga cuiusq(ue) ordinis homines beneficis**), reflecting the continued importance given to beneficence among the imperial family, as among the elite of Rome more widely (Griffin, 2003b). The principle of reciprocity that underpins the giving of benefits (*beneficia*) justifies the Senate's giving of thanks to Tiberius in return for Rome's current tranquillity. The use of the word here also, however, marks a fundamental shift away from *beneficia* being characteristic of personal relationships which are based upon *amicitia* towards it being a feature of the political relationship between *princeps* and Senate. Tiberius' unique position is clear from the fact that he can bestow the *beneficium* of tranquillity upon the whole of Roman society: this calls into question the extent to which the *princeps* was in fact limited to displays of *civilitas* within a network of peers (raising doubts about the principle outlined by Griffin, 2003b: 109, 112: 'By making it clear that the *Princeps* was expected to practise beneficence according to that code and relate to his peers as they did to each other, he was strengthening the social side of *civilitas*'). Grammatically, *quo* is an ablative of comparison following the comparative adjective *melior*, qualifying *status*. Eck, Caballos, and Fernández, 1996: 57–58 do not emend *pote*, taking it as an example of archaising language more commonly found in Roman comedy, with *pote* + passive infinitive meaning (*OLD* s.v. 'potis or pote' 1b: 'subject to the possibility of / liable to') (Lott, 2012: 265, who translates as 'can possibly be').

Line 15: principi nostro / our Princeps Copy A is inscribed here with the words *principi suo*, which are adopted by Eck, Caballos, Fernández (1996: 38), but Copy B (line 12) has *principi nostro*. Given that the *SCPP* consistently refers to Tiberius as *princeps noster*, this edition follows the text of Copy B here (cf. González, 2002: 360, 382). This phrase is used of Tiberius a further sixteen times in the decree (14, 38–39, 84–85, 94, 111, 116, 118, 124, 133, 143, 154, 156, 158, 160–61, 168), keeping the person of Tiberius in view throughout the Senate's deliberations. The same phrasing is also seen in the decree of honours to Germanicus from AD 19 (*Tabula Siarensis* = Crawford, 1996: no.37, frag. a line 23 = LACTOR 19, J8c, restored in other places as well) and the decree of honours for

Drusus from AD 23 (Crawford, 1996: no.38, frag.3/f col. 1, line 9). In the *Res Gestae*, Augustus refers to himself as *princeps*, whilst the earliest surviving epigraphic use of the phrase *princeps noster* is found in the letter of 8 BC (for this date, see Stern, 2012: 274–78) sent by the proconsul of Asia Minor, Paullus Fabius Maximus, introducing his proposals to reform the calendar of the province so as to make Augustus' birthday (the 'birthday of our princeps', *principis nostri natalis*, Sherk, 1969: 330–31) coincide with New Year's Day. That this is distinctive to the Latin original of the proconsul's letter is illustrated by the fact that the Greek version of the same letter uses a very different expression ('the birthday of the most divine Caesar', ἡ τοῦ θειοτάτου Καίσαρος γενέθλιος ἡμέρα, Sherk, 1969: 329). By 4 BC, however, the phrase 'our *princeps*' is found in Greek too (ἡγεμὼν ἡμέτερος), as used by the presiding consuls to describe Augustus in the senatorial decree on extortion inscribed at Cyrene (*SEG* IX.8, line 86 = LACTOR 17, M78; Corbier, 2001a: 311). Only once does the *SCPP* use the third-person pronoun in referring to both Augustus and Tiberius as *principibus suis* (92). On the ideological significance of this choice of wording, see Cooley 2009: 160–61 on *RGDA* 13, **me principe**.

Lines 15–17: quod earum rerum omnium, quae ad explorandam veritatem necessariae fuerunt, copiam senatui fecerit / because he made available to the Senate everything which was necessary for determining the truth As observed by Eck, Caballos, Fernández (1996: 143), this refers to Tiberius' actions in facilitating Piso's trial at the start of the judicial proceedings. A corrupted passage in Tacitus (*Ann.* 3.14.3), by contrast, appears to allude to the rejection by both Tiberius and Piso of some sort of written evidence produced at the trial, possibly letters written by Piso to Tiberius (Woodman and Martin, 1996: 159–62).

Line 17: aequitatem et patientiam / impartiality and patience Although the *SCPP* praises Tiberius for his display of many virtues (see §6), the two qualities mentioned here are specific to the circumstances around the continuation of Piso's trial after his suicide, rather than fitting into a broader framework of imperial virtues. The following clause in the decree explains that the Senate is specifically praising Tiberius for his impartiality and patience in allowing the trial to continue following Piso's suicide (see 6–7n., *et an merito sibi mortem conscisse videretur*). This is different from the Senate's later praise for the *aequitas* of Iulia Augusta and Drusus (see 135n., ***aequitatem in servandis integris iudicis suis***). Just as Tiberius shares *aequitas* with his mother and son, so he also shares *patientia* with Germanicus, although Germanicus' *patientia* is different in character from Tiberius' (see 26n., ***singularem moderationem patientiamq(ue) Germanici Caesaris***). In this way, the Senate is able to praise Tiberius and other members of his family for sharing the same qualities, marking them out as *exempla* for the rest of society, even though the precise behaviour manifested by these qualities can differ between them.

Line 18: admirarì senatum / the Senate wonders at   This choice of translation follows the *OLD* s.v. 'admiror': 1. To be surprised. Astonished at; marvel / wonder at' rather than '2. Show admiration for / admire / respect', which other editions adopt (Griffin, 1997: 250; Lott, 2012: 141). Applying this meaning also at line 26 removes the need to correct the verb *admirari* there (see 26n., *<senatum> admirari*).

Line 18: cum manufestissuma sint Cn(aei) Pisonis patris scelera / although the crimes of Gnaeus Piso Senior are most flagrant   This hyperbolic language is typical of the decree (see §5).

Line 19: et ipse de se supplicium sumpsisset / and although he had inflicted the death penalty on himself   Tacitus (*Ann.* 3.15) narrates that Piso committed suicide before the case for the defence had been fully presented. The Senate later adds to the punishment inflicted upon himself by Piso (see 71n., *non optulisse eum se de͗b͗itae poenae*). The Senate's emphasis on Piso's guilt in both of these passages was intended to justify the confiscation of his property (which would normally have been protected by his suicide before conviction: Tac., *Ann.* 6.29), even though this was subsequently returned to Piso's heirs, and for the additional, severe penalties imposed upon him by the Senate (Griffin, 1997: 261–63; see also §7). The Senate's insistence on the fact of suicide may reflect a desire to deflect any suspicion that Piso had actually been murdered (contrast Tacitus' wording at *Ann.* 3.15.3, 'designed precisely to raise questions about the manner of death' – Woodman and Martin, 1996: 170, cf. 168).

Line 20: filiosque eius accessitos hortatus sit, ut patris suì causam defenderent / having summoned his sons, urged them to defend their father's case   The third-century lawyer Marcianus suggests that a trial continues after a defendant's suicide if his heirs want to defend his innocence:

If the heirs of a person who has died under accusation, at his own hand and without sufficient prior cause, are prepared to take up the case and demonstrate the innocence of the deceased, should they be given a hearing and the property not seized for the imperial treasury until the charge is proved; or is the property absolutely forfeit? However, the deified Pius wrote in a rescript to Modestus Taurinus that if the heirs are prepared to take up the defense, the property should not be confiscated unless the charge is proved.

de illo uideamus, si quis conscita morte nulla iusta causa praecedente in reatu decesserit, an, si parati fuerint heredes causam suscipere et innocentem defunctum ostendere, audiendi sint nec prius bona in fiscum cogenda sint, quam si de crimine fuerit probatum: an uero omnimodo publicanda sunt. sed diuus Pius Modesto Taurino rescripsit, si parati sint heredes defensiones suscipere, non esse bona publicanda, nisi de crimine fuerit probatum. (*Dig.* 48.21.3.8, trans. Watson)

Otherwise, he is treated as guilty and his property confiscated. This principle, however, may not date back as far as the Tiberian era, since Marcianus mentions the role of Antoninus Pius in establishing this rule.

Line 21: qui ordinis senatori nondum esset / who was not yet a member of the senatorial body   This refers to Piso's younger son, Marcus, who would not normally therefore have been permitted to speak at the trial held in the Senate, unless as a witness (Eck, Caballos, Fernández, 1996: 143–44).

Line 22: copiam utriq(ue) dicendi pro patre et pro matre ipsorum et pro M(arco) Pisone faceret / gave them both the opportunity to speak on behalf of their father, on behalf of their mother, and on behalf of Marcus Piso   Mixed messages emerge about the continuation of Piso's trial after his suicide. Tiberius requests that Piso's two sons should continue to defend the case against him, even though Piso's suicide could have been interpreted as an admission of guilt, whilst their defence of Plancina and Marcus might have seemed superfluous given that Tiberius himself had already spoken on their behalf (see 8n., ***uti precum suarum pro adulescente memor is ordo esset***; 9–10n., ***pro qua persona, quid petisset et quas propter causas, exposuisset antea***). The Senate's emphasis upon the fact that all relevant evidence had been made available to them and that Tiberius actively encouraged Piso's sons to continue his defence may reflect contemporary anxieties about secret instructions having been given to Piso by Tiberius (Potter, 1999: 72–73; Tac., *Ann.* 3.16.1, with Woodman and Martin, 1996: 168–70 on Tacitus' care to present this as authentic contemporary evidence).

LINES 23–70 DESCRIPTION OF THE CIRCUMSTANCES THAT LED TO PISO'S PROSECUTION

The Senate now addresses in turn the four issues raised by Tiberius in his *relatio*, starting with the evidence against Piso himself. There are two main themes: Piso's hostility towards Germanicus both during his lifetime and after his death, and Piso's stirring up of unrest in Syria by supporting Vonones' attempts to regain the throne of Armenia and by himself attempting to wrest back control of the province by military force after Germanicus' death. The charges in the central sections (lines 37–57) of disturbing the peace and provoking civil war, which clearly fall into the traditional framework of *maiestas* charges (see Castro-Camero, 2000: 39–44 for an overview of *maiestas* charges; 44–50 for Piso's liability under the *lex maiestatis*), are framed by Piso's hostile attitude to Germanicus (lines 23–37, 57–70), which is, by contrast, an illustration of how *maiestas* was developing in new directions under Tiberius. Eck, Caballos, and Fernández (1996: 145–46) discern a different structure in these lines, with 25–37 presenting the premises on which the charges were being based and then 37–70 (or perhaps only from 45) dealing with the charges themselves, but this arguably underestimates the charges against Piso detailed in 32–37 (see 32–33n., **ne͡g͡lecta maiestate domus Aug(ustae)**, 33n., **ne͡g͡lecto etiam iure publico**). For a table setting out the key differences between the charges outlined in the decree and in Tacitus, see Lott (2012: 269).

Lines 23–37 Piso's relationship with Germanicus

First of all, this section summarises what evidence had been heard at the trial (letters, memoranda, witnesses) before turning to an account of how the relationship between Piso and Germanicus had irrevocably broken down. This is consistent with the picture of personal animosity between the two men drawn by Tacitus, who, in addition, describes similar hostility between their wives, Plancina and Agrippina (Shotter, 1968: 208–14; 1974). It then proceeds to explain how the problem was of more than personal significance, given that offences against Germanicus were also regarded as offences against the *domus Augusta* and the Roman Senate and people. This gives us contemporary insight into how the *maiestas* law was changing during these years, complementing the central role played by *maiestas* in Tacitus' Tiberian hexad. The charge that Piso murdered Germanicus is mentioned only in the form of an accusation made by the dying Germanicus.

Lines 23–24: itaque, cum per aliquot dies acta causa sit, ab accusatoribus Cn(aei) Pisonis patris et ab ipso Cn(aeo) Pisone patre recitatae epistulae recitata exemplaria codicillorum / when the case was pleaded over a number of days, by the prosecutors of Gnaeus Piso Senior and by Gnaeus Piso Senior himself letters were read out, and copies of the memoranda were read out On both Copy A and B, the beginning of the word *itaque* projects into the left margin, in order to mark the start of a new paragraph. Piso's prosecutors at Rome were P. Vitellius, Q. Veranius, and Servaeus, who had accompanied Germanicus in Syria, and Fulcinius Trio, who charged him with offences pre-dating his governorship of Syria (Tac., *Ann.* 3.10.1, 13.2). The opening clauses of this subsection can be interpreted in different ways depending on how it is punctuated (various options reviewed by Talbert, 1999: 91–93; Mackay, 2003: 343 n.82). This edition suggests that a break should be inserted after the initial statement *cum per aliquot dies acta causa sit* / 'when the case was pleaded over a number of days' (cf. González, 2002: 383). In favour of this is the fact that the clause *ab accusatoribus ... patre* is not sandwiched within that clause (i.e., *cum per aliquot dies ab accusatoribus Cn. Pisonis patris et ab ipso Cn. Pisone patre acta causa sit*). This then creates the impression of both sides in the case producing documentary evidence and witnesses in their support, with *ab accusatoribus* and *ab ipso Cn. Pisone patre* referring to their activities during the trial. Only the memoranda (*exemplaria codicillorum*), as is clear from the subsequent relative pronoun, *quos*, are described as having been sent from Germanicus to Piso. Who had written the letters, by contrast, is not stated, but there seems to be a distinction being made between formal documents issued by Germanicus as magistrate and more informal letters. Eck, Caballos, and Fernández (1996: 152) argue that *epistulae* consisted of letters written by dictation, whereas *codicilli* were more personal, hand-written, documents (Lott, 2012: 267–68 suggests the opposite).

This interpretation of the sentence structure differs from that adopted by Eck, Caballos, and Fernández (1996: 123; cf. also Griffin, 1997: 250), who take the temporal clause without a break with *ab accusatoribus Cn. Pisonis patris et ab ipso Cn(aeo) Pisone patre* / 'when the case was pleaded over a number of days by the prosecutors of Gnaeus Piso Senior and by Gnaeus Piso Senior himself'. This gives the impression that the case for the defence was put only by Piso himself, whereas he was defended by his brother L. Calpurnius Piso Augur, M. Aemilius Lepidus, and Livineius Regulus (Tac., *Ann.* 3.11.2). This is important, since Eck, Caballos, and Fernández (1996: 149–51) also assume on this basis that the whole of the trial's proceedings – prosecution and defence – was accomplished in under a fortnight, from 29 November to 10 December ('over a number of days') (cf. Mackay, 2003: 356). This allocates two days for the prosecution followed by a break of six days, then a further two days out of the three initially assigned to the defence, interrupted by Piso's suicide. Finally, the trial continued for two more days beyond Piso's suicide (Tac., *Ann.* 3.17.3). There was possibly one additional day at the start for a speech by Tiberius. Talbert (1999: 93), however, questions whether the trial proceedings could have been wrapped up so speedily, pointing out that time would have been needed for hearing the evidence, on days separate from those allocated to prosecution or defence: 'The total of five meeting-days was only for the advocates' speeches. Reading of documents and testimony from witnesses comprised separate, subsequent stages (the *probatio*), without any fixed time-limit.' Lott (2012: 142–43) punctuates the Latin with a comma after *causa sit*, but translates without the comma; his commentary on the phrase (267) shows, however, that he follows Talbert.

Talbert (1999: 92) further contends that 'the stage of the proceedings referred to seems to be after his suicide anyway' and considers that *ab accusatoribus* and *ab ipso Cn. Pisone patre* refer to the act of sending the letters rather than to their being read out in the Senate. This suggests that the *accusatores* in question are not the individuals prosecuting Piso in Rome, but his detractors in Syria (although they could also be the same).

Line 25: Germanicus Caesar / Germanicus Caesar This is the first mention of Germanicus in the decree, reflecting the way in which the Senate's focus upon Piso's crimes in Syria is not based around his relationship with Germanicus to the same extent as in Tacitus (as discussed by Giua, 2000: 270–71), but rather highlights his offences in the military sphere.

Line 25: producti testes cuiusq(ue) ordinis sint / when witnesses of each order were brought before the court Eck, Caballos, and Fernández (1996: 24, 58) read Copy B line 20 as *quoiusque ii ordinis sint*, concluding from this and from the historical context of the case that witnesses of all social status appeared in the Senate, not just senators and equestrians (which would have been indicated by *utriusque ordinis*) (Mackay, 2003: 365). Autopsy of Copy B reveals that the text reads *quoiusque ll ordinis*, with the two uprights consisting of the letter L, not I. This is an engraver's error, possibly as the result of the fact that the letters LLOR in line 20 of Copy B are engraved just to the left beneath the letters LLOR in *codicillorum* in line 19. Tacitus relates (*Ann.* 3.7.2) how the witness Martina, a notorious poisoner from Syria (who would have been neither senatorial nor equestrian in rank) died suddenly at Brundisium before she could travel to Rome to appear in court.

Line 26: <senatum> admirari / the Senate wonders at Both Copy A and Copy B have the verb *admirari* here, and neither has the word *senatum*, which has been supplied. The verb is emended by Eck, Caballos, and Fernández (1996: 58; followed by Griffin, 1997: 250 and Lott, 2012: 268) to *arbitrari*, but retained by González (2002: 360, 384) and Gil (1999: 218). Although the verb *admirari* does not make sense in this context if taken to mean 'show admiration for / admire' (*OLD* s.v. 'admiror' 2), it does work if interpreted as 'to be surprised; astonished at; marvel / wonder at' (*OLD* s.v. 'admiror' 1). This meaning for the verb can also be applied to the Senate's previous use of it at line 18 (***admirari senatum***). Elsewhere in the decree, the Senate uses the verbs *probare* and *laudare* where it wishes to praise qualities shown by members of the imperial family.

Line 26: singularem moderationem patientiamq(ue) Germanici Caesaris / the exceptional restraint and patience of Germanicus Caesar Eck, Caballos, and Fernández (1996: 292–93) observe that the decree actually shows the limits of Germanicus' *moderatio* and *patientia*, which fail when faced with Piso's extreme behaviour. Damon (1999a: 337) explains this as 'not precisely praise but rather part of a judgement about his behaviour towards Piso', and yet the Senate concludes at lines 166–67 that its aim in publishing its decree is precisely to inform future generations 'what the Senate's judgement was concerning the exceptional restraint of Germanicus Caesar'. Retaining the verb *admirari* in the sense of 'wonders at' helps to account for this, if we understand that the Senate is expressing its amazement at the fact that even Germanicus' exceptional restraint and patience were, in the end, overcome by Piso's behaviour. This means that this comment should not be considered a criticism of Germanicus, but evidence of the uniquely wicked character shown by Piso. Damon (1999a: 337) considers that the Senate's comment on Germanicus' *moderatio* might reflect a separate speech delivered by Tiberius rather than the one introducing the *relatio*.

Line 27: feritate morum Cn(aei) Pisonis patris / by the brutish behaviour of Gnaeus Piso Senior This illustrates the extreme language used by the Senate to condemn Piso's character, to dehumanise him (see 61n., ***humanitatis***), and to isolate him from the rest of humanity (see 57–58n., ***cuius interitum non p(opulus) R(omanus) modo, sed exterae quoq(ue) gentes luxserunt***) (Cooley, 1998). The noun *feritas* ('brutish behaviour') aligns Piso with barbarians and wild beasts: 'More often used of mythological monsters or barbarian tribes than of a member the Roman elite, it reduces Piso to subhuman status' (Cooley, 1998: 200). The Senate's choice of language is much more extreme than and quite different in tone from the attribution of *ferocia* to Piso by Tacitus, a word which can refer to an independent, insubordinate, indomitable spirit. The word *ferocia* is therefore equally applicable to other characters in Tacitus who are defiant in the face of being ruled by others, including other Pisones (see §2 and §8), Agrippina the Elder, Sejanus, C. Asinius Gallus, and Agrippa Postumus (Cooley, 1998: 204; cf. Traub, 1953 for a detailed study of Tacitus' use of the word).

Line 28: cuius mortis fuisse causam Cn(aeum) Pisonem patrem ipse testatus sit / of whose death he himself bore witness that Gnaeus Piso was the cause According to Tacitus (*Ann.* 3.14.1), the charge of poisoning was the only charge not proven against Piso. Nevertheless, the suspicion that Piso and Plancina did murder Germanicus fundamentally shapes Tacitus' account. He concludes his narrative of the trial of Piso ('the end of avenging the death of Germanicus', *is finis fuit ulciscenda Germanici morte*) with reflections on the difficulty of uncovering the truth about what really happened (*Ann.* 3.18.2). This claim in the decree echoes the death-bed scene in which Tacitus' Germanicus claims that he is being poisoned (*Ann.* 2.71). Pliny the Elder (*HN* 11.187 = LACTOR 19, P2c) records part of the case for poisoning presented by the prosecutor P. Vitellius at Piso's trial, namely, evidence relating to the fact that Germanicus' heart did not burn during cremation, thought to be an indication of poisoning. He also preserves Piso's defence case, that this phenomenon was related to the nature of Germanicus' illness. Suetonius repeats this observation about Germanicus' cremation, adding that Piso's poisoning of Germanicus had been instigated by Tiberius himself (*Calig.* 1–2; cf. *Tib.* 52, where the current phrase finds an echo: 'the cause of his death is also believed to have been through the agency of Gnaeus Piso, governor of Syria', *etiam causa mortis fuisse ei per Cn. Pisonem legatum Syraie creditur*). The fact that the Senate finds this way to allude to the charge of poisoning (cf. Eck, Caballos, and Fernández, 1996: 145–46) perhaps suggests that it still did not accept the not-guilty verdict on this point. The tradition that Germanicus had been poisoned by Piso persisted for many years, recorded, for example, also by Josephus (*AJ* 18.2.5). Tacitus (*Ann.* 2.69) further describes how magical practices had hastened Germanicus' death (Tupet, 1980), but there is no reference to witchcraft in the decree. All of these elements then appear in the brief account by Cassius Dio (57.18.9–10). Eck, Caballos, and Fernández (1996: 155) note the different account of Germanicus' death in the *Tabula Siarensis* (Crawford, 1996: no.37, frag. a, line 18 = LACTOR 19, J8b), where he is said to have 'died in the service of the state'.

Line 29: amicitiam ei renuntiasse / renounced his friendship with him The act of formally renouncing friendship is also described by Tacitus (*Ann.* 2.70.2) and Suetonius (*Calig.* 3). Evidence for this practice clusters in the first centuries BC and AD (although Rogers, 1959 argues that it can be surmised to have continued down to the fourth century), and it is represented (as in the passage from Suetonius below) as a traditional practice (*mos maiorum*: cf. Tac., *Ann.* 6.29.2 in relation to Pomponius Labeo in AD 34; Kierdorf, [1983] 1987: 226–27). Suetonius (*Calig.* 3) presents this act as an illustration of Germanicus' self-restraint, in not exacting a worse penalty from Piso:

he was so mild and blameless that he did not resolve to be angry against Piso who was cancelling his decrees and harassing his entourage before he learnt that he was also being attacked by poisons and curses; and not even then did he go further than renouncing friendship with him, according to traditional practice, and instructing his friends to avenge him if anything should happen to him.

lenis adeo et innoxius, ut Pisoni decreta sua rescindenti, clientelas diuexanti non prius suscensere in animum induxerit, quam ueneficiis quoque et deuotionibus impugnari se comperisset; ac ne tunc quidem ultra progressus, quam ut amicitiam ei more maiorum renuntiaret mandaretque domesticis ultionem, si quid sibi accideret.

As Kierdorf ([1983] 1987: 238) observes, the removal of the *princeps'* friendship from a member of the elite who was standing trial would have been tantamount to a conviction, but the full impact of Germanicus' renunciation is less clear. Unlike the parallel case of M. Lollius who was sent to the East to act as Gaius Caesar's *adiutor* but ended up poisoning himself after friendship was renounced (Plin., *HN* 9.118 = LACTOR 17, P17), Piso did not commit suicide after having been rejected by Germanicus, perhaps assuming he could rely on Tiberius' support, but may have taken it as an implicit instruction to leave the province (see 47n., ***repetendo provinciam***

Syriam). Tacitus (*Ann.* 3.12.2) narrates how at the start of Piso's trial Tiberius threatens to withdraw his friendship from Piso in the future, banning him from entering his house: 'For if he cast aside the boundaries of a legate's duties and the obedience due to a commanding officer and if he rejoiced at the death of that same individual and at my grief, I shall hate him and remove him from my house and I shall take vengeance for private acts of hostility not as the *princeps*' (*nam si legatus officii terminos, obsequium erga imperatorem exuit eiusdemque morte et luctu meo laetatus est, odero seponamque a domo mea et priuatas inimicitias non ut princeps ulciscar*). Although Tiberius here presents the action of potentially renouncing his friendship with Piso as essentially a private matter, separate from his rank as *princeps*, this is a false distinction (contra, Rogers, 1959, who maintains that renouncing friendship was essentially a private matter). As Kierdorf ([1983] 1987: 225) points out, the oath of loyalty sworn to Tiberius after Augustus' death promised to regard the same people as friends or enemies as the *princeps*: 'we ourselves and our descendants swear ... to have the same man as friend and enemy' (Mitford, 1960 = LACTOR 19, J2b). It is possible that Tacitus has introduced this theme himself in order to illustrate Tiberius' hypocrisy, but it would cause no surprise if this threat, if delivered in this way, may in due course have influenced Piso to take his own life.

Lines 29–30: adiutorem se datum esse / he had been assigned as an aide The Senate states that Piso had been instructed to act as Germanicus' 'aide' (*adiutor*), a term which denoted that he had a formal duty to work with Germanicus, beyond his role as imperial legate (Eck, Caballos, Fernández, 1996: 157–58; Damon, 1999b: 150 n.15). This dates back to AD 17 (see §2 for the partial parallels with Marcus Lollius, *adiutor* to Gaius Caesar in 1 BC: their relationship could have been less problematic since, unlike Piso, Lollius was not also a provincial governor, whilst Gaius was still young and inexperienced). Given the significant age difference between Germanicus and Piso (possibly around twenty-five years), the scope for tensions between the two to develop from such a mentoring arrangement is clear (Eck, 2002: 149), especially if Piso considered himself to be answerable directly to Tiberius (Lamberti, 2006: 140) and given that Germanicus was far from inexperienced and so may have resented being assigned an 'aide'. The role remained vaguely defined, however, since it could have encompassed both acting in important political or military matters and performing more mundane administrative tasks (De Martino, 1996: 480), and this lack of clarity is also likely to have contributed to the uneasiness of relations between Piso and Germanicus. This is one place where the language of the decree is closely mirrored in Tacitus (*Ann.* 3.12.1), where Tiberius also describes Piso as having been appointed jointly by himself and the Senate as *adiutor* ('aide') to Germanicus ('given as aide to Germanicus by himself, on the Senate's initiative, for administering affairs in the East', *adiutoremque Germanico datum a se auctore senatu rebus apud Orientem administrandis*). Woodman and Martin (1996: 141) remind us that we cannot be sure whether the involvement of the Senate in Piso's appointment as *adiutor* is authentic or a Tacitean invention. The importance of this term lies in its ambiguity, as underlined by Potter (1998: 444): 'In ll. 29–37 the behavior of Piso is removed from the context of private relationships to that of public responsibility, and returned to the very gray area betwixt the two, for we are told that Piso failed both in his personal duty to Germanicus as his *adiutor*, and with respect to the law that granted Germanicus superior *imperium* to himself' (see 34n., **lex ad populum lata esset**).

Line 30: a principe nostro ex auctoritate huius ordinis / by our Princeps in accordance with the authority of this body This phrase illustrates how the Senate represents itself as collaborating with Tiberius in appointing Germanicus to a special mission to sort out affairs in the eastern provinces (see 30–31n., **ad rerum transmarinarum statum componendum**; cf. also the pairing of **ex voluntate patris sui senatusq(ue)** at line 44). In referring to its *auctoritas*, the Senate alludes to its passing of a decree recommending that Germanicus should be appointed directly to his special post, whilst reference to Tiberius' role relates to the instructions (*mandata*) which he gave to Germanicus, outlining his duties in more detail (Hurlet, 1997: 192–3). These instructions were of fundamental importance in directing Germanicus, who was not simply being sent out with enhanced powers, but was tasked with completing a specific set of duties (see 30–31n., **ad rerum transmarinarum statum componendum**). Further detail is given in the *Tabula Siarensis*, where Germanicus is said to have acted 'in setting in order the overseas provinces and the kingdoms of that region in accordance with the instructions of Tiberius Caesar Augustus' (Crawford, 1996: no.37, frag. a, line 16 = LACTOR 19, J8b: *in conformandis iis regnisque eiusdem tractus ex mandatis Ti(berii) C<a>esaris Au[g(usti)]*). A few lines later (Crawford, 1996: no.37, frag. a, line 24), the Senate refers in more general terms to the 'care and guardianship' for these regions entrusted to Germanicus by Tiberius in accordance with the authority of the Senate (a likely restoration of the missing word) (*curam et tutelam Germanico Caesari ex auctori[tate senatus ipse mandasset]*; for further analysis, see Lebek, 1991: esp. 113–14). The picture of collaboration between Senate and *princeps* in making this appointment differs from that in Tacitus (*Ann.* 2.43), who gives the impression that the Senate alone was responsible for Germanicus' appointment.

Lines 30–31: ad rerum transmarinarum statum componendum / to put overseas affairs in order Germanicus' sphere of responsibility is referred to in this way in other contemporary documentary sources too, such as in his speech at Alexandria, where he describes himself as 'sent by my father

Commentary on 31–32

to settle the overseas provinces' (*P.Oxy.* no.2435 recto = LACTOR 19, J7e: πεμφθεὶς ... ὑπὸ τοῦ πατρὸς [ἐ]πὶ τὸ καταστησάσθαι τα{ῖ}ς πέραν θαλάσ<σ>ης ἐπαρχίας) and the *Tabula Siarensis* ('sent as proconsul to the overseas provinces', Crawford, 1996: no.37, frag. a line 15 = LACTOR 19, J8b: *pro co(n)s(ule) missus in transmarinas pro[uincias]*; cf. Crawford, 1996, no.37, Rome Fragment c, line 10). Although this expression appears to us to be rather a vague geographical description, Arnaud (1994) has argued that it did have a precise geographical meaning during the Augustan and Tiberian eras, referring to the provinces in the eastern Mediterranean beyond the Adriatic and the strait of Otranto, as distinguished from the transalpine provinces (cf. Goodyear, 1981: 323–24 on Tac., *Ann.* 2.43.1; Crawford, 1996: 533 on *Tabula Siarensis*). Moreover, the expression was associated with particular political circumstances, whereby a member of the imperial family was given powers above those of normal provincial governors when sent on special missions to the East. Germanicus was the last to have held this position (Arnaud, 1994: 243; on Germanicus' mission, see Arnaud, 1994: 232–36). Gaius Caesar had previously been given similar power, and this might have led Germanicus to assume that his authority similarly extended to Egypt, even though his instructions from Tiberius may not have related to that province (Arnaud, 1994: 230). Germanicus may be understood to have been given specific tasks to complete in the East (forming his *provincia* in its original sense: Richardson, 2008: 8-9) rather than simply being sent eastwards with enhanced powers to settle affairs as he saw fit (Arnaud, 1994: 246). If Germanicus had, however, exceeded his specific instructions from Tiberius by intervening in Egypt on his own initiative, this explains why this may have been a cause of tension between the two men. Velleius echoes this technical language in using it four times for defining the sphere of authority for an individual's overseas command, in relation in turn to Pompey, Antony, Tiberius, and Germanicus (Vell. Pat. 2.44.2, 2.78.1, 2.99.4, 2.129.3: 'with what great honour he sent his Germanicus into the overseas provinces', *quanto cum honore Germanicum suum in transmarinas misit provincias*; Arnaud, 1994: 221–23). By contrast, Tacitus (*Ann.* 2.43.1) seems deliberately to avoid echoing the official language, using instead the phrase 'the provinces which are divided off by the sea' (*prouinciae quae mari diuiduntur*). Germanicus' mission had several strands: to stabilise the client kingdom of Armenia (see 37–38n., **bellum {cum} Armeniacum et Parthicum**, 39n., **Vononem**), to consolidate a positive relationship between Rome and Parthia, and to reorganise the kingdoms of Cappadocia, Commagene, and Cilicia into provinces (Tac., *Ann.* 2.42.; Suet., *Calig.* 1.2; Eck, Caballos, Fernández, 1997: 216; Olbrycht, 2016).

Lines 31–32: desiderantium praesentiam aut ipsius Ti(beri) Caesaris Aug(usti) aut filiorum alterius utrius / affairs which called for the presence either of Tiberius Caesar Augustus himself or of one of his two

sons This seems to preserve an echo of the debate in the Senate in AD 17 over how to put eastern affairs in order (Eck, Caballos, Fernández, 1996: 159), illustrating how Tiberius, Germanicus, and Drusus were promoted by the Senate as individuals of unique influence (see §5). The tendency for members of the imperial family to be regarded as having the potential to solve intractable problems in the East goes back to the special missions under Augustus of Agrippa, Tiberius, and Gaius Caesar (cf. *RGDA* 27.2). Tacitus (*Ann.* 2.43.1) presents similar sentiments concerning the choice being just between Germanicus and Drusus, with the latter regarded as too young still in AD 17 to undertake such a responsibility (as Goodyear, 1981: 322 observes, though, it was less the case that Drusus was too young; rather he was merely the junior of the two). The problems posed in the East required not just military campaigns, but delicate diplomatic solutions, given that they affected more than a single province in the region and also involved dealings with Parthia, beyond the Roman empire (Arnaud, 1994: 250–52).

Lines 32–33: ne ̆g ̄lecta maiestate domus Aug(ustae) / without regard for the majesty of the House of Augustus Two absolute ablative clauses summarise Piso's crimes against the imperial family (mentioned first and foremost) and then against the Roman people. This is the first known use of the phrase 'majesty of the House of Augustus' (*maiestas domus Augustae*), reflecting the way in which *maiestas* began to play an even greater role than before in defining imperial power during this period (Corbier, 2001b; Suspène, 2010: 864) (see further discussion on *domus Augusta* in §5 and on the shifting meaning of *maiestas* in §6).

Line 33: ne ̆g ̄lecto etiam iure publico / without regard even for public law This refers to the charges against Piso of not having respected the authority of Germanicus in his capacity as a magistrate (proconsul) appointed by the Roman people (see 34n., *lex ad populum lata esset*), of stirring up unrest in Parthia and Armenia (see 37–38n., *bellum {cum} Armeniacum et Parthicum*), and of embarking upon a civil war by seeking to regain Syria by force (see 45–46n., *bellum etiam civile excitare conatus sit*) (Griffin, 1997: 263).

Line 33: adle ̆c ̄t(us) pro co(n)s(uli) / inasmuch as he had been assigned to a proconsul The abbreviation *procos* should be expanded in the dative case, referring to Piso's appointment as aide to Germanicus as proconsul. This description of Germanicus as proconsul also appears on the fragmentary inscription from Augustus' Mausoleum identified as an inscription set up in his honour after his death (*CIL* VI 40367) and in Greek (ἀνθύπατος) in the edicts issued by Germanicus in Egypt (Hunt and Edgar, 1956: no.211 = LACTOR 19, J7d, M59). Damon (1999b: 150–51) notes that the Senate dodges the question of who appointed Piso to be assigned to Germanicus as proconsul, but it is likely that the sole responsibility for the appointment of Piso lay with Tiberius. His role as Germanicus' *adiutor*, however, probably remained vaguely defined (see 29–30n., **adiutorem se datum esse**).

Line 34: lex ad populum lata esset / a law had been passed by the people A *lex* approving Germanicus' special powers and mission had been passed by the Roman people in AD 17. Together with the evidence from the *Tabula Siarensis* (Crawford, 1996: no.37, frag. b, col. ii, lines 27–31 = LACTOR 19, J8h), where the consuls are instructed by the Senate to ratify the honours for Germanicus before the people, this reference to a *lex* shows the continuing participation of the Roman people in the popular assembly (*comitia centuriata*). Even though the Senate appears to take for granted the people's approval of its decrees, this evidence illustrates the continued importance of political participation by the Roman people under Tiberius (Millar, [1988] 2002: 635–39). This phrase is crucial in explaining why Piso's disregard for Germanicus' authority was not just a matter of personal hostility but could also be seen as undermining the authority of the Roman people (Griffin, 1997: 255). The involvement of the Roman people in assigning *imperium* (magisterial legal authority) can be paralleled in the grant of *imperium* to Tiberius in AD 14 (Suet., *Tib.* 21) and to Agrippa before his death in 12 BC (as revealed by Augustus' funeral oration for him, partially preserved on papyrus: *P.Köln.* 4701 + 4722; Gronewald, 1983). By contrast, Tacitus refers only to the role of the Senate in granting *imperium* to Germanicus (*Ann.* 2.43). As Griffin (1997: 258) observes, 'This is in line with his general tendency to report political reality rather than legal formalities.'

Lines 34–35: maius ei imperium quam ei qui eam provinciam proco(n)s(ul) optineret / greater *imperium* than the person who was governing this province as proconsul The description of Germanicus' *imperium* here (and of Tiberius' *imperium* in lines 35–36) confirms the view that there was no such thing as *imperium maius* as a specific power, but that it was always to be understood in comparison with something else (Béranger, 1953: 74–96, esp. 82–84; Lebek, 1991: 120–23; Girardet, 2000: esp. 219–27 on Germanicus, qualified by Ferrary, 2001: 135–37; Paschoud, 2005). Copy B contains a bizarre error here, describing Germanicus' *imperium* as 'lesser' (*minus*) rather than 'greater' (*maius*) (Caballos Rufino, 2009: 146 comments that Copy B tends to be closer to the prototype text of the decree as distributed from Rome, so it is odd that the inscriber did not correct this error, even though it misrepresents Germanicus' power as *minus ei imperium quam sibi* [Copy B, line 28] in place of *maius ei imperium quam ei*). Tacitus adds the detail that Germanicus would have greater *imperium* than any official appointed either by lot or by the *princeps* (*Ann.* 2.43.1: 'greater *imperium* wherever he should go, than those who obtained their *imperium* by lot or by being sent by the *princeps*', *maiusque imperium quoquo adisset, quam iis, qui sorte aut missu principis obtinerent*). In other words, Tacitus explicitly refers both to proconsuls and legates, whereas the Senate does not feel the need to include legates in its definition. This is because only proconsuls could hold *imperium* in their own right (Eck, Caballos, Fernández, 1996: 161). This provision therefore extended to the proconsuls of Asia, Bithynia/Pontus, Cyprus, and Crete/Cyrene (Girardet, 2000: 224) and was necessary since otherwise they and Germanicus would potentially have held equal authority. It was unnecessary to mention legates like Piso, who by contrast held only *imperium* delegated to them by the *princeps*. Tacitus mentions both types of provincial governor, perhaps to underline the way in which Piso stepped out of line in opposing Germanicus' instructions, but the fact that Piso should have behaved as subordinate to Germanicus was in no doubt.

Lines 35–36: dum in omni re maius imperium Ti(berio) Caesari Aug(usto) quam Germanico Caesari esset / with the proviso that in every respect Tiberius Caesar Augustus had greater *imperium* than Germanicus Caesar *Imperium maius* was not therefore a distinct power, but defined an individual's *imperium* in relation to that held by others (see 34–35n., *maius ei imperium quam ei qui eam provinciam proco(n)s(ul) optineret*). This is the first known articulation of a threefold hierarchy, consisting of Tiberius, then Germanicus, and finally provincial governors (Eck, Caballos, Fernández, 1996: 160), but probably reflects the wording of the *lex* passed in AD 17. It makes clear that Germanicus is not being given powers as Tiberius' co-regent, but is still subordinate to his authority (cf. Arnaud, 1994: 246).

Lines 36–37: tamquam ipsius arbitri et potestatis omnia esse deberent / as if everything ought to be a matter for his decision and authority This highlights the problem as being that Piso had behaved as if he had enjoyed *imperium* equal to Germanicus' (Eck, Caballos, Fernández, 1996: 161).

Lines 37–45 Piso and Vonones

Grave charges are laid against Piso in this section, including disobeying his instructions from Tiberius and Germanicus, trying to stir up unrest in Armenia and Parthia by championing the cause of the deposed King Vonones, opposing the settlement of the Armenian throne which had been approved by Tiberius and the Senate, and accepting bribes from Vonones. These were all the more serious because of the sensitive nature of the region, with Parthia and Rome having long been in contention for influence in

Armenia (Wheeler, 2007: 239). By contrast, Tacitus alludes only briefly to contact between Piso and Vonones in his narrative about Germanicus' negotiations with the Parthian king (*Ann.* 2.58.2) and does not mention these charges in his account of the trial.

Lines 37–38: bellum {cum} Armeniacum et Parthicum / war with Armenia and Parthia   The accusation that Piso promoted war between Armenia and Parthia, in trying to replace Artaxias III with Vonones, would have made Piso liable to the charge under the *lex maiestatis* of having alienated allies of the Roman people (*Dig.* 48.4.4pr. [Scaevola]: 'or who so acts that allies of the Roman people become their enemies', *utve ex amicis hostes populi Romani fiant*; Castro-Camero, 2000: 46), as well as of having waged a war without an order to do so from the *princeps* (*Dig.* 48.4.3 [Marcian]: 'under the same law who, without the command of the emperor, wages war', *eadem lege tenetur et qui iniussu principis bellum gesserit*; Potter, 1996: 56). The tendentious nature of the charge by the Senate is revealed, however, by the qualifying remark, 'as far as lay within his power' (*quantum in ipso fuerit*).

Lines 38–39: ex mandatis principis nostri / in accordance with the instructions of our Princeps   This refers to the instructions given by Tiberius to Piso as his legate in Syria, before he set out from Rome.

Line 39: epistulisq(ue) frequentibus Germanici Caesaris / and with the many letters of Germanicus Caesar   The letters sent to Piso by Germanicus may have been prompted by the need to modify Tiberius' initial set of instructions to him in the light of Germanicus' negotiations with the king of Parthia (Potter, 1996: 49). This would have been consistent with the practice of clarifying existing instructions from the *princeps* by issuing follow-up letters (Potter, 1996: 51). By juxtaposing in this way the instructions of Tiberius and letters of Germanicus, the Senate creates the impression that they were both working towards the same ends (Eck, Caballos, Fernández, 1996: 166). The decree does not mention what Tacitus narrates (*Ann.* 2.57.1): how Piso refused to obey Germanicus' instruction to convey troops to him in Armenia either under his own leadership or under that of his son Marcus.

Line 39: cum is abesset / when he was away   This refers to Germanicus' absence from Syria either when he was in Armenia in 18 or on tour in Egypt in 19 (or both).

Line 39: Vononem/ Vonones   Vonones (*PIR*² V994; see family tree in Cooley, 2009: 252, fig.29) was the eldest son of King Phraates IV of Parthia (reg. 38–2 BC). Together with his three brothers, Vonones had been brought up in Rome as part of Augustus' household. After his half-brother, Phraates V, was deposed in AD 4, Vonones returned to rule Parthia at the Parthians' request, but his pro-Roman outlook did not appeal to the Parthian nobility, who deposed him a few years later (reg. AD *c*.9–11/12; cf. *RGDA* 33, with Cooley, 2009: 255; his protracted power struggle with Artabanus III of Parthia makes their relative regnal years unclear: Pani, 1972: 173–74). He then assumed the role of king of Armenia (reg. AD *c*.12–15/16; again, the exact chronology is unclear: Pani, 1972: 175), but military pressure from the Parthian king (see 39–40n., **suspectus regi Part(h)orum erat**) forced him to flee to Syria, where he was placed under 'Roman protection' (i.e., imprisoned by the Roman governor), in an attempt to prevent an outbreak of fighting in the region (Tac., *Ann.* 2.1–4, with Andrade, 2012 on Tacitus' depiction of the eastern rulers; Joseph., *AJ* 18.46–52; Eck, Caballos, Fernández, 1996: 106–07).

Lines 39–40: suspectus regi Part(h)orum erat / was an object of suspicion to the king of the Parthians King Artabanus III of Parthia (reg. AD *c*.12–39/40; mistitled Artabanus II by Eck, Caballos, Fernández, 1996: 107) (*PIR*² A 1155), who had deposed Vonones in Parthia, was not comfortable with his predecessor controlling neighbouring Armenia, and so threatened military action against him. This led the Roman governor of Syria, Creticus Silanus, to take Vonones under Roman protection in Syria (Tac., *Ann.* 2.4.3; Joseph., *AJ* 18.52) (cf. 43n., **vel occiso vel expulso rege Armeniae**).

Line 40: longius removeri / be moved further away In AD 18, Germanicus received an embassy from the Parthian king, Artabanus III, requesting him to remove Vonones further from Parthia and Armenia, to prevent him from stirring up trouble. Consequently, Germanicus transferred Vonones to Pompeiopolis in Cilicia (Tac., *Ann.* 2.58; Eck, Caballos, Fernández, 1996: 164). There is a discrepancy between the accounts in Tacitus and the decree, as summarised by Griffin (1997: 260): 'Tacitus says that Germanicus moved Vonones out of Syria to spite Piso (2.58), whereas the inscription says that Piso disobeyed orders to move Vonones, implying that Piso thereby made possible his escape.'

Lines 40–41: ne profugere ex custodia posset, id quod fecit / so that he might be unable to escape from custody (something which he actually did) Vonones escaped from captivity at Pompeiopolis whilst Germanicus was in Egypt, according to Tacitus by bribing his guards (Tac., *Ann.* 2.68), but was intercepted whilst still in Cilicia and killed by Roman soldiers as he tried to travel towards Armenia and Scythia. The switch to the indicative (*fecit*) emphasises that this actually happened. It is unclear how Piso can have been held responsible for Vonones' escape from imprisonment in Cilicia, an area beyond his jurisdiction: the decree is vague about where exactly Vonones escaped from, perhaps deliberately, so as to be able to cast suspicion on Piso (Eck, Caballos, Fernández, 1996: 164). The Senate fails to mention that Vonones was killed during his attempt to escape, which potentially would have undermined the impression it creates of Piso and Vonones jointly plotting unrest in the region. Suetonius (*Tib.* 49.2) offers a different version of events, which attributes Vonones' death to Tiberius' desire to acquire his wealth.

Lines 41–42: et conloqui quosdam ex numero Armeniorum malos et audaces cum Vonone passus sit / he allowed some evil and reckless persons from the body of the Armenians to converse with Vonones The Senate characterises Vonones' supporters among the Armenians in negative moralising terms.

Line 43: vel occiso vel expulso rege Armeniae / once the king of Armenia … had been killed or expelled Zeno, the son of King Polemo of Pontus and stepson of King Archelaus of Cappadocia, may already have been made ruler of Armenia before being confirmed on the throne of Armenia as King Artaxias (*PIR*[2] A1168) by Germanicus in AD 18 (Tac., *Ann.* 2.56.3; Pani, 1972: 187–91, 211–12; Olbrycht, 2016: 608, 619, 621, 624). He replaced Vonones, who had caused tension with Parthia (Tac., *Ann.* 2.56, 64; Hurlet, 1997: 201). This was commemorated by silver drachms and didrachms depicting Germanicus crowning the new king of Armenia, minted at Caesarea in Cappadocia (Fig. 8). The date of their minting is unclear, with arguments being put forward for them being produced on Germanicus' orders in AD 18 (Olbrycht, 2016: 624–26), or later

Fig. 8. Silver didrachm, mint of Caesarea in Cappadocia, depicting the coronation of Artaxias by Germanicus. Obverse (A): head of Germanicus, with the legend GERMANICVS CAESAR TI(BERI) AVG(VSTI) F(ILIVS) CO(N)S(VL) II ('Germanicus Caesar, son of Tiberius Augustus, consul for the second time'). Reverse (B): Germanicus, standing on the right, crowning Artaxias with a diadem, with the legend ARTAXIAS GERMANICVS. *RPC* I 3629,2 (Münzkabinett, Staatliche Museen zu Berlin, 18200231). Photograph by Lutz-Jürgen Lübke (Lübke und Wiedemann). Courtesy of Dr Karsten Dahmen (Münzkabinett, Staatliche Museen zu Berlin).

under Claudius (*RPC* I nos 3629–30, with discussion of the problem of dating the issues on 554–55), or less likely in AD *c*.37–38 under Gaius Caligula (*RIC* I² Gaius 59 = LACTOR 19, M43). This diplomatic solution is visually reflected in the way in which Germanicus and Artaxias are treated as equals on the coins: both are depicted of equal height standing side by side, wearing a military cuirass, and both are involved in the act of Artaxias being crowned with a diadem, with Germanicus placing the diadem on top of Artaxias' tiara whilst Artaxias also supports the diadem with his right hand. Artaxias' coronation was the result of a diplomatic agreement between Armenia, Parthia, and Rome, sealed by a meeting between Germanicus and the king of the Parthians, Artabanus III, on the banks of the river Euphrates (Tac., *Ann.* 2.58). A crucial part of this agreement between Parthia and Rome was that Rome guaranteed the removal of Vonones from Syria, since that geographical proximity had enabled him to cause tensions in Armenia (see 40n., **longius removeri**). Vonones' alleged plan to remove the king of Armenia failed, since in the end Vonones was put to flight and killed during the first half of AD 19 (see 40–41n., **ne profugere ex custodia posset, id quod fecit**). Instead, it turned out that Germanicus had set up a successful arrangement, with Artaxias remaining king of Armenia until he died in AD 34 (Olbrycht, 2016).

Line 44: ex voluntate patris sui senatusq(ue) / in accordance with the wishes of his father and of the Senate   On the representation of collaboration between Senate and *princeps*, see 30n., **a principe nostro ex auctoritate huius ordinis**. In the *Tabula Siarensis*, by contrast, the appointment of a king in Armenia is juxtaposed with instructions of Tiberius alone: 'in accordance with the instructions of Tiberius Caesar Augustus a king having been appointed for Armenia' (*ex mandatis Ti. C<a>esaris Au[g. imposito re]g<e> Armeniae*) (Eck, Caballos, Fernández, 1996: 166; Crawford, 1996: no.37, frag. a, lines 16–17 offers a slightly different reading: *ex mandatis Ti(berii) C<a>esaris Au[g(usti), dato etiam re]g<e> Armeniae*).

Line 45: eaq(ue) magnis muneribus Vononis corruptus fecerit / and these things he did, corrupted by large bribes from Vonones   Tacitus alludes to Vonones winning goodwill from Piso by making lavish gifts to Plancina (Tac., *Ann.* 2.58.2), contravening the spirit of the law restricting the value of gifts made to provincial governors: 'A proconsul is not absolutely obliged to decline gifts, but he should aim for a mean, neither sulkily holding completely back nor greedily going beyond a reasonable level for gifts' (*non uero in totum xeniis abstinere debebit proconsul, sed modum adicere, ut neque morose in totum abstineat neque auare modum xeniorum excedat*; *Dig.* 1.16.6.3 [Ulpian], trans. Watson; Eck, Caballos, Fernández, 1996: 166).

Lines 45–57 Piso's stirring up of civil war

At this point, the Senate reverses the chronological order of events, first charging Piso with his activities in Syria following Germanicus' death (lines 45–57), before proceeding to give details of how Piso responded to news of his death (lines 57–70). In this way, the Senate links the charges of stirring up civil war and undermining military discipline to the previous section on Piso's alleged collusion with Vonones and attempt to provoke war in Armenia and Parthia (see 37–38n., **bellum {cum} Armeniacum et Parthicum**), making this latter claim more plausible in light of Piso's later military intervention in Syria, even though no war had actually been provoked. In this way the Senate also retains for the final sub-section of its charges against Piso the most emotionally charged section describing his behaviour immediately following Germanicus' death. The Senate's focus upon Piso's insurrection (Cooley, 1998: 202–03) contrasts strongly with its minor role in the narrative of Tacitus, who instead focuses upon the charge of poisoning (Giua, 2000: 270–71).

Lines 45–46: bellum etiam civile excitare conatus sit / he also tried to foment civil war   Piso had left Syria after Germanicus fell ill, ending up on the island of Cos (Tac., *Ann.* 2.75.2), a significant distance away. Given that it would have taken several days to travel from Antioch to Cos, covering a distance of more than 900 km (cf. The Stanford Orbis Project, http://orbis.stanford.edu/, accessed 23/03/21), Piso had removed himself far away and was not lurking nearby awaiting news of his death. There is a lack of clarity as to whether Germanicus directly ordered him to leave the province or whether Piso left of his own accord (see 48–49n., ***quam vivo eo pessumo et animo et exemplo reliquerat***). After Germanicus' death, the leading Romans present in Syria appointed Cn. Sentius Saturninus as the new governor of Syria (*PIR*[2] S395; Tac., *Ann.* 2.74), but at the same time Piso decided to return to the province as its governor. Initially, the appointment of Saturninus may have been somewhat irregular (as the choice of a group of senators rather than of Germanicus himself or Tiberius) (De Martino, 1996: 485–87), perhaps explaining why Piso considered that he was still the acting governor of Syria, but it was retrospectively sanctioned by Tiberius. Sentius continued in post at least until AD 21 (cf. his dedication of the *aqua Augusta* at Syrian Nicopolis in Tiberius' fourth consulship, which commenced at the start of AD 21: *CIL* III 6703). Eck (2002: 158) argues that Piso cannot have expected that he would become embroiled in a civil war, since it seems that his troops and officers supported his command, with centurions visiting him on Cos to persuade him to resume his command in Syria (Tac., *Ann.* 2.76.1). Tacitus attributes to one of Piso's friends, Domitius Celer (*PIR*[2] D140), a speech setting out the reasons why Piso should regard himself as still the legitimate governor of Syria (*Ann.*

2.77). Nevertheless, it must have become clear to Piso at some point that his actions in returning towards Syria were in fact resulting in conflict between different units of the Roman army. Even so, he did not refrain from trying to reassert his authority.

Lines 46–47: iam pridem numine divi Aug(usti) virtutibusq(ue) Ti(beri) Caesaris Aug(usti) omnibus civilis belli sepultis malis / even though all the evils of civil war had long since been buried through the divine power of deified Augustus and the virtues of Tiberius Caesar Augustus The horrors of civil war had been a common topic among the poets of the triumviral and Augustan eras, inspiring some of the most vivid imagery of the age, whether of a charioteer spinning out of control (Verg., *G.* 1.513–16 = LACTOR 17, G9), Romans rushing headlong towards self-destruction (Hor., *Epod.* 7 = LACTOR 17, G3), or the fields around Perusia polluted by the bones of the unburied casualties of civil conflict (Prop. 1.21 and 1.22 = LACTOR 17, G13–14). Augustus' ending of the civil wars through his victory at Actium was much celebrated by himself (*RGDA* 4.1, 25.2, 34.2) and others (Gurval, 1995). The transitory spectacle of the triple triumph in 29 BC was consolidated in 27 BC by awarding him the civic crown (*corona civica*) for saving the lives of citizens, displayed above the entrance to his house and on many coin issues (Cooley, 2009: 264–66). Further acknowledgement of Augustus' achievement in putting an end to civil strife came in 8 BC, when the Senate decreed that the month of Sextilis should be renamed August because (among other reasons) 'in this month an end was brought to civil wars' (Macrob., *Sat.* 1.12.35: *finisque hoc mense bellis civilibus impositus sit*). Furthermore, Augustus' permanent settling of civil conflicts was still being recalled in the final years of his life by Ovid from his exile at Tomis as a means of conjuring up Augustus' lenient nature, inasmuch as he 'has shut up civil wars with a permanent bolt' (Ov., *Pont.* 1.2.124: *clausit et aeterna civica bella sera*).

Referring to the civil wars as 'long since' buried by Augustus recalls his victories of fifty years earlier. As Osgood (2015: 1691–92) points out, the celebration of Augustus' ending of civil wars was particularly loud in the early years of the Tiberian era, with Velleius Paterculus offering a close echo of the language used here by the Senate in relating Augustus' pacification of the world: 'once the civil wars had been buried, as I mentioned earlier' (Vell. Pat. 2.90.1: *sepultis, ut praediximus, bellis civilibus*; cf. 2.87.1 for the capture of Alexandria in 30 BC putting an end to civil wars, and 2.89.3 [with Woodman, 1983: 251] for the symbolic closing of the gates of Janus on 11 January 29 BC marking the end of civil wars).

The expression 'through the divine power of deified Augustus' / *numine divi Aug(usti)* gives retrospective dignity to the power struggle between Imperator Caesar and Antony, anticipating the Senate's later claim that

Piso had offended against Augustus' 'divine power' in other ways too (see 68n., **numen quoq(ue) divi Aug(usti) violatum esse ab eo**). The drafters of the senatorial decree of AD 20 anachronistically retrojected the language of their own times, in which to speak of the *numen divi Augusti* was a standard element, onto an earlier period where it did not apply (Fishwick, 2007: 297–98). This did not matter, though, since the Senate's aim was to magnify Piso's transgressions by enhancing the status of Augustus and Tiberius.

In referring to Tiberius' role in putting an end to civil wars, the Senate may be alluding to the mutinies among the legions in Germania and Pannonia following Augustus' death (Tac., *Ann.* 1.16–52; Pettinger, 2012: chapter 11; Eck, Caballos, Fernández, 1996: 168). Although the Senate fulsomely expresses its appreciation of the current peaceful state of affairs (see 13–14n., **tranquillitatem praesentis status r(ei) p(ublicae)**, 14n., **quo melior optari non pote<st> ʿeʾt quo beneficio principis nostri frui contigit**), other contemporary voices – notably Valerius Maximus and Velleius Paterculus – betray continuing anxieties about the potential return of civil conflict. Both of these authors share the sentiment of the Senate that Rome could depend upon Tiberius to avert civil war through his virtues (Gowing, 2010). In addition, the threat may have continued beyond AD 15, since Pettinger (2012: chapter 2) makes a case for taking seriously the conspiracy of Clemens, who took on the role of Agrippa Postumus. He argues that M. Scribonius Drusus Libo was regarded as one of Clemens' supporters, with the result that a sense of foreboding emerged in AD 16, as fears of civil war breaking out once more re-emerged (as reflected in the later accounts of Tac., *Ann.* 2.39.1; Suet., *Tib.* 25.1). It is against this background of continued anxiety, therefore, that the Senate's praise for Tiberius in AD 20 should be understood.

Line 47: repetendo provinciam Syriam / by trying to regain ... the province of Syria Piso's attempt to regain control of Syria by force laid him open to two counts of *maiestas*: firstly, in causing his troops to bear arms against the state (cf. *Dig.* 48.4.1.1 [Ulpian], trans. Watson: anyone is liable to a charge of *maiestas* who 'bears arms against the state ... or who persuades or incites troops to make a sedition or tumult against the state', *quoue quis contra rem publicam arma ferat ... quiue milites sollicitauerit concitaueritve, quo seditio tumultusue adversus rem publicam fiat*), and secondly, in refusing to hand over his province to a successor (*Dig.* 48.4.2 [Ulpian], trans. Watson: 'or who has failed to relinquish his province although his successor has arrived', *quiue de prouincia, cum ei successum esset, non discessit*) (Castro-Camero, 2000: 47). On the circumstances surrounding Piso's initial departure from Syria, see 48–49n., **quam vivo eo pessumo et animo et exemplo reliquerat**. From Tacitus' narrative, it seems that Piso made it as far as Cilicia before being compelled to surrender to Sentius at the coastal stronghold of Celenderis (Tac., *Ann.* 2.80–81).

Lines 47–48 post mortem Germanici Caesaris / after the death of Germanicus Caesar Germanicus died in Antioch on the Orontes on 10 October AD 19 (Degrassi, 1963: 209 – *Fasti Antiates Ministrorum* = LACTOR 19, J7g; Suet., *Calig.* 1.2).

Lines 48–49 quam vivo eo pessumo et animo et exemplo reliquerat / which he had abandoned, demonstrating both the worst frame of mind and example, while Germanicus was still alive The Senate states that Piso left Syria on his own initiative, arguing that this was an indication of his wicked character. Abandoning his province whilst in post would in itself also constitute a crime under the *maiestas* law (Eck, Caballos, Fernández, 1996: 167, with reference to the *lex Cornelia de maiestate* of 81 BC, as cited in Cic., *Pis.* 50; cf. *Dig.* 1.16.10 [Ulpian] on the importance of maintaining continuity between the changeover in governors of a province). In Tacitus' account, by contrast, there is a distinct lack of clarity: whereas the narrative relates that 'Piso decided to leave Syria' (*Ann.* 2.69.2: *Piso abire Suria statuit*), Tacitus also records that 'many people add that he was ordered to leave the province' (*Ann.* 2.70.2: *addunt plerique iussum prouincia decedere*) (Giua, 2000: 265–66). One way of reconciling the two versions of events is to suggest that Germanicus did not directly command Piso to leave Syria, but that Piso interpreted Germanicus' act in formally withdrawing his friendship (see 29n., ***amicitiam ei renuntiasse***) as requiring him implicitly to leave (De Martino, 1996: 485). Although Eck (2002: 158; cf. Eck, Caballos, Fernández, 1996: 156) suggests that Germanicus overstepped his authority if he ordered Piso to leave the province to which he had been appointed directly by Tiberius, the potential ambiguity regarding Germanicus' powers suggests that this may not have been clearly the case (see 34–35n., ***maius ei imperium quam ei qui eam provinciam proco(n)s(ul) optineret***).

Line 49: milites Romani inter se concurrere coacti sunt / Roman soldiers were forced into conflict with each other The Senate alludes to Roman soldiers being 'forced into conflict with each other' to downplay the idea that Piso may have had genuine supporters in the army (Eck, Caballos, Fernández, 1996: 169; Lott, 2012: 276–77). One of the distinctive features of the decree is the Senate's desire to shore up military loyalty towards the Tiberian regime (see 159–65n.; 172n., ***item(que) hoc s(enatus) c(onsultum) in hibernis cuiusq(ue) legionis at signa figeretur***; for continued anxiety about the potential for civil war, see 46–47n., ***iam pridem numine divi Aug(usti) virtutibusq(ue) Ti(beri) Caesaris Aug(usti) omnibus civilis belli sepultis malis***).

Lines 49–50: perspecta etiam crudelitate unica / when he had also manifested his unparalleled cruelty The Senate continues to emphasise Piso's uniquely wicked character (see 13n., **nefaris consilis Cn(aei) Pisonis patris**).

Line 50: incognita causa, sine consili sententia / without hearing their cases, without consulting his council It was standard practice for a provincial governor to have a group of advisors with him for discussing judicial and administrative affairs (Lott, 2012: 277; Crook, 1955: 5; Amarelli, 1983: 63–69 on the consultation of their *consilium* by various Roman magistrates). In particular, a magistrate would be expected to consult his *consilium* if capital penalties were envisaged (Crifò, 1963: esp. 306–07).

Lines 50–51: plurimos capitis supplicio adfecisset / inasmuch as he had inflicted the death penalty on very many This statement continues the hyperbolic style of the Senate's condemnation of Piso, with the vague use of the superlative 'very many' complementing the description of Piso having shown his 'unique cruelty' (see 49–50, **perspecta etiam crudelitate unica**) and 'worst frame of mind' (48, **pessumo et animo**).

Lines 51–52: neq(ue) externos tantummodo, sed etiam centurionem c(ivem) R(omanum) cruci fixsisset / and had crucified not only foreigners but also a centurion, a Roman citizen This charge relates to the period when Piso was trying to return to Syria, so reference to 'foreigners' (*externi*) in this context should be understood as auxiliary troops (Eck, Caballos, Fernández, 1996: 170). Only the very worst offences connected with desertion were regarded as liable for the death penalty (*Dig.* 49.16.3 [Modestinus]), but in other contexts being prepared to punish centurions for deserting their post could be viewed as a positive trait (cf. Suet., *Aug.* 24). The charge of crucifying a Roman citizen is particularly shocking, since anyone with the status of a Roman citizen should have been exempt from this kind of capital punishment, which was usually reserved for slaves (Garnsey, 1970: 126–29). Furthermore, a centurion was of relatively high social status. Seneca the Younger (*De Ira* 1.18.3–6, 19.3 = LACTOR 19, P2b, with Kaster and Nussbaum, 2010: 107 n.108) mentions the summary execution of three soldiers, including a centurion, by Cn. Piso in a complicated episode of mistaken accusation. Seneca comments (1.18.3), 'Cn. Piso was in our memory a man free from many faults, but mistaken inasmuch as inflexibility pleased him in place of steadfastness' (*Cn. Piso fuit memoria nostra uir a multis uitiis integer, sed prauus et cui placebat pro constantia rigor*). Seneca's episode does not relate to the current charges about Piso's behaviour in the East, since he is referred to as proconsul, and since the executions do not take the form of crucifixion. This suggests that similar charges were believed to relate to Piso's earlier career as proconsular governor of Africa (Eck, Caballos, Fernández, 1996: 170 with n.454).

Lines 52–53: qui militarem disciplinam a divo Aug(usto) institutam et servatam a Ti(berio) Caesare Aug(usto) corrupisset / he had damaged the military discipline which had been established by deified Augustus and maintained by Tiberius Caesar Augustus It has been suggested that from this point in their list of charges, the Senate appears to go back to the period when Piso was in command of his troops in Syria before Germanicus' death, as narrated by Tacitus (*Ann.* 2.55.5; Eck, Caballos, Fernández, 1996: 169, 171). Nevertheless, elements of the charges recorded here, including distributing bribes to the soldiers to encourage them to mutiny (see 54–55n., ***donativa suo nomine ex fisco principis nostri dando***), also correspond to Tacitus' narrative of Piso's actions in seeking to return to Syria (*Ann.* 2.81). Augustus' reputation for having strengthened discipline within the army is also recorded in the second century by Suetonius (*Aug.* 24–25) and Polyaenus (*Strat.* 8.24). These measures, alongside his professionalisation of the army, helped to maintain Augustus' leadership of Rome via his control of the army (Raaflaub, 1980: 1005–13). Any interference in military matters that might undermine discipline was viewed with suspicion by Tiberius, as illustrated by his negative reception of the misguided attempt by Iunius Gallio to promote Tiberius' interests by proposing that ex-praetorians be rewarded with special seats in the theatre (Tac., *Ann.* 6.3, with Woodman, 2017: ad loc.; Cooley 1998: 202).

Lines 53–54: indulgendo militibus, <ne> his, qui ipsis praesunt, more vetustissumo parerent / by allowing soldiers not to obey in the traditional manner those in command of them Tacitus (*Ann.* 2.55.5) expands upon the charges made against Piso in relation to his command of the Syrian legions. Roman elite culture held ancestral tradition (*mos maiorum*) in the deepest respect, as illustrated in Augustus' repeated allusions to ancestral practice in his *Res Gestae* (6.1, 8.5, 13, 27.2, with Cooley, 2009: 38). Syntactically, the Senate constructs a tricolon of three gerunds with which to describe Piso's offences in undermining military discipline: *indulgendo, dando, honorando*.

Lines 54–55: donativa suo nomine ex fisco principis nostri dando / but also by giving donatives in his own name from the treasury of our Princeps This is the earliest known use of the word *donativum* meaning a special gift of cash made to soldiers (Eck, Caballos, Fernández, 1996: 179). Augustus had set the pattern that donatives to the military should come only from him, to mark victories and important political events (Raaflaub, 1980: 1011). Piso's distribution of donatives in his own name therefore seriously encroaches upon politically sensitive ground (Eck, Caballos, Fernández, 1996: 173; cf. Campbell, 1984: 183–94 on the continuing close association between emperors and donatives). The use of the plural 'donatives' (*donativa*) underlines the irregularity of Piso's actions. It is unlikely that he was giving cash rewards to all the soldiers in the Syrian legions on multiple occasions, so the Senate appears to be alluding to sums of money being given only to certain individuals or units, emphasising Piso's attempts to subvert their loyalty (Eck, Caballos, Fernández, 1996: 172).

The phrase 'treasury of our Princeps' (*fiscus principis*) is the earliest example of *fiscus* used in close association with the *princeps* (Eck, Caballos, Fernández, 1996: 174, 179–80; Alpers, 1995: 59–60). In appearing to designate the emperor's own personal treasury, this ostensibly solves a debate of many decades surrounding the organisation of imperial finances (cf. Garzetti, 1953, with a summary of previous scholarship; Jones, 1950; Millar, 1963; Brunt, 1966; Alpers, 1995), by demonstrating that already by AD 20 there was a clear distinction between the *aerarium* – the public treasury of the Roman people housed in the Temple of Saturn at Rome – and the *fiscus* containing private funds belonging to Tiberius (Castro-Camero, 2000: 85–87). This would support the view of Millar (1963) that already at this date the *fiscus* contained Tiberius' private property (excluding the possibility that the *fiscus* also contained tax revenues from an imperial province such as Syria; cf. Alpers, 1995: 274). It seems clear, however, that we should not think in terms of **the** *fiscus*, meaning a separate central treasury at Rome containing Tiberius' private wealth, but multiple *fisci* (Garzetti, 1953: 308), and that the term *fiscus* can have different meanings. Firstly, it was used to refer to the private funds of the *princeps*; secondly, a provincial treasury containing public funds; and lastly, the whole financial administration controlled by the *princeps* (Brunt, 1966: 75). In fact, as Millar (1963: 29) argued, there was no moment at which an institution called 'the Fiscus' was created, but this term gradually came to be used to refer to imperial wealth. Already under Augustus the distinction between his own private wealth and public funds had become blurred: as the *Res Gestae* illustrates, Augustus used his own private wealth for public purposes (most notably in setting up the military treasury / *aerarium militare*), and he had control over all revenues, both public and private (Millar, 1963: 29). Suetonius (*Aug.* 101.4) records a division between *aerarium* (state treasury) and *fisci* (imperial treasuries) in language that may well be derived from contemporary Augustan documentation (Alpers, 1995: 274).

Although the decree may well refer to personal funds belonging to Tiberius, an alternative interpretation cannot be excluded given that the word *fiscus* could also be used at this time to refer to the treasury based in a province, which could be drawn upon by the provincial governor (Garzetti,

1953: 323). Under Tiberius, for example, an inscription refers to the Gallic *fiscus* of the province of Lugdunensis (*fiscus Gallicus provinciae Lugdunensis*: *CIL* VI 5197 = LACTOR 19, S5). In this instance, therefore, the *fiscus* from which Piso funded the donatives might have been a similar provincial treasury based in Syria, containing public revenues gathered in the province (Castro-Camero, 2000: 87; Lo Cascio, 2000: 167). This might explain Piso's access to these funds, as provincial legate, although he may have had to access them via the imperial procurator (of unknown identity at this date) (Eck, Caballos, Fernández, 1996: 173; Lo Cascio, 2000: 169; Lott, 2012: 278–79). Even if he had legitimately accessed the funds, it is clear that Piso abused this right by distributing them to the military in his own name. Such a misuse of public funds would have made him liable to the Iulian law on embezzlement (*lex Iulia de peculatu*) (Castro-Camero, 2000: 48; *Dig.* 48.13.1). Moreover, although provincial governors were authorised to use revenues in their province, it is less clear whether Piso would have been authorised to access Tiberius' private wealth, if the *fiscus* were instead a treasury containing his personal funds (Castro-Camero, 2000: 87; Lo Cascio, 2000: 169). In the latter case, Piso's offence in distributing the donatives is, according to the Senate, compounded by appropriating the private resources of Tiberius, even though he may actually have had permission to access those funds at the time (Eck, Caballos, Fernández, 1996: 174, 180; Potter, 1998: 446). In summarising previous scholarship on this question, Lo Cascio (2000: 163–74) agrees that the *SCPP* demonstrates that there was already a distinction between *aerarium* and *fiscus* by AD 20, but that the question remains as to whether the *fiscus* held only private funds belonging personally to the *princeps* or whether the *fiscus* was also in receipt of public revenue. He concludes differently from Eck, Caballos, and Fernández (1996: 180), who argued that the decree refers to the personal treasury of Tiberius, that the phrase *fiscus principis nostri* refers to the provincial treasury of the imperial province of Syria.

Lines 55–56: milites alios Pisonianos, alios Caesarianos dicì laetatus sit / he was pleased to see some soldiers being called 'Pisonians', others 'Caesarians' Tacitus does not record this detail, stating instead that Piso had been called 'father of the legions' (*parens legionum*) during his command of the Syrian legions before Germanicus' death, in recognition of his corrupt attitude to military discipline (*Ann.* 2.55.5). As Goodyear (1981: 363) observed, however, this title had 'old and respectable precedent'. The Senate's reference to 'Pisonians' and 'Caesareans', by contrast, evoked only the troubles of civil strife, as illustrated in Velleius' contemporary references (2.51.3; 2.63.3) to the *Pompeiani* and *Iuliani* of an earlier era. In this way, the troops identified their interests either with Piso or Germanicus (Caesar). Consequently, this charge must date back to before Germanicus' death (Eck, Caballos, Fernández, 1996: 175–77). It is possible that the splitting of the army into Caesarians and Pisonians may also have underlain Piso's letter to Tiberius accusing Germanicus after his death of arrogance and even of plotting a revolt (Tac., *Ann.* 2.78.1; Eck, Caballos, Fernández, 1996: 176 n.477; see 59n., ***libellum, quo eum accusaret***). A later echo of a similar expression of loyalty among soldiers embroiled in a civil war may also be found in the epitaph from Clunia (Hispania Tarraconensis) of a soldier, who identifies himself with his commander, Otho: *T. Cantio Nasonis f(ilio) mil(iti) Ot<h>oniano* (*AE* 1988, 788; Abramenko, 1993: 'To Titus Cantius Othonianus, son of Naso, soldier' or 'To Titus Cantius, son of Naso, Othonian soldier').

Lines 57–70 Piso's response to Germanicus' death

In this final subsection of charges (lines 57–68), the Senate turns away from crimes liable under the *lex maiestatis* towards aspects of Piso's behaviour which show him to have been a uniquely wicked character. These include not mourning Germanicus, sending a letter to Tiberius criticising Germanicus after his death, and giving a tip to the messenger who brought news of his death. Most of these offences appear to relate to the period when Piso was still on the island of Cos, before he set off towards Syria, as narrated by Tacitus (*Ann.* 2.75.2). Tacitus also depicts Tiberius at the start of Piso's trial as raising the question of how Piso had responded to Germanicus' death, but as relevant to Tiberius' private relationship with Piso rather than to his guilt under law (*Ann.* 3.12.1–2). It is unclear when Piso is supposed to have committed the final offences listed, against the *numen* of Augustus (lines 68–70).

Lines 57–58: cuius interitum non p(opulus) R(omanus) modo, sed exterae quoq(ue) gentes luxserunt / whose loss not only the Roman people but foreign nations too mourned Precedents for the widespread expression of grief at the death of a member of the imperial family are found in reactions to the deaths of Lucius and Gaius Caesar in AD 2 and 4, as attested in the decrees passed by the town council of Pisa (*CIL* XI 1420–21 = LACTOR 17, J61, J64). The contemporary evidence of the *fasti Ostienses* (Bargagli and Grosso, 1997: 23, frag. Cd left/Ce 33–34 = LACTOR 19, J7h) and the senatorial decree on honours for Germanicus preserved on the *Tabulae Siarensis* and *Hebana* give an impression of the extraordinary reactions to Germanicus' death at Rome (Crawford, 1996: no.37 = LACTOR 19, J8). This is made even more vivid by later accounts of the ways in which Germanicus' death was interpreted as a moment of crisis for the state, as social disintegration accompanied unrestrained displays of grief (Versnel, 1980; Joseph., *AJ* 18.209; Tac., *Ann.* 2.72–73, 82–83; Suet., *Calig.* 1–6). The Senate's allusion here to grief displayed by 'foreign nations' (*exterae gentes*) probably relates to the Parthians, with whom Germanicus had built up a positive relationship (see 43n., ***vel occiso vel expulso rege Armeniae***). Suetonius describes how the Parthians mourned Germanicus' death in ways that are represented as both typically alien to Rome (for example, cutting off a beard rather than growing one as a sign of grief) and yet equivalent to the Roman declaration of a period of official mourning, or *iustitium*:

Moreover, they say that even the barbarians, among whom there was either internal war or war against us, agreed upon a truce as if in a domestic and shared sorrow; that some chieftains cut their beards and shaved their wives' heads as a sign of the deepest grief; that even the king of kings {i.e., the king of Parthia, Artabanus III} refrained from hunting-practice and from socialising with the noblemen, which among the Parthians is like official mourning

quin et barbaros ferunt, quibus intestinum quibusque aduersus nos bellum esset, uelut in domestico communique maerore consensisse ad indutias; regulos quosdam barbam posuisse et uxorum capita rasisse ad indicium maximi luctus; regum etiam regem et exercitatione uenandi et conuictu megistanum abstinuisse, quod apud Parthos iustiti instar est. (*Calig.* 5)

Lines 58–59: patri optumo et indulgentissumo / to Germanicus' most excellent and most forbearing parent This is the first known use of the word *indulgentia* in an inscription, in reference to the expectation of indulgence in the relationship between a father and his son (cf. Cic., *De Or.* 2.168) rather than to the later political phenomenon of imperial *indulgentia*, which came to refer to benefits generously given by the *princeps* (Griffin, 2003b: 110–11; Eck, Caballos, Fernández, 1996: 182). In a striking reversal of the norm later in the decree, Tiberius is on the receiving end of the Senate's *indulgentia* (see 118–19n., ***principis nostri summa\<e\> erga matrem suam pietati suffragandum indulgendumq(ue) esse***). The Senate emphasises the excellent relationship between Tiberius and his (adopted) son Germanicus, in contrast to Tacitus' depiction of a rather fraught relationship between the two (*Ann.* 1.31.1, 1.33, 1.52.1, 2.59; Shotter, 1968; O'Gorman, 2000: 46–69; Pelling, 2012).

Line 59: libellum, quo eum accusaret / a document in which he made accusations about Germanicus It is possible that this was read out during the trial as part of the documentary evidence presented in the Senate (see 23–24n., ***cum per aliquot dies acta causa sit, ab accusatoribus Cn(aei) Pisonis patris et ab ipso Cn(aeo) Pisone patre recitatae epistulae recitata exemplaria codicillorum***). Tacitus (*Ann.* 2.78.1) also mentions a letter critical of Germanicus sent after his death by Piso to Tiberius. Whereas the Senate mentions no details about the nature of Piso's accusations against Germanicus, Tacitus relates that Piso accused Germanicus of arrogance and luxury, as well as of revolutionary plans (Eck, Caballos, Fernández, 1996: 182).

Lines 59–60: oblitus non tantum venerationis caritatisq(ue), quae principis filio debebantur / forgetting not only the respect and affection which were owed to the son of the Princeps In other contexts, it was considered natural for someone to express their delight at the death of another person acknowledged to be an enemy, as argued by Kierdorf ([1983] 1987: 231). The examples he cites are not straightforward, however. Cicero's joy at the death of Clodius is justified by his representation of Clodius as a public enemy (Cic., *Phil.* 2.21), but neither M. Antonius rejoicing at the death of Servius Sulpicius (Cic., *Phil.* 9.7) nor Otho at the murder of Piso (Tac., *Hist.* 1.44.1) is described in positive terms. Given that Germanicus had formally renounced his friendship with Piso (see 29n., ***amicitiam ei renuntiasse***), it is not perhaps surprising if Piso had been pleased to hear of his death. The Senate's view here, however, of the affection owed to the son of the *princeps* illustrates the way in which members of the Augustan household (*domus Augusta*) were assuming unique status in Roman society (see §5).

Line 61: humanitatis / common humanity The Romans regarded *humanitas* as at the core of their civilising mission in ruling over their empire (Woolf, 1994: 119–21). By denying that Piso possessed this fundamental quality, the Senate excludes him from one of the defining characteristics of what it was to be Roman, isolating him from the rest of society.

Lines 62–63: nefaria sacrificia / wicked sacrifices Describing the sacrifices oxymoronically as *nefaria* underlines the point that they were a subversion of the norm. Tacitus (*Ann.* 2.75.2) relates that Piso performed sacrifices on Cos on hearing the news of Germanicus' death. Goodyear (1981: 422) comments 'Here, as elsewhere, his conduct seems little short of demented': this is certainly the impression which the Senate is trying to create.

Line 63: naves, quibus vehebatur, ornatae sint / the ships in which he sailed were decorated This is obviously not a criminal activity, but is included as an indication of Piso's wicked character.

Lines 63–64: recluserit deorum immortalium templa / he reopened the temples of the immortal gods The Senate declared a *iustitium* on 8 December when news reached Rome of Germanicus' death in AD 19 (*Tabula Hebana* lines 54–55 = Crawford, 1996: no.37, 512, with commentary on 540–41 = LACTOR 19, J8p). This involved closing all temples and suspending public business in Rome and in communities of Roman citizens until Germanicus' burial should take place in Rome (at some point before 4 April the following year), but these measures were not formally required elsewhere. Instead, the Senate alludes here to the spontaneous decision to close temples in mourning which was taken by people in the provinces. Given uncertainties over the timing and location of these events (were temples in the provinces closed even before the declaration of the *iustitium* at Rome in December? would Piso have had the authority to order temples on Cos to be reopened?), it seems that the Senate may well be exaggerating Piso's actions here (Eck, Caballos, Fernández, 1996: 184).

Lines 64–65: totius imperi Romani constantissuma pietas clauserat / the most unwavering devotion of the whole Roman empire had closed The Senate continues its use of hyperbolic language, with the superlative adjective 'most unwavering' (*constantissuma*) to emphasise the universal feelings of devotion towards Germanicus throughout the Roman empire. This is the first of nine references to *pietas*, which has two main characteristics in the decree. Firstly, it is the quality of loyalty and affection shown between members of the *domus Augusta* towards each other (Tiberius towards Germanicus, lines 123–24; Tiberius towards Iulia Augusta, line 119; Iulia Augusta and Drusus towards Germanicus, line 134). In this way, members of the imperial family inspire emulation among the rest of Roman society, with the Senate displaying its *pietas* towards Germanicus (line 72), the equestrian order perceiving that the trial was of the utmost importance and relevant to the safety and *pietas* of all of Roman society (line 152), the *plebs* demonstrating *pietas* towards Tiberius and Germanicus (line 155), the army maintaining its *pietas* towards the *domus Augusta* (line 161), and finally army officers remaining loyal to the name of the Caesars (line 164) (cf. Severy, 2000: 335, 'The authors also use *pietas*, a term of familial and religious devotion, to describe ties of traditional political institutions, such as the equestrian order and the *plebs*, to the imperial house'). The quality of *pietas* – 'dutiful respect' (*OLD* s.v. 'pietas') – which had always been multivalent in application (compare the copy from Arles of the shield granted in honour of Augustus, which includes 'piety towards gods and country', *pietas erga deos patriamque*, *AE* 1952, 165 = LACTOR 17, H24), becomes more closely refocused in the decree upon defining correct behaviour towards members of Tiberius' family, embedding the *domus Augusta* at the heart of Roman society. Whereas the *Res Gestae* had emphasised universal support and consensus towards Augustus himself as an individual (34–35), the safety of Rome is now depicted as dependent upon the imperial family more broadly (see §5). As Severy (2000: 329) states, 'In general, the rhetoric of the decree thus constructs the state as a hierarchy based on familial devotion (*pietas*) and the demonstration of virtues learned from (paternal) superiors'.

Lines 65–66: quod dedisset congiarium / the fact that he had given a gift of money The Senate cites this action by Piso as another instance of his wicked character, rather than as an example of an actual crime. Lott (2012: 281) suggests that the choice of wording is intended to intimate Piso's ambitions, given that *congiarium* was used as the technical word to describe public cash handouts from the *princeps* in the city of Rome, but it can equally be used to denote an individual gift (*OLD* s.v. 'congiarium', 2).

Lines 66–67: frequenter{q(ue)} convivia habuisse / on several occasions he had held banquets Tacitus (*Ann.* 3.9.3) narrates how Piso caused offence on his return to Rome in AD 20 by holding banquets in his house overlooking the Roman Forum.

Line 68: numen quoq(ue) divi Aug(usti) violatum esse ab eo / the divine spirit of deified Augustus had been violated by him Offences against the *lex maiestatis* developed in significant ways during this period: 'Allowing disrespect to Augustus and later to Tiberius to be understood as a slight against the *maiestas* of the Roman people forms part of a conceptual and social revolution that received only gradual articulation in contemporary political theoretical discourse' (Ando, 2011: 105). There has been much debate about how to understand the reference to the *numen divi Augusti* here (Eck, Caballos, Fernández, 1996: 186–88; Fishwick, 2007; Lott, 2012: 282; Marcone, 2015). Whereas Eck, Caballos, and Fernández argue that *numen* can only apply to Augustus in his lifetime, Fishwick contends that it is associated with divus Augustus. The Senate in the decree, however, calls it the *numen divi Augusti* simply because Augustus had become *divus* by the time of writing, not because the *numen* belonged to Augustus in his deified form. The offences, therefore, may in fact relate to the *numen Augusti*. The Senate once again increases the seriousness of Piso's actions by applying anachronistic language to Augustus (see 46–47n., **iam pridem numine divi Aug(usti) virtutibusq(ue) Ti(beri) Caesaris Aug(usti) omnibus civilis belli sepultis malis**). The reason why this is important is in trying to work out when Piso is supposed to have committed these offences against the *numen divi Augusti*. It is possible that these are historic charges against Piso, resurrected when he comes to trial in AD 20, but which relate to his behaviour during Augustus' lifetime. It is not difficult to imagine that Piso may have been outspoken in opposing innovations in honouring Augustus' *numen* at some point, but it is not impossible either to suppose that Piso may have done or said things even after Augustus had been deified (or during the debate about that deification) that were later interpreted as offences against Augustus' *numen* (on the chronology, see further 69–70n., **qui aut memoriae eius aut imaginibus, quae, antequam in deorum numerum referre{n}tur, ei r[eddi]tae erant**). It is not necessary, therefore, to identify Piso's offences against Augustus' *imagines* as belonging only to a brief time frame, between Augustus' death on 19 August and his deification on 17 September in AD 14 (cf. Fishwick, 2007). Moreover, *numen* was not used as a technical term for some sort of divine property assigned to Augustus during his lifetime (nor was it equivalent to his *genius*): 'worshipping the emperor's divinity (*numen*) was simply synonymous with worshipping him directly, as a god' (Gradel, 2002: chapter 10, esp. 245). Offences against the *numen* of Augustus emerged, according to Tacitus, shortly after Augustus' death and deification, with the equestrian Rubrius accused in AD 15 of having offended against the *numen* of Augustus by perjury (*Ann.* 1.73.2, *Rubrio crimini dabatur uiolatum periurio numen Augusti*; cf. *Ann.* 3.66 in AD 22, C. Iunius Silanus accused of having offended against Augustus' *numen* and Tiberius' *maiestas*: *uiolatum Augusti numen, spretam Tiberii maiestatem*). Tiberius, however, intervened by writing to the consuls to dismiss this charge against Rubrius.

Lines 69–70: qui aut memoriae eius aut imaginibus, quae, antequam in deorum numerum referre{n}tur, eì r[eddi]tae erant / which was being accorded either to his memory or to those portraits which had been [set up] to him before he was entered into the number of the gods The Senate does not specify exactly how Piso offended against the *numen Augusti*, but the implication of 'either to his memory or to those portraits which had been set up to him before he was entered into the number of the gods' is that the offences took place on more than one occasion and related in some cases to Piso's treatment of likenesses of Augustus which had been set up before his deification. On this basis, Piso may have committed at least some of the offences during Augustus' lifetime (Eck, Caballos, Fernández, 1996: 187), but it seems equally possible that Piso was accused of offences which took place after Augustus' death and deification but concerned images of Augustus set up during his lifetime. At line 70 we encounter one of the rare places where the text of the decree remains doubtful. Copy A omits in error the words *ei r[---]tae erant* entirely, whilst Copy B is damaged. The lacuna within *ei r[---]tae erant* could be completed as *r[ecep]tae*, *r[eddi]tae*, or *r[ela]tae* (interpreted by Eck, Caballos, Fernández, 1996: 186 as 'promised', 'granted', or 'dedicated'), but the general sense is clear nonetheless.

LINES 71–123 SENATE'S RECOMMENDATIONS ON THE FOUR ITEMS UNDER DISCUSSION

Lines 71–90 Posthumous punishments for Piso

The Senate responds in this section specifically to Tiberius' instruction in his *relatio* that it consider 'whether Piso was regarded as having taken his own life deservedly' (see 6–7n., **et an merito sibi mortem conscisse videretur**). The change in topic is indicated in Copy A by extending the start of the line into the left margin and in Copy B by leaving a blank space (*vacat*). For an extensive discussion of this section, see §7. There are also excellent overviews of this section by Bodel (1999) and by Flower (1996: 23–31; 1998), who points out that the order in which the penalties are listed reflects the chronological order in which they were to be imposed, starting with a ban on mourning at Piso's death and ending with confiscation of property in Illyricum. By committing suicide, Piso might have expected his will to be valid and his property to be inherited by his heirs: Tacitus comments in relation to the suicides of Pomponius Labeo and his wife Paxaea in AD 34 that only those who had already been condemned at the time of their deaths would normally expect to have their property confiscated and burial forbidden (*Ann.* 6.29). Besides confiscating his property (the majority of which was then returned to the family), the Senate imposes other penalties, which also go beyond what might have been expected after Piso's suicide (Griffin, 1997: 261). The Senate therefore justifies the harshness of these penalties by stating that Piso was clearly conscious of his own guilt and only committed suicide in order to try to avoid these penalties (see 71n., **non optulisse eum se de͡b͡itae poenae**). By confiscating property, banning his *imago* and *praenomen*, erasing his name from inscriptions, and destroying statues set up in his honour, the Senate effectively prevents Piso's family from remembering him in all the traditional ways normally adopted by Rome's senatorial elite (Flower, 1998: 181). The overall impact of the penalties upon Piso was 'to remove an erring citizen while enabling both the family of the traitor and the larger community to continue as if the offender had never existed' (Flower, 1998: 155). Tacitus' account of the penalties is selective (*Ann.* 3.17–18), differing from the *SCPP* by recording the punishments proposed by the consul M. Aurelius Cotta Maximus Messallinus and other senators along with Tiberius' response to them, whereas the decree includes only those which were agreed upon between the Senate and Tiberius.

Line 71: non optulisse eum se de͡b͡itae poenae / he had not undergone the punishment he deserved The Senate offers special pleading to justify its imposition of a series of harsh penalties against Piso, even though he remained unconvicted at the time of his suicide.

Line 72: ab pietate et severitate iudicantium / from the devotion to duty and the strictness of the judges *Severitas* is a positive trait. It 'indicated uncompromising strictness and, in the administration of punishment, a desire to follow the letter of the law' (Cowan, 2016: 80). Consequently, according to Velleius Paterculus, it was a quality needed in the Senate when it was making decisions in judicial affairs, allowing it to suppress threats to Rome's wellbeing effectively (Cowan 2016: 86). Accordingly, the Senate prides itself on its uncompromising attitude towards Piso's crimes, as a result of which it proceeds to impose an unprecedented set of punishments upon him. By contrast, in dealing with Plancina and Marcus Piso, the Senate represents itself as influenced by the *clementia* it has learnt from Augustus and Tiberius (see 90–91n., **memorem clementiae suae iustitiaeq(ue) \<atq(ue)\> animi magnitudinis**). What the Senate considers to be indicative of its *severitas*, however, could later be interpreted by Tacitus as a symptom of its *saevitia* (Cowan, 2016: 91, on Tac., *Ann.* 3.15.2).

(See further Cowan, 2016 for an analysis of *severitas* under Tiberius, with specific discussion of the *SCPP* at 90–92; Langlands, 2008 on *severitas* in Valerius Maximus.)

Lines 73–74: ne quis luctus mortis eius causa a feminis / that no mourning for his death be undertaken by the women Mourning was traditionally regarded as a female duty (Flower, 1998), with professional female mourners being hired to lead the mourning at the funeral (van Sickle, 1987: 45–46). From the detailed instructions here, we might deduce that the Senate did not ban all mourning at the funeral, but was instead concerned with curtailing the year-long mourning customary among the women of the deceased's household, believed to have been sanctioned by Rome's second king, Numa (Plut., *Vit. Num.* 12; cf. Sen., *Ep.* 63.13 on this being the maximum period of mourning by women). This would explain both why mourning is mentioned in a decree that (on the interpretation of its chronology offered in this edition) was issued some months after Piso's actual demise and why nothing is said to prohibit Piso's burial, presumably because this had already been accomplished before the Senate issued this decree (Flower, 1996: 28–29). The women covered by this prohibition may have included all adult female relations of Piso, his freedwomen and female slaves, and any other women living in his household. They would otherwise have displayed their mourning for the deceased for twelve months via their plain dark clothing. In this, as in the following additional penalties it imposes, the Senate unexpectedly regulates the behaviour that was normally controlled by families (Bodel, 1999: 47–48).

Line 74: more maiorum / in accordance with ancestral custom This is the earliest example of the Senate altering a practice laid down by the *mos maiorum* (Bodel, 1999: 48). Earlier bans on mourning were more focused upon mourning in the public sphere (Flower, 1999: 102).

Lines 75–76: utiq(ue) statuae et imagines Cn(aei) Pisonis patris, quae ubiq(ue) positae essent, tollerentur / and that the statues and portraits of Gnaeus Piso Senior, wherever they had been placed, be removed The Senate gives thorough instructions for the destruction of Piso's images, referring both to statues in bronze or marble and to the wax masks traditionally displayed in the *atria* of aristocratic houses (see 80–81n., ***ne inter reliquas imagines, \<quibus\> exequias eorum funerum celebrare solent, imago Cn(aei) Pisonis patris duceretur***). Any inscription on the base of such a statue would also have been destroyed in this process. The Senate's specification that this instruction relates to statues 'wherever they had been placed' ensures the destruction of statues on display in private as well as public spaces (Eck, Caballos, Fernández, 1996: 194). Tacitus (*Ann.* 3.14.4) narrates how statues of Piso were attacked by the urban plebs whilst his trial was ongoing, with Tiberius interceding to prevent Piso's statues from being hauled down to the Gemonian steps on the Tiber and destroyed in a 'ritualised public execution' (Gregory, 1994: 96–97; Flower, 2006: 10; see also §7). Perhaps the Senate has such a traitor's death in mind when it states that by his suicide Piso rescued himself from the punishment he deserved (see 71n., **non optulisse eum se debitae poenae**).

Line 76: recte et ordine facturos / will have acted rightly and properly There are different ways of interpreting the phrasing of this recommendation (summarised by Lott, 2012: 286). It is possible that the Senate respectfully expresses its desire to intervene in family ritual as a recommendation rather than as an instruction, reflecting the unprecedented nature of this request, given that the Senate did not have the power to intervene in a family's religious activities (Bodel, 1999: 48–49; González, 2002: 255). Alternatively, the Senate is using this phrase not because it lacks power in this sphere, but because it wishes to express itself using a polite formula in addressing fellow-senators (Eck, Caballos, Fernández, 1996: 195–96). As Flower (1996: 30) observes, 'The branch of the Pisones is, therefore, singled out for punishment, while the family in general including its other branches are addressed separately and in a respectful tone.' The Senate has no intention of implying that the Calpurnian family as a whole should be punished, but at the same time does wish to ensure that all trace of Piso is removed from his family, both close and more remote. The Senate uses the same expression in directing Piso's elder son to change his *praenomen* (see 99–100n., **recte atque ordine facturum, si praenomen patris mutasset**), whilst in the *Tabula Siarensis* (frag. b, col. II, 26–27 = Crawford, 1996: no.37 = LACTOR 19, J8h) the Senate uses it in addressing provincial governors: 'that those who were in charge of the provinces would be acting properly and correctly if they took pains to see that this senatorial decree should be fixed in as crowded a place as possible', *eos quoque in provinc<i><i>s praessent* **recte atque ordine facturos** *si hoc s(enatus) c(onsultum) dedisse<n>t <operam ut> quam celeberrumo loco figeretur*. By contrast, in the same passage of the *Tabula Siarensis* (frag. b, col. II, 24–25 = Crawford, 1996: no.37 = LACTOR 19, J8h) the Senate agrees that the consuls 'should order the magistrates and ambassadors of the municipalities and colonies' (*iuberentque mag(istratus) et legatos municipiorum et coloniarum*).

Lines 76–77: qui quandoq(ue) familiae Calpurniae essent / that whoever shall at any time belong to the Calpurnian family The Senate extends its instructions to a very wide definition of who is to be regarded as a member of the Calpurnian family. This would have included other branches of the Calpurnii beyond the Pisones, such as the Bestiae, Bibuli, and Frugi (Flower, 1996: 30).

Lines 77–78: quive eam familiam cognatione adfinitateve contingerent / or be connected to the family by blood or marriage The Senate includes in its definition of members of the Calpurnian family those descended from a shared male ancestor whether through the male or female line, and whether they are related by blood or marriage (Flower, 1998: 161).

Lines 80–81: ne inter reliquas imagines, <quibus> exequias eorum funerum celebrare solent, imago Cn(aei) Pisonis patris duceretur / that the portrait of Gnaeus Piso Senior should not be brought out with the rest of the portraits with which they customarily solemnise the processions at their funerals An *imago* was not a death-mask but a realistic wax mask made during the person's lifetime. It could be worn by actors at funerals to impersonate the deceased's ancestors (Flower, 1996: 2). In earlier times, the decision to exclude an *imago* from a funeral was made by the *paterfamilias* (Bodel, 1999: 47, alluding to the case of T. Manlius Torquatus in 140 BC – Val. Max. 5.8.3), but here the Senate intervenes in this sphere, which was traditionally controlled by the family (Flower, 1996: 30; see 76n., **recte et ordine facturos**). Scribonius Libo Drusus had suffered the same penalty a few years earlier: after he committed suicide, his property was confiscated and his *imago* banned (Tac., *Ann.* 2.32.1: 'Then Cotta Messalinus proposed that the portrait of Libo should not accompany the funeral rites of his descendants', *tunc Cotta Messalinus, ne imago Libonis exsequias posterorum comitaretur, censuit*; Flower, 1999: 103; Pettinger, 2012: 38–40).

Lines 81–82: neve imaginibus familiae Calpurniae imago eius interponeretur / nor placed among the portraits of the Calpurnian family *Imagines* of distinguished ancestors who had held at least the office of aedile were stored in cupboards in the main reception room (*atrium*) of elite houses at Rome (Flower, 1996: 2, 4, 185–203). The Senate extends the ban beyond prohibiting the display of Piso's *imago* in public in also forbidding private possession of his *imago*. This was not always the case in penalties against *imagines*: in the case of Brutus and Cassius, for example, their *imagines* were allowed to be in their descendants' private possession but were prohibited from being displayed at family funerals (see discussion in Goodyear, 1981: 281 commenting on the case of Libo Drusus at *Ann.* 2.32). For Tacitus, in AD 22 the *imagines* of Cassius and Brutus at the funeral of Iunia – Cassius' wife and Brutus' sister – paradoxically 'shone out' through the very fact that they were not included in the distinguished parade of twenty *imagines* (*Ann.* 3.76: *sed praefulgebant Cassius atque Brutus eo ipso quod effigies eorum non uisebantur*). In AD 24, in contrast, the *imago* of C. Silius (*PIR*² S718), a friend of Germanicus who having held the consulship in AD 13 went on to a distinguished military career, only to be accused of *maiestas* and extortion on Sejanus' initiative (*Ann.* 4.18–20.1), was banned everywhere by decree of the Senate. Nevertheless, it was still found on display in his son's house in AD 48 (*Ann.* 11.35.1). The significance of the measures taken against Piso's *imago* by the Senate lies in the idea that an ancestor's *imago* is supposed to inspire future generations to emulate, or even better surpass, his achievements (see §7).

Lines 82–83: utiq(ue) nomen Cn(aei) Pisonis patris tolleretur ex titulo statuae Germanicì Caesaris / and that the name of Gnaeus Piso Senior be removed from the inscription on the statue of Germanicus Caesar This statue of Germanicus is likely to have been set up at the latest by AD 17, when both Piso and Germanicus departed for the East (Torelli, 1999: 165, emending the earlier suggestion by Torelli, 1992: 111 that it was set up only in AD 19, after Germanicus' death). The Senate is not advocating that Piso's name be removed only from this inscription (see 75–76n., *utiq(ue) statuae et imagines Cn(aei) Pisonis patris, quae ubiq(ue) positae essent, tollerentur*), but has to specify this erasure since it is on the base of a statue of Germanicus (not Piso). To remove all memory of Piso's involvement in setting up a statue to honour Germanicus as one of the *sodales Augustales* (see 83n., *sodales Augustales*) was evidently a priority for the Senate. Piso's name is similarly found erased in other contexts where it appears closely associated with members of the imperial family. At Rome, his name is erased where it appears alongside that of Tiberius on a base recording the undertaking of votive games on behalf of Augustus' safe return to Rome in 7 BC, when Tiberius and Piso were both consuls (*CIL* VI 385). In Hispania Tarraconensis, his name is erased from a monumental dedication to Augustus (*CIL* II 2703; see in general Kajava, 1995 on the erasure of Piso's name). Tacitus (*Ann.* 3.17.4) records how Tiberius vetoes the proposal by M. Aurelius Cotta Maximus Messallinus to erase Piso's name from the *fasti* at Rome.

Line 83: sodales Augustales / the *sodales Augustales* The *sodales Augustales* were a prestigious group of twenty-five senators established following Augustus' death and deification who were responsible for carrying out cult for deified Augustus. It included high-status senators ('drawn by lot from the leading-men of the state' according to Tac., *Ann.* 1.54.1: *sorte ducti e primoribus ciuitatis*; although exactly who these *primores ciuitatis* comprised is far from clear, as pointed out by Goodyear, 1972: 328), besides four members of the imperial family itself, namely Tiberius, Germanicus, Drusus, and Claudius (Di Vita-Évrard, 1993: 471). Piso's name may have been particularly prominent if, as suggested by Eck, Caballos, and Fernández (1996: 198), he was named on the inscription as *magister* of the *sodales* in charge of setting up the monument. Piso's membership of the *sodales* is the most striking evidence that he was high in Tiberius' favour during this period (Eck, Caballos, Fernández, 1996: 76). The *sodales Augustales* were responsible for carrying out annual sacrifices on the anniversary of Augustus' death, a day to be regarded as a day of ill-omen, or *dies nefas* (Eck, 2001: 544). Moreover, the Senate decreed in AD 19 that the *magistri* of the *sodales* were to make offerings to Germanicus' departed spirit at the mausoleum of Augustus every 10 October on the anniversary of his death and that Germanicus should be honoured on 28 October during the *ludi Augustales* with curule chairs placed among the seats of the *sodales* in the theatre, in memory of the fact that he had belonged to the priesthood (*Tabula Siarensis* b, col. 1, 1–4 and 11–14; *Tabula Hebana* 50–54, 59–60 = Crawford, 1996: no.37 = LACTOR J8). Consequently, the memory of Germanicus was publicly honoured during the month of October, perhaps prompting the Senate to create this decree at the start of December (see further the discussion on chronology: §3).

Lines 83–84: in campo ad aram Providentiae / in the Field of Mars next to the Altar of Foresight The Altar of Foresight was most likely built in AD 15, probably on the Senate's initiative, in the area of the Field of Mars (Campus Martius) known as the Field of Agrippa, *campus Agrippae*, a public park initiated by Agrippa to the east of the via Lata. After Agrippa's death, Augustus completed the complex and presented it to the Roman people in 7 BC (Cass. Dio 55.8.3; Coarelli, 1993; 2003: 66–67; Lott, 2014/15: 149) (Fig. 9). It is plausible that the altar was dedicated on 26 June AD 15 in commemoration of the imperial adoptions on that day in AD 4 (Barrandon, Suspène, Gaffiero, 2010: 166; slight variations on this proposed by Cox, 2005: 254–57, who suggests it may have been decreed on 17 September AD 14, along with other honours for Augustus, and subsequently dedicated on 26 June AD 16; Fishwick, 2010: 252 suggests it might have been voted before Augustus' death but built between AD 14 and 17; possibly set up in AD 4 according to Lott, 2012: 287; summary of chronological questions in Eck, Caballos, Fernández, 1996: 199–201). It was sited to the east of the via Lata, opposite the Altar of Augustan Peace (*ara Pacis Augustae*), both altars flanking the main road north out of Rome (leading onto the via Flaminia) in an area that was undeveloped at the time (Patterson, 1999: 136).

The quality of *providentia* could take on different significance according to context. Tiberius, for instance, as depicted by Velleius, was considered to have demonstrated *providentia* as a military general whilst on campaign (Hellegouarc'h, 1980: 171; Kuntze, 1985: 77–82; Balmaceda, 2014: 354–55; 2017: 149). For Valerius Maximus (1.praef.), Tiberius' heavenly foresight (*caelestis providentia*) is instead relevant to his role in fostering virtues among Roman society, and it steps into the limelight at the very start of this compilation of *exempla*. By a sort of ring composition, Tiberius' *providentia* then recurs towards the end of the work (9.11.ext.4), allowing him to suppress the conspiracy of Sejanus. Coinage (*asses*) issued in AD c.22/23–(?)30, moreover, which illustrates the altar on its reverse labelled PROVIDENT, along with a radiate head of *divus Augustus pater* on the obverse (*RIC* I² 99, nos 80–81), has been associated with the grant of tribunician power for Drusus the Younger (Cox, 2005; on the problems of dating these issues, see Klein and von Kaenel, 2000). By AD 38, the cult of *Providentia* at the altar was certainly focused upon celebrating imperial succession: sacrifices by the Arvals at the *ara Providentiae Augustae*

Commentary on 83–84 197

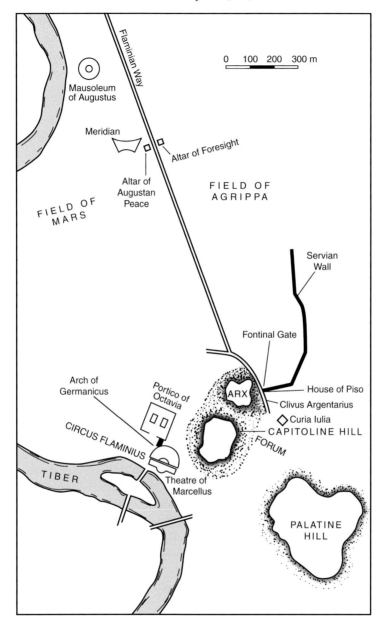

Fig. 9. Map of Rome (adapted from Bodel, 1999).

in AD 38 took place on 26 June, the day of Tiberius' adoption by Augustus (*CFA* 12c, 55–57). Similar sacrifices also occurred on 12 October AD 39 (*CFA* 13fgh, 5–6) to coincide with the *Augustalia* (Torelli, 1999). It is likely that this association with imperial succession was present from the time of the altar's foundation and that it had especially strong links with both Tiberius as the actual successor to Augustus and Germanicus as the presumptive successor to Tiberius (Torelli, 1992: 109–11; Bodel, 1999: 53–57). Punishing Piso in this way still evokes the charge against him of murdering Germanicus, given the altar's connection to Augustus' plans for the succession, which had now been rendered futile by Germanicus' death. See further on the altar of *Providentia*, §4.

Line 84: utiq(ue) bona Cn(aei) Pisonis patris publicarentur / and that the property of Gnaeus Piso Senior be declared public property This would involve auctioning off Piso's property, with the proceeds being assigned to the public treasury (Lamberti, 2006: 141). The decree records the final decision regarding Piso's property and gives more detail than is found in Tacitus (*Ann.* 3.17.4), who describes how M. Aurelius Cotta Maximus Messallinus proposed that only half of Piso's property should be confiscated, with the rest of it being given to his elder son, excepting five million sesterces for his younger son Marcus. This proposal was then modified, according to Tacitus (*Ann.* 3.18.1), by Tiberius, who wished to reinstate Marcus' right to a full share of his father's property. The decree now reveals that all of Piso's property was initially confiscated (despite his suicide before conviction) since the Senate takes for granted that he is guilty of *maiestas* (see 71n., ***non optulisse eum se de͡b͡itae poenae***), but that the Senate then divided it up between his heirs (see 102–03n., ***alteram partem dimidiam bonorum paternorum dari***; see 104–05n., ***n(ummum) (decies centena milia) dotis nomine Calpurniae Cn(aei) Pisonis filiae***), apart from an estate in Illyricum (see 85n., ***excepto saltu, qui esset in Hillyrico***).

Line 85: excepto saltu, qui esset in Hillyrico / with the exception of the woodland in Illyricum The term Illyricum/Hillyricum is used here to refer generically to the region of the northern and central Balkans rather than to a well-defined administrative province (Eck, Caballos, Fernández, 1996: 204–05). The word *saltus* refers to upland woodland containing rough pasturage (*OLD* s.v. 'saltus' 2 and 3). The Senate returns this individual property alone to Tiberius' ownership, on the grounds that complaints had been made by the neighbouring peoples against the management of the estate by Piso and his agents (see 88–89, *frequenter de iniuris Cn(aei) Pisonis patris libertorumq(ue) et servorum eius questae essent*). Nevertheless, the parallel with C. Silius in AD 24 (Tac., *Ann.* 4.20.1), whose property, which had originated as gifts from Augustus, was seized for the *fiscus*, suggests that the Senate is simply trying to put a positive spin on the confiscation in Illyricum (Eck, Caballos, Fernández, 1996: 202–04). There is epigraphic evidence that the Calpurnii Pisones owned land in the region, and it is possible that Piso spent some time on his estates there as he returned to Rome from the East in AD 20, whilst also taking the opportunity to visit Drusus the Younger in the hope of winning his support (Tac., *Ann.* 3.7–8; Wilkes, 1969: 331 n.5). A daughter of Piso's brother Lucius Calpurnius Piso Augur, Calpurnia, set up three dedications at Cissa on the isle of Pag. The best preserved of these reads: 'To the Good Goddess Mistress Heia Augusta Triumphant, ruler of land and sea, protector, powerful goddess of wisdom and medicine, well-judging. Calpurnia, daughter of Lucius Piso augur and granddaughter of Cn. Piso, gave this as a gift' (*B(onae) D(eae) Dom(inae) Heiae A[ug(ustae)]* / *triumphali terrae* / *marisq(ue) dominatric[i]* / *conservatrici* / *mentiumque bo[n]arum* / *ac remediorum potenti* / *deae bene iudicanti* / *[C]alpurnia L(uci) Pisonis aug(uris) f(ilia)* / *Cn(aei) Pisonis neptis* / *d(onum) d(edit)*: A. and J. Šašel, 1963: 90 no.260; Šašel, 1964: 363–67 = *AE* 1964, 270; Brouwer, 1989: no.127; cf. *AE* 1949, 199). Calpurnia's pride in her family is reflected in the fact that she does not simply give her filiation as 'daughter of Lucius', as would be the norm. Her use of the title 'Augusta' to describe the Good Goddess points to a willingness to honour the Imperial regime.

Line 86: cuius a patre divo Aug(usto) Cn(aeo) Pisoni patri donatus erat / by whose father deified Augustus it had been given to Gnaeus Piso Senior This is the first documented example of land outside Egypt given to a senator by Augustus, but it is probably typical of a more widespread pattern (Eck, Caballos, Fernández, 1996: 205–06). The gift of land in this area to Piso by Augustus suggests that Piso may have served in the army with Tiberius during the suppression of the Pannonian revolt in AD 6–9 (Eck, Caballos, Fernández, 1996: 204–05).

Line 87: is idcirco dari eum sibi desiderasset / he had expressed the wish that it be given to him This shows that Tiberius actively intervenes in the Senate to secure this property for himself.

Lines 87–88: quod <civitates>, quarum fines hos saltus contingerent / because the communities whose territory bordered that of the woodland A word is missing from both Copy A and Copy B of the inscription. This could be either *civitates* or *gentes*. Copy B has further errors at this point of the inscription, which require a sequence of editorial emendations as follows: *desideras<s>et, quod <civitates>, quarum <fines>* (Eck, Caballos, Fernández, 1996: 62). The difference is that *civitates* would evoke a more organised group of inhabitants, with some political structure (*OLD* s.v. 'civitas' 1–2), whereas *gentes* would evoke a less civilized, less Roman type of community (*OLD* s.v. 'gens' 3).

Lines 88–89: frequenter de iniuris Cn(aei) Pisonis patris libertorumq(ue) et servorum eius questae essent / had often complained of injuries from Gnaeus Piso Senior, his freedmen and slaves It is possible that the Senate represents common boundary disputes as injustices committed by Piso's agents for rhetorical effect (Eck, Caballos, Fernández, 1996: 206), implying that the rotten character of Piso had also infected his subordinates. A willingness to believe that freedmen and slaves acted badly is also typical of the senatorial elite distaste for the lower orders so obvious in Tacitus' *Annales* (for example in characterising the disaster at Fidenae amphitheatre as the result of a freedman's profiteering, *Ann.* 4.62, with Martin and Woodman, 1989: ad loc.).

Line 89: ob id providendum putaret / for this reason he thought that care should be taken If this is an echo of how Tiberius himself presented the case in the Senate, it illustrates how he depicted himself as demonstrating his quality of *providentia* in the context of caring for the inhabitants of the empire beyond Italy, fitting into the broader pattern of the promotion of *providentia* as a characteristically Tiberian quality (see §6).

Lines 89–90: ne postea iure meritoq(ue) soci p(opuli) R(omani) queri possent / that allies of the Roman people should no longer be able to complain with just cause In this way, the Senate presents Tiberius as protecting the interests of peoples allied to Rome in the provinces, removing any hint that he might have been guilty of coveting Piso's property.

Lines 90–108 Decisions about Piso's property

In this section, the Senate goes into more detail about what should happen to Piso's confiscated property. It emphasises that Piso's elder son, Gnaeus, has not been involved in his father's misdeeds in the slightest (see 93–94n., ***filio eius Pisoni maiori, de quo nihil esset dictum***), though appears to admit that his younger son Marcus is guilty but to be pardoned (see 100–01n., ***M(arco) etiam Pisoni, qu<o>i inpunitatem senatus humanitati et moderationi principis sui adsensus dandam esse{t} arbitraretur***). This corresponds to the second point raised in Tiberius' *relatio* (see 7n., ***qualis causa M(arci) Pisonis visa esset***). The Senate's attitude to Marcus, however, appears not to have been its initial response, but was adjusted only after Tiberius intervened to deflect the original punishment determined upon by the Senate (as also happened in the case of Plancina) (Cowan, 2016: 92). The Senate also decides to give a sizeable cash lump-sum to Calpurnia, who does not appear in Tacitus' narrative, and whose identity is unclear (see 104–05n., ***n(ummum) (decies centena milia) dotis nomine Calpurniae Cn(aei) Pisonis filiae***). Finally, the Senate orders the demolition of a specific part of Piso's house on the Capitol (see 106n., ***supra portam Fontinalem***).

Lines 90–91: memorem clementiae suae iustitiaeq(ue) <atq(ue)> animi magnitudinis / mindful of its clemency, justice, and generosity of spirit This ostensibly exemplifies the shift under Tiberius towards *clementia* being associated with legal trials (Cowan, 2016: 91), but see §6 for detailed discussion of the presentation of 'imperial virtues' in this section.

The Senate's reference to its 'clemency, justice, and generosity of spirit' prepares for the subsequent concessions to Piso's family, in contrast to the Senate's harsh treatment of Piso himself.

Lines 91–92: quas virtutes {quas} a maioribus suis accepisset / virtues which it had inherited from its ancestors The idea of following precedents set by the ancestors (*maiores*) was a highly valued ideological principle among Rome's elite through the ages. The idea that Rome's preeminence in the world was the result of the Romans' superiority to others, which they enjoyed thanks to their traditional code of behaviour, goes back at least to the poet Ennius, who wrote that 'Roman affairs rely upon traditional practices and its men' (*moribus antiquis res stat Romana virisque*, Enn., *Ann.* 5.1 = Skutsch, 1985: fr. 156). See further discussion in §7.

Line 92: tum praecipue ab divo Aug(usto) et Ti(berio) Caesare Aug(usto) principibus suis didicisset / then learned in particular from deified Augustus and Tiberius Caesar Augustus, its Principes In this way the Senate contributes to the justification of the special role played in Roman society by members of the imperial family. Whereas traditionally Romans would aim to emulate their own ancestors, senior members of the imperial family were now thought to have an exemplary role in disseminating their distinctive virtues to the rest of society (see 158n., *regi tamen exemplo equestris ordinis a principe nostro se passa sit*). See further §6.

Line 93: aequom humanumq(ue) censere / has deemed it fair and humane The Senate implicitly contrasts the inhumane behaviour of Piso following Germanicus' death with its own decency and humanity (see 61n., *humanitatis*).

Lines 93–94: filio eius Pisoni maiori, de quo nihil esset dictum / to his son the elder Piso, about whom nothing had been said This refers to Cn. Piso junior (*PIR*[2] C293), the elder son of Piso, perhaps around twenty-seven years old at this date (Eck, Caballos, Fernández, 1996: 77–80). He had remained in Rome throughout the period of tension between his father and Germanicus in Syria and the latter's death, as claimed by his father in the suicide note according to Tacitus (*Ann.* 3.16.3) (see 94n., *qui principis nostri q(uaestor) fuisset*).

Line 94: qui principis nostri q(uaestor) fuisset / who had served as quaestor of our Princeps Two of the twenty quaestors each year were allocated to support the *princeps*, whilst others went to the provinces to serve governors or stayed in Rome to act as the two urban quaestors or as quaestors to the two consuls (Cébeillac, 1972: 6). Cn. Piso junior is likely to have held the office of *quaestor Augusti* for a year from 5 December of AD 17 or 18 (Eck, Caballos, Fernández, 1996: 77–78, with doubts on the timing expressed by Champlin, 1999: 119). The post involved acting as liaison between the Senate and *princeps*, for example in reading out his letters or speeches in his absence (*Dig.* 1.13.1.4 [Ulpian]; Suet., *Aug.* 65.2; Cébeillac, 1972: 6–7). It was both a sign of enjoying Tiberius' confidence and a promise of a stellar career to come (cf. Cébeillac, 1972: 22 on Augustus' quaestors).

Lines 94–95: quem Germanicus <Caesar> quoq(ue) liberalitate sua honorasset / whom Germanicus Caesar also had honoured with his liberality He may have served under Germanicus as a military tribune or member of his staff (*comes*) in Germania during AD 13–16, before being appointed quaestor by Tiberius (Hofmann-Löbl, 1996: 262–63). The expression 'honoured with his liberality', however, seems more likely to refer to actual gifts from Germanicus than to an appointment (Eck, Caballos, Fernández, 1996: 212–13). These might be understood as an indication of continued favour. The Senate implies that the positive relationship between Piso's elder son and both Tiberius and Germanicus serves as the most convincing character reference for him.

Lines 95–96: qui complura modestiae suae posuisset pignora / who had given many indications of his restraint His *modestia* is in contrast to the excessive behaviour which the Senate earlier attributes to his father. By mentioning the 'many indications', the Senate makes the point that he consistently acted in a praiseworthy way.

Line 97: ex quibus sperari posset, dissimillumum eum patri suo futurum / which made it possible to hope that he would turn out very different from his father In Roman culture, it was usually the case that a son would emulate the behaviour of his father and ancestors. The embeddedness of this attitude can be seen from the way in which it is reflected in Tiberian literature with reference both to great Romans of the past (Scipio Aemilianus described in Vell. Pat. 1.12.3 as 'most alike in his virtues', *virtutibus simillimus*, to both his grandfather and father) and to contemporaries (Tiberius praised for being similar to Augustus in the representation of virtue, *tibi similem virtutis imagine*, Ov., *Pont.* 2.8.31) (see Galasso, 1995: 363 ad loc., for further parallels). In expressing this hope, therefore, the Senate strikingly inverts the norm (see further, Cooley, 1998).

Line 98: nomine principis et senatus / in the name of the Princeps and the Senate Most of Piso's property is returned to his sons and (grand-)daughter as a gift from the Senate and Tiberius. Piso's will would not have been valid, given that he was regarded as guilty of *maiestas* (even though he committed suicide before his formal conviction), and so his property is treated as if he had died intestate, in which case it would pass to the individuals who were in his *potestas* at the time of his death. This excludes his wife Plancina, other relations, and his freedmen and freedwomen. It also ensures that Tiberius did not have to manage the potential embarrassment of himself being named one of Piso's heirs, as would have been expected in the will (Flower, 1998: 165–69). As Flower (1998: 166) observes, 'As a result his relationships are disrupted not only within his family but also in the wider circle of people with whom he was connected.'

Lines 99–100: recte atque ordine facturum, si praenomen patris mutasset / would be behaving rightly and appropriately, if he changed his first name, that of his father Cn. Piso junior did change his *praenomen* to Lucius, going on to enjoy a successful political career as consul in AD 27, urban prefect, proconsul of Africa (one of the most prestigious posts open to senators), and perhaps governor of Dalmatia (Eck, Caballos, Fernández, 1996: 79; see also §8). Even though the *praenomen* Gnaeus had been used regularly by members of the Calpurnii Pisones since the mid-third century BC, it seems that it dropped out of use completely from the rest of the family (Flower, 1998: 165). In the Ephesos Customs Law from AD 62 (*AE* (2008) 1353, line 109), the name even of Cn. Piso *pater* appears as Lucius, showing that his name too was retrospectively changed in some official documentary contexts at Rome. Recent precedents for such a change could be found in the case of Marcus Antonius, whose *praenomen* was banned from future generations of his family following his defeat by Augustus (Cass. Dio 51.19.3), and M. Scribonius Libo Drusus, whose cognomen was likewise banned (Tac., *Ann.* 2.32.1, with Goodyear, 1981: 282). See further §7 and Eck, Caballos, Fernández, 1996: 214–15. On the phrasing *recte atque ordine factum*, which may reflect the Senate's approach to addressing its peers, see 76n., **recte et ordine facturos**. *Mutasset* is a contracted form of *mutavisset*.

Lines 100–01: M(arco) etiam Pisoni, qu<o>i inpunitatem senatus humanitati et moderationi principis sui adsensus dandam esse{t} arbitraretur / to Marcus Piso, to whom the Senate, in agreement with the humanity and restraint of its Princeps, thought that impunity should be given The Senate here responds to one of the points raised by Tiberius in his *relatio*, where Tiberius' insistent intervention on Marcus' behalf is also recorded (see 8n., **uti precum suarum pro adulescente memor is ordo esset**). The Senate represents itself as acting in agreement with Tiberius, but in theory he could have imposed a veto on its decisions had it not done so. The slightly contorted expression which the Senate uses to describe the cases of both Marcus and (especially) Plancina betrays its desire to disguise the real impact of Tiberius' interventions in them:

It would appear, then, that there was an effort to avoid stating clearly what the decision about Piso's son and wife was. The reason for this procedure shows that the senate were to a large extent governed by political considerations …. From the point of view of the author of the SCPP, the interference of emperor and his mother would have been underlined with uncomfortable clarity if the document had baldly stated that though found guilty, the defendants were not to be punished because of deprecations of the Imperial family. (Mackay, 2003: 349)

In this way, the Senate tries to emphasise its own agency in deciding the outcome of its deliberations about them, and states that Marcus owed his pardon to the Senate's 'favour' (see 102, **benificium**; Eck, Caballos, Fernández, 1996: 218). Marcus' case (like that of his mother and Piso's staff members) is not separate from Piso's (Mackay, 2003: 347), but the Senate's responses to the cases of Marcus and Plancina are based upon its sense of its own 'clemency, justice, and generosity of spirit', in stark contrast to its attitude towards Piso, which is governed by its *pietas* and *severitas* (see 72n., **ab pietate et severitate iudicantium**). Marcus' guilt is implicitly recognised (as also is Plancina's later), but the Senate is more concerned with expressing the political situation than with legal niceties (Mackay, 2003: 349; Cowan, 2016: 92). The term 'impunity' reveals clearly that Marcus had initially been found guilty of abetting his father's treasonous activities in Syria (as narrated in Tac., *Ann.* 2.78.2), but it is likely that he was pardoned on the grounds that he was bound to obey his father's instructions (Tac., *Ann.* 3.17.1; Flower, 1998: 168). From Tacitus (*Ann.* 2.76.2–3, 3.16.3) it appears that the case was made for Marcus that he had also tried to dissuade his father from returning to Syria after Germanicus' death. Nothing is known about his career after this date (Eck, Caballos, Fernández, 1996: 81), whether because he deliberately kept a low profile or met an early death (Syme, 1986: 375).

In dealing with Piso's property the Senate uses two different verbs: *donari* and *dari*, the former relating to the Senate's gift of one half of his property to his elder son (line 96), and the latter in relation to the other half of the property being given to Marcus (line 102). This distinction does not lie in any legal difference, but the choice of wording may have been of political significance, with the use of *donari* indicating that the transfer of property to the elder son was to be regarded as a particular privilege, and the use of *dari* intended to avoid any implication that Marcus was somehow being rewarded with the property (Lamberti, 2006: 142).

Lines 102–03: alteram partem dimidiam bonorum paternorum dari / the other half of his father's property should be given Returning half of his father's property to him is the logical result of the decision to pardon him, given that Marcus would not have been able to retain his status in society without also receiving a substantial portion of his father's property (Eck, Caballos, Fernández, 1996: 218).

Lines 104–05: n(ummum) (decies centena milia) dotis nomine Calpurniae Cn(aei) Pisonis filiae / one million sesterces be given to

Calpurnia, the daughter of Gnaeus Piso, as dowry Calpurnia is not mentioned in Tacitus and is otherwise unknown. Strong arguments have been presented for identifying her as the daughter of Cn. Piso *pater* himself (Hofmann-Löbl, 1996: 264; Champlin, 1999: 119; Grelle, 2000: 228; Corbier, 2001b: 166 n.33; González, 2002: 264; Lamberti, 2006: 143–47), or as his granddaughter, the daughter of Cn. Piso junior, at the time only a young child (Eck, Caballos, Fernández, 1996: 83–87; Flower, 1998: 166; Castro-Camero, 2000: 98–100, 212), who may perhaps have gone on to marry Nonius Asprenas, consul in AD 29, who was one of the drafters of this decree (see 3–4n., ***L(ucius) Nonius L(uci) f(ilius) Pom(ptina tribu) Asprenas q(uaestor)***) (Eck, Caballos, Fernández 1996: 85–87; Dowling, 2006: 173). The suggestion that Calpurnia is included here because she had been named in Piso's will (Eck, Caballos, Fernández, 1996: 218) sits uncomfortably with the Senate's insistence that it is not following the terms of a will, but making gifts on its own account (see 98n., ***nomine principis et senatus***), along with the idea that precisely the inability to leave his property in a will is one of the penalties incurred by Piso, despite his suicide.

The most straightforward solution to this question is to assume that she is the daughter of Piso, and that the Senate's provision reflects the importance of ensuring a dowry for the daughters of high-ranking families at Rome, even in cases where the father loses his status through deportation or exile (*Dig.* 24.3.42 pr. [Papinian]; *Dig.* 24.3.22.4 [Ulpian]; Fayer, 1994: 673–731). On marriage, a husband was obliged to preserve the capital of the dowry, but could spend any income derived from it, for as long as the marriage continued (Csillag, 1976: 91–94). Admittedly, the Senate calls her simply 'daughter of Gnaeus Piso', without the usual addition of *pater* to designate the Piso on trial, but it might have seemed odd to use the phrase 'Calpurnia daughter of Gnaeus Piso the father'. This also follows close on the Senate's instruction to Gnaeus junior to change his *praenomen*, whilst he is never otherwise named as Gnaeus in the decree (González, 2002: 264). Furthermore, if she were the granddaughter, it might have seemed more natural for the Senate to describe her as 'granddaughter of Piso (*pater*)' (*neptis*), rather than as 'daughter of Gnaeus' (Lamberti, 2006: 145). It would also be appropriate for a daughter of Piso to receive such a generous financial settlement, and for the Senate to do this even before turning to the sons (her brothers on this scenario). It would seem odd if a granddaughter's financial affairs were settled before those of Piso's sons (Hofmann-Löbl, 1996: 264) and for a granddaughter to benefit from the whole estate (her allowance is allocated before the rest is divided between the two sons of Piso), whilst her own father was still alive (Eck, Caballos, Fernández, 1996: 84). The amount of money settled on her – five million sesterces in total – is the same as was initially proposed for Marcus in the Senate (Tac., *Ann* 3.17.4; Corbier, 2001b: 166 n.33). This is in line for other senatorial dowries of the time: compare, for example, the one million sesterces allocated as a dowry for the daughter of the senator Fonteius Agrippa in AD 19 (Tac., *Ann.* 2.86; see also Saller, 1994: 213–16 for evidence regarding the size of dowries at Rome). The main problem with this hypothesis is how to explain that she is given both a dowry and *peculium* (see 105n., **item peculi nomine n(ummum) (quadragies centena milia) daretur**).

In terms of her potential age, it is not impossible that Calpurnia is Piso's daughter. Gnaeus Piso junior is thought to have been born around 7 BC (Eck, Caballos, Fernández, 1996: 78), and so Calpurnia could have been born as late as AD 5, assuming a period of about a dozen years during which Plancina may have been active in childbirth (compare Agrippina the Elder's nine children in a period of about thirteen years: Lindsay, 1995: 4–5). This fits the suggestion that Plancina was younger than her husband, and not his first wife (a Roman senator would expect to marry first in his early twenties: Treggiari, 1991: 93; Shaw, 1987: 43–44). At the time of the trial, therefore, Calpurnia could have been of an age at which elite daughters were normally married (legal minimum of twelve: Treggiari, 1991: 39–42, but mid/late teens as the norm at Rome, with a tendency for earlier marriage at around fourteen among the upper classes: Syme, 1987: 318; Shaw, 1987; cf. review by Frier, 2015, with brief analysis of modern comparative data). If she is instead Piso's granddaughter, then it is unlikely that she is more than five years old (Eck, Caballos, Fernández, 1996: 83; Lucius Piso, consul AD 57, who would on this account be her brother, was born in around AD 23 – Eck, Caballos, Fernández, 1996: 85), although betrothing a girl aged as young as this (and younger) was acceptable (Treggiari, 1991: 153–54). Providing her with a dowry appears to imply that she is not as yet married, but she might well have already been betrothed (the dowry promised on betrothal but paid only on marriage: Treggiari, 1991: 96, 142). Furthermore, a dowry was not necessarily given as a single lump-sum at the time of the wedding (Saller, 1994: 207–09).

Line 105: item peculi nomine n(ummum) (quadragies centena milia) daretur / and likewise four million sesterces as her *peculium* A *peculium* is a cash allowance made to individuals who were not of legally independent status (*sui iuris*) and so could not legally own property but could manage this cash allowance themselves. It has been suggested that if Calpurnia were Piso's daughter, she would have become *sui iuris* on his suicide, and so would not normally then have been eligible to receive a *peculium* (Eck, Caballos, Fernández, 1996: 84; Castro-Camero, 2000: 99, 212). Furthermore, the provision of a dowry might suggest that she is not yet married and consequently would be independent on her father's death and so ineligible for a *peculium*. This is the main reason for disallowing her identity as Piso's daughter and suggesting that she must be his granddaughter (Eck, Caballos, Fernández, 1996: 84). There are, however, possible ways of reconciling these contradictions: the grant of *peculium* after Piso's death might have been a confirmation of continuing an arrangement made during his lifetime for an unmarried daughter; or she may have been betrothed but not yet married (see Lamberti, 2006: 143–47 for a summary of different scenarios; compare Saller, 1994: 219 for ways in which a daughter might be in receipt of both dowry and *peculium*). Furthermore, an arrangement could have been made for the payment of a dowry to be postponed until a father's death (Saller, 1994: 222). The identity of Calpurnia ultimately remains unverifiable for now, but overall it seems more logical that she was Piso's daughter rather than granddaughter.

Line 106: supra portam Fontinalem / above the Fontinal Gate The Fontinal Gate was located in the Servian Wall beneath the part of the Capitol Hill known as the *Arx*, next to the *Clivus Argentarius*, where the Flaminian Way began, to the north-east of the Roman Forum (Eck, Caballos, Fernández, 1996: 209) (Fig. 9). Piso's house therefore was located on the *Arx* itself (Coarelli, 1996; 2003: 68–74) (Fig. 10). This phrasing does not make it clear whether the Senate refers to a structure built directly on top of the Fontinal Gate or on the slope above it (Coarelli, 2003: 68; see, however, 106–07n., ***quae inaedificasset iungendarum domum privatarum causa***). Bodel (1999: 59–60) suggests that the destruction of Piso's property may have been prompted by the fact that it faced the houses of Tiberius and Germanicus opposite on the Palatine, but there are other factors to consider as well. The most significant offence to which this is a response is Piso's encroachment upon public space (see 106–07n., ***quae inaedificasset iungendarum domum privatarum causa***), but it is likely that this penalty will have evoked house-destruction as an accepted punishment for traitors of the state (see §7), as well as perhaps being a reaction to Piso having a

Fig. 10. Modern view of area of Piso's house on the Capitoline Hill, overlooking the Roman Forum, with the *curia Iulia* to the left (photograph: A.E. Cooley).

house on the Capitol even though this had been prohibited to individuals of patrician status since the times of Manlius Capitolinus in the fourth century BC (Livy 6.20.13; Val. Max. 6.3.1a). In any case, it seems that the Senate took advantage of Piso's trial for *maiestas* in AD 20 to order the destruction of a structure that had probably been built some time before.

Lines 106–07: quae inaedificasset iungendarum domum privatarum causa / the structure which Gnaeus Piso Senior had built … to connect private residences The word order lacks coherence, perhaps as a result of a desire to focus upon the person of Cn. Piso, presenting the relative clause first and delaying *ea* and the subject of the *ut* clause, *curatores*. Piso's house, described by Tacitus (*Ann*. 3.9.3) as 'a house overhanging the forum' (*domus foro imminens*), was the setting for a lavish party on Piso's return to Rome in AD 20, which may have inspired the Senate to order this demolition (Eck, 1995a; 1995b: 5–7). It must have been conspicuous in both scale and location (Bodel, 1999: 58–60), with this particular part of it being a structure between the Capitol and Quirinal hills linking two properties (Eck, Caballos, Fernández, 1996: 207–08; Coarelli, 2003: 74). The Senate's use of the verb *inaedificare* supports the view that Piso's structure was built directly on top of the Fontinal Gate. In legal terms, therefore, since Piso had built on top of a public structure and given that ownership of the land upon which a structure is built further encompasses any addition made to it, Piso's ownership of the additional structure could be contested, and the structure itself demolished (Eck, Caballos, Fernández, 1996: 208; Flower, 1998: 169).

Lines 107–08: curatores locorum publicorum iudicandorum / the superintendents responsible for adjudicating public places The superintendents (*curatores*) belonged to a board of senators (*collegium*), one of a whole series of new administrative posts introduced by Augustus (Suet., *Aug*. 37; Eck, 1992). They were responsible for ensuring the integrity of public space in Rome (Lott, 2012: 293). This is exceptional evidence for the *curatores* taking charge of demolishing a structure: the rest of our epigraphic evidence attests to their granting permission for the setting up of a monument or building on public space (Bruun, 2006: 99). The *curatores locorum publicorum iudicandorum* were later titled, from the Claudian period, the *curatores aedium sacrarum et operum locorumque publicorum* ('superintendents of sacred buildings, works, and public spaces': Eck, Caballos, Fernández, 1996: 210).

Line 108: tollenda dimolienda curarent / should see to it that … be removed and destroyed As Eck, Caballos, and Fernández (1996: 209–10) observe, it is likely that a blind eye had been turned towards Piso's offence of building above the *porta Fontinalis* until it became politically expedient because of the *maiestas* trial to remedy the situation, perhaps also because Piso's lavish partying drew attention to his house on the Capitol (see 106–07n., ***quae inaedificasset iungendarum domum privatarum causa***).

Lines 109–20 Pardon for Plancina

Here the Senate turns to the third element introduced by Tiberius in his *relatio*, namely its verdict on the case of Piso's wife, Plancina (see 8–9n., ***qualis causa Plancinae visa esset***). This subsection of the decree is the most surprising in an inscription that is full of novelties, since it sheds unexpected light upon the way in which Iulia Augusta intervened in the trial. It reveals how 'the frontier between the domestic and the public' was negotiated, to use Purcell's phrase in a prescient article written before this decree was discovered ([1986] 2009: 168). On the one hand, the Senate's publicly proclaimed reason for granting pardon to Plancina reveals Iulia Augusta's ability to influence even the most delicate of political trials. On the other, that the Senate was aware of the delicacy of the situation and indeed felt embarrassed by her intervention is clearly revealed by the tortuous nature of the syntax in this subsection, with its five levels of subordination (as analysed earlier, see §5). Its use of language in relation to Iulia Augusta, however, justifies her intervention by balancing expressions associated with the male political world (see 115n., ***Iuliae Aug(ustae), optume de r(e) p(ublica) meritae***, 116–17n., ***sed etiam multis magnisq(ue) erga cuiusq(ue) ordinis homines beneficis***) with sentiments associated with the domestic world of the family (see 118–19n., ***principis nostri summa<e> erga matrem suam pietati suffragandum indulgendumq(ue) esse***; cf. the exploration of Livia's dual role as patron and mediator by Purcell, [1986] 2009: 179–80). The extensive special pleading of this section reflects a deep sense of unease on the Senate's part in pardoning Plancina in this way (Mackay, 2003: 349–50) and also suggests that Tiberius left the Senate to find its own reasons to explain why Iulia Augusta's request for Plancina to be pardoned should be granted (114–15, ***quam ob rem ˹id˺ mater sua inpetrari vellet, iustissumas ab ea causas sibi expositas acceperit***). The Senate implicitly acknowledges Plancina's guilt, as it had also done in the case of her son (see 100–01n., ***M(arco) etiam Pisoni, qu<o>i inpunitatem senatus humanitati et moderationi principis sui adsensus dandam esse{t} arbitraretur***), but unlike Marcus, Plancina's activities could not be excused in any way. Although the Senate's decree does not deal directly with the charge of murdering Germanicus, it may have been difficult for the Senate to refer to the 'very many extremely serious charges' placed against Plancina without his death lurking in the background (González, 2003: 297–98).

Lines 109–10: quod ad Plancinae causam pertineret, qu<o>i pluruma et gravissuma crimina obiecta essent / That as regarded the case of

Plancina, against whom very many extremely serious charges had been brought In contrast to the Senate's long list of detailed charges against Piso which appears earlier in the decree (lines 23–70), nowhere does the Senate specify with what charges Plancina is accused. Tacitus, however, reveals two main charges against Plancina: firstly, that she had received bribes from Vonones (see 39n., **Vononem**, 45n., **eaq(ue) magnis muneribus Vononis corruptus fecerit**), which persuaded Piso to champion his cause in Armenia (*Ann.* 2.58.2). She thus appears involved in the charge of stirring up war between Parthia and Armenia (see 37–38n., **bellum {cum} Armeniacum et Parthicum**). Secondly, that she had associated with the poisoner Martina, and so was suspected of poisoning Germanicus (*Ann.* 2.74.2). She was also implicated in undermining military discipline (*Ann.* 2.55.6) and rejoicing at Germanicus' death (*Ann.* 2.75.2) and had supplied slaves to Piso for his military action in Syria (*Ann.* 2.80.1), supporting what the Senate considered to be civil war (see 45–46n., **bellum etiam civile excitare conatus sit**). Moreover, her case was so inextricably linked to that of her husband (cf. Mackay, 2003: 345) that the Senate's declaration of his guilt likewise entailed Plancina's guilt. After the trial, she continued to benefit from the protection of Iulia Augusta (who died in AD 29) (see 113n., **pro Plancina rogatu matris suae depreca´tus` s´it`**), but then committed suicide in AD 33. Tacitus suggests that Plancina survived this long after Iulia Augusta's death because her hatred for Agrippina protected her, but once Agrippina died in AD 33, Plancina's position became untenable (Tac., *Ann.* 6.26.3; Cass. Dio 58.22.5). Tacitus further suggests that her suicide was not prompted by new charges laid against her, but by the charges from AD 20 still being in the public's consciousness and her guilt now catching up with her (Flower, 1998: 175).

Lines 110–11: quoniam confiteretur se omnem spem in misericordia{m} principis nostri et senatus habere / since she was now admitting that she placed all her hope in the mercy of our Princeps and the Senate In reality, Plancina was relying upon the influence of Iulia Augusta (see 113n., **pro Plancina rogatu matris suae depreca´tus` s´it`**), but it seems that Plancina's tactic in appealing for pardon was not to name Iulia Augusta herself, forcing Tiberius to be the one to raise his mother's name (Eck, Caballos, Fernández, 1996: 224).

Lines 111–12: et saepe princeps noster accurateq(ue) ab eo ordine petierit / and since our Princeps has often and pressingly requested from this body The addition of the adverbs 'often and pressingly' (*saepe accurateque*) implies that Tiberius had experienced some trouble in persuading the Senate to pardon Plancina, reflecting its reluctance to come to this decision (see 9–10n., ***pro qua persona, quid petisset et quas propter causas, exposuisset antea***).

Lines 112–13: uxori ⌈e⌉ius sic uti M(arco) filio parceret / spare his wife as it was sparing his son Marcus This sets up a false parallel, since, unlike Plancina, Marcus could be excused on the grounds that he had been obeying his father (see 100–01n., ***M(arco) etiam Pisoni, qu<o>i inpunitatem senatus humanitati et moderationi principis sui adsensus esse{t} arbitraretur***). It shows, though, that the Senate's decision to excuse Marcus was made before it turned to Plancina (Eck, Caballos, Fernández, 1996: 224).

Line 113: pro Plancina rogatu matris suae depreca⌈tus⌉ s⌈it⌉ / since he pleaded himself for Plancina at the request of his mother The verb *deprecari* is a technical term, as explained by Cicero (*Inv. rhet.* 2.104): 'A plea for mercy is one in which there is no defence of what has been done, but the request is confined to one for pardon' (*deprecatio est in qua non defensio facti, sed ignoscendi postulatio continetur*; cf. Quint. *Inst.* 5.13.5; Eck, Caballos, Fernández, 1996: 225). By using it, therefore, Tiberius himself clearly admits Plancina's guilt. Iulia Augusta's defence of Plancina is not an isolated instance of her intervention at law on behalf of a friend: in AD 16, she similarly exerted herself in defence of Urgulania (*PIR*² V1010), whom L. Calpurnius Piso Augur had summoned to court in a provocative way (Tac., *Ann.* 2.34.2–4, with Goodyear, 1981: 293–94, ad loc. on how Piso was being deliberately provocative). The language which Tacitus uses of Tiberius' deference to his mother in the matter ('thinking it proper to indulge his mother to this extent', *hactenus indulgere matri ciuile ratus*) echoes that now documented in this decree (see 118–19n., ***principis nostri summa<e> erga matrem suam pietati suffragandum indulgendumq(ue) esse***). Iulia Augusta's willingness to rescue someone from danger is described in positive terms by Velleius Paterculus (2.130.5), suggesting that there may have been further instances of similar behaviour: the most celebrated instance was her intervention with Augustus to obtain mercy for the conspirator Cn. Cornelius Cinna in 16 BC (Sen., *Clem.* 1.9 = LACTOR 17, P11) (see 116–17n., ***sed etiam multis magnisq(ue) erga cuiusq(ue) ordinis homines beneficis***).

Lines 114–15: quam ob rem ⌈id⌉ mater sua inpetrari vellet, iustissumas ab ea causas sibi expositas acceperit / had very just reasons presented to him by her for wanting to secure her request This phrasing suggests that Tiberius did not go into detail before the Senate about the reasons why Iulia Augusta had persuaded him to defend Plancina. This leaves the Senate with the responsibility of justifying its decision to grant the request presented on Iulia Augusta's behalf by Tiberius (115–18). On Livia's links with justice, see Purcell, [1986] 2009: 187–88.

Line 115: Iuliae Aug(ustae), optume de r(e) p(ublica) meritae / to Iulia Augusta, who has served the state superlatively Whereas Tacitus suggests that Iulia Augusta worked behind the scenes in securing Plancina's pardon, 'with secret pleas of Augusta' (*secretis Augustae precibus*, *Ann*. 3.15.1), it is one of the revelations of this decree that, on the contrary, her role is publicly recognised by the Senate (Lott, 2012: 294). The language used by the Senate to describe Iulia Augusta unexpectedly aligns her with male officeholders, of whom alone the formula *optume de re publica meritus* had previously been used (Eck, Caballos, Fernández, 1996: 228; Barrett, 2002: 169–70 for examples of the customary usage). It had generally therefore been used to recognise outstanding public service to Rome by magistrates. This assimilation of Iulia Augusta into the world of male magistrates goes right back to 35 BC, when along with Octavia she was granted sacrosanctity, a privilege which had previously been reserved for tribunes of the plebs (Cass. Dio 49.38.1; Frei-Stolba, 1998: 72–76). This encroachment upon the world of male officeholders had been reiterated with the grant of a lictor to her as priestess of Augustus in AD 14 (Cass. Dio 56.46.2; Purcell, [1986] 2009: 178–79).

Lines 115–16: non partu tantum modo principis nostri / not only in giving birth to our Princeps The Senate's choice of explanation for why Iulia Augusta deserves to influence the Senate's decision-making – that she had given birth to Tiberius and that she had bestowed favours upon men of every rank – demonstrates that the Senate was left by Tiberius to devise its own form of words to explain why Iulia Augusta's request to pardon Plancina should be granted, suggesting in turn that Tiberius did not divulge the 'very just reasons' which she had offered to him.

Lines 116–17: sed etiam multis magnisq(ue) erga cuius(que) ordinis homines beneficis / but also through her many great favours towards men of every rank It is surprising to find the Senate formally acknowledging favours (*beneficia*) from Iulia Augusta in its decree (cf. Eck, Caballos, Fernández, 1996: 225–27 for context). As a result, 'The Senate represents the senatorial pardon of Plancina, not as their response to an exercise of power by Livia [Iulia Augusta] (and the Princeps), but as an act of reciprocation, a favour earned by Livia' (Griffin, 2003b: 112). This wording continues to apply formulae from the male political sphere to Iulia Augusta and her relationship to individual senators (see 115n., ***Iuliae Aug(ustae), optume de r(e) p(ublica) meritae***; Severy, 2003: 239). Other sources attest to her financial aid and social patronage towards individual senators, including the later emperor Galba (Suet., *Galb.* 5.2), M. Salvius Otho (grandfather of the later emperor: Suet. *Otho* 1.1), Q. Haterius (*PIR*² H24; Tac., *Ann.* 1.13.6) and C. Fufius Geminus (*PIR*² 511; Tac., *Ann.* 5.2.2), who became consul in the year she died, AD 29. In Dio's account of the honours proposed for her in the Senate after her death (58.2.3), he alludes to her help in raising senators' children and in providing dowries for daughters. Dio further narrates how she had proposed to put on a banquet for senators, equestrians, and their wives on the occasion of dedicating a statue of Augustus after his death, but Tiberius insisted that she invite only the women, whilst he invite the men (Cass. Dio 57.12.5, discussed by Purcell, [1986] 2009: 184). Her financial aid extended more widely in AD 16 too, as she provided relief to victims of a fire that broke out in Rome (Cass. Dio 57.16.2). It is easy to believe, therefore, that by AD 20 Iulia Augusta had already put many senators in her debt.

Lines 117–18: cum iure meritoq(ue) plurumum posse in eo, quod a senatu petere\<t\> deberet, parcissume uteretur eo / who rightly and deservedly ought to have supreme influence in what she asked from the Senate, but used that influence sparingly Although the word *iure* can mean 'according to the law', it here means 'with good reason / deservedly' (*OLD* s.v. 'iure' 1, 2; Barrett, 2002: 170; Lott, 2012: 294). The idea that Iulia Augusta should be praised for her restrained use of power finds echoes in the contemporary words of Velleius (2.130.5), written shortly after her death: 'the loss of his mother has increased the distress of this time, a most eminent woman, more like the gods than men in everything, whose power no-one felt unless it was for the relief from danger or the increase of rank' (*cuius temporis aegritudinem auxit amissa mater, eminentissima et per omnia deis quam hominibus similior femina, cuius potentiam nemo sensit nisi aut leuatione periculi aut accessione dignitatis*). Velleius' direct reference to Iulia Augusta's *potentia* is in contrast to the Senate's roundabout way of broaching the subject of her influence. A similar sentiment is found in the *Consolatio ad Liviam* (47–49), a work ostensibly composed to console Livia in 9 BC on the death of her son Drusus, where the author asks what the point has been 'not to have harmed anyone and yet to have had the occasion of harming; nor that anyone feared your strength; and that your power did not wander over Campus or forum' (*nec nocuisse ulli et fortunam habuisse nocendi, nec quemquam neruos extimuisse tuos? nec uires errasse tuas campoue foroue*). This is a work of anonymous authorship and of unknown date of composition (with possibilities ranging from 9 BC down to the Neronian period, as reviewed by Schoonhoven, 1992: 22–39, Fraschetti, 1995 and 1996 arguing for composition shortly after Drusus' death). Even if the work is a later rhetorical composition, its language may reflect the ideas thought to be appropriate to its dramatic date (Flory, 1993: 298).

Written from an equestrian perspective (*Consolatio*, 202), the *Consolatio* complements the senatorial viewpoint of Velleius and suggests that Iulia Augusta's influence was appreciated already during her lifetime, even if (or perhaps, because of which) the Senate in its decree touches upon it obliquely. In effect, the Senate is praising Iulia Augusta for showing *moderatio* in the exercise of her power, but the problem is that such a quality would normally be praised in holders of *imperium* (see above, §6), whereas her power exists outside the framework of male political office-holding.

Lines 118–19: principis nostri summa<e> erga matrem suam pietati suffragandum indulgendumq(ue) esse / and to the supreme piety of our Princeps towards his mother, support and indulgence should be accorded This phrase is key to appreciating how the Senate explains its pardon of Plancina, not by presenting Tiberius' intervention on her behalf in juridical terms but by presenting his piety (*pietas*) as the reason for his intervention on behalf of Iulia Augusta. 'In asking her son to protect her friend, she was operating within the family sphere, but because her son was the emperor and the imperial family part of the state, she was operating within the political sphere as well' (Severy, 2003: 239). In this way, Iulia Augusta can be presented as essentially wielding influence within her family, but this just happens to have political consequences, given that her family is no ordinary family but the *domus Augusta* (Frei-Stolba, 1998: 88–89; Purcell, [1986] 2009: 183–84).

Lines 119–20: remittiq(ue) poenam Plancinae placere / has decided that the punishment of Plancina should be waived The Senate ends by acknowledging that a penalty had already been decided upon for Plancina, but that this is now being waived.

Rhetorically, this both underlined the senate's commitment to *severitas* and highlighted the extent to which the *princeps* was responsible for the outcome in her case … Procedurally, the views of the *princeps* were accommodated after the senate had come to a decision about punishment. His recommendations modified or overturned the senate's decisions. The fact that the *SCPP* is decidedly vague about this procedure and mentions no actual sentence recorded against Marcus or Plancina suggests manifest unease about advertising the real consequences of the *princeps*' intervention. (Cowan, 2016: 92)

Lines 120–23 Penalties for Visellius Karus and Sempronius Bassus

The Senate now turns to the final matter raised by Tiberius in his *relatio*, namely its verdict on Piso's associates (see 10–11n., **quid de Visellio Karo et de Sempronio Basso, comitibus Cn(aei) Pisonis patris, iudicaret senatus**). These individuals are not named by Tacitus, whilst Domitius Celer, who does feature in his account, encouraging Piso that he is within his rights to re-enter Syria (*Ann.* 2.77.1), is not mentioned in the decree. Visellius Karus and Sempronius Bassus may be equestrian in rank, which would be normal for *comites* of a governor (Eck, Caballos, Fernández, 1996: 99), and which is suggested by the Senate naming them by *nomen* and *cognomen* in contrast to other individuals in the text, who are named by *praenomen* and *cognomen*. This pattern suggests that they are not otherwise known to the Senate (Eck, Caballos, Fernández, 1996: 229–30). The recommendation made by the Senate for penalties to be imposed shows that Piso's associates had already been found guilty of the charges against them. The praetor in charge of the lawcourt along with the praetors in charge of the treasury are delegated by the Senate with implementing the penalties imposed on Piso's associates.

Lines 120–21: Visellio Karo et Sempronio Basso, comitibus Cn(aei) Pisonis patris et omnium malificiorum socis ac ministris / On Visellius Karus and Sempronius Bassus, members of the staff of Gnaeus Piso Senior and his associates and allies in all his misdeeds As discussed earlier (see 10–11n., *quid de Visellio Karo et de Sempronio Basso, comitibus Cn(aei) Pisonis patris, iudicaret senatus*), the language which Tiberius uses to introduce the cases of Visellius Karus and Sempronius Bassus for discussion in the Senate, and with which the Senate here expresses its view on their cases, differs markedly from how both Tiberius and the Senate introduce and discuss the cases of Piso and his family. No specific charges are raised against Piso's two associates beyond their collusion in his misdeeds (probably in the context of his attempt to regain Syria after Germanicus' death or in stirring up unrest in Armenia and Parthia: Eck, Caballos, Fernández, 1996: 99), but once Piso was judged guilty, this was enough to ensure their conviction for *maiestas*.

Line 121: aqua et igne interdici oportere / that the penalty of interdiction from water and fire should be imposed The Senate imposes upon Piso's associates the standard penalty under the *lex Iulia de maiestate* (Richardson, 1997: 515; cf. Cic., *Phil.* 1.9.23). Interdiction entailed exiling an individual, banning him or her from returning to Roman territory, but it was not equivalent to a death sentence, given that the convicted person could still live in an area outside Rome's jurisdiction (G.P. Kelly, 2006: 19). The penalty prevented an individual from being regarded as part of the Roman citizen body, confiscating his or her property (Williamson, 2016: 340).

Line 122: ab eo pr(aetore), qu ̔i ̓ lege{m} maiestatis quaereret / by the praetor presiding over cases under the law of *maiestas* The Senate delegates the task of implementing the penalties (imposing exile upon Piso's associates and selling off their property) to one of the two praetors

216   *Commentary on 122–23*

in charge of the lawcourt that hears treason charges (*quaestio maiestatis*) (contradicting Talbert, 1984: 466, who suggests that the *quaestio* may have ceased to operate beyond AD 15). The relationship between the Senate and the *quaestio* in this decree has been much debated (Eck, Caballos, Fernández, 1996: 230–32; Richardson, 1997; Ermann, 2002; Mackay, 2003: 350–56; G.P. Kelly, 2006: 45 n.112; Lott, 2012: 296–97), but the clearest explanation is that 'The senate passed its judgement on the guilt of the accused and prescribed the appropriate punishment, but the legal implementation of these decisions required the *quaestio*' (Pettinger, 2012: 17).

Lines 122–23: bonaq(ue) eorum ab pr(aetoribus), qui aerario praeesse<n>t, venire et in aerarium redigi placere / and that their goods should be sold and the profits consigned to the public treasury by the praetors in charge of the public treasury   The Senate also delegates to the praetors in charge of the public treasury the task of confiscating property belonging to Piso's associates, selling it, and giving the proceeds to the public treasury. Eck, Caballos, and Fernández (1996: 63–64, followed by Lott, 2012: 297) change the singular verb *praeesset* to the plural *praeesse<n>t*, consequently also expanding the abbreviation as *pr(aetoribus)* rather than *pr(aetore)*, although Mackay (2003: 352–53, n.97) argues that the Senate's instructions only need to be carried out by one of the two praetors assigned to the treasury and so there is no need to modify the inscribed text as preserved on both Copy A and Copy B. The two praetors in charge of the *aerarium* in AD 20 are named as Q. Arquinius and L. Pontius Ni[grinus?] on an inscription found in fragments near the Temple of Saturn where the *aerarium* was located in the Roman Forum, listing its annual officeholders (*fasti scribarum quaestoriorum, CIL* VI 1496 = *Inscr.It.* XIII.1, 305, no.27; Corbier, 1974: 33, 52–54; Eck, Caballos, Fernández, 1996: 234).

LINES 123–51 PRAISE FOR MEMBERS OF THE IMPERIAL FAMILY

This passage has been regarded by some as the second part of the expression of thanks (*gratiarum actio*: Eck, Caballos, Fernández 1996: 234–38; Lott, 2012: 297), which begins in lines 12–22, where the Senate expresses its thanks to the gods for foiling Piso's dastardly plots and to Tiberius for ensuring a fair trial. This runs the risk of misidentifying the Senate's declared purpose, however (Lebek, 1999: 193–95). Tacitus' narrative has led scholars to map this subsection of the decree onto the proposal (*sententia*) of Valerius Messallinus to offer thanks to members of the imperial family for avenging the death of Germanicus (*ob uindictam Germanici grates agendas, Ann.* 3.18; see also lines 12–22n.). On this interpretation, the Senate recapitulates the topic of thanksgiving from lines 12–22, having dealt in turn with each matter raised by Tiberius in his *relatio*. Whereas the Senate does give thanks to the immortal gods and to Tiberius at the very start of its decree following the *relatio* (see lines 12, 15), the Senate does not use a verb of thanking anywhere in this section, instead focusing upon its desire to praise and commend the behaviour of the imperial family (Eck, Caballos, Fernández, 1996: 235 argue, however, that this is still consistent with its being part of a *gratiarum actio*). There is also a mismatch between the scope of the decree and the thanksgiving proposed by Messallinus, who does not include (in Tacitus) Germanicus' sister, his children, the equestrian order, the plebs, or the army. Further, the language is consistent between different members of the imperial family (with the exception of Tiberius: see lines 123–32n.). The Senate 'offers abundant praise of the restraint of Iulia Augusta and Drusus Caesar' (lines 132–33, *laudare magnopere ... moderationem*); it 'greatly approves of' Germanicus' kin (line 137, *magnopere probare*), naming first the women of his family – Agrippina, Antonia, and Livi(ll)a (his wife, mother, and sister) – whom 'the Senate greatly approves of in equal measure for their most loyal grief and their moderation in that grief' (lines 145–46, *quarum aeq(ue) et dolor˙e˙m fidelissumum et in dolore moderatione<m> senatum probare*); and it finally turns to Germanicus' sons and brother, whom 'it reckons ought to be praised' (lines 150–51, *laudandum existumare*) for holding back their grief within the proper limits. This then links directly into the following sections in which the Senate goes on to approve of the behaviour of the equestrian order (line 151, *probari*), to praise the plebs of Rome (line 155, *laudare*), and finally to approve of the army (line 159, *probare*). The Senate's commentary on members of the imperial family, therefore, is not self-contained, but is the first element in an extended passage that takes us through the hierarchy of Roman society. Despite the fact that the decree up to this point has focused upon Piso's crimes against Rome, this section refocuses upon Germanicus' death, as the Senate praises individual members of the imperial family for their restraint in grieving for Germanicus, and then commends groups from the rest of Roman society for their emulation of that behaviour and for their continuing loyalty towards Tiberius and his family.

Lines 123–32 Exhortation of Tiberius

The Senate opens by making a strong plea and requesting (line 126, *magnopere rogare et petere*) that Tiberius cease mourning for Germanicus, so that he can refocus his energies upon his sole surviving son, Drusus. This section is neither in the form of thanking Tiberius nor praising him (although the Senate obliquely comments on his exemplary *pietas*), but of exhorting him to resume his public duties. It is tempting to view this public declaration by the Senate of the depth of Tiberius' grief as a counter to rumours that he had on the contrary rejoiced at Germanicus' death (Eck,

Caballos, Fernández 1996: 239) (see 125n., *tant⌐i⌐ et ⌐t⌐am aequali<s> dolor⌐i⌐<s eius indicis> totiens conspectis*).

Lines 123–24: item cum iudic<ar>et senatus omnium partium pietatem antecessisse Ti(berium) Caesarem Aug(ustum) principem nostrum / Likewise, since it was the judgement of the Senate that Tiberius Caesar Augustus our Princeps has surpassed all parties in his devotion to duty The Senate's reference to Tiberius' outstanding *pietas* appears in relation to his heartfelt grief at the death of his son Germanicus.

Line 125: tant⌐i⌐ et ⌐t⌐am aequali<s> dolor⌐i⌐<s eius indicis> totiens conspectis / after witnessing so often the signs of his grief, so great and of such intensity This picture of Tiberius wracked with grief at Germanicus' death contrasts with Tacitus' portrayal of his failure to disguise his joy at his death: 'everyone was aware that Germanicus' death being a source of happiness to Tiberius was barely disguised' (*gnaris omnibus laetam Tiberio Germanici mortem male dissimulari*, *Ann*. 3.2.3). The Senate's reference to the fact that it has witnessed signs of Tiberius' grief also contradicts Tacitus' hypothesis that Tiberius may have remained in private so as not to betray his lack of grief (*Ann*. 3.3.1). Compare Lott, 2012: 299 for an alternative interpretation of *tam aequalis*.

Lines 126–27: ut omnem curam, quam in duos quondam filios suos partitus erat, ad eum, quem haberet, converteret / that he devote all the care which he previously divided between his two sons to the one whom he still has The Senate refers to Germanicus and Drusus (the Younger) in the same terms, as sons of Tiberius. Germanicus was adopted by Tiberius in AD 4, whereas Drusus was his son by birth. In AD 22, Drusus was given tribunician power, another sign of his status as successor to Tiberius, but he died only a year later (Rogers, 1940 on the chronology; Cox, 2005 on tribunician power). The Senate then honoured the deceased Drusus in ways similar to those already used in the cases of Germanicus, Gaius Caesar, and Lucius Caesar (Crawford, 1996: no.38; cf. Tac., *Ann*. 4.9.2, 'The same things were decreed for the memory of Drusus as for Germanicus, and more elements were added on', *memoriae Drusi eadem quae in Germanicum decernuntur, plerique additis*).

Lines 128–29: sperareq(ue) senatum eum, qui supersit, ⌐t⌐anto maior⌐i⌐ curae dis immortalibus fore / and the Senate hopes that the immortal gods will devote all the more care to the one who remains The idea that the gods had a special interest in protecting Drusus, as successor to Tiberius, proceeds from the sentiment that Augustus was especially favoured and supported by the gods, and that this consequently put him in a unique position to protect Rome (Cooley, 2019; cf. Ov., *Fast*. 2.63–66 for the mutual protection of Augustus and the gods). Tiberian authors elaborated on this idea, with Valerius Maximus attributing the downfall of an enemy of the state (most likely Sejanus) to the watchfulness of the gods (9.11 ext.4), and Velleius ending his whole work with a prayer to the gods to protect Tiberius (2.131) (see 12n., **senatum populumq(ue) Romanum ante omnia dis immortalibus gratias agere**).

Lines 129–30: omnem spem futuram paternae pro r(e) p(ublica) stationis in uno repos[i]ta\<m\> / that all hope for the position which his father holds to the benefit of the state has rested for the future on one person alone The language used by the Senate here to refer to the idea of hereditary succession goes back to Augustus, as shown by a letter recorded by Aulus Gellius, in which Augustus expresses his hope that Gaius and Lucius will succeed to his 'post' (*statio*, *NA* 15.7.3). There is a hint that Augustus' *statio* was incompatible with also being regarded as *princeps* in an ironic comment in Ovid's *Tristia* (2.219–20: note the heavily ironic *scilicet*), where the exiled poet imagines the (unthinkable) circumstances in which Augustus might now read his poetry (and so implies that there is in reality no chance that Augustus will again read his verses): 'doubtless, though *princeps* of the empire, if your *statio* were relinquished, you might read my verses composed in unequal measures' (*scilicet imperii princeps statione relicta / imparibus legeres carmina facta modis*, with Ingleheart, 2010: ad loc.). This idea was continued under Tiberius, as Velleius Paterculus also refers to Tiberius taking over his *paterna statio* from Augustus in AD 14: 'There was, however, one wrestling match as it were in the state, of the Senate and the Roman people struggling with Caesar to induce him to succeed to his father's *statio*, while he on his side strove for permission to play the part of equal citizen rather than of outstanding leader' (*una tamen ueluti luctatio ciuitatis fuit, pugnantis cum Caesare senatus populique Romani, ut* **stationi paternae** *succederet, illius, ut potius aequalem ciuem quam eminentem liceret agere principem*, 2.124.2). This is just one of many examples where the decree offers valuable insight into contemporary official political usage, providing a corrective to the later language of Tacitus in particular (Griffin, 1997: 257; see §6). Rather than seeing Tiberius as inheriting from Augustus a new constitution in the form of the Principate, therefore, his contemporaries considered that Tiberius succeeded to his *paterna statio*. This decree shows that in AD 20 this was still the way in which the Senate understood Drusus' potential succession to Tiberius too (Cooley, 2019; for a survey of uses of the word *statio*, see Köstermann, 1932). That Tiberius in turn was to pass on his *statio* is apparent from the final prayer to the gods in Velleius Paterculus with which he ends his work: 'On you I call and to you I pray with public voice: guard, preserve, protect this state of things, this peace, this leader, and, when he has completed the longest possible mortal *statio*, grant him successors at the latest time' (*uos publica uoce obtestor atque precor custodite, seruate, protegite hunc statum, hanc pacem, hunc principem, eique functo longissima statione mortali destinate successores quam serissimos*, 2.131.1–2).

Line 130: quo nomine debere eum finire dolorem / for which reason he should end his grief   The Senate having to urge Tiberius to end his grief is in effect a mirror-image of the edict issued by Tiberius in Tacitus, by which he urges the populace of Rome to put an end to its grief for Germanicus (*Ann.* 3.6).

Lines 131–32: ac restituere patriae suae non tantum animum, sed etiam voltum, qui publicae felicitati conueniret / and regain for his country not only the frame of mind, but also the appearance appropriate to public happiness   One of the main motifs in Tacitus' Tiberian narrative is the inscrutability of Tiberius' *vultus*, which defeated usual expectations that someone's wishes would be visible from their face (Corbeill, 2004: 20 on the etymology of *vultus* 'facial expression' from *volo* 'I want'; see also §3; Goodyear, 1981: 366–67 on the prevalence of the *vultus* in Tacitus more generally; extended analysis in Bloomer, 1997: chapter 5 'The imperial mask of rhetoric: *animus* and *vultus* in the *Annales* of Tacitus' and Corbeill, 2004: 157–67). For Tacitus' Piso, the emotionless face of Tiberius was the main factor that propelled him towards suicide: 'nothing terrified him more than the fact that he saw Tiberius without pity, without anger, inflexible and closed up, so that he might not be broken through by any emotion' (*nullo magis exterritus est quam quod Tiberium sine miseratione, sine ira, obstinatum clausumque uidit, ne quo adfectu perrumperetur*, *Ann.* 3.15.2). Tiberius' unchanging expression at Piso's trial recalls his similar behaviour towards Libo Drusus, who likewise took this as a cue to commit suicide (*Ann.* 2.29.2).

Lines 132–36 Praise of Iulia Augusta and Drusus

The Senate praises members of the imperial family in hierarchical order, starting with Iulia Augusta and Drusus (*PIR*² 219). It tackles the potential clash between showing both devotion (*pietas*) towards Germanicus and fairness (*aequitas*) in the conduct of Piso's trial (Eck, Caballos, Fernández, 1996: 300).

Lines 132–33: item senatum laudare magnopere Iuliae Aug(ustae) Drusiq(ue) Caesaris moderationem / likewise, the Senate offers abundant praise of the restraint of Iulia Augusta and Drusus Caesar   The pairing of Drusus with Iulia Augusta differs from Tacitus' account of Valerius Messallinus' proposal to thank the imperial family for avenging Germanicus' death (*Ann.* 3.18.3), where Drusus is listed last. Indeed, Messallinus only names Tiberius, Iulia Augusta, Antonia, Agrippina, and Drusus, with

Claudius added in amendment by Nonius Asprenas. This is another indication that Messallinus' proposal does not map in a straightforward way onto the senatorial decree, where the Senate's praise extends to a much wider selection of the imperial family (see 123–51n. and 146–51n.). Whereas the following sub-sections specify that the 'restraint' shown by Germanicus' family, which is being praised by the Senate, relates to their restraint in mourning him – 'their moderation in grief' (*in dolore moderatione<m>*, lines 145–46); cf. lines 146–48 (in contrast to the excessive lamentation shown by the plebs, line 157) – the context in which the Senate praises Iulia Augusta and Drusus for what at first appears to be the same virtue of *moderatio* leaves open the possibility that they may have shown restraint instead in their attitude towards Piso and in not influencing his trial (see 135n., ***aequitatem in servandis integris iudicis suis***).

Line 133: imitantium principis nostri iustitiam / as they imitate the justice of our Princeps The Senate suggests in this way that Iulia Augusta and Drusus model their behaviour upon Tiberius' example. This is rather topsy-turvy as far as Tiberius' mother is concerned but can be explained as being specific to this situation. Tiberius' sense of justice has been demonstrated in allowing Piso's trial to continue after his suicide and in encouraging his sons to plead on behalf of Piso himself, as well as of Marcus and Plancina (see lines 15–22). The Senate is not alluding to a general principle of behaviour being imitated but is acknowledging that Iulia Augusta and Drusus too have not pre-judged Piso's case, but allowed his trial to unfold (see 135n., ***aequitatem in servandis integris iudicis suis***).

Lines 133–34: quos animadvertere{t} hunc ordinem non maiorem pietatem in Germanicum / this body recognises that they have equalled their devotion towards Germanicus On *pietas* in the decree, see 64–65n., ***totius imperi R(omani) constantissuma pietas clauserat***. Although it is possible that their *pietas* relates only to their condemnation of Piso's hostile behaviour towards Germanicus, the charge of poisoning may also lurk in the background here. Drusus' *pietas* towards Germanicus had been demonstrated through his presentation of a document in the Senate during the meetings to discuss honours for the deceased Germanicus in December AD 19. This was then to be inscribed on bronze and put on public display so that it might reach a wider audience too: 'likewise, so that the loyalty of Drusus Caesar might be better attested, it was agreed that the pamphlet which he had read out at the most recent meeting of the Senate should be inscribed on bronze and fixed in the place decided upon by his father and himself' (*item quo testatior esset Drusi Caesaris pietas placere uti libellus quem is proxumo senatu recitasset in aere incideretur eoque loco figeretur quo patri eius ipsique placuisset*, Tabula Siarensis = Crawford (1996) no.37, frag. b, col. II, lines 18–19 = LACTOR 19, J8g).

Line 135: aequitatem in servandis integrìs iudicìs suis / with their impartiality in reserving their own judgement intact   It is typical of the decree that the Senate uses what appears to be technical legal language (*aequitatem ... iudicìs*) in unexpected contexts (see 10–11n., **quid de Visellio Karo et de Sempronio Basso, comitibus Cn(aei) Pisonis patris, iudicaret senatus**), as here in praising Iulia Augusta and Drusus for not allowing their devotion towards Germanicus to have inclined them towards condemning Piso even before his case had been heard. Iulia Augusta for certain and probably Drusus (if the trial occurred before he returned to Rome to celebrate his triumph in May) were not involved in the formal judicial proceedings, so strictly speaking the Senate is using the word 'judgement' in a non-legal sense. The problem is, of course, that Iulia Augusta has shortly before been shown to have had an impact upon formal legal proceedings in successfully requesting pardon for Plancina (see lines 109–20).

Lines 136–46 Praise for Germanicus' Wife, Mother, and Sister

One of the consistent features of the Senate's response to Germanicus' death is its involvement of his family members in mourning and honouring him. As noted above, the individuals mentioned by the Senate in this part of its decree do not map across neatly onto the proposal made by Messallinus as recorded by Tacitus (*Ann.* 3.18.3; see 123–51n.). The overall concept of the *domus Augusta* consistently embraced the men and women, adults, and children as part of a family with a unique exemplary role to play in Roman society, but the precise membership of that family varied according to context (see §5). At the end of AD 19, the Senate had convened a consultative group to discuss honours for Germanicus, which consisted of Tiberius, Iulia Augusta, Drusus, Antonia, and possibly Agrippina (*Tabula Siarensis* = Crawford, 1996: no.37, frag. a, 4–8 = LACTOR 19, J8a). Here, however, the Senate includes a wider range of family members, adding Germanicus' sons, his sister Livi(ll)a, and his brother Claudius. This recalls the statues on the arch set up in Germanicus' honour decreed at the end of AD 19 by the Senate, which offered an alternative focus upon Germanicus' immediate family by including his original father Drusus rather than his adoptive father Tiberius alongside his mother Antonia, his sister and brother, and all his children (girls and boys alike) and by excluding Iulia Augusta (*Tabula Siarensis* = Crawford, 1996: no.37, frag. a, 18–21 = LACTOR 19, J8b).

Lines 136–37: ceterorum quoq(ue) contingentium Germanicum Caesarem necessitudine magnopere probare / likewise, of the others related by kinship to Germanicus Caesar, the Senate greatly approves   The term *necessitudo* is used here because it can encompass both individuals who share a male ancestor (*cognati* – i.e. Antonia and Livi(ll)a) and those who are related by marriage (*adfines* – i.e. Agrippina) (Corbier, 2001b: 176; see 77–78n., ***quive eam familiam cognatione adfinitateve contingerent***) (Fig. 1).

Lines 137–38: Agrippinae, quam senatui memoria{m} divi Aug(usti), qu<o>i fuisset probatissuma / of Agrippina, whom the memory of deified Augustus, by whom she was most highly approved As a direct descendant of Augustus by blood (daughter of his daughter Iulia and Agrippa), Agrippina was the dynastic lynchpin joining together the Iulians and Claudians via her marriage to Germanicus, as observed by Tacitus (*Ann.* 5.1.2; Shotter, 2000: 343; *PIR*² V682; Raepsaet-Charlier, 1987: no.812). This created the potential for Tiberius' heirs to be direct descendants of Augustus himself (as did subsequently happen in the case of the son of Germanicus and Agrippina, Gaius Caligula). Agrippina's sister Iulia, exiled for adultery in AD 7/8, is a reminder that being Augustus' granddaughter did not guarantee his approval (Fig. 1).

Lines 138–39: et viri Germanici, cum quo unica concordia vixsisset / and of her husband Germanicus, with whom she had lived in unique harmony The Latin word *concordia* is the common term used to allude to marital harmony based upon 'trust and sympathy' and often also the result of equality between husband and wife and many happy years of marriage (Treggiari, 1991: 245–46, 251–53). Germanicus and Agrippina were married for roughly fifteen years (AD 4/5–19; on the date see Lindsay, 1995: 3). The ideal had come to prominence with the marriage partnership of Augustus and Livia, who were celebrated for their harmonious relationship, with Livia building a shrine of *Concordia* 'to her dear husband' (*caro viro*) in public commemoration of her ideal marriage within the portico built by Augustus in her name (Ov., *Fast.* 6.637–48, with Flory, 1984). Agrippina continued in this tradition, being seen to be supportive of Germanicus in accompanying her husband on tours of duty to Germania even when heavily pregnant (*Ann.* 1.40.2) and to the eastern provinces (including his detour to Egypt). After his death she made an impressive display of her grief by escorting his ashes from Brundisium to Rome (*Ann.* 3.1; Wood, 2001: 203–07).

Line 139: et tot pignora edita partu felicissumo eorum, qui superessent / and the many children born of their most fortunate union, who survived Agrippina and Germanicus had nine children: three sons died in infancy or childhood (*CIL* VI 888–90 = LACTOR J9a), but six children survived (in brackets, their approximate ages in December AD 20): Nero (14), Drusus (12/13), Gaius (8), Agrippina (5), Drusilla (4), and Iulia Livilla (2) (Lindsay, 1995) (Fig. 1). Agrippina retained a lasting reputation for her exceptional fertility and fidelity (Tac., *Ann.* 1.41.2). After Germanicus' death, Agrippina was not permitted by Tiberius to remarry (Tac., *Ann.*

4.53.2), continuing a fractious relationship with Tiberius which ended in her exile and death in AD 33 (*Ann.* 6.25; Shotter, 2000: 349–55, following Tacitus' narrative). The use of the Latin word *pignora* to refer to the children alludes to the idea that the offspring of a marriage are 'tokens' of the mutual affection felt between the couple, continuing the sentiment of *concordia* (cf. *TLL* X,1 fasc. xiv, col. 2125 s.v. 'pignus' II.2.b; whereas *OLD* s.v. 'pignus' 4a suggests that as applied to children, they represent a 'guarantee of the reality of a marriage'; cf. Eck, Caballos, Fernández, 1996: 244).

Line 140: itemq(ue) Antoniae, Germanicì Caesaris matris / and further the Senate greatly approves of Antonia, the mother of Germanicus Caesar Antonia was the younger daughter of Marcus Antonius and Augustus' sister Octavia (*PIR*² A885; Raepsaet-Charlier, 1987: no.73). She had been married to Tiberius' younger brother Drusus, who died in 9 BC. They had three surviving children: Germanicus, Livi(ll)a, and Claudius (Kokkinos, 1992: 11–13) (Fig. 1). Her continuing influence is clearly reflected in her role in engineering the downfall of Sejanus in AD 31, which she achieved by sending a letter to Tiberius on Capri in which she warned of his conspiracy (Joseph., *AJ* 18.181–82 = LACTOR 19, P4e).

Lines 140–41: quae unum matrimonium Drusi Germ(anici) patris experta / whose only marriage was to Drusus the father of Germanicus A woman who had been married only once (*univira*) was regarded as having a special moral and ritual status (Treggiari, 1991: 233–37; Wood, 2001: 76, 143). The idea was so valued (despite its contradiction of the Augustan marriage legislation requiring widows to remarry) that Livia was hailed as 'a woman rejoicing in only one husband' (*unico gaudens mulier marito*: Hor., *Carm.* 3.14.5) even though Augustus was her second husband. The marriage of Antonia and Drusus was used by Valerius Maximus (4.3.3) as an exemplar of conjugal loyalty, with Antonia being praised for her outstanding loyalty to Drusus. After his death Antonia did not ever remarry, despite being only twenty-seven years old at the time of his death, living instead with Livia/Iulia Augusta.

Lines 141–42: sanctitate morum dignam se divo Aug(usto) tam arta propinquitate exhibuerit / through the excellence of her moral character, demonstrated herself to deified Augustus worthy of so close a relationship The suspicion that the Senate is indulging in special pleading is only enhanced by the fact that as Augustus' niece Antonia was already in a closer relationship to him than as the wife of his stepson when she married Drusus. Nevertheless, Antonia's reputation for her strict morality was confirmed by her decision to starve to death her daughter Livi(ll)a, accused of having been seduced by Sejanus and being complicit in the death of her husband Drusus (Cass. Dio 58.11.7; Kokkinos, 1992: 30).

Lines 142–43: et Liviae, sororis Germ(anici) Caesar(is), de qua optume et avia sua et socer idemq(ue) patruos, princeps noster, iudicaret / and of Livia, the sister of Germanicus Caesar, whom her grandmother and her father-in-law, who is also her uncle, our Princeps, held in the highest esteem Germanicus' sister Livi(ll)a is called Livia in Tacitus and inscriptions, and Livilla in Suetonius and Dio (Eck, Caballos, Fernández, 1996: 245; *PIR*² L303, (Claudia) Livia Iulia; Raepsaet-Charlier, 1987: no.239). Her importance within the imperial family is illustrated by the fact that she was initially betrothed in 1 BC to Augustus' oldest grandson/adopted son Gaius Caesar. After his death in AD 4, she was then married to Tiberius' son Drusus (i.e., her cousin). She was celebrated for giving birth in AD 19 to twin boys, Drusus Gemellus and Tiberius Gemellus (in addition to an earlier daughter Iulia in AD 6/7; their birth was commemorated a couple of years later on coinage, *RIC*² Tiberius 42) (Fig. 1). After Drusus' death in AD 23, Livi(ll)a suffered disgrace in connection with Sejanus' downfall and was put to death in AD 31 (Cass. Dio 58.11.7), when the Senate also decreed the destruction of her statues, an unprecedented step for a woman (Tac., *Ann.* 6.2, with Woodman, 2017: 96–97, ad loc. on problems of interpreting the evidence about Livi(ll)a's punishment). This may explain why she is omitted by Tacitus in his list of members of the imperial family included in Messallinus' proposal to be honoured by the Senate in AD 20 (Corbier, 2006: 194; useful summary of evidence for Livi(ll)a in Wood, 2001: 180–82, albeit with some factual errors). Her grandmother is Iulia Augusta; her father-in-law/uncle is Tiberius. In addition, Augustus is her great-uncle.

Lines 143–45: quorum iudicis, etiam si non contingere{n}t domum eorum, merito gloriari posset, nedum tam coniunctis necessitudinibus inligata femina / whose esteem, even if she did not belong to their family, she could deservedly vaunt, all the more as she is a woman attached by such family ties Livi(ll)a belonged to the Claudian gens, but could only be regarded as a member of the *domus Augusta* by marriage (see 142–43n., *et Liviae, sororis Germ(anici) Caesar(is), de qua optume et avia sua et socer idemq(ue) patruos, princeps noster, iudicaret*).

Lines 146–51 Praise for Germanicus' sons and brother

In December AD 19, the Senate had also added Germanicus' daughters to its design for the arch to be set up in honour of Germanicus in the Circus Flaminius (*Tabula Siarensis* = Crawford, 1996: no.37, frag. a, 18–21 = LACTOR 19, J8b), but they were too young for it to make sense to mention them in this decree (see 139n., ***et tot pignora edita partu felicissumo eorum, qui superessent***).

Lines 146–47: item quod filiorum Germanici puerilis et praecipue in Nerone{m} Caesare{m} iam etiam iu<v>enis dolor amisso patre tali / Likewise the fact that the child's grief felt by the sons of Germanicus at the loss of such a father and especially the grief which is, in the case of Nero Caesar, already that of a young man This refers firstly to Germanicus' sons, Drusus Iulius Caesar, at this time aged about twelve (cf. Tac., *Ann.* 4.4.1 on Drusus assuming his adult toga in AD 23; *PIR*² I220), and Gaius (the future emperor, also known as Caligula; *PIR*² I217), aged eight. Their grief is described as 'a child's' (*puerilis*) to distinguish them from their elder brother Nero, who had assumed his adult toga in June AD 20 (Fig. 1). They are not mentioned in Tacitus' account of Messallinus' proposal. Nero Iulius Caesar, eldest child of Germanicus and Agrippina, born in AD 6 (or AD 5 – Lindsay, 1995: 5), is singled out as already being a *iuvenis* (the word here used as an adjective, qualifying the noun 'grief', *dolor*) in contrast to his brothers, who remain *pueri* (as is appropriate to the *SCPP* being published in December) (*PIR*² I223; Eck, Caballos, Fernández, 1996: 112). He is likewise not mentioned in Tacitus. He married his cousin Iulia in AD 20 (Tac., *Ann.* 3.29.4), following his assumption of his adult toga on 7 June 20 (Bargagli and Grosso, 1997: 23 – *Fasti Ostienses* frag. Ce, lines 40–41 = LACTOR J17b). He was attacked in the Senate along with his mother Agrippina by a letter sent from Tiberius in AD 29 and died in exile in AD 31 (Tac., *Ann.* 5.3–5; Vell. Pat. 130.4).

Line 148: itemq(ue) <Ti(beri) Germanici> fratrˉiˉs {Ti(beri)} Germ(anici) Caesar(is) non excˉeˉsserit modum probabilem / and similarly the grief of Tiberius Germanicus, the brother of Germanicus Caesar, has not exceeded the proper limits The wording is rather confused here and has to be emended. Germanicus' brother, Tiberius Claudius Germanicus (the later emperor Claudius: *PIR*² C942), was included by the Senate in its design for the arch in the Circus Flaminius, where he is named as 'Tiberius Germanicus, his brother' (*Ti. Germanici fratris eius*: *Tabula Siarensis* = Crawford, 1996: no.37, frag. a, 21 = LACTOR 19, J8b). The appearance of Claudius' name only at the end of the list of members of the imperial family who are praised for exercising restraint in their grief might seem to fit Tacitus' narrative, where Claudius is initially omitted by Messallinus and added only through the intervention of Nonius Asprenas (Tac., *Ann.* 3.18.3–4). This in turn has appeared to suit Claudius' marginal place in the imperial family, as discussed by Augustus in letters to Claudius' grandmother, Livia (Suet., *Claud.* 4). Uncertainties over Claudius' name in the decree have accordingly been interpreted as indicating his relative obscurity at this date (Meyer, 1998: 317). Although this is one possible interpretation of Claudius' appearance, the rhetorical flow of the decree also supports the view that Claudius is included appropriately rather than as an afterthought: the Senate has grouped together Iulia Augusta and Drusus; Agrippina, Antonia, and Livi(ll)a; and Germanicus' sons and brother. The decision of the Senate, after having chosen to mention the three female relatives of Germanicus as a unit, to mention likewise his male relatives makes sense, whilst the Senate might well have considered it right to mention Germanicus' sons before his brother in this context dealing with the impact of his death upon his family. The different order in the *Tabula Siarensis* – Germanicus' father and mother, his wife, sister, brother, sons, and daughters – reflects the different message of the arch, which is intended to celebrate Germanicus' close family (González, 2002: 274).

Lines 148–50: iudicare senatum referendum quidem esse acceptum maxume discipulinae avi ⸢e⸣orum et patrui et Iuliae Aug(ustae) / the Senate judges that it ought primarily to be traced back to the training of their grandfather and uncle and of Iulia Augusta   Tiberius was grandfather to Germanicus' sons (by adoption) and uncle of Claudius. As discussed earlier (see §5), the Senate contributes to the distinctive view that members of the *domus Augusta* held a unique role as exemplary models for the rest of Roman society precisely because of their unique opportunity to develop shared virtues from living in a household first with Augustus, then Tiberius and Iulia Augusta.

LINES 151–53 PRAISE FOR THE EQUESTRIAN ORDER

The equestrian order had attained a new importance under Augustus, playing a prominent part in public life and developing a corporate identity (Rowe, 2002: chapter 2). Augustus carried out a 'review of the equestrians' (*recognitio equitum*) in 13 BC and probably at five-yearly intervals thereafter in order to define membership of the order. He also revived the order's annual parade on horseback (*transvectio*), held each on 15 July (Suet., *Aug.* 38–39; cf. Ov., *Tr.* 2.89–91 = LACTOR 17, G56; Ov., *Tr.* 2.541–42; Nicolet, 1984: 96–98). It was the equestrians who hailed Gaius and Lucius Caesar as 'leaders of the youth' (*principes iuventutis*) and presented them with silver shields and spears (*RGDA* 14.2). The final section of the *Res Gestae* (35.1) illustrates how integral the equestrian order had become to conceptions of the state, given that Augustus presents his acclamation as 'father of the country' (*pater patriae*) as carried out by 'the Roman Senate and equestrian order and people all together' (*senatus et equester ordo populusque Romanus universus*), in a striking deviation from the traditional formula 'the Roman Senate and people' (*senatus populusque Romanus*). At the end of AD 19, the equestrian order assumed a special role in honouring the memory of Germanicus, renaming a section of their reserved seating in the theatre (previously, the *cuneus iuniorum*) after Germanicus, and having his statue accompany their annual procession for the *transvectio* (Tac., *Ann.* 2.83.4).

It also seems likely that they had some specific role to play in his burial at the mausoleum (*Tabula Hebana* 54–57 = Crawford, 1996: no.37 = LACTOR 19, J8p).

Line 151: item equestris ordinis curam et industriam unic⌈e⌉ senatui probari / likewise the Senate particularly approves of the conscientious efforts of the equestrian order The equestrian order relevant here consisted of a couple of thousand freeborn men of proven morality with property worth 400,000 sesterces or more in the city of Rome (Lebek, 1993: 85). This is the implication of the ensuing description of how the equestrian order had expressed its views via repeated acclamations (see 153–54n., *et quod frequentibus adclamationibus adfectum animi sui et dolorem de principis nostri filiq(ue) eius iniuris ac pro r(ei) p(ublicae) utilitate testatus sit*; contra Eck, Caballos, Fernández, 1996: 247 n.815).

Lines 152–53: quanta res et quam ad omnium salutem pietatemq(ue) pertinens ageretur/ how important a matter and how relevant to the safety and devotion of all was at stake The Senate continues to emphasise how the welfare of Tiberius and his family is critical for the safety of Rome as a whole.

Lines 153–54: et quod frequentibus adclamationibus adfectum animi sui et dolorem de principis nostri filiq(ue) eius iniuris ac pro r(ei) p(ublicae) utilitate testatus sit / and because it declared with repeated acclamations its sentiments and its grief for the wrongs against our Princeps and his son and did this to the advantage of the state Although the Senate does not specify the context in which the equestrian order made these 'repeated acclamations', this may allude to demonstrations of equestrian opinion in the theatre. The potential for this had been illustrated by equestrian protests in the theatre against Augustus' marriage legislation (Suet., *Aug.* 34.2).

LINES 155–58 PRAISE FOR THE PLEBS OF ROME

The plebs had expressed its deep grief at the unexpected death of Germanicus when news of it reached Rome in December AD 19 (Tac., *Ann.* 2.82; Versnel, 1980). Demonstrations of sorrow continued for several months until Tiberius issued an edict just before the festival of the Great Mother in April AD 20, urging the plebs to put an end to its grief (Tac., *Ann.* 3.6) (see further §2). The plebs had been involved in passing the *lex* determining honours for the deceased Germanicus at the start of AD 20 and had pledged to set up statues in his memory (*Tabula Siarensis* = Crawford, 1996: no.37, frag. b, col. ii, lines 27–31 and lines 5–10 = LACTOR 19, J8; Nicolet, 1995). One surviving statue base honouring Germanicus, set up by the urban plebs belonging to the thirty-five voting-tribes (*plebs urbana quinque et triginta tribuum*), appears to have been decided upon after his death (*CIL* VI 909, with Lebek, 1993: 119) and is a pair with another statue base honouring Drusus, which was probably also set up after his death in AD 23 (*CIL* VI 910). The plebs had also attended Germanicus' funeral 'by voting-tribe' (*per tribus*, Tac., *Ann.* 3.4.1), illustrating how these groups provided a focus for their participation in imperial ritual (on the urban plebs acting within their voting-tribes, see Nicolet, 1995).

Lines 155–56: quod cum equestre ordine consenserit pietatemq(ue) suam erga principem nostrum memoriamq(ue) fili eius significaverit / because it joined with the equestrian order in demonstrating its devotion towards our Princeps and the memory of his son Consensus among Rome's social orders was key to supporting the emergence of the imperial family as leaders of Rome (Lobur, 2008: chapter 1). In the final two chapters of the *Res Gestae*, where Augustus summed up his leadership at Rome, he emphasised that he had gained control at Rome in 28/27 BC and continued to be hailed as the 'father of the country' (*pater patriae*) in 2 BC, because he enjoyed the support of the whole of Roman society. In the first instance, he describes his rise to power as 'although by everyone's agreement I had power over everything' (*per consensum universorum potens rerum omnium*, *RGDA* 34.1, with Cooley, 2009: 257–58), whilst his ultimate accolade as 'father of the fatherland' (*pater patriae*) is described as being delivered by 'the Roman Senate and equestrian order and people all together' (*senatus et equester ordo populusque Romanus universus*, *RGDA* 35.1, with Cooley, 2009: 272–73). The importance of consensus continued under Tiberius: in its publication clause at the end of the *Tabula Siarensis*, the Senate explains that its distribution of the decree was intended to demonstrate for all to see how all orders in Roman society shared loyalty (*pietas*) towards the imperial family as well as consensus about the honours being granted to Germanicus: 'And likewise it was agreed that the Senate wished and considered it right, so that the loyalty of all orders towards the Augustan household and the consensus of all citizens in honouring the memory of Germanicus Caesar might more readily be apparent, that the consuls should publish this senatorial decree beneath their edict' (*item senatum uelle atque aequom censere, quo facilius pietas omnium ordinum erga domum Augustam et consensu<s> uniuersorum ciuium memoria honoranda Germanici Caesaris apparet, uti co(n)s(ules) hoc s(enatus) c(onsultum) sub edicto suo proponerent*, Crawford, 1996: no.37, frag. b, col. ii, lines 22–24 = LACTOR 19, J8h). Indeed, the Senate's unusual instructions about distributing copies of its decrees concerning honours for Germanicus and concerning Piso around the empire reflect its eagerness to foster the impression of consensus at a time when consensus was not perhaps guaranteed among the plebs (see 156–58n., **et cum effusissumis studis ad repraesentandam poenam Cn(aei) Pisonis patris ab semet ipsa accensa**

esset; 158n., ***regi tamen exemplo equestris ordinis a principe nostro se passa sit***) and army in particular (see 159–65n.).

Lines 156–58: et cum effusissumis studis ad repraesentandam poenam Cn(aei) Pisonis patris ab semet ipsa accensa esset / and, although with its unrestrained enthusiasm it had roused itself to the point of itself carrying out the punishment of Gnaeus Piso Senior The theme of the plebs' enthusiasm for taking vengeance upon Piso echoes the Senate's praise in the *Tabula Siarensis* for the plebs' enthusiastic commitment to honouring the deceased Germanicus ('{the Senate} praises its {i.e. the plebs'} enthusiasm', *[studi]umque eius probare*, *Tabula Siarensis* = Crawford, 1996: no.37, frag. b, col. ii, line 5 = LACTOR 19, J8g). During Piso's trial, the plebs expressed its hostility towards him in violent demonstrations outside the Senate's meeting-place even whilst the trial was in session. Further, the plebs threatened to carry out a symbolic execution of Piso by toppling his statues from their plinths and dragging them towards the Tiber (Tac., *Ann.* 3.14.4–5; see §7). It was not unlikely that the plebs might even have seized the person of Piso himself to carry out his summary execution had he not been escorted home from the trial by the praetorian guard (Mackay, 2003: 366–67; cf. Suet., *Calig.* 2: 'on account of these things, when Piso returned to Rome, having been almost torn apart by the people, he was condemned by the Senate', *propter quae, ut Romam rediit, paene discerptus a populo, a senatu capitis damnatus est*).

Line 158: regi tamen exemplo equestris ordinis a principe nostro se passa sit / it allowed itself, nevertheless, to follow the example of the equestrian order and be governed by our Princeps The Senate praises the plebs for following the example of the equestrian order in expressing its loyalty towards Tiberius and Germanicus, but at the same time praises it for being governed by Tiberius. This presumably alludes to his edict suspending mourning for Germanicus (Tac., *Ann.* 3.6) and perhaps to his stopping the plebs from destroying Piso's statues whilst the trial was in session (Tac., *Ann.* 3.14.4–5; Lott, 2012: 306). Overall, the demonstrations by the plebs around the trial, as well as the Senate's specific inclusion of the plebs in its decree, illustrate that the plebs at Rome retained political influence in indirect ways, even if not via the voting-system (Eck, 1995b: 7–10). The potential seriousness of the plebs' intention to attack Piso is supported by Tacitus' reference to the need to deploy praetorians to escort him safely home from the trial (*Ann.* 3.14.4).

LINES 159–65 PRAISE FOR THE ARMY

Up to this point, the Senate has focused upon praising constituencies based in Rome – the imperial family, equestrian order, plebs – for their restraint in mourning Germanicus. It now turns to express its expectations of the legions, which were based in the provinces. Whereas also the previous sections focus more upon praising behaviour in the past, this shifts towards expressing hopes for the future (Eck, Caballos, Fernández, 1996: 251). This section is critical for understanding the threat which Piso's activities in Syria were felt to have posed (Rowe, 2002: 165–68). This is also reflected by the Senate's exceptional requirement that the decree should be displayed in legionary winter quarters (see 172n., ***item(que) hoc s(enatus) c(onsultum) in hibernis cuiusq(ue) legionis at signa figeretur***).

Line 159: item senatum probare eorum militum fidem / that likewise the Senate approves of the loyalty of those soldiers All soldiers owed loyalty to Tiberius on at least two counts, since they had sworn the standard military oath of allegiance (*sacramentum*) to him as their commander (cf. *RGDA* 3.3), and since they had probably also pledged their allegiance to him as successor to Augustus (Tac., *Ann.* 1.7.2; Campbell, 1984: 22–27).

Lines 159–60: quorum animi frustra sollicitati essent scelere Cn(aei) Pisonis patris / whose hearts had been tempted in vain by the criminal activity of Gnaeus Piso Senior Piso's criminal activity, as outlined earlier, consisted in corrupting military discipline (see 52–53n., ***qui militarem disciplinam a divo Aug(usto) institutam et servatam a Ti(berio) Caesare Aug(usto) corrupisset***) and distributing bribes to his men before Germanicus' death (see 54–55n., ***donativa suo nomine ex fisco principis nostri dando***) and afterwards seeking to recover Syria, thus provoking civil war (see 45–46n., ***bellum etiam civile excitare conatus sit***). The Senate first focuses its comments only upon those soldiers who had not supported Piso. The report that a few years later the legions of Syria were the only ones not to have placed statues of Sejanus in their legionary shrines (Suet., *Tib.* 48.2) suggests that they did learn a lesson from having been under Piso's command, being much less ready in the future to back a horse not from the imperial stable.

Lines 160–62: omnesq(ue), qui sub auspiciìs et imperió principis nostri milites essent, quam fidem pietatemq(ue) domui Aug(ustae) par͡a͡rent, eam sperare perpetuo praestaturos / and hopes that all who were soldiers under the auspices and command of our Princeps will continue to manifest the same loyalty and devotion to the Imperial House which they used to deliver The Senate now turns to all soldiers. In its eagerness to emphasise that all soldiers had in the past been loyal towards the Imperial House, the Senate glosses over the accusations which it had made earlier, that Piso had successfully won over the support of at least some of his legions, those known as the *Pisoniani* (see 55–56n., ***milites alios Pisonianos, alios Caesarianos dicì laetatus sit***). Instead, the Senate implies here through its use of the verb *sollicitare* ('to tempt', with undertones of 'to pester / importune': *OLD* s.v. '*sollicito*') and elsewhere (see 49n., **milites Romani inter se concurrere coacti sunt**) that these soldiers were unwilling pawns in Piso's criminal game. The Senate thus obscures the risk that some of the army's loyalty had been turned away from Germanicus and even Tiberius, focusing instead upon an impression of the legions' loyal consensus (Lott, 2012: 307).

An army was traditionally thought to fight 'under the auspices' of its commander, but under Augustus it was established that all legions would fight under his auspices (cf. the celebration of thanksgiving sacrifices to the gods voted by the Senate 'on account of affairs successfully accomplished by land and sea by me or though my deputies under my auspices', *ob res a [me aut per legatos] meos auspicis meis terra ma[riqu]e pr[o]spere gestas*, *RGDA* 4.2, with Cooley, 2009: 124; *RGDA* 26.5, describing the armies led into Aethiopia and Arabia as 'under my command and auspices', *meo iussu et auspicio*), rather than those of the commander in the field. As a result, Augustus could claim that 'An army of Dacians which crossed over onto this side of that river was conquered and overwhelmed under my auspices, and afterwards my army was led across the Danube' (*RGDA* 30.2: *citr[a] quod [D]a[cor]u[m tr]an[s]gressus exercitus meis a[u]sp[iciis vict]us profligatusque [es]t, et pos[tea tran]s Danu<v>ium ductus ex[ercitus me]us*). This extended the traditional Roman religious custom whereby military commanders looked for favourable omens (auspices) before proceeding into battle. The phrase 'under the auspices and command of our Princeps' (*sub auspicis et imperio principis nostri*) alludes to Tiberius as supreme military commander by virtue of both his religious leadership in the state and his holding of military authority, formally bestowed upon him in the form of a grant of command over the army (*imperium*). All triumphs were therefore attributable ultimately to Augustus, or rather Tiberius now, instead of to the general in command. This is a further reminder of the idea that close links between Tiberius and the gods were a guarantee of prosperity for Rome (see 162–63n., **cum scirent salutem imperi nostri in eius dom ⌈u⌉ <s> custodia posita<m> esse{t}**).

Lines 162–63: cum scirent salutem imperi nostri in eius dom ⌈u⌉ <s> custodia posita<m> esse{t} / since they knew that the safety of our empire depends on the protection of that House The idea had already been established that Augustus was in a unique position to win the favour of the gods for Rome, consequently acting as the 'guardian of the Roman empire'. It is articulated in the decree from Pisa lamenting the death of Gaius Caesar in AD 4, who is described as the son of Augustus, 'protector of the Roman empire and guardian of the whole world' (*custodis imperi Romani totiusque orbis terrarum praesi[dis]*, *CIL* XI 1421 = LACTOR 17, J61). It is extended to include both Tiberius and other members of the imperial family (*domus Augusta*), an idea which is embedded in other

Tiberian texts too (Eck, Caballos, Fernández, 1996: 253–54, with further references; see §5). This language is echoed, for example, by Velleius Paterculus, who refers to Tiberius after his adoption by Augustus in AD 4 as the 'champion and guardian of Rome's empire' (2.104.2, *uindicem custodemque imperii sui*; on this theme in Velleius, see Schmitzer, 2000: 296). Such sentiments have precedents under the Republic (Woodman, 1977: 136), but what is new is the way in which they become monopolised under Tiberius for referring to members of the imperial family. In this context, the Senate is alluding to Germanicus' importance in successfully accomplishing his overseas mission (see 31–32n., ***desiderantium praesentiam aut ipsius Ti(beri) Caesaris Aug(usti) aut filiorum alterius utrius***) and to Drusus now representing the future of stability for Rome (see 126–27n., ***ut omnem curam, quam in duos quondam filios suos partitus erat, ad eum, quem haberet, converteret***, 128–29n., ***sperareq(ue) senatum eum, qui supersit, ⌈t⌉anto maior⌈i⌉ curae dis immortalibus fore***).

Lines 163–65: senatum arbitrari eorum curae atq(ue) offici esse, ut aput eos ii, qui quandoq(ue) e⌈i⌉<s> praessent, plurumum auctoritatis <haberent>, qui fidelissuma pietate salutare huic urbi imperioq(ue) p(opuli) R(omani) nomen Caesarum coluissent / The Senate believes that it belongs to their concern and duty that, among those who commanded them at any time, the greatest authority with them belonged to those who had with the most devoted loyalty cultivated the name of the Caesars, which gives protection to this city and to the empire of the Roman people Once again, the tortuous syntax of the Senate, piling up subordinate clauses, reflects the difficulties it faces in suggesting that soldiers should not necessarily respect commanders like Piso who do not demonstrate the devotion due to the Caesars (on the significance of syntactical complexity in the decree, see §5). The choice of the expression 'name of the Caesars' deliberately extends the principle of loyalty beyond Tiberius himself to others in the family (see 55–56n., ***milites alios Pisonianos, alios Caesarianos dici laetatus sit***), whilst the verb *colere* is flavoured with ideas of religious worship (Eck, Caballos, Fernández, 1996: 254). In this way, the Senate implicitly supports the position of Germanicus' loyal friend Sentius Saturninus, who took over the governorship of Syria following Germanicus' death, in contrast to Piso, whose disaffection vis-à-vis Germanicus was notorious (Potter, 1999: 74).

LINES 165–72 INSTRUCTIONS FOR PUBLICATION OF THE DECREE

The Senate gives instructions for publishing a variety of documents relating to the trial of Piso. This is far from standard procedure, given that the vast majority of senatorial decrees was never disseminated in this way (Cooley, 2012). Firstly, a speech delivered by Tiberius and the Senate's decree(s) inscribed on bronze (see 169n., ***itemq(ue) haec senatus consulta in {h}aere incisa***) are to be put on display at Rome in a location of Tiberius' choosing. Secondly, the Senate's decree is to be inscribed on bronze and set up in the most frequented place of the most populous city of each province (see 170–72n., ***item hoc s(enatus) c(onsultum) {hic} in cuiusque provinciae celeberruma{e} urbe eiusque i<n> urbis ipsius celeberrimo loco in aere incisum figeretur***). It is also to be set up at the winter quarters of each legion, possibly on whiteboards rather than inscribed on bronze (see 172n., ***item(que) hoc s(enatus) c(onsultum) in hibernis cuiusq(ue) legionis at signa figeretur***). If the Senate's instructions for publication were followed, the decree would have been displayed in over fifty different places (in thirty provincial cities and twenty-five legionary camps, on the estimate of Hurlet, 2006: 56 n.28), whilst the fact that so many copies have been identified in the province of Baetica alone (see §4) suggests that this total may have been exceeded. The Senate's instructions for publishing its decree in multiple places in a monumental format are explicit in aiming to record its version of events for the instruction of later generations (see 165–66n., ***et quo facilius totius actae rei ordo posterorum memoriae tradi posset***). This is a distinctive feature of the crisis around the death of Germanicus. In the *Tabula Siarensis*, likewise, the Senate states that its aim in publishing its decree is to illustrate remembrance of Germanicus: 'And likewise it was agreed that the Senate wished and considered it right, so that the loyalty of all orders towards the Augustan household and the consensus of all citizens in honouring the memory of Germanicus Caesar might more readily be apparent, that the consuls should publish this senatorial decree beneath their edict' (*item senatum uelle atque aequom censere, quo facilius pietas omnium ordinum erga domum Augustam et consensu<s> uniuersorum ciuium memoria honoranda Germanici Caesaris apparet, uti co(n)s(ules) hoc s(enatus) c(onsultum) sub edicto suo proponerent*, Crawford, 1996: no.37, frag. b, col. ii, lines 22–24 = LACTOR 19, J8h). In that case, however, the Senate does not mandate its monumentalisation via a bronze inscription; its publication instructions target audiences that are distinct from those covered by the *SCPP* (Eck, Caballos, Fernández, 1996: 265–66). This all marks a significant shift in senatorial procedure, with the *SCPP* disseminating a political message rather than simply being a summary record of deliberations held in the Senate (Giua, 2002: 112–14).

Lines 165–66: et quo facilius totius actae rei ordo posterorum memoriae tradi posset / And in order that the course of the proceedings as a whole might be more easily transmitted to the memory of future generations The Senate explicitly addresses future generations, just as Tiberius had declared a similar purpose for his eulogy of Germanicus, which he had delivered in the Senate in AD 19: he 'judged it to be useful to the youth of the next generation and of generations to come' (*esse utile iuuentuti liberorum* *posteriorumque nostrorum iudicaret, Tabula Siarensis* = Crawford, 1996: no.37, frag. b, col. ii, line 17 = LACTOR 19, J8g).

Lines 166–68: atque hi scire\<nt\>, quid et de singulari moderatione Germ(anici) Caesa(ris) et de sceleribus Cn(aei) Pisonis patris senatus iudicasset / and so that they might know what the Senate's judgement was concerning the exceptional restraint of Germanicus Caesar and the crimes of Gnaeus Piso Senior Whereas the heading of Copy A (see note on Heading, *s(enatus) c(onsultum) de Cn(aeo) Pisone patre*) gives the impression that the *SCPP* is focused upon Piso himself, the Senate summarises the decree as demonstrating both Germanicus' exceptional restraint and Piso's crimes.

Line 168: placere uti oratio, quam recitasset princeps noster / the Senate has decided that the speech which our Princeps had delivered The Senate does not specify which speech delivered by Tiberius is to be put on display. Although it has been suggested (Mackay, 2003: 315) that the Senate's vagueness in this respect is surprising if Tiberius delivered more than one speech and that consequently the speech which he made at the start of the trial (of which Tacitus gives us a version, *Ann.* 3.12) must be the one in view here (compare also Eck, Caballos, Fernández, 1996: 136), it does seem more likely that Tiberius did speak more than once at the trial. In addition to his opening speech, it seems that he intervened on more than one occasion for Marcus Piso (see 8n., **uti precum suarum pro adulescente memor is ordo esset**) and Plancina (see 111–12n., **et saepe princeps noster accurateq(ue) ab eo ordine petierit**) and also made a speech on 10 December after Piso's suicide introducing the *relatio* of the present decree. It is unlikely that Tiberius' speeches in favour of Marcus or Plancina were to be memorialised, but it seems equally possible that the inscription was to display either the speech which he made right at the start of the trial or the one which he delivered after Piso's suicide (Eck, Caballos, Fernández, 1996: 258, however, conclude in favour of his opening speech). The decision to display this speech in the city of Rome (and not elsewhere) suggests that the Senate regarded the speech as relevant to the capital, perhaps as an illustration of Tiberius' justice and moderation in his treatment of a high-ranking senator (Mackay, 2003: 315) or as an attempt to persuade the plebs that the due process of law had been observed. Similarly, in December AD 19, the Senate had instructed that Tiberius' eulogy of Germanicus, which he had delivered in the Senate, was to be inscribed on bronze and displayed publicly (*Tabula Siarensis* = Crawford, 1996: no.37, frag. b, col. ii, lines 11–13 = LACTOR 19, J8g).

Line 169: itemq(ue) haec senatus consulta in {h}aere incisa / and also these decrees of the Senate, inscribed on bronze The reference here to the plural, 'these decrees of the Senate', has provoked debate about the nature of this inscription (see 11n., *d(e) i(is) r(ebus) i(ta) c(ensuerunt)*). The most straightforward interpretation (Eck, Caballos, Fernández, 1996: 259–64; Griffin, 1997: 254; Barnes, 1998: 128) sees this as an allusion to multiple decrees to be displayed in Rome, which are distinct from the present decree, referred to in the singular (see 74–75, ***si hoc senatus consultum factum non esset***, 170–72n., ***item hoc s(enatus) c(onsultum) {hic} in cuiusque provinciae celeberruma{e} urbe eiusque i<n> urbis ipsius celeberrimo loco in aere incisum figeretur***), which was sent to the provinces and the legions' winter quarters. Mackay (2003: 315) argues, however, that the wording 'these decrees' (*haec senatus consulta*) also refers to the current decree, alluding to different clauses in a single decree rather than to multiple decrees. It would be unexpected if the demonstrative pronoun, 'these'/'this' (*haec/hoc*), were to have a different meaning within the space of two lines. It is also possible that the plural is an error of engraving, given that a singular verb (*poneretur*) is used in both Copy A and Copy B (which is editorially corrected to *ponere<n>tur*). Mackay (2003: 319) concludes: 'Thus, when conceived of in terms of the subcategory *relationes*, the senate passed several *senatus consulta*, but when the totality of the subcategory *relationes* is viewed as a single *relatio*, then one *senatus consultum* resulted.' What is clear, though, is that the text that we have preserved on bronze is an account of the Senate's proceedings which has been edited specifically for distribution in the provinces and to the army.

Lines 169–70: quo loco Ti(berio) Caes(ari) Aug(usto) videretur, ponere<n>tur / should be set up in whatever place seemed best to Tiberius Caesar Augustus The Senate's deference to Tiberius recalls its similar request in the *Tabula Siarensis* for Tiberius to feel free to change the proposed location of the arch honouring Germanicus in Syria and its referral to him of the decision of where to display an inscribed copy of his speech honouring Germanicus which he had delivered in the Senate (Crawford, 1996: no.37, frag. a, lines 22–24 and frag. b, col. ii, lines 12–13 = LACTOR 19, J8c, J8g). Two obvious possibilities would be outside the Mausoleum of Augustus or in the portico of the Temple of Apollo on the Palatine, to complement the previous display of inscriptions honouring Germanicus in those two locations (*Tabula Siarensis*: Crawford, 1996: no.37, frag. b, col. i, lines 5–6; frag. b, col. ii, lines 20–21 = LACTOR 19, J8f, J8h).

Lines 170–72: item hoc s(enatus) c(onsultum) {hic} in cuiusque provinciae celeberruma{e} urbe eiusque i<n> urbis ipsius celeberrimo loco in aere incisum figeretur / and that likewise this decree of the Senate, inscribed on bronze, should be set up in the most frequented city of each province and in the most frequented place in that city The requirement to set up an inscription or statue in the 'most frequented place' of a city is a standard formula, as also seen, for example, in the municipal decree honouring M. Nonius Balbus, the preeminent benefactor at Herculaneum during the Augustan era: 'it pleases the town councillors that an equestrian statue be set up to him in the most frequented place' (*placere decurionibus statuam equestrem ei poni quam celeberrimo loco*, *AE* 1976, 144 = LACTOR 17, K73). Later examples include the publication clause for the Flavian municipal law on the *Tabula Irnitana*, section 95 (González and Crawford, 1986 = LACTOR 20, Section F) and a bronze tablet inscribed with a copy of a letter from Sex. Fadius Secundus Musa (*CIL* XII 4393, AD 149, Narbo). The requirement for the *SCPP* to be set up in the most frequented city of each province is paralleled in the *Tabula Siarensis*, but in that case there is no mention of inscribing on bronze, so it is more likely that the text of the decree concerning honours for Germanicus was published on whiteboards only and so implicitly intended only for temporary display (Eck, Caballos, Fernández, 1996: 256 n.835).

Line 172: item(que) hoc s(enatus) c(onsultum) in hibernis cuiusq(ue) legionis at signa figeretur / and that likewise this decree of the Senate should be set up in the winter quarters of each legion where the standards are kept   Each legion had a permanent base where it spent the winter months when it was not on campaign. Each base included a legionary shrine containing the legion's standards and images of Tiberius and his family (Eck, Caballos, Fernández, 1996: 269–70; Lott, 2012: 310). The unparalleled publication of the *SCPP* in legionary winter quarters reflects the deep concerns felt about Piso's alleged interference with military discipline and attempts to align his soldiers more closely with his own interests (Eck, Caballos, Fernández, 1996: 266–67). This potentially threatened Tiberius' position, given that maintaining the loyalty of the army was the basis of his own authority (Zecchini, 1999: 330–31). These copies were not necessarily on bronze, given that the Senate does not specify a medium; it is more likely that they were displayed on whiteboards. In addition, the text of the *SCPP* may have been read out aloud before the troops (Eck, Caballos, Fernández, 1996: 270).

LINE 172–73 SENATORIAL PROCEDURE

Lines 172–73: censuerunt. in senatu fuerunt CCCI / Decree passed. There were 301 present in the Senate   This statistic about the number of senators present in the Senate to pass the decree hints at a lack of enthusiasm on the part of the senatorial order for taking part in this business, given that 301 senators would represent only about half the total number of roughly 600 members (Eck, 1997: 133). Even though it would have been routine for around eighty senators to be absent from Rome, on service abroad (Talbert, 1984: 145), the number voting on Piso's decree is significantly fewer than could be expected. Similarly, only 285 senators were present to vote honours for Germanicus in December AD 19 (*Tabula Siarensis* = Crawford, 1996: no.37, frag. b, col. ii, line 30 = LACTOR 19, J8h). Although we do not have many details of numbers present at individual senatorial meetings, it is striking that higher numbers are attested in cases of voting for routine business in the Senate. In AD 26, for example, 407 senators voted on allowing a second temple to be built for Augustus in Asia (Aristid., *Or.* 19.13), whilst in AD 47, 383 senators voted on building-regulations (*CIL* X 1401 = LACTOR 19, K33; Eck, Caballos, Fernández, 1996: 270–71; Zecchini, 1999: 326). Despite the fulsome rhetoric composed by the drafting committee, therefore, the absence of a large number of senators suggests that support for Tiberius was not perhaps as strong as the *SCPP* implies (Zecchini, 1999). This may also account for the tendency towards using hyperbolic language, as the drafting committee tried to compensate for the lack of senators attending the meeting.

Line 173: hoc s(enatus) c(onsultum) factum est per relationem solum / This senatorial decree was passed in accordance with a single proposal There has been considerable debate about the meaning of the phrase *per relationem solum* here and the similar phrase *h(oc) s(enatus) c(onsultum) per relationem secundam factum est unum* in the *Tabula Siarensis* (frag. II, col. b, line 30 = Crawford, 1996: no.37 = LACTOR 19, J8h; debate summarised in Lott, 2012: 236–37, who translates this at 97 as 'This senate decree alone was approved in accordance with the second *relatio*', in contrast to 'This decree of the senate was made one by a second *relatio*' in Crawford, 1996: 529). Initially, it was suggested that the phrase in the *SCPP* means 'by proposal only' (Griffin, 1997: 253; Potter, 1998: 457, both following Eck, Caballos, Fernández, 1996: 51, 271–72). In other words, there was neither discussion nor voting on the matters presented to the Senate in Tiberius' proposal (*relatio*), and the decree was passed without any debate (cf. Nicolet, 1988: 839; Barnes, 1998: 128). In a detailed discussion, however, Mackay (2003, 322–37) argues that such a process would be designated instead by the phrase *per discessionem* ('in accordance with a division', i.e. with senators indicating how they were voting on the matter without any preceding discussion). A discussion of senatorial procedure in Aulus Gellius (*NA* 14.7.12), a second-century AD antiquarian, which draws upon both Varro and Ateius Capito, is not quite as decisive as we would like in helping to explain the phrase. On the one hand, Varro is cited as describing how there were two methods of passing a senatorial decree – either by the giving of opinions or by division for a vote (*aut conquisitis sententiis aut per discessionem*) – but Gellius goes on to observe that, according to Ateius Capito, all decrees required a division for voting. The context of the phrase in the *SCPP* also challenges the original interpretation, given that it is clear from both Tacitus and from the

SCPP itself that, on the contrary, there had been discussion about how the Senate should respond to Piso's case in its decree. Crucially, the format of Tiberius' *relatio* itself makes it clear that he was requiring the Senate to express views on the questions in hand: he did not phrase it in such a way that the Senate could simply parrot it as an answer (see 4–11n.). In conclusion, the phrase in the *SCPP* indicates that the Senate passed its decree following debate and a vote on the basis of a single proposal (*relatio*) put to it by Tiberius, in contrast to the situation in the *Tabula Siarensis,* where Tiberius brought two proposals (*relationes*) before the Senate on the day of the debate.

LINES 174–76 ADDENDUM (*SUBSCRIPTIO*) BY TIBERIUS

This final subsection is unparalleled in any other extant senatorial decree. Tiberius personally vouches for the accuracy of the decree and instructs for it to be deposited formally in the archives. These three lines of text are the first utterance of Tiberius known in Latin from an inscription. Brief though they are, they can give some insight into Tiberius' self-presentation (see 174n., **Ti(berius) Caesar Aug(ustus) trib(unicia) potestate XXII manu mea scripsi**; Eck, Caballos, Fernández, 1996: 275). The personal tone of the subscript, which is written in the first person, is a formal indication that Tiberius himself has approved the text of the decree, which had been passed in response to a motion which he himself had introduced to the Senate, but at whose drafting he had not been present. This is contrary to the norm, since usually a convenor (*relator*) would be expected to chair the drafting committee: his absence therefore perhaps prompted the need for him to approve the decree in this subscript (Eck, 1993b: 204). It demonstrates Tiberius' active collaboration with the Senate, since he represents himself as approving the decree before giving instructions for it to be archived.

Line 174: Ti(berius) Caesar Aug(ustus) trib(unicia) potestate XXII manu mea scripsi / I, Tiberius Caesar Augustus, holder of tribunician power for the twenty-second time, wrote this with my own hand The fact that Tiberius here records only his tribunician power (contrast the fuller set of titles at the start of the decree in the *relatio*) reflects the fact that he must have summoned the Senate to a meeting and put his proposal (*relatio*) for discussion to it by virtue of his tribunician power (see 5n., **tribunicia potestate XXII**; Meyer, 1998: 317). On his use of the title Augustus, see 4n., **Ti(berius) Caesar divi Aug(usti) f(ilius) Aug(ustus)**. The editing of senatorial decrees was usually chaired by the magistrate who had presided over the meeting of the Senate (Coudry, 1994: 71–72). By contrast, Tiberius does not appear to have been involved in the editing process, even though he had introduced the matters for discussion to the Senate. This addendum may therefore have seemed necessary in order to confirm that the convenor (*relator*) had read and approved of the committee's version of events.

Line 175: Cotta et Messalla co(n)s(ulibus) / in the year when Cotta and Messalla were consuls Both consuls of AD 20 – M. Aurelius Cotta Maximus Messallinus (*PIR*² A1487) and his nephew M. Valerius Messalla Messallinus (*PIR*² V145) – were related to the distinguished consul of 31 BC, M. Valerius Messalla Corvinus (Lebek, 1999: 184–85), the former his son and the latter his grandson (as son of the senator named first in the list of the drafting committee; see 2n., **M(arcus) Valerius M(arci) f(ilius) Lem(onia tribu) Messallinus**; Eck, Caballos, Fernández, 1996: 100–01). Tacitus records that Aurelius Cotta was invited to give the first response in the debate about Piso following his suicide (*Ann.* 3. 17.4).

Lines 175–76: scriptum manu Auli q(uaestoris) mei in tabellis XIIII / copied by the hand of my quaestor Aulus on fourteen tablets This quaestor named Aulus is probably to be identified with Aulus Plautius, who went on to be urban praetor in AD 26 and then suffect consul in the second half of AD 29 (Eck, Caballos, Fernández, 1996: 104–05; *PIR*² P457). He would have taken up his post as one of two *quaestores Augusti* on 5 December of AD 20. Tiberius delegated to him the task of writing out the decree on wooden tablets coated with wax: the use of the verb *scriptum* rather than *descriptum*, which is the normal verb to indicate the making of an official copy of a text, suggests that Aulus Plautius may actually have written out the text as Tiberius' representative in the presence of the drafting committee, even though he is not named in the prescript (Eck, Caballos, Fernández, 1996: 274–75). Although De Martino (1996: 468–69) wonders whether 176 lines of text (as in Copy A) would be too tight a squeeze to fit on fourteen tablets, Eck, Caballos, and Fernández (1996: 277–78) calculate that the *SCPP* contained around 12,500 characters in total, including spaces, and suggest that each tablet would have been double-faced, giving a total of twenty-eight sides of writing. They further reckon that around 445 characters per side is consistent with the amount of writing typically found on wax tablets from the Murecine archive of the Sulpicii. Given the emphasis on Tiberius having checked the copy of the decree being made by his quaestor, it is likely that the copy deposited in the archive was a complete version rather than a summary of what is inscribed. It would have been normal procedure for one of the two urban quaestors, who had also been involved in the drafting process, to be charged with depositing the decree in the archives (Lott, 2012: 32). It is likely, therefore, that Aulus Plautius only wrote out the decree, whilst one of the urban quaestors would have been in charge of archiving it in the *aerarium* (see 176n., ***referri in tabulas pub<l>icas***). It is odd that Tiberius alludes to his quaestor by *praenomen* only: this could be an indication of the level of trust between *princeps* and quaestor (Eck, Caballos, Fernández, 1996: 103), or of the fact that this subscript was not perhaps intended to be included in the publication of the decree (Eck, Caballos, Fernández, 1996: 272).

Line 176: referri in tabulas pub<l>icas / should be placed in the public archives A senatorial decree was only valid once it had been deposited in the public archive of the treasury at the Temple of Saturn (*aerarium Saturni*) in the Roman Forum, under the supervision of the urban quaestors (Talbert, 1984: 303).

Bibliography

Abramenko, A. (1993) 'Othonianus. Zur Genese von cognomina aus militärischer Terminologie', *Zeitschrift für Papyrologie und Epigraphik* 95: 226–28.

Allison, J.E. and Cloud, D. (1962) 'The *lex Julia Maiestatis*', *Latomus* 21.4: 711–31.

Alpers, M. (1995) *Das nachrepublikanische Finanzsystem. Fiscus und Fisci in der frühen Kaiserzeit* (Berlin / New York: De Gruyter).

Amarelli, F. (1983) *Consilia principum* (Naples: Jovene).

Ando, C. (2011) *Law, Language, and Empire in the Roman Tradition* (Philadelphia, PA: University of Pennsylvania Press).

Andrade, N. (2012) 'Seducing autocracy: Tacitus and the dynasts of the Near East', *American Journal of Philology* 133.3: 441–75.

Arnaud, P. (1994) '"Transmarinae provinciae": réflexions sur les limites géographiques et sur la nature des pouvoirs en Orient des "corégents" sous les règnes d'Auguste et de Tibère', *Cahiers du Centre Gustave Glotz* 5: 221–53.

Balmaceda, C. (2014) 'The virtues of Tiberius in Velleius' "Histories"', *Historia* 63.3: 340–63.

Balmaceda, C. (2017) Virtus Romana: *Politics and Morality in the Roman Historians* (Chapel Hill, NC: University of North Carolina Press).

Bargagli, B. and Grosso, C. (1997) *I Fasti Ostienses*, Itinerari Ostiensi 8 (Rome: Ministero per i beni culturali e ambientali, Soprintendenza archeologica di Ostia).

Barnes, T.D. (1998) 'Tacitus and the "Senatus Consultum de Cn. Pisone Patre"', *Phoenix* 52: 125–48.

Barrandon, J.-N., Suspène, A., Gaffiero, A. (2010) 'Les émissions d'as au type Divvs Avgvstvs Pater frappées sous Tibère: l'apport des analyses à leur datation et à leur interprétation', *Revue numismatique* 166: 149–73.

Barrett, A. (2002) *Livia: First Lady of Imperial Rome* (New Haven, CT: Yale University Press).

Bartels, J. (2009) 'Der Tod des Germanicus und seine epigraphische Dokumentation: Ein neues Exemplar des *senatus consultum de Cn. Pisone patre* aus Genf', *Chiron* 39: 1–9.

Bauman, R.A. (1989) *Lawyers and Politics in the Early Roman Empire: A Study of Relations between the Roman Jurists and the Emperors from Augustus to Hadrian* (Munich: C.H. Beck).

Bauman, R.A. (1996) *Crime and Punishment in Ancient Rome* (London: Routledge).

Bellemore, J. (1989) 'When did Valerius Maximus write the *Dicta et Facta Memorabilia*?', *Antichthon* 23: 67–80.

Bennett, A. (2015) '"It's readable all right, but it's not history." Robert Graves's Claudius novels and the impossibility of historical fiction', in A.G.G. Gibson (ed.), *Robert Graves and the Classical Tradition*, 21–41 (Oxford: Oxford University Press).

Béranger, J. (1953) *Recherches sur l'aspect idéologique du principat* (Basel: F. Reinhardt).

Bird, H.W. (1987) 'Tiberius, Piso and Germanicus: further considerations', *Acta Classica* 30: 72–75.

Bloomer, W.M. (1992) *Valerius Maximus and the Rhetoric of the New Nobility* (Chapel Hill, NC and London: University of North Carolina Press).

Bloomer, W.M. (1997) *Latinity and Literary Society at Rome* (Philadelphia, PA: University of Pennsylvania Press).

Boatwright, M.T. (2021) *Imperial Women of Rome. Power, Gender, Context* (New York: Oxford University Press).

Bodel, J. (1999) 'Punishing Piso', *American Journal of Philology* 120.1: 43–63.

Bonnefond-Coudry, M. (1989) *Le Sénat de la République Romaine de la Guerre d'Hannibal à Auguste: pratiques délibératives et prise de décision* (Rome: École française de Rome).

Briscoe, J. (2019) *Valerius Maximus, 'Facta et Dicta Memorabilia', Book 8. Text, Introduction, and Commentary*, Untersuchungen zur antiken Literatur und Geschichte 141 (Berlin / Boston, MA: De Gruyter).

Broughton, T.R.S. (1952) *The Magistrates of the Roman Republic*, vol. 2 (New York: American Philological Association).

Brouwer, H.H.J. (1989) *Bona Dea. The Sources and a Description of the Cult*, Études préliminaires aux religions orientales dans l'empire romain 110 (Leiden: Brill).

Brunt, P.A. (1966) 'The "fiscus" and its development', *Journal of Roman Studies* 56: 75–91.

Bruun, C. (2006) 'Der Kaiser und die stadtrömischen *curae*: Geschichte und Bedeutung', in A. Kolb (ed.), *Herrschaftsstrukturen und Herrschaftspraxis. Konzepte, Prinzipien und Strategien der Administration im römischen Kaiserreich*, 89–114 (Berlin: Akademie Verlag).

Burnett, A. (1977) 'The authority to coin in the late Republic and early Empire', *Numismatic Chronicle* 17.137: 37–63.

Burnett, A., Amandry, M., Ripollès, P.P. (1992) *Roman Provincial Coinage*, vol. 1: *From the Death of Caesar to the Death of Vitellius (44 BC–AD 69). Part I: Introduction and Catalogue* (London / Paris: British Museum Press / Bibliothèque nationale de France) [=*RPC* I].

Burton, P. (1995) 'The values of a classical education: satirical elements in Robert Graves's *Claudius* novels', *Review of English Studies* n.s. 46.182: 191–218.

Caballos, A. (2002) 'El Senatconsult de Gneu Pisó pare / El senadoconsulto de Gneo Pisón padre', in R. Comes, I. Rodà (eds), Scripta Manent. *La memòria escrita dels romans/ La memoria escrita de los romanos*, 78–109 (Barcelona: Museu d'Arqueologia de Catalunya).

Caballos, A., Eck, W., Fernández, F. (1996) *El Senadoconsulto de Gneo Pisón Padre* (Seville: Universidad de Sevilla / Consejería de Cultura, Junta de Andalucía).

Caballos Rufino, A. (2009) 'Publicación de documentos públicos en las ciudades del Occidente romano: el ejemplo de la Bética', in R. Haensch (ed.), *Selbstdarstellung und Kommunikation. Die Veröffentlichung staatlicher Urkunden auf Stein und Bronze in der römischen Welt*, Vestigia 61, 131–72 (Munich: C.H. Beck).

Caballos Rufino, A. (2018) 'Monumenta fatiscunt. Meaning and fate of legal inscriptions on bronze: the Baetica', in A. Kolb (ed.), *Literacy in Ancient Everyday Life*, 289–317 (Berlin / Boston, MA: De Gruyter).

Caballos Rufino, A., Eck, W., Fernández Gómez, F. (1994a) 'Senatus consultum de Cn. Pisone patre. Informe preliminar', in *Actas del II Congreso de Historia de Andalucía. Cordoba, 1991. Historia antigua*, 159–71 (Córdoba: Instituto de Historia de Andalucia).

Caballos Rufino, A., Eck, W., Fernández Gómez, F. (1994b) 'Nuevas aportaciones al análisis del s.c. de Cn. Pisone patre', in P. Sáez and S. Ordóñez (eds), *Homenaje al Profesor Presedo*, 319–32 (Seville: Universidad de Sevilla).

Caballos Rufino, A., Fernández Gómez, F. (1999) 'Novedades, estado de la cuestión y expectativas de la epigrafía en bronce en Andalucía', in *XI Congresso Internazionale di Epigrafia Greca e Latina. Roma, 28–24 settembre 1997. Atti I*, 653–60 (Rome: Quasar).

Calboli, G. (1998) 'Le *Senatus Consultum de Cn. Pisone patre*, quelques considérations linguistiques', in B. Bureau, C. Nicolas (eds), *Moussyllanea. Mélanges de linguistique et de littérature anciennes offerts à Claude Moussy*, 117–30 (Louvain / Paris: Editions Peeters).

Calomino, D. (2015) 'Emperor or god? The posthumous commemoration of Augustus in Rome and the provinces', *Numismatic Chronicle* 175: 57–82.

Camodeca, G. (2008) *I ceti dirigenti di rango senatorio equestre e decurionale della Campania romana* (Naples: Satura Editrice).

Campbell, J.B. (1984) *The Emperor and the Roman Army, 31 BC–AD 235* (Oxford: Clarendon Press).

Carroll, K.K. (1979) 'The date of Boudicca's revolt', *Britannia* 10: 197–202.

Castro-Camero, R. de (2000) *El crimen maiestatis a la luz del senatus consultum de Cn. Pisone patre* (Seville: Universidad de Sevilla).

Cébeillac, M. (1972) *Les "Quaestores principis et candidati" aux Ier et IIème siècles de l'Empire* (Milan: Cisalpino-Goliardica).

Champlin, E. (1999) 'The first (1996) edition of the "Senatus Consultum de Cn. Pisone Patre": a review', *American Journal of Philology* 120.1: 117–22.

Chilton, C.W. (1955) 'The Roman law of treason under the early Principate', *Journal of Roman Studies* 45: 73–81.

Chilver, G.E.F. (1979) *A Historical Commentary on Tacitus' Histories I and II* (Oxford: Clarendon Press).

Chilver, G.E.F. and Townsend, G.B. (1985) *A Historical Commentary on Tacitus' Histories IV and V* (Oxford: Clarendon Press).

Christes, J. (1994) 'Tacitus und die *moderatio* des Tiberius', *Gymnasium* 101: 112–35.

Cipollone, M. (2012) 'Un frammento del *senatus consultum de honoribus Germanici* al Museo Archeologico di Perugia', *Epigraphica* 74: 83–107.

Clark, A.J. (2007) *Divine Qualities. Cult and Community in Republican Rome*, Oxford Classical Monographs (Oxford: Oxford University Press).

Classen, C.J. (1991) 'Virtutes imperatoriae', *Arctos* 25: 17–39.

Coarelli, F. (1993) 'Campus Agrippae', in *LTUR* I, 217.

Coarelli, F. (1996) 'Porta Fontinalis', in *LTUR* III, 329.

Coarelli, F. (2003) 'Il *s.c. de Cn. Pisone patre*. I dati topografici', *Eutopia* ns 3.1–2: 65–74.

Cooley, A.E. (1998) 'The moralizing message of the *senatus consultum de Cn. Pisone patre*', *Greece and Rome* 45.2: 199–212.

Cooley, A.E. (2007) 'The publication of Roman official documents in the Greek East', in K. Lomas, R.D. Whitehouse, J.B. Wilkins (eds), *Literacy and the State in the Ancient Mediterranean*, Accordia Specialist Studies on the Mediterranean 7, 203–16 (London: Accordia Research Institute).

Cooley, A.E. (2009) Res Gestae divi Augusti*: Text, Translation, and Commentary* (Cambridge: Cambridge University Press).

Cooley, A.E. (2012) 'From document to monument: inscribing Roman official documents in the Greek East', in J.K. Davies, J. Wilkes (eds), *Epigraphy and the Historical Sciences*, Proceedings of the British Academy 177, 159–82 (Oxford: Oxford University Press).

Cooley, A.E. (2014) 'Paratextual perspectives upon the *SC de Pisone patre*', in L. Jansen (ed.), *The Roman Paratext: Frame, Texts, Readers*, 143–55 (Cambridge: Cambridge University Press).

Cooley, A.E. (2015) 'Paratextual readings of imperial discourse in the *Res Gestae divi Augusti*', *Cahiers du Centre Gustave Glotz* 25 [2014]: 215–30.

Cooley, A.E. (2019) 'From the Augustan Principate to the invention of the age of Augustus', *Journal of Roman Studies* 109: 71–87.

Cooley, A.E. (forthcoming) 'Debating Tiberian political discourse', in C. Kuhn (ed.).

Corbeill, A. (2004) *Nature Embodied. Gesture in Ancient Rome* (Princeton, NJ / Oxford: Princeton University Press).

Corbier, M. (1974) *L'aerarium Saturni et l'aerarium militare: administration et prosopographie sénatoriale* (Rome: École française de Rome).

Corbier, M. (1992) 'De la maison d'Hortensius à la *curia* sur la Palatin', *Mélanges de l'École française de Rome* 104.2: 871–916.

Corbier, M. (1994) 'A propos de la Tabula Siarensis: le Sénat, Germanicus et la domus Augusta', in J. González (ed.), *Roma y las provincias. Realidad administrativa e ideología imperial*, 39–85 (Madrid: Ediciones Clásicas).

Corbier, M. (2001a) 'Le "Principatus" de Jean Béranger à la lumière des découvertes épigraphiques récentes', in R. Frei-Stolba, K. Gex (eds), *Recherches récentes sur le monde hellénistique. Actes du colloque international organisé à l'occasion du 60e anniversaire de Pierre Ducrey (Lausanne, 20–21 novembre 1998)*, 309–20 (Bern: Peter Lang).

Corbier, M. (2001b) '*Maiestas domus Augustae*', in G. Angeli Bertinelli, A. Donati (eds), *Varia Epigraphica. Atti del Colloquio Internazionale di Epigrafia Bertinoro, 8–10 giugno 2000*, Epigrafia e Antichità 17, 155–99 (Faenza: Fratelli Lega Editori).

Corbier, M. (2006) *Donner à voir, donner à lire. Mémoire et communication dans la Rome ancienne* (Paris: CNRS Editions).

Coudry, M. (1994) 'Sénatus-consultes et *acta senatus*: rédaction, conservation et archivage des documents émanant du sénat, de l'époque de César à celle des Sévères', in S. Demougin (ed.), *La mémoire perdue. A la recherche des archives oubliées, publiques et privées, de la Rome antique*, 65–102 (Paris: Publications de la Sorbonne).

Cowan, E. (2009a) 'Tacitus, Tiberius and Augustus', *Classical Antiquity* 28.2: 179–210.

Cowan, E. (2009b) 'Tiberius and Augustus in Tiberian sources', *Historia* 58.4: 468–85.

Cowan, E. (2011a) 'Introduction', in E. Cowan (ed.), *Velleius Paterculus: Making History*, ix–xiii (Swansea: The Classical Press of Wales).

Cowan, E. (ed.) (2011b) *Velleius Paterculus: Making History* (Swansea: The Classical Press of Wales).
Cowan, E. (2016) 'Contesting *clementia*: the rhetoric of *severitas* in Tiberian Rome before and after the trial of Clutorius Priscus', *Journal of Roman Studies* 106: 77–101.
Cox, S.E. (2005) 'The mark of the successor: tribunician power and the *ara Providentia* under Tiberius and Vespasian', *Numismatica e Antichità Classiche* 34: 251–70.
Crawford, M.H. (ed.) (1996) *Roman Statutes*, vol. 1, Bulletin of the Institute of Classical Studies Suppl. 64 (London: Institute of Classical Studies).
Crifò, G. (1963) 'Sul "consilium" del magistrato', *Studia et documenta historiae et iuris* 29: 296–309.
Crook, J.A. (1955) *Consilium principis: Imperial Councils and Counsellors from Augustus to Diocletian* (Cambridge: Cambridge University Press).
Csillag, P. (1976) *The Augustan Laws on Family Relations* (Budapest: Akadémiai Kiadó).
Daitz, S.G. (1960) 'Tacitus' technique of character portrayal', *American Journal of Philology* 81: 30–52.
Damon, C. (1999a) '*Relatio* vs. *oratio*: Tacitus, *Ann.* 3.12 and the *senatus consultum de Cn. Pisone patre*', *Classical Quarterly* 49.1: 336–38.
Damon, C. (1999b) 'The trial of Cn. Piso in Tacitus' Annals and the "Senatus Consultum de Cn. Pisone Patre": new light on narrative technique', *American Journal of Philology* 120.1: 143–62.
Damon, C. and Takács, S. (1999) 'Introduction', *American Journal of Philology* 120.1: 1–12.
David, J.-M. (1998) 'Les enjeux de l'exemplarité à la fin de la République et au début du Principat', in J.-M. David (ed.), *Valeurs et mémoire à Rome. Valère Maxime ou la vertu recomposée*, 9–17 (Paris: De Boccard).
De Martino, F. (1996) 'Intorno al senatusconsulto *de Pisone patre*', in L.B. Pulci Doria (ed.), *L'incidenza dell'antico. Studi in memoria di Ettore Lepore*, vol. 2, 465–88 (Naples: Luciano Editore).
De Monte, J. (1999) 'Velleius Paterculus and "Triumphal History"', *Ancient History Bulletin* 13.4: 121–35.
Degrassi, A. (1963) *Inscriptiones Italiae XIII, Fasti et Elogia. Fasc. II, Fasti Anni Numani et Iuliani* (Rome: Istituto Poligrafico dello Stato / Libreria dello Stato).
Devillers, O. (2003) *Tacite et les sources des* Annales. *Enquêtes sur la méthode historique* (Louvain / Paris / Dudley, MA: Peeters).
Di Vita-Évrard, G. (1990) 'IRT 520, le proconsulat de Cn. Calpurnius Piso et l'insertion de Lepcis Magna dans la provincia Africa', in *L'Afrique dans l'Occident romain (Ier siècle av. J.-C.–IVe siècle ap. J.-C.). Actes du colloque organisé par l'École française de Rome sous le patronage de l'Institut national d'archéologie et d'art de Tunis (Rome, 3–5 décembre 1987)*, 315–31 (Rome: École française de Rome).
Di Vita-Évrard, G. (1993) 'Les fastes des *sodales Augustales*', in M. Mayer (ed.), Religio Deorum. *Actas del coloquio internacional de epigrafía culto y sociedad en occidente*, 471–84 (Barcelona: Editorial Ausa).
Dowling, M.B. (2006) *Clemency and Cruelty in the Roman World* (Ann Arbor, MI: University of Michigan Press).
Drogula, F.K. (2015) 'Who was watching whom? A reassessment of the conflict between Germanicus and Piso', *American Journal of Philology* 136.1: 121–53.

Du Pont, O. (2005) 'Robert Graves's Claudian novels. A case of pseudotranslation', *Target* 17.2: 327–47.
Eck, W. (1992) '*Cura viarum* und *cura operum publicorum* als kollegiale Ämter im frühen Prinzipat', *Klio* 74: 237–45.
Eck, W. (1993a) 'Un *senatus consultum* sul processo di Cn. Calpurnius Piso', *Atti della Pontificia Accademia Romana di Archeologia. Rendiconti* 63 [1990–91]: 91–94.
Eck, W. (1993b) 'Das s.c. de Cn. Pisone patre und seine Publikation in der Baetica', *Cahiers du Centre Gustave Glotz* 4: 189–208.
Eck, W. (1995a) 'Domus: Cn. Calpurnius Piso', in *LTUR* II, 76.
Eck, W. (1995b) 'Plebs und Princeps nach dem Tod des Germanicus', in I. Malkin, Z.W. Rubinsohn (eds), *Leaders and Masses in the Roman World. Studies in Honor of Zvi Yavetz* (Leiden / New York / Cologne: E.J. Brill), 1–10.
Eck, W. (1997) 'Die Täuschung der Öffentlichkeit. Der Prozeß gegen Cnaeus Calpurnius Piso im Jahre 20 n. Chr.', in U. Manthe, J. von Ungern-Sternberg (eds), *Große Prozesse der römischen Antike*, 128–45 (Munich: C.H. Beck).
Eck, W. (2001) 'Der Blick nach Rom. Die Affäre um den Tod des Germanicus und ihr Reflex in der Baetica', in A. Caballos Rufino (ed.), *Carmona Romana. Actas del II congreso de historia de Carmona*, 543–57 (Carmona: Delegación de Carmona, Excmo / Seville: Universidad de Sevilla).
Eck, W. (2002) 'Cheating the public, or: Tacitus vindicated', *Scripta Classica Israelica* 21: 149–64.
Eck, W., Caballos, A., Fernández, F. (1996) *Das senatus consultum de Cn. Pisone patre*, Vestigia 48 (Munich: C.H. Beck).
Eck, W., Caballos, A., Fernández, F. (1997) 'Il senatus consultum de Cn. Pisone patre', in J. Arce, S. Ensoli, E. La Rocca (eds), *Hispania Romana. Da terra di conquista a provincia dell'impero*, 215–21 (Milan: Electa).
Eich, A. (2009) 'Diplomatische Genauigkeit oder inhaltliche Richtigkeit? Das Verhältnis von Original und Abschrift', in R. Haensch (ed.), *Selbstdarstellung und Kommunikation: Die Veröffentlichung staatlicher Urkunden auf Stein und Bronze in der römischen Welt*, Vestigia 61, 267–99 (Munich: C.H. Beck).
Ermann, J. (2002) 'Das senatus consultum de Cn. Pisone patre und die Funktion des Consilium im römischen Strafprozess', *Zeitschrift der Savigny-Stiftung für Rechtsgeschichte Romanistische Abteilung* 119: 380–88.
Fayer, C. (1994) *La familia romana: aspetti giuridici ed antiquari*, vol. 2 (Rome: 'L'Erma' di Bretschneider).
Fernández Ochoa, C., Morillo Cerdán, A., Villa Valdés, A. (2005) 'La Torre de Augusto en la Campa Torres (Gijón, Asturias). Las antiguas excavaciones y el epígrafe de Calpurnio Pisón', *Archivio Español de Arqueología* 78: 129–46.
Ferrary, J.-L. (2001) 'A propos des pouvoirs d'Auguste', *Cahiers du Centre Gustave Glotz* 12: 101–54 (abridged and trans., 'The powers of Augustus', in J. Edmondson (ed.) (2009) *Augustus*, 90–136 (Edinburgh: Edinburgh University Press)).
Firla, I. (2000) 'The historical novels: motives for an end', in I. Firla (ed.), *Robert Graves's Historical Novels*, 29–53 (Frankfurt am Main: Peter Lang).
Fishwick, D. (2007) 'Cn. Piso pater and the *numen divi Augusti*', *Zeitschrift für Papyrologie und Epigraphik* 159: 297–300.
Fishwick, D. (2010) 'Agrippa and the Ara Providentiae at Rome', *Zeitschrift für Papyrologie und Epigraphik* 174: 251–58.
Flory, M.B. (1984) '*Sic exempla parantur*: Livia's shrine to Concordia and the Porticus Liviae', *Historia* 33.3: 309–30.

Flory, M.B. (1993) 'Livia and the history of public honorific statues for women in Rome', *Transactions of the American Philological Association* 123: 287–308.
Flower, H.I. (1996) *Ancestor Masks and Aristocratic Power in Roman Culture* (Oxford: Clarendon Press).
Flower, H.I. (1998) 'Rethinking "damnatio memoriae": the case of Cn. Calpurnius Piso Pater in AD 20', *Classical Antiquity* 17.2: 155–87.
Flower, H.I. (1999) 'Piso in Chicago: a commentary on the APA/AIA joint seminar on the "Senatus Consultum de Cn. Pisone Patre"', *American Journal of Philology* 120.1: 99–115.
Flower, H.I. (2006) *The Art of Forgetting* (Chapel Hill, NC: University of North Carolina Press).
Fónagy, I. (2001) *Languages within Language. An Evolutive Approach* (Amsterdam / Philadelphia, PA: John Benjamins).
Fraschetti, A. (1988) 'La *Tabula Hebana*, la *Tabula Siarensis* e il *iustitium* per la morte di Germanico', *Mélanges de l'École française de Rome. Antiquité* 100.2: 867–89.
Fraschetti, A. (1995) 'Sulla datazione della *Consolatio ad Liviam*', *Rivista di Filologia e di Istruzione Classica* 123: 409–27.
Fraschetti, A. (1996) 'Indice analitico della *consolatio ad Liviam Augustam de morte Drusi Neronis filii eius qui in Germania de morbo periit*', *Mélanges de l'École française de Rome. Antiquité* 108: 191–239.
Frei-Stolba, R. (1998) 'Recherches sur la position juridique et sociale de Livie, l'épouse d'Auguste', in R. Frei-Stolba, A. Bielman, M. Corbier (eds), *Femmes et vie publique dans l'antiquité gréco-romaine*, 65–90 (Lausanne: Faculté des lettres de l'Université de Lausanne).
Frenz, H.G. (1989) 'The honorary arch at Mainz-Kastel', *Journal of Roman Archaeology* 2: 120–25.
Frier, B.W. (2015) 'Roman law and the marriage of underage girls', *Journal of Roman Archaeology* 28: 652–64.
Fulkerson, L. (2006) 'Staging a mutiny: competitive roleplaying on the Rhine (Annals 1.31–51)', *Ramus* 35.2: 169–92.
Fullerton, M.D. (1985) 'The *domus Augusti* in imperial iconography of 13–12 B.C.', *American Journal of Archaeology*, 89.3: 473–83.
Furbank P.N. (2004) 'On the historical novel', *Raritan: A Quarterly Review* 23.3: 94–114.
Galasso, L. (1995) *P. Ovidii Nasonis Epistularum ex Ponto liber II* (Florence: Le Monnier / Trieste: Università degli studi di Trieste, Dipartimento di studi dell'Antichità).
Galimberti, A. (1998) '"Clementia" e "moderatio" in Tiberio', in M. Sordi (ed.), *Responsabilità perdono e vendetta nel mondo antico*, Contributi dell'Istituto di storia antica vol. 24, 175–90 (Milan: Vita e Pensiero).
Garnsey, P. (1970) *Social Status and Legal Privilege in the Roman Empire* (Oxford: Clarendon Press).
Garzetti, A. (1953) 'Aerarium e fiscus sotto Augusto: storia di una questione in parte di nomi', *Athenaeum* 31: 298–327.
Genette, G. (1997) *Paratexts: Thresholds of Interpretation*, trans. J.E. Lewin (Cambridge: Cambridge University Press) [originally published as *Seuils*, Paris: Editions du Seuil, 1987].
Gesche, H. (1971) 'Datierung und Deutung der CLEMENTIAE – MODERATIONI – Dupondien', *Jahrbuch für Numismatik und Geldgeschichte* 21: 37–80.

Gibson, A.G.G. (2015) 'Josef von Sternberg and the cinematizing of *I, Claudius*', in A.G.G. Gibson (ed.), *Robert Graves and the Classical Tradition*, 275–95 (Oxford: Oxford University Press).

Gil, J. (1999) '*Lanx satura*. De El Saucejo a Barcarrota', *Habis* 30: 217–23.

Ginsburg, J. (1981) *Tradition and Theme in the Annals of Tacitus* (New York: Arno Press).

Girardet, K.M. (2000) '*Imperium "maius"*: Politische und verfassungsrechtliche Aspekte. Versuch einer Klärung', in A. Giovanini (ed.), *La révolution romaine après Ronald Syme. Bilans et perspectives*, 167–236 (Geneva: Fondation Hardt).

Giua, M.A. (2000) 'Tra storiografia e comunicazione ufficiale', *Athenaeum* 88.1: 253–75.

Giua, M.A. (2002) 'Strategie della comunicazione ufficiale. Osservazioni sulla pubblicità dei senatoconsulti in età giulio-claudia', *Rendiconti dell'Accademia Nazionale dei Lincei, Cl. di Scienze Morali, Storiche e Filologiche* ser.9 no.13: 95–138.

González, J. (1999) 'Tacitus, Germanicus Piso, and the Tabula Siarensis', *American Journal of Philology* 120.1: 123–42.

González, J. (2002) *Tácito y las fuentes documentales: SS.CC. de honoribus Germanici decernendis (Tabula Siarensis) y de Cn. Pisone Patre* (Seville: Universidad de Sevilla, Fundación el Monte).

González, J. (2003) 'El *S.C. de Pisone Patre*: problemas textuales', in M.G. Angeli Bertinelli, A. Donati (eds), *Usi e abusi epigrafici. Atti del Colloquio Internazionale di Epigrafia Latina (Genova 20–22 settembre 2001)*, Serta Antiqua et Mediaevalia vol. 6, 287–99 (Rome: Bretschneider).

González, J., Arce, J. (eds) (1988) *Estudios sobre la* Tabula Siarensis, Anejos de Archivo Español de Arqueología 9 (Madrid: Consejo Superior de Investigaciones Científicas, Centro de Estudios Históricos).

González, J., Crawford, M.H. (1986) 'The *Lex Irnitana*: a new copy of the Flavian municipal law', *Journal of Roman Studies* 76: 147–243.

Goodyear, F.R.D. (1972) *The Annals of Tacitus Books 1–6*, vol. 1: *Annals 1.1–54* (Cambridge: Cambridge University Press).

Goodyear, F.R.D. (1981) *The Annals of Tacitus Books 1–6*, vol. 2: *Annals 1.55–81 and Annals 2* (Cambridge: Cambridge University Press).

Gordon, R.L., Simón, F.M. (2010) 'Introduction', in R.L. Gordon, F.M. Simón (eds), *Magical Practice in the Latin West. Papers from the International Conference Held at the University of Zaragoza 30 Sept.–1 Oct. 2005*, 1–49 (Leiden / Boston, MA: Brill).

Gowing, A.M. (2005) *Empire and Memory. The Representation of the Roman Republic in Imperial Literature* (Cambridge: Cambridge University Press).

Gowing, A.M. (2007) 'The Imperial Republic of Velleius Paterculus', in J. Marincola (ed.), *A Companion to Greek and Roman Historiography*, Blackwell Companions to the Ancient World, vol. 2, 411–18 (Malden, MA / Oxford: Blackwell).

Gowing, A.M. (2010) '"Caesar grabs my pen": writing civil war under Tiberius', in B. Breed, C. Damon, A. Rossi (eds), *Citizens of Discord: Rome and its Civil Wars*, 249–60 (Oxford: Oxford University Press).

Gradel, I. (2002) *Emperor Worship and Roman Religion* (Oxford: Oxford University Press).

Gradel, I. (2014) 'A new fragment of Copy A of the Senatus Consultum de Cn. Pisone Patre', *Zeitschrift für Papyrologie und Epigraphik* 192: 284–86.

Graves, L. (ed.) [1995] (2008) *Robert Graves. Complete Short Stories* (London: Penguin Classics).
Graves, Richard P. (1990) *Robert Graves. The Years with Laura, 1926–40* (London: Weidenfeld and Nicholson).
Graves, Robert [1929] (1957, revised edn) *Goodbye to All That* (London: Penguin Books).
Graves, Robert [1934] (1953) *I, Claudius* (London: Penguin Books).
Graves, Robert [1934] (1978) *I, Claudius* (Harmondsworth: Penguin Books).
Gregory, A.P. (1994) '"Powerful images": responses to portraits and the political uses of images in Rome', *Journal of Roman Archaeology* 7: 80–99.
Grelle, F. (2000) 'Il senatus consultum de Cn. Pisone patre', *Studia et documenta historiae et juris* 66: 223–30.
Griffin, M.T. (1982) 'The Lyons tablet and Tacitean hindsight', *Classical Quarterly* 32: 404–18.
Griffin, M.T. (1997) 'The senate's story', *Journal of Roman Studies* 87: 249–63.
Griffin, M.T. (2003a) '*Clementia* after Caesar: from politics to philosophy', in F. Cairns, E. Fantham (eds), *Caesar against Liberty? Perspectives on His Autocracy*, Papers of the Langford Latin Seminar 11, 157–82 (Cambridge: Francis Cairns Publications) [repr. in *Politics and Philosophy at Rome. Collected Papers*, ed. C. Balmaceda, 570–86 (Oxford: Oxford University Press, 2018)].
Griffin, M.T. (2003b) '*De Beneficiis* and Roman society', *Journal of Roman Studies* 93: 92–113.
Grimal, P. (1980) 'Du nouveau sur les *Fables* de Phèdre?', in *Mélanges de littérature et d'épigraphie latines, d'histoire ancienne et d'archéologie: hommage à la mémoire de Pierre Wuilleumier*, 143–49 (Paris: Belles Lettres).
Gronewald, M. (1983) 'Ein neues Fragment der Laudatio Funebris des Augustus auf Agrippa', *Zeitschrift für Papyrologie und Epigraphik* 52: 61–62.
Gros, P. (1993) 'Apollo Palatinus', in *LTUR* I, 54–57.
Gunderson, E. (2014) 'E.g. Augustus: exemplum in the Augustus and Tiberius', in T. Power, R.K. Gibson (eds), *Suetonius the Biographer: Studies in Roman Lives*, 130–45 (Oxford: Oxford University Press).
Gurval, R.A. (1995) *Actium and Augustus: The Politics and Emotions of Civil War* (Ann Arbor, MI: University of Michigan Press).
Hellegouarc'h, J. (1980) 'La figure de Tibère chez Tacite et Velleius Paterculus', in *Mélanges de littérature et d'épigraphie latines d'histoire ancienne et d'archéologie. Hommage à la mémoire de Pierre Wuilleumier*, 167–83 (Paris: Belles Lettres).
Henderson, J. (2001) *Telling Tales on Caesar. Roman Stories from Phaedrus* (Oxford: Oxford University Press).
Herbert-Brown, G. (1994) *Ovid and the* Fasti. *An Historical Study* (Oxford: Clarendon Press).
Higginson, F.H. (1987) *A Bibliography of the Writings of Robert Graves*, revised by W.P. Williams, 2nd edn (Winchester: St Paul's Bibliographies).
Hofmann-Löbl, I. (1996) *Die Calpurnii. Politisches Wirken und familiäre Kontinuität* (Frankfurt am Main: Peter Lang).
Hopkins, C. (1999) 'Robert Graves and the historical novel in the 1930s', in P.J. Quinn (ed.), *New Perspectives on Robert Graves*, 128–35 (London: Associated University Presses).
Humphrey, J.W. (1976) 'An historical commentary on Cassius Dio's "Roman History" Book 59, Gaius Caligula', PhD thesis, University of British Columbia.

Hunt, A.S., Edgar, C.C. (1956) *Select Papyri*, vol. 2, Loeb Classical Library 282 (Cambridge, MA: Heinemann / Harvard University Press).

Hurlet, F. (1997) *Les Collègues du Prince sous Auguste et Tibère*, Collection de l'École française de Rome 227 (Rome: École française de Rome).

Hurlet, F. (2006) 'Les modalités de la diffusion et de la réception de l'image et de l'idéologie impériale en occident sous le haut-empire', in M. Navarro Caballero, J.-M. Roddaz (eds), *La transmission de l'idéologie impériale dans l'occident romain*, 49–68 (Bordeaux / Paris: Ausonius).

Ingleheart, J. (2010) *A Commentary on Ovid, Tristia, Book 2* (Oxford / New York: Oxford University Press).

Jacquemin, A. (1998) 'Valère Maxime et Velleius Paterculus', in J.-M. David (ed.), *Valeurs et Mémoire à Rome. Valère Maxime ou la vertu recomposée*, 147–56 (Paris: De Boccard).

Jansen, L. (2014) 'Introduction: approaches to Roman paratextuality', in L. Jansen (ed.), *The Roman Paratext. Frame, Texts, Readers*, 1–18 (Cambridge: Cambridge University Press).

Jones, A.H.M. (1950) 'The aerarium and the fiscus', *Journal of Roman Studies* 40: 22–29.

Jongeling, K. (2008) *Handbook of Neo-Punic Inscriptions* (Tübingen: Mohr Siebeck).

Joshel, S. (2001) '*I, Claudius*. Projection and imperial soap opera', in S.R. Joshel, M. Malamud, D.T. McGuire (eds), *Imperial Projections: Ancient Rome in Modern Popular Culture*, 119–61 (Baltimore, MD: Johns Hopkins University Press).

Kajava, M. (1995) 'Some remarks on the erasure of inscriptions in the Roman world (with special reference to the case of Cn. Piso, cos. 7 B.C.', in H. Solin, O. Salomies, U.-M. Liertz (eds), *Acta Colloquii Epigraphici Latini*, Commentationes Humanarum Litterarum 104, 201–10 (Helsinki: Societas Scientiarum Fennica).

Kaster, R.A., Nussbaum, M.C. (2010) *Seneca. Anger, Mercy, Revenge* (Chicago, IL and London: University of Chicago Press).

Kelly, B. (2010) 'Tacitus, Germanicus and the kings of Egypt (Tac. *Ann.* 2.59–61)', *Classical Quarterly* 60.1: 221–37.

Kelly, G.P. (2006) *A History of Exile in the Roman Republic* (Cambridge: Cambridge University Press).

Kennedy, D. and O'Gorman, E. (2015) 'Claudius in the library', in A.G.G. Gibson (ed.), *Robert Graves and the Classical Tradition*, 43–55 (Oxford: Oxford University Press).

Kersnowski, F. (ed.) (1989) *Conversations with Robert Graves* (Jackson, MS / London: University Press of Mississippi).

Kierdorf, W. [1983] (1987) 'Freundschaft und Freundschaftskündigung von der Republik zum Prinzipat', in G. Binder (ed.), *Saeculum Augustum*, vol. 1, 223–45 (Darmstadt: Wissenschaftliche Buchgesellschaft).

Klein, S., Kaenel, H.-M. von (2000) 'The early Roman Imperial *aes* coinage: metal analysis and numismatic studies. Part one', *Schweizerische numismatische Rundschau* 79: 53–106.

Koelb, C. (2000) 'The medium of history: Robert Graves and the ancient past', in J.L. Halio, B. Siegel (eds), *Comparative Literary Dimensions. Essays in Honor of Melvin I. Friedman*, 31–47 (London: Associated University Presses).

Kokkinos, N. (1992) *Antonia Augusta. Portrait of a Great Roman Lady* (London / New York: Routledge).
Konstan, D. (2005) 'Clemency as a virtue', *Classical Philology* 100.4: 337–46.
Köstermann, E. (1932) '*Statio principis*', *Philologus* 87: 358–68, 430–44.
Köstermann, E. (1937) '"Status" als politischer Terminus in der Antike', *Rheinisches Museum für Philologie* 86.3: 225–40.
Köstermann, E. (1958) 'Die Mission des Germanicus im Orient', *Historia* 7: 331–75.
Kuntze, C. (1985) *Zur Darstellung des Kaisers Tiberius und seiner Zeit bei Velleius Paterculus*, Europäische Hochschulschriften vol. 247 (Frankfurt / Berlin / New York: Peter Lang).
L'Hoir, F.S. (1994) 'Tacitus and women's usurpation of power', *The Classical World* 88.1: 5–25.
Lamberti, F. (2006) 'Questioni aperte sul *SC. de Cneo Pisone patre*', in M. Silvestrini, T. Spagnuolo Vigorita, G. Volpe (eds), *Studi in onore di Francesco Grelle*, 139–48 (Bari: Edipuglia).
Lana, I. (1952) *Velleio Patercolo o della propaganda*, Pubblicazioni della Facoltà di lettere e filosofia vol. 4 (Turin: Università di Torino).
Langlands, R. (2008) '"Reading for the moral" in Valerius Maximus: the case of *severitas*', *The Cambridge Classical Journal* 54: 160–87.
Langlands, R. (2011) 'Roman exempla and situation ethics: Valerius Maximus and Cicero *de Officiis*', *Journal of Roman Studies* 101: 100–22.
Langlands, R. (2018) *Exemplary Ethics in Ancient Rome* (Cambridge: Cambridge University Press).
Lasserre, F. (1983) 'Strabon devant l'empire romain', *Aufstieg und Niedergang der römischen Welt* II.30.1: 867–96.
Lawrence, A.W. (ed.) (1962) *Letters to T.E. Lawrence* (London: Jonathan Cape).
Lawrence, T.E. (1963) *T.E. Lawrence to His Biographers Robert Graves and Liddell Hart* (Garden City, NY: Doubleday & Company).
Lebek, W.D. (1991) 'Der Proconsulat des Germanicus und die *Auctoritas* des Senats: Tab. Siar. Frg. I 22–24', *Zeitschrift für Papyrologie und Epigraphik* 87: 103–24.
Lebek, W.D. (1993) 'Roms Ritter und Roms Pleps in den Senatsbeschlüssen für Germanicus Caesar und Drusus Caesar', *Zeitschrift für Papyrologie und Epigraphik* 95: 81–120.
Lebek, W.D. (1999) 'Das Senatus consultum de Cn. Pisone patre und Tacitus', *Zeitschrift für Papyrologie und Epigraphik* 128: 183–211.
Levick, B. (1966) 'Drusus Caesar and the adoptions of A.D. 4', *Latomus* 25: 227–44.
Levick B. (1975) 'Mercy and moderation on the coinage of Tiberius', in B. Levick (ed.), *The Ancient Historian and His Materials. Essays in Honour of C.E. Stevens on His Seventieth Birthday*, 123–37 (Farnborough: Gregg International).
Levick, B. (1979) '*Poena legis maiestatis*', *Historia* 28.3: 358–79.
Levick, B. (1999) *Tiberius the Politician* (London / New York: Routledge).
Lindsay, H. (1995) 'A fertile marriage: Agrippina and the chronology of her children by Germanicus', *Latomus* 54.1: 3–17.
Liverani, P. (2012) 'V,4. Un calendario dei *magistri vici*', in R. Friggeri, M.G. Granino Cecere, G.L. Gregori (eds), *Terme di Diocleziano: la collezione epigrafica*, 262–67 (Milan: Electa).

Lo Cascio, E. (2000) *Il* princeps *e il suo impero. Studi di storia amministrativa e finanziaria romana* (Bari: Edipuglia).

Lobur, J.A. (2007) '*Festinatio* (haste), *brevitas* (concision), and the generation of imperial ideology in Velleius Paterculus', *Transactions of the American Philological Association* 137.1: 211–30.

Lobur, J.A. (2008) Consensus, Concordia, *and the Formation of Roman Imperial Ideology* (New York / London: Routledge).

Lott, J.B. (2012) *Death and Dynasty in Early Imperial Rome. Key Sources, with Text, Translation, and Commentary* (Cambridge: Cambridge University Press).

Lott, J.B. (2014/15) 'The earliest Augustan gods outside of Rome', *Classical Journal* 110.2: 129–58.

Low, K. (2016) 'Germanicus on tour: history, diplomacy and the promotion of a dynasty', *Classical Quarterly* 66.1: 222–38.

Lucarelli, U. (2007) *Exemplarische Vergangenheit. Valerius Maximus und die Konstruktion des sozialen Raumes in der frühen Kaiserzeit* (Göttingen: Vandenhoeck & Ruprecht).

Mackay, C.S. (2003) '*Quaestiones Pisonianae*: procedural and chronological notes on the *S.C. de Cn. Pisone Patre*', *Harvard Studies in Classical Philology* 101: 311–70.

Malloch, S.J.V. (2013) *The Annals of Tacitus. Book 11* (Cambridge: Cambridge University Press).

Malloch, S.J.V. (2020) *The* Tabula Lugdunensis. *A Critical Edition with Translation and Commentary* (Cambridge: Cambridge University Press).

Marcone, A. (2015) 'Il *Numen Augusti* nel *senatus consultum de Cn. Pisone patre*', in K.-D. Fischer, B. Holmes (eds), *The Frontiers of Ancient Science: Essays in Honor of Heinrich von Staden*, 397–406 (Berlin / Boston, MA: De Gruyter).

Márquez, C. (2019) 'The seated statue of Divus Augustus Pater found in the province of Baetica', in B. Porod and P. Scherrer (eds), *Akten des 15. Internationalen Kolloquiums zum provinzialrömischen Kunstschaffen. Der Stifter und sein Monument. Gesellschaft – Ikonographie – Chronologie*, 262–72 (Graz: Universalmuseum Joanneum).

Martin, J.-P. (1982) Providentia deorum. *Recherches sur certains aspects religieux du pouvoir impérial romain*, Collection de l'École française de Rome 61 (Rome: École française de Rome).

Martin, R.H., Woodman, A.J. (1989) *Tacitus. Annals Book IV* (Cambridge: Cambridge University Press).

Meyer, E.A. (1998) Review of *Das Senatus Consultum de Cn. Pisone patre* by Werner Eck, Antonio Caballos and Fernando Fernández, *The Classical Journal* 93.3: 315–24.

Millar, F. (1963) 'The fiscus in the first two centuries', *Journal of Roman Studies* 53: 29–42.

Millar, F. (1988) 'Imperial ideology in the *Tabula Siarensis*', in J. González, J. Arce (eds), *Estudios sobre la Tabula Siarensis*, 11–19 (Madrid: Consejo Superior de Investigaciones Científicas, Centro de Estudios Históricos) [repr. in G.M. Rogers, H.M. Cotton (eds), *Rome, the Greek World, and the East*, vol. 1: *The Roman Republic and the Augustan Revolution*, 633–49 (Chapel Hill, NC: University of North Carolina Press, 2002)].

Millar, F. (1993) 'Ovid and the *Domus Augusta*: Rome seen from Tomoi', *Journal of Roman Studies* 83: 1–17.

Miller, N.P. (1956) 'The Claudian tablet and Tacitus: a reconsideration', *Rheinisches Museum für Philologie* 99: 304–15.
Mitchell, H. (2019) 'The reputation of L. Munatius Plancus and the idea of "serving the times"', in J. Osgood, K. Morrell, K. Welch (eds), *The Alternative Augustan Age*, 163–81 (Oxford: Oxford University Press).
Mitchell, S. (1976) 'Requisitioned transport in the Roman empire: a new inscription from Pisidia', *Journal of Roman Studies* 66: 106–31.
Mitford, T.B. (1960) 'A Cypriot oath of allegiance to Tiberius', *Journal of Roman Studies* 50: 75–79.
Momigliano, A. (1990) *The Classical Foundations of Modern Historiography* (Berkeley, CA / Los Angeles, CA: University of California Press).
Mommsen, T. (1891) *Le droit public romain*, trans. P.F. Girard (Paris: Ernest Thorin) [repr. Paris: De Boccard, 1985].
Mommsen, T. [1887] (1906) 'Der Rechenschaftsbericht des Augustus', in *Gesammelte Schriften* IV: *Historische Schriften* I, 247–58 (Berlin: Weidmann).
Moralejo, J.L. (2009) 'Una nota de ecdótica epigráfica', in *Espacios, usos y formas de la epigrafía hispana en épocas antigua y tardoantigua. Homenaje al D. Armin U. Stylow*, Anejos de Archivo Español de Arqueología 48, 21–25 (Mérida: Consejo Superior de Investigaciones Científicas, Instituto de Arqueología de Mérida).
Morgan, T. (2007) *Popular Morality in the Early Roman Empire* (Cambridge: Cambridge University Press).
Myers, K.S. (2014) 'Ovid, *Epistulae ex Ponto* 4.8, Germanicus, and the *Fasti*', *Classical Quarterly* 64.2: 725–34.
Nakagawa, A. (2002) 'L'imperatore Tiberio e la virtù della *moderatio*', *Acme* 55.3: 219–35.
Nemesi, A.L. (2004) 'What discourse goals can be accomplished by the use of hyperbole?', *Acta Linguistica Hungarica* 51.3–4: 351–78.
Nicolet, C. (1984) 'Augustus, government, and the propertied classes', in F. Millar, E. Segal (eds), *Caesar Augustus. Seven Aspects*, 89–128 (Oxford: Clarendon Press).
Nicolet, C. (1988) 'La *Tabula Siarensis*, la *lex de imperio Vespasiani*, et le *jus relationis* de l'empereur au Sénat', *Mélanges de l'École française de Rome. Antiquité* 100.2: 827–66.
Nicolet, C. (1995) 'La *tabula Siarensis*, la plèbe et les statues de Germanicus', in I. Malkin, Z.W. Rubinsohn (eds), *Leaders and Masses in the Roman World. Studies in Honor of Zvi Yavetz*, 115–27 (Leiden / New York / Cologne: Brill).
Nikulin, D. (2015) 'Introduction: memory in recollection of itself', in D. Nikulin (ed.), *Memory. A History*, Oxford Philosophical Concepts, 3–34 (Oxford: Oxford University Press).
Nogales Basarrate, T. (2000) 'Un altar en el foro de Augusta Emerita', in P. León Alonso, T. Nogales Basarrate (eds), *Actas de la III reunión sobre escultura romana en Hispania*, 25–46 (Madrid: Ministerio de Educación, Cultura y Deporte).
Noreña, C. (2001) 'The communication of the emperor's virtues', *Journal of Roman Studies* 91: 146–68.
Noreña, C. (2011) 'Coins and communication', in M. Peachin (ed.), *The Oxford Handbook of Social Relations in the Roman World*, 248–68 (New York / Oxford: Oxford University Press).
O'Gorman, E. (2000) *Irony and Misreading in the Annals of Tacitus* (Cambridge: Cambridge University Press).

O'Gorman, E. (2006) 'Alternative empires: Tacitus's virtual history of the Pisonian principate', *Arethusa* 39.2: 281–301.
O'Prey, P. (ed.) (1982) *In Broken Images. Selected Letters of Robert Graves 1914–1946* (London: Hutchinson).
Olbrycht, M.J. (2016) 'Germanicus, Artabanos II of Parthia, and Zeno Artaxias in Armenia', *Klio* 98.2: 605–33.
Osgood, J. (2015) 'Ending civil war at Rome: rhetoric and reality, 88 B.C.E.–197 C.E.', *The American Historical Review* 120.5: 1683–95.
Östenberg, I. (2019) '*Damnatio memoriae* inscribed: the materiality of cultural repression', in A. Petrovic, I. Petrovic, E. Thomas (eds), *The Materiality of Text: Placement, Perception, and Presence of Inscribed Texts in Classical Antiquity*, 324–47 (Leiden / Boston, MA: Brill).
Pagán, V.E. (2012) 'Introduction', in V.E. Pagán (ed.), *A Companion to Tacitus*, 1–12 (Chichester / Malden, MA: Blackwell-Wiley).
Paladini, M.L. (1996) 'Il processo Pisoniano nella Roma di Tiberio', in M. Sordi (ed.), *Processi e politica nel mondo antico*, Contributi dell'Istituto di storia antica vol. 22, 219–36 (Milan: Vita e Pensiero).
Palombi, D. (1993a) 'Clementia Caesaris, aedes', in *LTUR* I, 279–80.
Palombi, D. (1993b) 'Curia in Palatio', in *LTUR* I, 334.
Pani, M. (1972) *Roma e i re d'Oriente da Augusto a Tiberio: (Cappadocia, Armenia, Media Atropatene)* (Bari: Adriatica).
Pani, M. (1987) 'La missione di Germanico in Oriente: politica estera e politica interna', in G. Bonamente, M.P. Segoloni (eds), *Germanico. La persona, la personalità, il personaggio nel bimillenario dalla nascita*, 1–23 (Rome: Bretschneider).
Pani, M. (1993) *Potere e valori a Roma fra Augusto e Traiano* (Bari: Edipuglia).
Pani, M. (2000) 'Principato e logica familiare nel *s.c.* su Gneo Calpurnio Pisone', in G. Paci (ed.), Ἐπιγραφαί. *Miscellanea epigrafica in onore di Lidio Gasperino*, vol. 2, Ichnia vol. 5, 685–93 (Tivoli: Editrice Tipigraf).
Paschoud, F. (2005) 'À propos d'*imperium maius*: nil sub sole nouum', *Zeitschrift für Papyrologie und Epigraphik* 153: 280–82.
Patterson, J.R. (1999) 'Via Flaminia', in *LTUR* V, 135–37.
Pelling, C. (2012) 'Tacitus and Germanicus', in R. Ash (ed.), *Oxford Readings in Classical Studies. Tacitus*, 281–313 (Oxford: Oxford University Press) [updated reprint of chapter in A.J. Woodman, T.J. Luce (eds), *Tacitus and the Tacitean Tradition*, 59–85 (Princeton, NJ: Princeton University Press, 1993)].
Perry, J. (2015) '"Con beffarda irriverenza": Graves's Augustus in Mussolini's Italy', in A.G.G. Gibson (ed.), *Robert Graves and the Classical Tradition*, 255–73 (Oxford: Oxford University Press).
Pettinger, A. (2012) *The Republic in Danger: Drusus Libo and the Succession of Tiberius* (Oxford: Oxford University Press).
Polleichtner, W. (2003) 'Das *Senatus Consultum de Cn. Pisone Patre* und Tacitus' Bericht vom Prozess gegen Piso', *Philologus* 147: 289–306.
Post, L.A. (1944) 'A new reading of the Germanicus papyrus', *American Journal of Philology* 64.1: 80–82.
Potter, D.S. (1987) 'The Tabula Siarensis, Tiberius, the Senate, and the eastern boundary of the Roman Empire', *Zeitschrift für Papyrologie und Epigraphik* 69: 269–76.
Potter, D.S (1996) 'Emperors, their borders and their neighbours: the scope of imperial *mandata*', in D.L. Kennedy (ed.), *The Roman Army in the East*, Journal

of Roman Archaeology Suppl.18, 49–66 (Ann Arbor, MI: Journal of Roman Archaeology).

Potter, D.S. (1998) '*Senatus consultum de Cn. Pisone*', *Journal of Roman Archaeology* 11: 437–57.

Potter, D.S. (1999) 'Political theory in the "senatus consultum Pisonianum"', *American Journal of Philology* 120.1: 65–88.

Potter, D.S. (2012) 'Tacitus' sources', in V.E. Pagán (ed.), *A Companion to Tacitus*, 125–40 (Chichester / Malden, MA: Blackwell-Wiley).

Potter, D.S., Damon, C. (1999) 'The "Senatus Consultum de Cn. Pisone Patre"', *American Journal of Philology* 120.1: 13–42.

Poulsen, A.D. (2020) 'Teleology with a human face: "side-shadowing" and its effects in Tacitus' treatment of Germanicus (*Annals* 1–2)', in A. Turner (ed.), *Reconciling Ancient and Modern Philosophies of History*, 149–82 (Berlin / Boston, MA: De Gruyter).

Purcell, N. (2009) 'Livia and the womanhood of Rome', in J. Edmondson (ed.), *Augustus*, Edinburgh Readings on the Ancient World, 165–94 (Edinburgh: Edinburgh University Press) [= *Proceedings of the Cambridge Philological Society*, n.s. 32 (1986), 78–105].

Raaflaub, K.A. (1980) 'The political significance of Augustus' military reforms', in W.S. Hanson, L.J.F. Keppie (eds), *Roman Frontier Studies 1979*, BAR International Series 71.iii, 1005–25 (Oxford: British Archaeological Reports).

Raepsaet-Charlier, M.-T. (1987) *Prosopographie des femmes de l'ordre sénatorial: Ier–IIe siècles* (Leuven: Peeters).

Ramsey, J.T. (2007) *Sallust's Bellum Catilinae*, 2nd edn (Oxford: Oxford University Press).

Rapke, T.T. (1982) 'Tiberius, Piso, and Germanicus', *Acta Classica* 25: 61–69.

Rich, J. (2011) 'Velleius' history: genre and purpose', in E. Cowan (ed.), *Velleius Paterculus: Making History*, 73–92 (Swansea: The Classical Press of Wales).

Richardson, J.S. (1997) 'The senate, the courts, and the *SC de Cn. Pisone patre*', *Classical Quarterly* 47.2: 510–18.

Richardson, J.S. (2008) *The Language of Empire: Rome and the Idea of Empire from the Third Century BC to the Second Century AD* (Cambridge: Cambridge University Press).

Riess, W. (2003) 'Die Rede des Claudius über das ius honorum der gallischen Notabeln: Forschungsstand und Perspektiven', *Revue des Etudes Anciennes* 105: 211–49.

Ripollès, P.P. (2005) 'Coinage and identity in the Roman provinces: Spain', in C. Howgego, V. Heuchert, A. Burnett (eds), *Coinage and Identity*, 79–93 (Oxford: Oxford University Press).

Rogers, R.S. (1940) 'Drusus Caesar's tribunician power', *American Journal of Philology* 61.4: 457–59.

Rogers, R.S. (1943) *Studies in the Reign of Tiberius. Some Imperial Virtues of Tiberius and Drusus Julius Caesar* (Baltimore, MD: The Johns Hopkins Press).

Rogers, R.S. (1959) 'The emperor's displeasure – *amicitiam renuntiare*', *Transactions of the American Philological Association* 90: 224–37.

Roller, M.B. (2010) 'Demolished houses, monumentality, and memory in Roman culture', *Classical Antiquity* 29.1: 117–80.

Roller, M.B. (2018) *Models from the Past in Roman Culture. A World of Exempla* (Cambridge: Cambridge University Press).

Rose, C.B. (1997) *Dynastic Commemoration and Imperial Portraiture in the Julio-Claudian Period* (Cambridge: Cambridge University Press).
Ross, D.O., Jr (1973) 'The Tacitean Germanicus', in T. Cole, D. Ross (eds), *Studies in Latin Language and Literature*, Yale Classical Studies 23, 209–28 (Cambridge: Cambridge University Press).
Rowe, G. (2002) *Princes and Political Cultures: The New Tiberian Senatorial Decrees* (Ann Arbor, MI: University of Michigan Press).
Ruiz Castellanos, A., Lomas Salmonte, F.J. (2002) 'El *status qualitatis* de la *relatio* en el texto epigráfico del senado-consulto de Gneo Pisón Padre', *Gerión* 20.1: 389–411.
Rüpke, J. (2008) *Fasti Sacerdotum. A Prosopography of Pagan, Jewish, and Christian Religious Officials in the City of Rome, 300 BC to AD 499*, trans. D.M.B. Richardson (Oxford: Oxford University Press).
Rutland, L.W. (1987) 'The Tacitean Germanicus: suggestions for a re-evaluation', *Rheinisches Museum für Philologie* 130.2: 153–64.
Rutledge, S.H. (2001) *Imperial Inquisitions. Prosecutors and Informants from Tiberius to Domitian* (London / New York: Routledge).
Saller, R.P. (1994) *Patriarchy, Property, and Death in the Roman Family* (Cambridge: Cambridge University Press).
Šašel, A. and J. (1963) *Inscriptiones Latinae quae in Iugoslavia inter annos MCMXL et MCMLX repertae et editae sunt*, Situla 5 (Ljubljana: Razprave Narodnega Muzeja v Ljubljani).
Šašel, J. (1964) 'Probleme und Möglichkeiten onomastischer Forschung', in *Akte des IV. internationalen Kongresses für griechische und lateinische Epigraphik*, 352–68 (Graz / Vienna / Cologne: Hermann Böohlaus Nachf.).
Sawiński, P. (2021) *Holders of Extraordinary* Imperium *under Augustus and Tiberius. A Study into the Beginnings of the Principate*, trans. M. Jarczyk (London / New York: Routledge).
Scheid, J. (1998) Commentarii fratrum Arvalium qui supersunt. *Les copies épigraphiques des protocoles annuels de la confrérie arvale (21 av.–304 ap. J.-C.)*. (Rome: École française de Rome / Soprintendenza archeologica di Roma) [= *CFA*].
Scheid, J. (2007) *Res Gestae Divi Augusti. Hauts faits du divin Auguste* (Paris: Les Belles Lettres).
Schillinger-Häfele, U. (1965) 'Claudius und Tacitus über die Aufnahme von Galliern in den Senat', *Historia* 14: 443–54.
Schmitzer, U. (2000) *Velleius Paterculus und das Interesse an der Geschichte im Zeitalter des Tiberius* (Heidelberg: C. Winter).
Schoonhoven, H. (1992) *The Pseudo-Ovidian ad Liviam de Morte Drusi (Consolatio ad Liviam, Epicedium Drusi): A Critical Text with Introduction and Commentary* (Groningen: E. Forsten).
Seager, R. (2005) *Tiberius*, 2nd edn (Oxford: Blackwell).
Seager, R. (2013) 'Perceptions of the *domus Augusta*, AD 4–24', in A.G.G. Gibson (ed.), *The Julio-Claudian Succession: Reality and Perception of the "Augustan model"*, 41–58 (Leiden / Boston, MA: Brill).
Sensi, L. (1982) 'Praescriptio del S.C. Larinate', in *Atti del Colloquio internazionale AIEGL su epigrafia e ordine senatorio, Roma, 14–20 maggio 1981*, vol. 1, 515–20 (Rome: Edizioni di storia e letteratura).
Severy, B. (2000) 'Family and state in the early imperial monarchy: the *senatus consultum de Pisone Patre*, *Tabula Siarensis*, and *Tabula Hebana*', *Classical Philology*, 95.3: 318–37.

Severy, B. (2003) *Augustus and the Family at the Birth of the Roman Empire* (New York: Routledge).
Seymour, M. (1995) *Robert Graves: Life on the Edge* (London: Doubleday).
Seymour-Smith, M. (1982) *Robert Graves. His Life and Work* (London: Hutchinson).
Shackleton Bailey, D.R. (2000) *Valerius Maximus. Memorable Doings and Sayings*, Loeb Classical Library 492–93 (Cambridge, MA / London: Harvard University Press).
Shaw, B.D. (1987) 'The age of Roman girls at marriage: some reconsiderations', *Journal of Roman Studies* 77: 30–46.
Sherk, R.K. (1969) *Roman Documents from the Greek East.* Senatus Consulta *and* Epistulae *to the Age of Augustus* (Baltimore, MD: Johns Hopkins University Press).
Sherwin-White, A.N. (1966) *The Letters of Pliny: A Historical and Social Commentary* (Oxford: Clarendon Press).
Shotter, D.C.A. (1968) 'Tacitus, Tiberius and Germanicus', *Historia* 17.2: 194–214.
Shotter, D.C.A. (1974) 'Cnaeus Calpurnius Piso, legate of Syria', *Historia* 23.2: 229–45.
Shotter, D.C.A. (2000) 'Agrippina the Elder: a woman in a man's world', *Historia* 49.3: 341–57.
Sickle, J. van (1987) 'The elogia of the Cornelii Scipiones and the origin of epigram at Rome', *American Journal of Philology* 108: 41–55.
Skutsch, O. (1985) *The* Annals *of Q. Ennius* (Oxford: Clarendon Press).
Solin, H. (1986) 'Obbligo o libertà? Sull'onomastica dell'aristocrazia romana', *Opuscula Instituti Romani Finlandiae* 3: 69–80.
Solin, H. (1989) 'Namenwechsel und besondere Vornamen römischer Senatoren', *Philologus* 133: 252–59.
Solin, H. (1995) 'Namensgebung und Politik. Zum Namenswechsel und zu besonderen Vornamen römischer Senatoren', *Tyche* 10: 185–210.
Stern, S. (2012) *Calendars in Antiquity: Empires, States, and Societies* (Oxford: Oxford University Press).
Strzelecki, W. (1967) *C. Atei Capitonis Fragmenta* (Leipzig: Teubner).
Stylow, A.U., Corzo Pérez, S. (1999) 'Eine neue Kopie des senatus consultum de Cn. Pisone patre', *Chiron* 29: 24–28.
Suerbaum, W. (1999) 'Schwierigkeiten bei der Lektüre des SC de Cn. Pisone patre durch die Zeitgenossen um 20 n. Chr., durch Tacitus und durch heutige Leser', *Zeitschrift für Papyrologie und Epigraphik* 128: 213–34.
Sumner, G.V. (1967) 'Germanicus and Drusus Caesar', *Latomus* 26: 413–35.
Sumner, G.V. (1970) 'The truth about Velleius Paterculus: prolegomena', *Harvard Studies in Classical Philology* 74: 257–97.
Suspène, A. (2010) 'Un "procès politique" au début de l'Empire romain: le cas de Pison Père', *Revue Historique* 312.4 [656]: 845–71.
Sutherland, C.H.V. (1979) 'The *Clementiae* and *Moderationi* dupondii of Tiberius: more thoughts on the chronology', *Numismatic Chronicle* 139: 21–25.
Syme, R. (1939) *The Roman Revolution* (Oxford: Clarendon Press).
Syme, R. (1956) 'Some Pisones in Tacitus', *Journal of Roman Studies* 46: 17–21.
Syme, R. (1958) *Tacitus*, 2 vols (Oxford: Clarendon Press).
Syme, R. (1977) 'How Tacitus wrote *Annals* I–III', in *Historiographia Antiqua. Commentationes Lovanienses in honorem W. Peremans septuagenarii editae*, 231–63 (Leuven: Leuven University Press) [= A.R. Birley (ed.), *Roman Papers* III, 1014–42 (Oxford: Clarendon Press, 1984)].

Syme, R. (1978) 'Mendacity in Velleius', *American Journal of Philology* 99.1: 45–63.

Syme, R. (1982) 'Tacitus: some sources of his information', *Journal of Roman Studies* 72: 68–82 [= A.R. Birley (ed.), *Roman Papers* IV, 199–222. (Oxford: Clarendon Press, 1988)].

Syme, R. (1986) *The Augustan Aristocracy* (Oxford: Clarendon Press).

Syme, R. (1987) 'Marriage ages for Roman senators', *Historia* 36.3: 318–32 [= A.R. Birley (ed.), *Roman Papers* VI: 232–46 (Oxford: Clarendon Press, 1991)].

Takács, S.A. (2000) 'Politics and religion in the Bacchanalian affair of 186 B.C.E.', *Harvard Studies in Classical Philology* 100: 301–10.

Talbert, R.J.A. (1984) *The Senate of Imperial Rome* (Princeton, NJ: Princeton University Press).

Talbert, R.J.A. (1999) 'Tacitus and the "Senatus Consultum de Cn. Pisone Patre"', *American Journal of Philology* 120.1: 89–97.

Torelli, M. (1992) 'Topografia e iconologia. Arco di Portogallo, *Ara Pacis, Ara Providentiae, Templum Solis*', *Ostraka* 1.1: 105–31.

Torelli, M. (1999) 'Providentia, ara', in *LTUR* IV, 165–66.

Toynbee, J.M.C. (1944) *Roman Medallions*, Numismatic Studies no. 5 (New York: The American Numismatic Society).

Traub, H.W. (1953) 'Tacitus' use of *ferocia*', *Transactions and Proceedings of the American Philological Association* 84: 250–61.

Treggiari, S. (1991) *Roman Marriage. Iusti coniuges from the Time of Cicero to the Time of Ulpian* (Oxford: Clarendon Press).

Tucci, P.L. (2019) 'Living on the Capitoline Hill: the *domus* of the Aracoeli and its sculptural and painted decoration', *Papers of the British School at Rome* 87: 71–144.

Tupet, A.-M. (1980) 'Les pratiques magiques à la mort de Germanicus', in *Mélanges de littérature et d'épigraphie latines, d'histoire ancienne et d'archéologie: hommage à la mémoire de Pierre Wuilleumier*, 345–52 (Paris: Belles Lettres).

Turcan, R. (2011) 'Notions romaines de l'État: de la "Res Publica" au "Status Romanus"', *Latomus* 70.3: 621–41.

Versnel, H.S. (1980) 'Destruction, *devotio* and despair in a situation of anomy: the mourning of Germanicus in triple perspective', in *Perennitas. Studi in onore di Angelo Brelich*, 541–618 (Rome: Edizioni dell'Ateneo).

Volterra, E. (1993) 'Senatus consulta', in *Scritti giuridici*, vol. 5: *Le fonti*, Antiqua 65, 193–297 (Naples: Jovene Editore).

Wallace-Hadrill, A. (1981) 'The emperor and his virtues', *Historia* 30.3: 298–323.

Wardle, D. (1994) *Suetonius' Life of Caligula. A Commentary*, Collection Latomus 225 (Brussels: Latomus).

Wardle, D. (1997) '"The Sainted Julius": Valerius Maximus and the Dictator', *Classical Philology* 92.4: 323–45.

Watson, A. (trans.) (2009) *The Digest of Justinian*, Latin text edited by T. Mommsen with the aid of P. Krueger, vol. 4, revised edition (Philadelphia, PA: University of Pennsylvania Press) [= *Dig.*].

Weinstock, S. (1971) *Divus Julius* (Oxford: Clarendon Press).

Wells, C. (1984) *The Roman Empire*, Fontana History of the Ancient World (London: Fontana).

Westphal, H. (2015) '*Imperium suum paulatim destruxit*: the concept of *moderatio* in Valerius Maximus' *Facta et dicta memorabilia*', *Acta Classica* 58: 191–208.

Wheeler, E.L. (2007) 'The army and the *limes* in the East', in P. Erdkamp (ed.), *A Companion to the Roman Army*, 235–66 (Malden, MA / Oxford: Blackwell-Wiley).

Wilamowitz-Moellendorff, U. von, Zucker, F. (1911) 'Zwei Edikte des Germanicus auf einem Papyrus des Berliner Museums', *Sitzungsberichte der Königlich Preussischen Akademie der Wissenschaften zu Berlin* 38: 794–821.

Wilcken, U. (1928) 'Zum Germanicus-Papyrus', *Hermes* 63.4: 48–65.

Wilkes, J.J. (1969) *Dalmatia* (London: Routledge and Kegan Paul).

Williams, K.F. (2009) 'Tacitus' Germanicus and the Principate', *Latomus* 68: 117–30.

Williamson, C. (1987) 'Monuments of bronze: Roman legal documents on bronze tablets', *Classical Antiquity* 6: 160–83.

Williamson, C. (2016) 'Crimes against the State', in P.J. du Plessis, C. Ando, K. Tuori (eds), *The Oxford Handbook of Roman Law and Society*, 333–44 (Oxford: Oxford University Press).

Wirszubski, C. (1950) *Libertas as a Political Idea at Rome* (Cambridge: Cambridge University Press).

Wirszubski, C. (1954) 'Cicero's *cum dignitate otium*: a reconsideration', *Journal of Roman Studies* 44: 1–13.

Wiseman, T.P. (2019) *The House of Augustus. A Historical Detective Story* (Princeton, NJ / Oxford: Princeton University Press).

Wood, S.E. (2001) *Imperial Women: A Study in Public Images, 40 BC–AD 68*, 2nd edn (Leiden / Boston, MA: Brill).

Woodman, A.J. (1975a) 'Velleius Paterculus', in T.A. Dorey (ed.), *Empire and Aftermath. Silver Latin II*, 1–25 (London: Routledge & Kegan Paul).

Woodman, A.J. (1975b) 'Questions of date, genre, and style in Velleius: some literary answers', *Classical Quarterly*, 25.2: 272–306.

Woodman, A.J. (1977) *Velleius Paterculus: The Tiberian Narrative (2.94–131)* (Cambridge: Cambridge University Press).

Woodman, A.J. (1979) 'Self-imitation and the substance of history (*Annals* 1.61–5 and *Histories* 2.70, 5.14–15)', in D. West, T. Woodman (eds), *Creative Imitation and Latin Literature*, 143–55 (Cambridge: Cambridge University Press) [reprinted in A.J. Woodman, *Tacitus Reviewed*, 70–85 (Oxford: Clarendon Press, 1998)].

Woodman, A.J. (1983) *Velleius Paterculus: The Caesarian and Augustan Narrative (2.41–93)* (Cambridge: Cambridge University Press).

Woodman, A.J. (2015) 'Tacitus and Germanicus', in R. Ash, J. Mossman, F. Titchener (eds), *Fame and Infamy: Essays on Characterization in Greek and Roman Biography and Historiography*, 255–68 (Oxford: Oxford University Press).

Woodman, A.J. (2017) *The Annals of Tacitus. Books 5 and 6*, Cambridge Classical Texts and Commentaries 55 (Cambridge: Cambridge University Press).

Woodman, A.J. (2018) *The Annals of Tacitus. Book 4*, Cambridge Classical Texts and Commentaries 58 (Cambridge: Cambridge University Press).

Woodman, A.J., Martin, R.H. (1996) *The Annals of Tacitus. Book 3*, Cambridge Classical Texts and Commentaries 32 (Cambridge: Cambridge University Press).

Woolf, G. (1994) 'Becoming Roman, staying Greek: culture, identity and the civilizing process in the Greek East', *Proceedings of the Cambridge Philological Society* 40: 116–43.

Woytek B.E. (2017) 'Tiberian pseudo medallions of the CLEMENTIAE/MODERATIONI(S) group and the problem of chronology', *The Numismatic Chronicle* 177: 83–92.

Yakobson, A. (1998) 'The princess of inscriptions: *senatus consultum de Cn. Pisone patre* and the early years of Tiberius' reign', *Scripta Classica Israelica* 17: 206–24.

Yakobson, A. (2003) '*Maiestas*, the imperial ideology and the imperial family: the evidence of the *senatus consultum de Cn. Pisone patre*', *Eutopia* ns 3.1–2: 75–107.

Zecchini, G. (1999) 'Regime e opposizioni nel 20 d. C.: dal S.C. "de Cn. Pisone patre" a Tacito', in M. Sordi (ed.), *Fazioni e congiure nel mondo antico*, Contributi dell'Istituto di storia antica 25, 309–35 (Milan: Vita e Pensiero).

Index Locorum

AE
  1952.165 188
  1976.144 237
  1976.653 63
  1983.210 143, 146, 147, 148, 149
  1988.788 185
  2006.305 144
  2008.387 92
  2008.1353 lines 1–3 and line 109 92
  2012.467 6

Cass. Dio
  57.15.9 13
  57.18.9 8
  59.20.7 97

CFA
  2 col.1 20–22 16, 157
  13fgh lines 17–19 156

Cicero
  Inv. Rhet. 2.104 211
  Rab. Post. 9.24 87

CIL
  II², 5.64 37
  V.5050
  VI.2023a 16
  VI.5197 184
  VI.7461 88
  VI.31199 6
  VI.32323 144
  VI.32346 156
  XI.1421 92, 232
  XIII.1668 20–21

Dig.
  1.16.6.3 (Ulpian) 176
  9.2.50 (Ulpian) 90
  14.6.1.pr. (Ulpian) 143
  21.2.31 (Ulpian) 144
  48.4.1.1 (Ulpian) 18, 179
  48.4.2 (Ulpian) 19, 179
  48.4.3 (Marcianus) 173
  48.4.4 (Scaevola) 19, 173
  48.21.3.8 (Marcianus) 46, 160–61

Enn. *Ann.* 5.1 201

Fasti Ostienses
  Frag. Ce lines 37–39 28
  Frag. Ce lines 40–41 28

Gell. *NA* 15.7.3 157

Hunt and Edgar (1956) no.211 5

ILS 5026 16
Inscr. It. 13.2 193, no.25 84, 156

Livy
  4.13.9 90
  9.46 144

Macrob. *Sat* 1.12.35 178
Mitford 1960 167

Ovid
  Pont. 1.2.124 178
  Pont. 2.8.31 202
  Pont. 4.5.25–26 148
  Pont. 4.8.27–88 2
  Pont. 4.9.68–69 78–79
  Tr. 2.41–42 72
  Tr. 2.219–20 219

Palatine Anthology 7.391 6
Phaedrus *Fables* 2.5.23 79
Pliny the Elder, *HN* 11.187 7
Pliny the Younger *Ep.*
  3.7.12 98
  8.6 27, 54
Polybius 6.53–54 85
P.Oxy. no.2435 recto 5, 10, 11, 168–69

RGDA
  4.2 232
  26.5 232
  30.2 232
  34–35 229
RIC I² Augustus 358 157
  Tiberius nos 80–81 42, 43
RPC I.64
  I.3629,2 175–76

Index Locorum

Sallust
   Cat. 18.4–5 12–13, 96–97
   Jug. 4.5–6 86
SEG
   9.8 159
   26.1392 63
Seneca
   Apocol. 11 99
   De Ira 1.18.3 181–82
   Ep. 70.10 84
Sherk 1969, 329–331 159
Strabo *Geography* 6.4.2 2, 4
Suetonius
   Tib. 26 150
   Tib. 52 165–66
   Calig. 2 230
   Calig. 3 8, 166
   Calig. 5 6, 186
   Calig. 16.1 144

Tabula Siarensis
   Frag. A, lines 6–8 47, 64
   Frag. A, lines 15–16 9, 168, 169
   Frag. A, lines 22–24 47, 168
   Frag. B, col. 2, line 5 230
   Frag. B, col. 2, lines 11–13 47
   Frag. B, col. 2 line 17 235
   Frag. B, col. 2, lines 18–19 221
   Frag. B, col. 2, lines 22–24 229, 234
   Frag. B, col. 2, lines 24–25 193
   Frag. B, col. 2, lines 26–27 193
   Frag. B, col. 2, lines 27–39 147
   Frag. B, col. 2, line 30 238

Tacitus
   Annales
   1.33.2 4–5
   1.54.1 195
   1.62.2 23
   1.69 11
   1.73.2 190
   1.74.5 13
   2.27.2 84, 86
   2.32.1 194
   2.35 13
   2.37.2 146
   2.43 9, 11, 14, 97, 169
   2.50.1 78
   2.53.3/ 2.55.1–2 108
   2.64.1 28
   2.70.2 180
   2.71.1 27
   2.72.2 24
   2.75.2 26
   2.76.2 24
   2.78.1 14, 26
   2.88.1 21
   3.1.1 28

3.2.3 28, 218
3.3.1 25
3.6.3 28
3.9.1. 32
3.9.3 90, 208
3.11.1 28
3.12 23, 167
3.14.4 146
3.15.1 212, 220
3.16.1 22
3.16.4 15
3.17.4–18.2 83, 88, 147, 165, 216
3.19.2 7, 107
3.19.3 28
3.33.3 153
3.29.3 28
3.65.1 22
3.66 190
3.75 147
3.76 86, 194
4.9.2 218
4.13 144
4.21 14, 96
4.28–30 144
6.3 20
11.23–25 20–21
14.29.1 29
Hist.
2.70 23
4.38 98
4.48.1 97

Valerius Maximus
   1 *praef.* 65–66, 196
   1.8.1b 79
   2 *praef.* 79
   2.2.2 79
   2.2.8 79
   2.10 79–80
   3.4.6 80
   4.1 75–77
   4.3.3 59
   4.8.5 80
   5.1.*praef.* 71
   5.1.4–5 71
   5.1.10 71
   5.1.ext.6 71
   6.2.4 13
   6.3.3a 80
   6.4.2a 80
   6.5.4 80
   8.1.damn.3 87
   8.5 80
   9.2.3 80
   9.5.1 80
   9.8.2 81
Velleius Paterculus
   1.12 71, 202

2.55.2 71
2.69.6 71
2.83.2 71
2.86.2 71
2.89.3 62
2.90.1 178
2.100.4 71
2.104.2 233
2.122.1 73
2.124 65, 81, 219
2.126 62, 64–65
2.129.3 169
2.130.5 213
2.131 72, 156, 220

Thematic Index

Ad Gemellas 35, 38
Aemilius Lepidus, M. (cos. AD 6) 19, 163
Aemilius Paullus 80
Aequitas 159–60, 220, 222
Aerarium 30
Africa, Roman province of 12, 15, 97, 203
Agrippa, M. 65, 170, 171, 196, 223
Agrippa Postumus 108, 165, 179
Agrippina (the Elder) 46, 66, 89, 104, 220, 222, 226
    Characterisation in Tacitus 11, 15, 165, 223–24
    Hostility towards Plancina 11, 14, 161, 210
    Journey back to Rome 17, 28, 223
    Praised by Senate 55, 60–61, 73, 74, 217, 223–24, 227
    Wife of Germanicus 2, 11, 55, 109, 206, 223–24, 227
Agrippina (the Younger) 21, 104, 109, 223
Alexander the Great 11
Alexandria 5, 10–11, 168–69
Amicitiae renuntiatio see friendship
Antioch on the Orontes 2, 6, 7, 17, 177, 180
Antiochus, King 77, 80
Antonia (mother of Germanicus) 2, 46, 60–61, 65, 73, 74, 89, 217, 220, 222, 224, 227
Antony, M. 14, 88, 91, 169, 178, 187, 203, 224
Antonius Primus 99
Appuleius Saturninus, L. 86–87
Arles 188
Armenia 8, 10, 18, 33, 61, 152, 161, 169, 170, 172–76, 177, 210, 215
Army 51, 60, 94, 108, 181–85, 188, 199, 217, 230–33 *see also* civil war; donatives; mutiny
    Auxiliaries 181
    Ninth Hispanica Legion 32
    Rival allegiances in 12, 184–85, 231–32, 237
    Velleius Paterculus' career 65
    Winter headquarters 32, 45, 48, 58, 231, 234, 236, 237
Arquinius, Q. 216
Arrenus Gallus, C. 148
Artabanus III, King of Parthia 8, 174, 176
Artaxias III, King of Armenia 173, 175–76
Arvals 16, 43, 96, 156, 157, 196–97
Asinius Pollio (historian) 100–01, 105

Asinius Gallus, C. 165
Astrologers 13
Ateius Capito, C. (cos. AD 5) 147–48, 238
Athens 80, 108
Aufidius Bassus, historian 21
Augustus 65, 88, 89, 92, 97, 108, 146, 148, 150, 157, 170, 182, 183, 196, 198, 199, 208, 211, 212, 213, 218–19, 232
Auspices 232
Calendar of Asia Minor 159
Civic crown 70, 178
Clementia 69–70, 71, 191
Consecratio 43
Death 2, 63, 94, 167, 179, 189, 190, 195
Deified Augustus (*divus Augustus*) 18, 42, 45, 46, 55, 59, 63, 83, 182, 189, 190, 195, 196, 223 *see also* numen
Equestrian order 227, 228
Friendship with Piso *pater* 15, 89, 94, 199
Golden shield 66, 69, 188
Marriage to Livia 223
Moderatio 72
Parallelism with Tiberius 59, 60, 62–63, 150, 178–79, 182
Principate 2, 4, 63, 158, 159, 219
Res Gestae 40, 72, 143, 159, 182, 183, 188, 227, 229
Statio 219
Succession planning 43–44, 92, 100, 196–98, 219, 226
Supported by Munatius Plancus 14
Temple in Asia 238
Temple of Palatine Apollo 50, 145–46
Votive games 88, 195
Aurelius Cotta Maximus Messallinus, M. (cos. AD 20) 147, 191, 194, 195, 198, 240

Baetica 144 *see also Tabula Siarensis*
    Coins 2, 41–44
    Local elite 2, 41, 43, 44
    Providentia Augusti 41–44
    SCPP copies 38, 40–41, 58, 234
    Relationship with Rome 2, 41–44
Bassus, epigram on Germanicus' death 6
Beneficium 158, 212–13
Bibulus, M. 77

Bona Dea (Good goddess) 199
Brundisium 17
Brutus 13, 71, 86, 97, 194
Buchan, John 103

Caecilius Metellus Creticus Silanus, Q. (Roman governor) 8, 9, 174
Caecina Severus 153
Calpurnia (daughter of Cn. Piso) 83, 200, 204–07
Calpurnia (niece of Cn. Piso) 198–99
Calpurnii Pisones 12–14, 95–100, 193, 198, 203
Calpurnius Piso, C. 99
Calpurnius Piso, Cn. (grandfather of Piso *pater*) 12–13, 96–97
Calpurnius Piso, Cn. (*cos.* 23 BC, father of Piso *pater*) 12, 199
  Brutus and Cassius, supporter of 13, 97
  Character 13, 96
  Proquaestor in Spain 12
  Prosecutes supporter of Pompeius Magnus 13
Calpurnius Piso *pater*, Cn. (*cos.* 7 BC) 97
  Adiutor of Germanicus 9–10, 11, 12, 23, 167–68, 170–71
  Arval? 16
  Augustus, friendship with 15, 83, 89, 93–94, 199
  Characterisation in Robert Graves 108–09
  Characterisation in *SCPP* 31, 165, 179, 180, 181–2, 187, 199–200, 231–32
  Characterisation in Tacitus 13, 26–27, 165, 174–75, 202
  Charges against 18–20, 45, 59, 62, 161–90, 231
  Civil war, accused of 17, 18, 19–20, 177–80, 210, 215, 231
  Early career 12, 15, 88, 89, 162, 181–82
  Family background 12–14
  Germanicus' death, response to 17, 26–27, 177, 185–89, 201
  Germanicus, hostility towards 8, 10, 11–12, 15, 18, 50–51, 55, 88, 109, 161, 162–72, 186–98, 201, 221, 233
  Germanicus, suspected of poisoning 7–8, 15, 18, 19, 27, 28, 51, 74, 110, 162, 165–66, 198, 209, 221
  House at Rome 83, 89–91, 93, 189, 200, 207–09
  Legate of Syria 9, 10, 16–17, 24, 153, 166, 167, 173, 177–85, 231
  Name changed 92, 203
  Name erased 40, 83, 87–89, 191
  Patrician? 91
  Penalties against 20, 27, 43, 47, 50, 82–94, 143, 147, 160, 190–200, 207–09
  Property of 20, 46, 82, 83, 90–91, 94, 152, 160, 191, 198–200, 202–03, 204, 205
  Return to Rome in AD 20 17, 18, 28, 32, 33, 189, 198, 208
  Suicide 20, 27, 33, 45, 82–83, 87, 93, 94, 150, 151–52, 155, 159, 160–61, 163, 166, 190–91, 193, 198, 201, 202, 205, 206, 221, 235, 240
  Tiberius, relationship with 10, 13, 14, 15–16, 20, 26, 27, 28, 88, 89, 93–94, 167, 184, 195
  Trial 1, 7, 18–20, 24, 27–28, 44–47, 51, 96, 107, 148, 155, 159, 160–61, 164, 220, 230, 235
  Chronology of 28–33, 162, 192, 196, 222
  Jack Pulman's BBC script 110
Calpurnius Piso, Cn. (L.) (*cos.* AD 27) (elder son of Piso *pater*) 20, 45, 70, 83, 91–92, 93, 95, 97–98, 193, 198, 200, 201–03, 205, 206
Calpurnius Piso Augur, L. (*cos.* 1 BC) (brother of Piso *pater*) 13–14, 19, 96, 109–10, 163, 198–99, 211
Calpurnius Piso, L. (nephew of Piso *pater*) 96
Calpurnius Piso, L. (*cos.* AD 57) (grandson of Piso *pater*) 16, 96, 97–98, 99, 206
Calpurnius Piso, M. (younger son of Piso *pater*) 17, 24, 45–46, 51, 95–96, 149–50, 152, 161, 173, 198, 205, 209, 222, 235
  Pardoned by Senate 20, 57, 70, 74–75, 83, 96, 191, 200, 203–04, 211, 214
Calpurnius Piso Crassus Frugi Licinianus (*cos.* AD 87) 99
Calpurnius Piso Frugi Licinianus, L. (Galba's heir) 99, 187
Calpurnius Piso Galerianus 99
Campa Torres 40, 89
Caninius, L. 89
Cantius Othonianus, T. 185
Cappadocia 8–9, 10, 18, 169, 175
Cassius 13, 71, 86, 97, 194
Cassius Dio 8, 13, 63, 97, 110, 166, 213
Cassius, Sp. 90
Catiline 12, 96–97
Cato the Younger 76, 80
Centobriga 71
Cicero 69, 157, 187
Cilicia 8–9, 10, 169, 174, 180
Cissa 199
Civil war 17, 62, 69, 70, 98, 157, 161, 170, 177–80, 184–85, 210
Claudius (brother of Germanicus, later *princeps*) 54, 73, 74, 98–99, 176, 221, 222, 224, 226–27
  I, Claudius 100–10
  Sodalis Augustalis 16, 195
  Speech as *princeps* on admitting Gauls to the Senate 20–21, 23
Claudius Nero, C. 76
Clemens, conspiracy of 179
Clementia (clemency) 46, 64, 65, 66–72, 83, 191, 200–01, 204
  Clementia Caesaris 69
Cleopatra 77
Clodius 187

Thematic Index

Clunia 185
Clutorius Priscus, poem on Germanicus' death 6
Coins, 63, 64, 150, 225 *see also* donatives
    Caesarian 69
    Clementia and *moderatio* 66–69
    Divus Augustus pater 63
    Minted at Caesarea in Cappadocia 175–76
    Minted at Rome 42–43, 44, 178, 196
    Minted by Cn. Calpurnius Piso *pater* 12
    Minted in the Hispanic provinces 41–44
Commagene 8–9, 18, 169
Concordia 223
Congiarium 188–89
Consensus 53–54, 58, 78, 188, 229
Consilium 181
Consolatio ad Liviam 213–14
Conventus Astiganus 37
Corduba, Roman provincial capital of Baetica 38, 44, 144
Cornelius Cinna, Cn. 211
Córdoba, modern province of 35
Cos 17, 177, 185, 187, 188
Crassus 96
Curatores locorum publicorum 108
Customs law of Asia of AD 62 92, 203
Cyrene, *SC* from 159

Divine qualities 66, 69, 70, 72, 78
Domitian, imperial titles omitted 92
Domitius Celer 177–78, 214–15
Domus Augusta 44, 59–62, 64, 69, 73, 77–78, 81–82, 156, 162, 170, 187, 188, 214, 222, 225, 227, 229, 232–33 *see also* imperial family
Donatives 182–83
Dowry 205–06
Drusilla (daughter of Germanicus) 223
Drusus Gemellus (son of Drusus the Younger) 225
Drusus Iulius Caesar (son of Germanicus) 223, 226–27
Drusus (the Elder) 2, 7, 65, 108, 145, 213, 222, 224
Drusus (the Younger) 13, 33, 42, 69, 89, 104, 148, 222, 224, 225
    Honorary magistrate at Carteia 42
    Honours after death 68, 158–59, 218, 229
    Meeting with Piso *pater* 17, 198
    Mutiny, suppression of 5
    Ovatio 28, 30, 32–33, 222
    Political importance 2, 4, 170, 196, 217, 218, 219, 233
    Portrait on *dupondii*? 67–68
    Praised by Senate 24, 60, 73, 159, 188, 217, 220–22, 227
    Sodalis Augustalis 16, 195
Dupondii, Tiberian 67–68, 69

Egypt 10, 12, 169, 170, 173, 174, 199
Emerita 42
Ephesos 92, 203
Equestrians 51, 55, 60, 188, 214, 215, 217, 227–28, 229–30
Erasures from inscriptions 16, 40, 43, 87–89, 93, 192, 195
Exemplarity 60–61, 64–66, 73, 82, 92, 159–60, 201, 221, 222, 227
    Valerius Maximus, in 13, 65–66, 75–78, 79–81, 196, 224

Fabius Maximus 75
Fabius Maximus, Paullus 159
Fadius Secundus Musa, Sex. 237
Families, shared characteristics in 14, 81, 85–86, 92, 93–94, 95–100, 109, 195, 202
Fasti 83, 88, 89, 92, 216
Fasti Amiterni 84, 156
Fasti Ostienses 28, 30, 92, 185
Feritas 54–55
Ferocia 14, 15, 26, 96, 165
Fidenae 200
Firmius Catus 86
Fiscus 183–84, 198
Flavius, Cn. (aedile) 144
Fonteius Agrippa 206
Friendship 86
    Renunciation of 11, 12, 16, 23–24, 74, 88, 166–67, 180, 187
Fufius, C. 89
Fufius Geminus, C. 213
Fulcinius Trio, L. (prosecutor of Piso *pater*) 18, 162
Fulvius Flaccus, M. 90
Funerals 83, 84, 85–86
Furius Camillus 75, 91

Gaius (Caligula) 67, 95, 97, 109, 156, 176, 223, 226–27
Gaius Iulius Caesar, 219, 225, 227
    Activities in the East 11, 169, 170
    Honours after death 7, 92, 185, 218, 232
    Hostility towards Marcus Lollius 11, 167
Galatia, *Res Gestae* in 40
Galba (*princeps*) 99, 213
Gallia Comata, Claudius' speech 20–21
Gellius, Aulus 219, 238
Gemellus (grandson of Tiberius) 67
Geneva, copy of *SCPP* 39–40
Germania 4, 7, 179, 202, 223
Germanicus Iulius Caesar 89, 108, 146, 148, 202, 207
    Activities in the East 1, 5, 8–12, 18, 61, 62, 88, 152, 162, 168–73, 175–76, 223, 233
    Adoption by Tiberius 2, 15, 43
    Alexandria, visit to 5, 10–11, 173
    Antony's grandson 10
    Characterisation in *SCPP* 31, 73, 74, 159, 164–65
    Characterisation in Tacitus 4–5, 23
    Coins, on 42, 175–76

Death 1, 2, 5–8, 24, 26–27, 33, 40, 75, 85, 107, 152, 155, 161, 180, 187, 215, 216, 217, 222, 228, 234
Suspected poisoning 7–8, 15, 18, 19, 27, 28, 33, 51, 74, 75, 94, 109, 155, 162, 165–66, 209–19, 221
Dynastic importance 2, 43–44, 223
Early career 4
Egypt, visit to 10–11, 12, 173, 174
Equestrian statue at Irni? 34
Family 4, 55, 73, 74, 217, 222–27
Honorary magistrate at Carteia 42
Honours decreed after death 6–7, 47, 50, 53, 58, 145–46, 158, 185, 195–96, 218, 221, 222, 227–29, 236, 237 *see also* Tabula Hebana, Tabula Siarensis
Hostility towards Piso 8, 10, 11–12, 15, 23–24, 27, 74, 88, 109, 180
Imperium 9, 10, 62, 171–72
Military commander 4, 5, 14, 18, 23, 153, 223
Ovatio 28, 32
Poet 2
Political importance 2, 4, 44, 170, 197–98
Portrait on *dupondii*? 67–69
Sodalis Augustalis 16, 195
Statue in Rome 43, 83, 88, 94, 195, 228–29
Tiberius, relationship with 4, 10–11, 23, 43–44, 60, 173
Triumph 4
Gracchus, C. 85, 87
Gracchus, Ti. 76
Granius Marcellus, *maiestas* case 13
Graves, Robert (poet and novelist) 100–10
  I, Claudius 100–10
  Goodbye to All That 104, 107
  'The Tenement: a vision of imperial Rome' 106–07
  'To Bring the Dead to Life' 106

Hadrian (*princeps*) 95, 99
Hannibal 71
Harmodius and Aristogeiton 81
Haterius, Q. 213
Herculaneum 144, 237
Hispalis 42
Hispania Baetica *see* Baetica
Hispania Citerior 12
Hispania Lusitania 42
Hispania Tarraconensis 12, 40, 42, 89, 195
Humanitas 27, 70, 71, 72, 74, 77–78, 83, 94, 187

Illyria / Illyricum 17, 33, 83, 94, 191, 198–99
  Piso's estate in 15, 17
Imago 83, 84, 85–87, 93, 191, 192–93, 194–95
Imago clipeata (shield portrait) 67–68, 69, 145
Imperial family 88, 146, 237 *see also* Agrippina (the Elder); Agrippina (the Younger); Antonia; Augustus; Claudius; *Domus Augusta*; Drusus (the Elder); Drusus (the Younger); Gaius Iulius Caesar; Germanicus Iulius Caesar; Iulia Augusta; Livi(ll)a; Nero Iulius Caesar; Tiberius
Coins 42–44
Dynastic statuary groups 4
Place in Roman society 1, 2, 8, 13–14, 44–62, 65, 77–78, 81–82, 158, 170, 185–86, 188, 201, 229, 232–33
sodales Augustales 15–16
Imperium 9, 10, 16, 18, 62, 75, 80, 81, 171–72, 214
Indulgentia 186
Irni 34, 38, 41, 143
Italica 42–44
Iulia (daughter of Agrippa) 223
Iulia (daughter of Drusus the Younger) 225, 226
Iulia Augusta 46, 65, 89, 109, 154, 222, 225
  Characterisation in Tacitus 15
  Divine honours 10
  Friend of Plancina 14, 15, 20, 25–26, 94
  Friend of Urgulania 13–14, 96
  Germanicus' death, suspected involvement in 7, 15, 33, 110
  Trial of Plancina, intervention in 14, 25–26, 56–57, 107, 209–14, 222
  Marriage to Augustus 223
  Praised by Senate 24, 60, 73, 159, 188, 217, 220–22, 227
Iulia Livilla (daughter of Germanicus) 149, 223
Iulius Caesar 69, 70, 71, 81
Iunia, funeral of 86, 194
Iunius Gallio 20, 182
Iunius Silanus, M. 97, 190
Iustitia (justice) 66, 68, 83, 200–01, 204, 235
Iustitium 5, 33, 186, 187–88

Jaén, modern province of 39

Lawrence, T.E. 102, 103, 104, 105
Legate 9, 12, 96, 97, 150, 172, 173, 184
Lepcis Magna, inscription of Piso 89
Lex on Germanicus' *imperium* 9, 62, 171, 172
Lex Irnitana 34
Lex Iulia de peculatu 184
Lex Valeria Cornelia 7
Libertas 13–14, 15
Libo Drusus, M. Scribonius 86, 179
  Arval? 16
  Maiestas case 16, 18, 25, 38, 66, 82, 144, 156, 220
  Penalties 84–85, 194, 2–3
Libo Frugi 99
Licinia Magna 96, 99
Licinius Crassus Frugi, M. (*cos.* AD 27) 98–99
Licinius Crassus Frugi, M. (*cos.* AD 64) 99
Licinius Crassus Scribonianus, 99

Thematic Index

Livia (wife of Augustus) 223, 224, 226 *see also* Iulia Augusta
Livi(ll)a (sister of Germanicus) 60–61, 73, 74, 154, 217, 222, 224, 225, 227
Livineius Regulus (cos. AD 18) (defence of Piso) 19, 163
Livius Salinator 76
Livy 90, 100–01, 105
Lollius, Marcus (*adiutor* of Gaius Caesar) 11, 166, 167
Lucius Iulius Caesar 7, 185, 218, 219, 227
Ludi saeculares 144, 147
Ludi Megalenses 28
Lugdunum Tablet 20–21, 23, 104

Magic 8, 166
Maelius, Sp. 90
Maiestas 46–47, 70, 78–82, 96, 162, 185, 189–90, 215
   Domus Augusta, of 61–62, 77, 78, 81, 170
   Granius Marcellus, case of 13
   Legal definitions of 18–19, 82–83, 173, 179, 180
   Lex Cornelia de maiestate, 81 BC 180
   Libo Drusus, case of 16, 18, 25, 38, 66, 82, 144, 194
   Penalties for 46, 47, 215–16
   Piso *pater*, case of 17–20, 44–47, 82–94, 161–2, 173, 179, 202–03, 208
   Quaestio maiestatis 19, 45, 154, 216
   Rubrius, case of
   Senate 19, 25, 44–47, 62, 80, 150, 154
   Tacitus, in 13, 25, 162
   Tiberius, of 79, 81, 190
   Valerius Maximus, in 79–81
   Vibius Serenus, trial of 144
Manlius Capitolinus, M. 90, 91, 208
Manlius Torquatus, T. 194
Marcellus, M. 71, 75
Marcius Rutilus Censorinus 75
Marius 80, 81
Marsh, Edward 102, 103
Martina, suspected poisoner 7, 109, 110, 164, 210
Martos 37
Masinissa, King 80
Matthews, Julie and Tom 102–03
Medallion, pseudo 68–69
Memory sanctions 16, 20, 40, 50, 83, 88, 92–94, 143, 191–98, 225
Mescinius Rufus, coins of 157
Metellus, Q. 71, 79
Metellus Macedonicus 76
Metellus Numidicus 76
Moderatio (moderation) 64, 66–69, 70, 72–78, 83, 164–65, 214, 221, 235
Mos maiorum 192, 201
Mourning 83, 85, 93, 185–86, 187–88, 191, 192, 217, 221, 222, 231
Munatius Plancus, L. (*cos.* 42 BC) 14, 152
Munatius Plancus, L. (*cos.* AD 13) 14, 153

Murecine archive of wax tablets 240
Mutiny 4, 5, 14, 153, 179

Names 50, 52, 215, 233, 241
   Changes to 20, 83, 84–85, 91–92, 93, 193, 203, 205
   Erased from inscriptions 16, 83, 87–89, 191, 195
Narbo 237
Nero (*princeps*) 95, 96, 99
Nero Iulius Caesar (son of Germanicus) 9, 28, 223, 226–27
Nerva (*princeps*) 95, 99
Nicopolis (Syria) 177
Nonius Asprenas, L. (*cos.* AD 6) 149, 221, 226
Nonius Asprenas, L. (urban quaestor) 148–49, 205
Nonius Balbus, M. 237
Numa, King 12, 192
Numen 18, 59, 178–79, 185, 189–90
Nyon (*Colonia Iulia Equestris*) 39–40

Octavia (sister of Augustus) 212, 224
Otho (*princeps*) 185, 187
Ovid 2, 59, 72, 78, 178, 219

Pallas (imperial freedman) 27, 54
Pannonia 5, 179, 199
Papyri 5, 10
Paratexts 47–54
Parthia 8, 18, 33, 61, 169, 170, 172–76, 177, 185–86, 210, 215
Patientia 74, 78, 159, 164–65
Paxea 191
Peculium 206–07
Phaedrus 79
Phraates IV, King of Parthia 173
Pietas 57, 65, 68, 70, 77–78, 188, 204, 214, 218, 220, 221, 229
Pisa 185
Plancina, Munatia 51, 85, 97, 108, 109, 149–50, 161, 176, 203, 206, 222, 235
   Family background 12, 14, 152
   Friendship with Iulia Augusta 15, 20, 25–26, 94, 107, 222
   Hostility towards Agrippina the Elder 11, 14, 152, 161, 210
   Pardoned by the Senate 14, 20, 25–26, 27, 56–57, 70, 153, 191, 200, 203, 204, 209–14, 222
   Suicide 20, 210
   Suspected of poisoning Germanicus 7, 18, 27, 109, 165–66, 209–10
Plautius, A. 52, 240–41
Plebs 60, 85, 87, 188, 192–93, 217, 228–30, 235
Pliny the Elder 21, 165
Pliny the Younger 22, 27, 54
Political discourse, Tiberian 1, 23, 25, 33, 63–82, 148, 156–57, 200, 219
Pompeiopolis 174

Pompeius, Sex. (*cos.* AD 14) 148
Pompeius Magnus 13, 71, 96
Pompeius Magnus, Cn. 99, 169
Pompeius Priscus, M. 148
Pomponius Gracchus, C. 78
Pomponius Labeo 191
Pontius Ni[grinus?], L. 216
Populus Romanus 62, 79, 80, 155, 161, 170, 171, 183, 189, 219, 220, 227
    Ratification of *imperium* for Germanicus 62, 171
    Ratification of honours for Germanicus 6, 147, 155, 171, 228, 230
    Rioting (actual and potential) 20, 32, 55–56, 87, 98, 230
Praetor 19, 45, 65, 154, 215–16, 240
Principate 1, 2, 4, 73, 78 *see also statio*
Proconsul 9, 12, 15, 18, 41, 62, 95, 96, 97, 144, 148, 159, 169, 170, 172, 176, 181, 203
Providentia (foresight) 64, 66, 78, 196, 200
Providentia Augusta/Augusti 41–44, 196–98

Quaestor
    Augusti (imperial) 52, 201–02, 240
    Urban 30, 145, 148–49, 201, 240–41
Quinctius Cincinnatus, L. 75

Riding, Laura 101, 103, 106
Rome 234, 235
    Aerarium Saturni (treasury at Temple of Saturn) 145, 148, 183, 216, 241
    Altar of Augustan Peace 43, 69, 196
    Altar of *Clementia* 69, 71
    Altar of *Providentia* (Foresight) 42–44, 83, 196–98
    Altar of Vengeance 83
    Basilica Iulia 92
    Campus Martius (Field of Mars) 43, 83, 91, 196–97, 213
    Capitol 17, 90–91, 200, 207–09
    Circus Flaminius, arch for Germanicus 7, 222, 225, 226–27
    Coins minted at 42–43, 44
    Fire in AD 16 213
    Fontinal Gate 83, 89–90, 207–09
    Forum 17, 90–91, 189, 207, 208, 213, 241
    Gemonian steps 87, 193
    Mausoleum of Augustus 5, 17, 74, 170, 195, 228, 236
    Piso's house 83, 89–91, 93, 189, 200, 207–09
    Statue of Germanicus 43, 83, 88, 94, 195
    Temple of *Clementia Caesaris* (Clemency of Caesar) 69
    Temple of Mars the Avenger 83
    Temple of Palatine Apollo, Library 50–51, 58, 68, 105, 145–46, 236
    Tiber, River 87, 193, 230

Saevitia 191
Sagalassos, requisitioning edict 63
Salus Augusta 68
Salvius Otho, M. 213
Sassoon, Siegfried 101
Saturninus, L. 90
Scaevola, Q. 76
Scipio Aemilianus 80, 202
Scipio Africanus 71, 75, 76, 77, 80, 81
Scipio Asiaticus 76
SC de Bacchanalibus 58
SC from Cyrene 159
SC from Larinum 62, 143, 146, 147, 148, 149
SC Macedonianum 143
SCPP
    Authorship 1, 46, 47, 50, 53–54, 144–45, 146, 204, 239–40
    Bias 1, 26–27, 30–31, 33, 177
    Comparison with Tacitus 1, 15, 18–19, 23–33, 83, 88, 150, 155, 159, 160, 161, 162, 164, 166, 167–68, 169, 172, 173, 174, 177, 180, 184, 186, 189, 191, 212, 214, 216–17, 218, 220, 225, 238–39
    Copies 2, 34–40
    Gratiarum actio 216–17
    Heading/Title 41, 47, 50, 143–44, 235
    Language of 23–25, 26–27, 31, 45, 46, 54–57, 150, 151, 153–54, 155, 157, 158, 164, 165, 167, 210, 212, 215, 217, 222, 232
    Archaisms in 34, 56, 151, 158
    Anachronism in 179, 189
    Hyperbole 54–56, 160, 181, 188, 238
    Syntax 51, 52, 56–57, 158, 162–63, 170, 174, 182, 208, 209, 233
    Moderatio 73–74
    Moralising aims 30–31, 41, 44, 46, 50–51, 54–55, 92–94, 151–52, 164–65, 175, 179, 180, 235
    Murder of Germanicus 8, 18, 51
    Paragraphing 48–49, 52, 145, 156, 162, 190
    Paratextual interpretation 47–54
    Prescript 50–51, 53, 144–45
    Publication 32, 38–39, 40–41, 44, 45, 53, 58, 64, 93, 144, 229–30, 233–37
    Date of publication 25, 145
    Readership 52–53
    Relatio 32, 51, 146, 149–50, 155, 161, 190, 200, 203, 209, 214, 217, 235, 238–39
    Rhetoric 1, 26–27, 33, 54–55, 182, 199–200, 238
    Retrospective account of Piso's trial 19, 27, 28, 30–32, 51–52, 150, 154
    Subscriptio 52, 53, 64, 146, 239–41
    Tiberius' *vultus* 24–25, 220
Sejanus 72, 87, 165, 194, 196, 219, 224, 225, 231
Sempronius Bassus 82, 149, 153–54, 214–15
Senate 11 *see also* Lugdunum Tablet, *SC de Bacchanalibus, SC* from Cyrene, *SC* from Larinum, *SC Macedonianum*, SCPP, *Tabula Hebana, Tabula Siarensis*

Thematic Index

Acta senatus 22–23, 26–28
   Attendance at 54, 237–38
   Authority of 10, 13, 19, 45, 53, 58–59, 153,
      155–56, 168, 171, 176
   Germanicus' death, response to 5–8, 26–27,
      34
   Decrees on honours for Germanicus 6–7, 34,
      44, 49, 50, 53, 54, 58, 64, 68, 145–46, 185
   Honours for Iulius Caesar 69
   Imperial family, relationship with 1, 19,
      24–25, 33, 44–62, 81–82, 147, 149, 154,
      155–60, 168, 176, 179, 186, 188, 200,
      201, 202, 209–14, 215, 216–27, 228, 236,
      237–38
   Maiestas trials in 19–20, 24, 46–47, 82–83,
      150, 153–54
   Meeting-place 50, 144, 145–46, 230
   Publication of decrees 30–32, 38, 40–41,
      58–59, 81, 143, 155, 193, 229, 233–37
Seneca the Younger 84, 181
Sentius Saturninus, Cn. (governor of Syria) 17,
   177, 180, 233
Servaeus, Q. (prosecutor of Piso) 18, 162
Servilius Nonianus (historian) 21
Servius Sulpicius 187
Severitas 191–92, 204, 214
Seville, modern province of 34, 36
Siarum 44
Silius, C. 194, 198
Sinceritas 80
Sodales Augustales 15–16, 43, 83, 88, 94, 195–96
Sotidius Strabo Libuscidianus, Sex.,
   requisitioning edict 63, 150
Statio 4, 219
Strabo, view of Tiberian rule 2, 4, 62–63
Suetonius 6, 8, 23, 63, 165–66
Suicide 16, 20, 27, 46, 84
Syracuse 71
Syria 7, 12, 14, 16, 24, 152, 153, 173, 184, 185
   Germanicus' death 2, 17
   Civil war in 17, 19, 161, 170, 177–85, 204,
      210, 215
   Mount Amanus, arch for Germanicus 7, 47,
      236
   Vonones in 8, 161

Tabula Hebana 6–7, 34, 145–46, 185
Tabula Irnitana 237
Tabula Siarensis 6–7, 34, 146, 147, 158, 166,
   185, 227, 230, 236, 239
   Advisory board of imperial family 46–47,
      64, 222
   Germanicus' mission in the east 9, 168, 171,
      176
   Publication 32, 44, 58, 155, 229, 234, 237
Tacitus 63, 190, 219, 240
   Acta senatus, use of 22–23, 26–28
   Boudiccan revolt, chronology of 29
   Characterisation of
   Agrippina 11, 25, 223–24

   Germanicus 4–5, 9
   Iulia Augusta 15, 25, 212
   Libo Drusus 84, 86
   Piso 12–14, 15, 26–27, 28, 90, 108–09, 165,
      182, 220
   Tiberius 5, 9, 15, 24–25, 28, 167, 185, 220
   Chronology in the *Annales* 29–30
   Comparison with Lugdunum Tablet 20–21,
      23
   Comparison with *SCPP* 1, 15, 18–19, 23–33,
      83, 88, 150, 155, 159, 160, 161, 162, 163,
      164, 166, 167–68, 169, 172, 173, 174,
      177, 180, 184, 186, 189, 191, 212, 214,
      216–17, 218, 225, 238–39
   Comparison with *Tabula Hebana* and *Tabula
      Siarensis* 6–7, 34, 176
   Documentary sources, use of 20–33
   Ferocia in 14
   Germanicus' death 5, 7–8, 16–17, 26–27, 33
   Hostility between Piso/Plancina and
      Germanicus/ Agrippina 11–12, 15, 109,
      152–53, 162
   Maiestas 13, 19, 25, 78, 84
   Mirror narratives 11, 152
   Oral sources, use of 22
   Piso's trial 7, 18–20, 24, 25–33, 46, 83, 146,
      163, 167
   Pisones in 12–14, 95, 98–100, 108, 110
   Rumours 6, 7, 11, 100, 217
   Self-imitation in 23
Tarraco 42
Teanum Sidicum 92
Theopompus 77
Thrasybulus 77
Tiberius 89, 146, 148, 154, 157–58, 169, 207,
   225, 239–41
   Divine honours 10
   Edict suspending mourning for Germanicus
      5–6, 73–74, 228, 230
   Germanicus, attitude to 10–11, 16, 23, 55,
      60, 73–74, 110, 186, 188, 217–18, 220,
      234, 235
   Germanicus' death, suspected involvement in
      7, 15, 33, 94, 110
   Imperium 9, 232
   Iulia Augusta, relationship with 57, 70, 110,
      188, 210–12, 213, 214, 221
   Mutinies against 4, 5
   Oath of loyalty to 167, 231
   Ovatio for Pannonia 33
   Parallelism with Augustus 59, 60, 62–63,
      178–79, 181, 202
   Piso, relationship with 10, 12, 13, 14, 15–16,
      20, 45, 88, 89, 110, 173, 184, 193, 195,
      199, 203
   Piso's trial, at 19, 24, 159, 161, 163, 185,
      190
   Modifies penalties 20, 27, 83, 88, 147, 191,
      195, 198, 200
   Portrait on *dupondii*? 67

Senate, influence in 13, 31, 45–47, 51, 52, 57, 83, 94, 145, 150, 152, 153–54, 155, 158–59, 199, 222
  Relator 45, 46, 146, 149–50, 151, 155, 161, 165, 200, 203, 209, 214, 235, 238–40
  Speeches 31, 150, 152, 163, 165, 233–34, 235
  Subscriptio 52, 64, 146, 239–41
  Sodalis Augustalis 16, 195
  Subscriptio 31–32
  Successor of Augustus 2, 4, 43, 62–63, 73, 81, 150, 167, 171, 197–98, 219, 231, 232, 239
  Tacitus' characterisation of 5, 9, 15, 25, 46
  Tribunician power 45, 52, 145, 151, 239
  Virtues 59, 63, 65, 69, 73, 74, 75, 76, 78, 159–60, 191, 196, 202, 235
  Vultus 24–25
Tiberius Gemellus (son of Drusus the Younger) 225
Titius, Sex. 86–87
Trajan (*princeps*) 95, 99
Tucci Colonia Gemella 37
Turiaso 42

Urgulania, friend of Iulia Augusta 13–14, 96, 211

Valerius Festus 96, 97
Valerius Maximus 1, 64–66, 78, 158, 179, 192, 219, 224
  Characterisation of Cn. Calpurnius Piso (cos. 23 BC) 13
  Clementia in 70–71, 72, 75
  Maiestas in 79–81
  Moderatio in 75–77
  Work dedicated to Tiberius 61, 65–66, 196
Valerius Messallinus Corvinus, M. (*cos.* 31 BC) 148, 240
Valerius Messalla Messallinus, M. (*cos.* 3 BC) 147, 149, 155, 216, 217, 220–21, 222, 225, 226
Valerius Messalla Messallinus?, M. (*cos.* AD 20) 147, 240
Valerius Publicola, P. 75
Varro 238
Vatienus, P. 79
Velleius Paterculus 1, 56, 64–65, 149, 158, 169, 178, 184, 191, 211, 213–14
  Attitude to Tiberius 65, 71–72, 73, 76, 78, 81, 157, 179, 196, 219–20, 233
  Career 65
  Clementia in 71–72, 78
Veneratio 80
Veranius, Q. (prosecutor of Piso) 18, 162
Vespasian (*princeps*) 95
Vibius Serenus, N. (provincial governor of Baetica) 38–39, 40, 41, 44, 50, 144
Vinicius, M. (urban quaestor) 149
Virtus 66
Visellius Karus 82, 149, 153–54, 214–15
Vitellius, P. (prosecutor of Piso) 7, 18, 162, 165
Vonones 8, 108, 172–76, 177, 210

Xenocrates 80

Zeno, son of King Polemo of Pontus *see* Artaxias, King